HIDING THE WORLD
IN THE WORLD

SUNY series in Chinese Philosophy and Culture

Roger T. Ames, editor

HIDING THE WORLD IN THE WORLD

Uneven Discourses on the *Zhuangzi*

Edited by

SCOTT COOK

STATE UNIVERSITY OF NEW YORK PRESS

Published by
State University of New York Press, Albany

For information, address State University of New York Press,
194 Washington Avenue, Suite 305, Albany, NY 12210-2384

Production by Marilyn P. Semerad
Marketing by Michael Campochiaro

Library of Congress Cataloging-in-Publication Data

Hiding the world in the world : uneven discourses on the Zhuangzi / edited by Scott Cook
    p. cm. — (SUNY series in Chinese philosophy and culture)
    Includes bibliographical references and index.
    ISBN 0-7914-5865-2 (alk. paper) — ISBN 0-7914-5866-0 (pbk. : alk. paper)
    1. Zhuangzi. Nanhua jing.   2. Philosophy, Chinese.   I. Cook, Scott,   II. Series.

BL1900.C576H53 2003
299'.51482—dc21
                                                        2002045260
ISBN-13 978-0-7914-5865-5 (alk. paper) — 978-0-7914-5866-2 (pbk : alk. paper)
            10 9 8 7 6 5 4 3 2 1

Contents

Acknowledgments

The initial motivation for this volume grew out of a panel, entitled Who is it that Rouses Them Forth: Mysticism, Perspectivism, and Illumination in Zhuang Zi's "Qiwulun 齊物論," that was held at the Association for Asian Studies' forty-ninth Annual Meeting in Chicago on March 14, 1997. The chapters by Scott Cook, Harold D. Roth, and Brook Ziporyn in this volume were all first presented as papers on that occasion; we thank Shuen-fu Lin for serving as chair and John S. Major for the many insightful comments he provided as discussant. Seven of the ten chapters in this volume are appearing in print for the first time. We would like to thank the following for permission to reprint chapters that first appeared in journals: Jonathan Herman and the editors for permission to reprint the essay "Bimodal Mystical Experience in the 'Qiwulun' Chapter of the *Zhuangzi*," by Harold D. Roth, which appeared in *The Journal of Chinese Religions*, 28 (2000): 31–50; Liu Ching-chih, chief editor at the Honk Kong Translation Society Limited, for permission to reprint "Transforming the Dao: A Critique of A. C. Graham's Translation of the Inner Chapters of the *Chuang Tzu*," by Shuen-fu Lin, which appeared in *Translation Quarterly* 翻譯季刊 (Hong Kong), nos. 13 and 14 (1999): 63–96; and Taylor and Francis for permission to reprint "Reflex and Reflectivity: *Wuwei* in the *Zhuangzi*," by Alan Fox, which appeared in *Asian Philosophy* vol. 6 (1): 59–72—publisher's website can be found at http://www.tandf.co.uk.

We should also like to thank inclusively anyone and everyone who has ever helped us to better think through this most complex and wonderful of texts; one person we should like to single out by name, however, is the anonymous reader for State University of New York Press. Special thanks go to Ma Minghao 馬銘浩, whose calligraphy graces the cover of this book. On a personal level, let me also thank Shuen-fu Lin, who has long served as a mentor on *Zhuangzi* matters; Roger T. Ames, for all his encouragement in regard to this volume; and Wang Shu-min 王叔岷, whose rigor, dedication, and enthusiasm as both a scholar and a gentleman have been a constant and boundless source of inspiration.

A Note on Conventions

To facilitate comparison not only with the Chinese text of the *Zhuangzi* itself but also with some of the major traditional commentaries on the *Zhuangzi*, all references to the text are cited according to both page/chapter/line numbers of the Harvard-Yenching concordance *and* page numbers of Guo Qingfan's *Zhuangzi jishi*; in most cases, the Chinese title of the chapter from which the passage is taken is given as well. The following abbreviations are employed throughout:

HY = Harvard-Yenching Institute, *Zhuangzi yinde* 莊子引得 (A concordance to Chuang Tzu). Beijing: Yanjing daxue tushuguan yinde bianzuanju, 1947 (Taipei reprint: Chengwen Publishing Company, 1966).

ZZJS = Guo Qingfan 郭慶藩 (19th c.), *Zhuangzi jishi* 莊子集釋 (1895). Wang Xiaoyu 王孝魚, ed.; Beijing: Zhonghua shuju, 1961.

Graham = Graham, A. C. (Angus Charles), *Chuang-tzu: The Seven Inner Chapters and Other Writings from the Book of Chuang-tzu*. London: George Allen & Unwin, 1981.

Watson = Watson, Burton, tr. *The Complete Works of Chuang Tzu*. New York: Columbia University Press, 1968.

Mainland pinyin romanization is employed throughout; names and terms quoted from earlier English-language works using the Wade-Giles system have been converted to pinyin, except in the titles of such works, where the original romanizations are retained. Names of Chinese scholars are also given in pinyin, except for those who have lived outside of mainland China in which case, according to custom, Wade-Giles is employed (i.e., Ch'ien Mu)—or for those who have previously established a particular spelling for their own names (i.e., Fung Yu-lan). All Chinese names are listed surname first, except those of scholars who have adopted the reverse order for their English-language publications. All references are listed by author and title; the bibliography at the end of the book lists all the primary and secondary works on the *Zhuangzi* that are cited by the contributors to this volume.

Introduction

SCOTT COOK 顧史考

What, you may ask, is the purpose of this volume we now lay before you? Have we finally, after over two millennia of groping in the dark, gained the standard of clarity by which all paradoxes involved in interpreting the *Zhuangzi* 莊子[1] are suddenly resolved? Have we at last completed the task of properly asserting all negations and negating all assertions, so that we may ask the readers' indulgence as we proceed to sort the matter out for them? Are we entitled, in short, to justify our project with the further assertion that our audience will never attain to the ultimate and essential truths hidden deep within the *Zhuangzi* until it carefully pores over the meticulously crafted pages of scholarly wisdom we now dutifully present to it?

Far be it from us to make such a claim. Yet we trust that our patient readers will be rewarded for their efforts nonetheless. To those who find the *Zhuangzi* disconcerting and would approach it with the aim of simply explaining away the very paradoxes to which the text itself, with incessant playfulness, draws our attention, we may suggest reading no further. With those, however, who find the incongruities themselves a constant source of creative stimulus, as have countless generations of interpreters before them, let us proceed onward, for there yet remains much to be done. As with any text, especially one separated so far from us in time, space, and cultural context as the *Zhuangzi*, there is always the hermeneutical task of making sense—insofar as this term may be allowed here—of it in terms of our own particular cognitive frameworks and interpretive contexts. This is a task that has been ongoing for some time and will of necessity always

1

be ongoing. To the extent that the *Zhuangzi* can be *understood*, the interpretive imperative remains, and the text must continually be read against
itself, against its contemporary texts, against those of other philosophical
traditions, and against prior interpretations if it is to remain alive for us
as an unremitting source of philosophical inspiration. So while we can
certainly never hope to attain the final word on the subject, let us give it
a try anyway, shall we?

We should not be so rash as to deny that this process will invariably
involve, to a certain degree, the "righting of wrongs" and the "wronging of
rights," as hypocritical as this may be for a book purporting to illuminate
something of the spirit of a text that itself sought to move beyond all that.
As scholars of ancient texts, we face a constant dilemma in the fact that
we must continually correct the very problems in interpretation that we
have, collectively, imposed upon ourselves. To the extent that we progress
at all in our hermeneutic understanding, such progress never comes in a
straight line; as one school of interpretation manages to gain the stamp
of authority in its day, the next comes along to challenge its assumptions
and provide corrective measure for its excesses, while almost inevitably
substituting for them some of its own. Thus do we invariably proceed in
fitful turns and twists toward the destination that we may approach and
yet never actually reach, in a sort of process of scholarly dialectic that
never achieves its final resolution.

Scholarship on the *Zhuangzi* has continued in such fashion almost
incessantly over the past two millennia, and recent years have been no
exception. The present volume comes on the heels of two other compila-
tions, each of which has presented a somewhat different point of focus. In
Essays on Skepticism, Relativism, and Ethics in the Zhuangzi (Paul Kjellberg
and Philip J. Ivanhoe, eds. [SUNY 1996]), the particular source of concern
lay in "reconciling Zhuangzi's skepticism with his normative vision."[2]
Each of the chapters addressed, in different ways, the issue of how the
Zhuangzi is able to present a positive vision of how one should best live
one's life in the face of its relentless questioning of our ability to possess
any evaluative knowledge whatsoever, and all the chapters, despite their
mutual points of departure, show some agreement in their confirmation
of that "positive ethical project" and the view that that project is in some
sense "therapeutic." This insightful volume has proven provocative for a
number of the authors in the present volume, whose works continue
to attack the problem from somewhat different perspectives.[3] More recently, the volume *Wandering at Ease in the* Zhuangzi (Roger T. Ames, ed.
[SUNY 1998])—published just after the initial submission of the present

volume—has contributed to the collective scholarly enterprise with an engaging array of somewhat more eclectic pieces that, in the words of the editor, "reflect an overlapping and sometimes coherent interpretation of Zhuangzi that respects the bottomlessness of one of the world's great achievements in philosophical literature."[4]

As for the present volume, let us, too, not pretend we all approach the text from a single perspective, for such a claim would be neither truthful nor desirable. For what we may thereby gain in cohesiveness would be far outweighed by the artificial constraints such a unified approach would place upon our collective visions. Nonetheless, the articles will be found to naturally cohere with each other to the extent not only that they all revolve around the *Zhuangzi*, but also that they all grow out, in their own ways, of the accumulated body of interpretive "wisdom" that we have come to own at present, and of which we all partake in our ongoing enterprise of reading and rereading this most incessantly bountiful of ancient literary and philosophical texts.

Our volume opens with Harold D. Roth's "Bimodal Mystical Experience in the 'Qiwulun 齊物論' Chapter of the *Zhuangzi*," wherein the author attempts to reestablish the place of mysticism in the philosophy of Zhuangzi and his followers, a dimension largely neglected or denied in recent studies. Drawing upon his own recent research into Daoist mystical praxis and the analyses of mystical experience and mystical philosophy in the writings of Walter Stace and others, Roth demonstrates the presence of what he terms "bimodal mystical experience" in the "Qiwulun" and other chapters of the *Zhuangzi*. Such experience is marked, on the one hand, by a sense of tranquility and condition of unity resulting from the gradual emptying out of one's consciousness through meditative practices, which is then followed, on the other hand, by a return to "the dualistic world in a profoundly transformed fashion, often characterized by an unselfconscious ability to spontaneously respond to whatever situation one is facing"—two modes that can be viewed as elaborations on Stace's "introvertive" and "extrovertive" types of mystical experience. After analyzing the evidence indicating that the author of the Inner Chapters was involved in mystical praxis, Roth draws upon the distinction between the *weishi* 為是 and *yinshi* 因是 (the "contrived" and "adaptive" "that's it," as identified by A. C. Graham) modes of consciousness in the "Qiwulun" to show how Zhuangzi's "sage" is one who abandons attachment to his own individual viewpoint and achieves an "illumined" consciousness that responds freely and spontaneously to circumstances without being confined to any particular perspective. That is, he adopts the all-embracing, equalizing perspective of the Way, a distinctive form of cognition that makes use of the skeptical methods afforded through total self-forgetting. Following such introvertive experience, however, the sage ultimately returns to the world of everyday living, "while at the same time retaining" his "prior condition of contact with the Way, the 'great pervader' and unifier of all things"—a "condition of simultaneously seeing unity within multiplicity" that is characteristic of extrovertive mystical experience. Through such analysis, Roth hopes to explain the phenomenological origins of the distinctive blend of cosmology, humor, and religious transformation that mark the *Zhuangzi*, and further the process of bringing Chinese religious experience into dialogue with the religious experience of human beings the world over.

The issue of individual versus global perspectives is addressed more directly in Brook Ziporyn's "How Many Are the Ten Thousand Things and I? Relativism, Mysticism, and the Privileging of Oneness in the 'Inner Chapters.'" In this chapter, Ziporyn seeks to reconcile the privileged nature of such a "mystical" view that "all things are one" in the *Zhuangzi* with the inherent contradiction this would seemingly entail in light of its "position" that *all* perspectives are equally arbitrary (as insisted upon by Hansen, most notably). Rather than seeing the coexistence of the "mystical" and "skeptical/relativist" trends as an irreconcilable problem (an assumption implicit throughout the essays of the Kjellberg/Ivanhoe volume), Ziporyn argues that Zhuangzi both thoroughly rejects the possibility of an "objectively" universal perspective *and* privileges such a perspective (all things are one) at the same time. This he accomplishes through what Ziporyn terms an "omnicentric holism," a doctrine that holds that the whole is more than the sum of its parts, but where this is true "in so thorough a sense that each point in any whole is a center of that whole, such that each one adequately represents, perceives, includes the whole." For Zhuangzi, in other words, the privileged position amounts simply to the claim that "all positions are right," which would then hold true for this privileged position itself. Through an analysis of the "Qiwu-lun" and other Inner Chapters, Ziporyn shows how the "all-things-are-one" perspective, though still one of many equally valid perspectives, gets privileged by Zhuangzi because "its self-referential nature and pragmatic nondisconfirmability give it certain unique qualities, not the least of which is a kind of staying power in the midst of the transformation of perspectives, which amounts to a *performative* demonstration of its truth." It is precisely its ability to coexist in and as any other perspective, including its direct contradiction, that gives it the special skill-functions Zhuangzi describes so enthusiastically. The perspective of "oneness" amounts, then, not to any truth-claim about the nature of the world, but rather nothing more than the "complete absence of any definite knowledge." Functioning as a kind of "wild card" in the game of life, the sage's "regarding things as one" merely opens him up to the possibility of change throughout the entire spectrum of what life may deal him, thereby allowing him to be free and independent of the limitations inherent in all partial vantage points.

In my own chapter, "Harmony and Cacophony in the Panpipes of Heaven," I approach the issue of the "all-things-are-one" perspective from a somewhat different angle: the eternal dilemma over the search for individual worth and creation of value in our lives in the face of the inevitable, equalizing impermanence brought upon us all by death. In one of the greatest and most thought-provoking examples of early Chinese philosophical prose, the dialogue between Nanguo Ziqi and Yancheng Ziyou that opens the "Qiwulun" chapter, Nanguo Ziqi presents the image of the "panpipes of Heaven" (*tianlai* 天籟), in which he describes in vivid terms the multifarious sounds produced when the winds blow across myriad crevices of various shapes and sizes, and then poses the question: "who is it that rouses them forth?" My chapter inquires into the aesthetic nature of the image: is it a cacophony of worldly noise or a celebration of sounds? It suggests that the answer may well lie in the attitude of the listener: like Nanguo in his achieved state of self-forgetting, one comes to celebrate the diversity of the world precisely by "forgetting" the claims of its distinctive members to any form of absolute value, and, rather, enjoying them as temporal players in the unified, yet ever-changing, symphony of life and death. By losing both self and other, one finally awakens to the awareness that all things even out in death, in the return to "Heaven's Pool" of transformation, just as the numerous crevices all alike return to an even and vacuous silence once the storm has blown over and the musical tempest has reached its coda. By unfolding the import of this crucial, opening image, this chapter hopes to provide the basis for a better understanding of all that follows it in the celebrated "Qiwulun" chapter, as well as the variations this theme would come to play in the literature and philosophy of other cultures and epochs.

The mystical element of the *Zhuangzi* receives further elaboration in Rur-bin Yang's 楊儒賓 "From 'Merging the Body with the Mind' to 'Wandering in Unitary *Qi* 氣': A Discussion of Zhuangzi's Realm of the True Man and its Corporeal Basis" (first published in Chinese in 1989),

wherein Yang explores the concept of 'body' implicit throughout the
Zhuangzi and its relation to Zhuangzi's metaphysics. The *Zhuangzi* is rife
with passages speaking to the experience of Dao-embodiment, in which
the adept allows his perception and rationality to disintegrate, loses his
sense of personal identity, and thereupon gains a more "authentic knowledge," wherein he grasps the whole in a single moment, subject and object
disappear, and all of existence merges into a single entity. Here, perception
and rationality constitute a kind of impediment to mystical experience. Yet
there is another sense, Yang notes, in which Zhuangzi views the "ears, eyes,
and other sense organs" as "channels leading to deep-level consciousness,"
which, while disparate in function, "are the same in terms of their essential
qualities" and can "be transformed into a state identical in essence to deep-
level consciousness." Yang discusses how passages in the *Zhuangzi* calling
for the "ears and eyes" to "communicate with what is inside," or "listening
with the vital energy" have a physiological basis to them, descriptive of a
kind of unifying "common sense" that has parallels to the phenomenon of
"synesthesia" commonly found in religious experiences worldwide, as well
as to similar notions discussed by philosophers from Aristotle to Merleau-
Ponty. In such a state, all sensations—and indeed the entire body—"meld
into a single whole and are fully integrated by the vital energy." Many
texts of the period speak of cultivation in such terms, wherein the mind
(*xin* 心) first consciously transforms the body to work in coordination
with it and then in its turn gets "transformed and permeated" into the
body to merge with the flow of its vital energy (*qi* 氣), carrying with
it a kind of consciousness to every part of the body. In the *Zhuangzi*,
such a state is described as "developing what is natural to Heaven"—the
intuitive understanding of oxcarver Ding, which transcends all perceptual
boundaries and penetrates to the deepest levels of human existence,
wherein the entire body, indeed, becomes "perceptualized." The sense
organs and body no longer restrain the individual but now become the
channels through which one interconnects with the outer world; the limits
of "self" can no longer be demarcated, human consciousness and bodily
energy mix and flow together with the unitary circulation of the cosmos,
and one comes to "wander" (*you* 遊) through the concrete world in a kind
of superexperiential (yet still consciously individual) state. Having thus
described Zhuangzi's philosophy of bodily transformation, Yang concludes
by noting that aside from its clearly unique characteristics, it drew upon
a more widely shared metaphysics of bodily experience that was both
part of the "common discourse" among the various schools of pre-Qin
China and yet in some ways unique to the Chinese cultural milieu.

By way of contrast to the affirmation of this kind of "bimodal" mystical experience as variously described by both Yang and Roth, the next piece, by the arch "antimystic" of Chinese philosophical studies, Chad Hansen, presents a somewhat dissenting view. In "Guru or Skeptic? Relativistic Skepticism in the *Zhuangzi*," Hansen takes issue with recent arguments denying or diminishing the skeptical-relativistic thrust of certain sections of the *Zhuangzi*. He traces such resistance to misconceptions regarding the "principle of interpretive coherence" and to a failure to appreciate the philosophically subtle formulations and defenses available to Chinese skeptics, as well as how conceptual differences in our two traditions affect the inferential roles played by skeptical and relativist doctrines. Hansen argues that it is methodologically fallacious to demand a mutually consistent position throughout an entire text or even from a single author, and that we should instead seek to formulate an account of how a "representative, competent, and thoughtful" member of the contemporaneous "linguistic community" (in this case the ancient Chinese philosophical community) would understand the implied commitments of each passage or argument. He presents the contemporary context of these issues as centering on disputes about *dao* viewed as a social-political guide, a context that gave Chinese its "practical" characteristic and the distinctive way in which its language and discourse were analyzed; lacking the sentential focus familiar in the West, the focus is instead on the word as the primary unit. Borrowing Alvin Goldman's analysis of skepticism in terms of its themes, scope, and strength, Hansen goes on to argue that (1) Zhuangzi's skepticism cannot reasonably be taken to advocate suspending all judgment but instead concentrates on the theme of dependence or justification for our judgments; (2) while it broadly targets all conventional, practical wisdom in its scope, it signals no doubt about a "real-world context" in which our language operates; and (3) Zhuangzi's is a weak variety of skepticism insofar as it does not deny the possibility of knowledge but only the assurance that the way of life we know is the uniquely justifiable one or that we could justify it from the points of view of all others. After analyzing Zhuangzi's relativism (which fuels his skepticism) along similar terms, Hansen goes on to argue that Zhuangzi's skeptical relativism underlies the "liberal thrust" of Daoist social-political attitudes; as it develops no political theory of liberal justice, however, in the context of dominant Confucian-Mohist political assumptions, Zhuangzi's skepticism is implicitly a recommendation for anarchy.

Sticking with the theme of skepticism, the next chapter, Dan Lusthaus's "Aporetics Ethics in the *Zhuangzi*," argues that Zhuangzi is

not at all a "thoroughgoing" skeptic ("one who rejects the very possibility of any sort of valid claim") but rather a "critical thinker" who resists
"*certain* knowledge-claims while accepting others." Zhuangzi is said to use
skeptical rhetoric as a "transitional phase" in his arguments, employing
it to deconstruct what Hansen terms the "evaluative distinctions" made
by his contemporaries yet ultimately substituting for them his own "prescriptive discourse." The latter is characterized as an "aporetic stance," in
which we "relativize" all extremes and locate the limits of our knowledge
and then turn around to use these very limits as the basis for an ethical
orientation marked by the complete acceptance of uncertainty. Lusthaus
draws his conclusions primarily from his analysis of two key passages in
the *Zhuangzi*: the "butterfly dream" at the end of the "Qiwulun" chapter
and the conversation between the River and the Sea that opens the "Qiu
shui 秋水" chapter. In the former, Lusthaus argues that the resolution of
the butterfly story comes when the moment of undecidibility (aporia)
between dream and reality gives way to an acceptance and understanding
of the unpredictable transformation of things. In his analysis of the "Qiu
shui" dialogue, Lusthaus develops two models—the "Temporality Knowledge" model and the "Perspectival" model—which he sees as implying a
sort of "reasoning by charts," and himself makes extensive use of charts
to unpack all the possible implications of the dialogue. The culmination
of the various epistemological steps and levels suggested therein is the
enlightened ethical conduct of the "Great Man," an "Ethics of Aporia,"
which recognizes the perspectival limits of all standards of value and uses
the very indeterminacy of these limits as the "unshakable foundation" for
ethical action.

     This common theme of awakening to the recognition of perspec-
tival limits is once again explored in Alan Fox's "Reflex and Reflectivity:
Wuwei in the *Zhuangzi*." Therein, Fox proposes to offer a new and more
nuanced interpretation of Zhuangzi's conception of "non-action," which
consists in a flexible approach to the world and its infinite possibilities.
In this approach, each situation we encounter poses its own certain set
of constraints and inevitabilities, and our task is to adapt to such circumstances by finding the best "fit" in each particular instance, rather than
obstinately applying our own values and perspectives in situations where
they do not apply. The result of such an approach is freedom—not freedom *to* act however we so choose, but freedom *from* slavish commitment
to rigid formulae that cause us to act inappropriately. Zhuangzi articulates
wuwei in the image of the "hinge of *dao*," through which one may clearly
perceive the mutual interrelation of all distinctions and observe them re-

volve around a central standpoint. It is from such a position that the sage
finds the most appropriate responses to the inevitable, leading him to the
most efficient, unobtrusive, and effortless experience, wherein he comes
to expect the unexpected with open-minded equanimity. Having thus
described the *Zhuangzi's* notion of *wuwei*, Fox goes on to emphasize, in
contrast to some prior readings of the text that have Zhuangzi advocating
withdrawal from the world and mystical conjoinment with a transcendental *dao*, that Zhuangzi instead affirms the world and finds it wonderful,
espousing that we should "fully and completely integrate ourselves *within*
it." This last point, indeed, is one that all the essays of the present volume
thus far have in common: whether they view such experience as "mystical" or not, their shared conclusion is that "Zhuangzi" does *not* advocate
withdrawal and detachment from the world, but on the contrary calls for
us to experience it in all its fullness from—for some of us anyway—a
higher and more comprehensive plane.

The final three chapters explore somewhat different themes and
seek to analyze the *Zhuangzi* against the backdrop of its contemporary
discourse and historical environment. In "A Mind-Body Problem in the
Zhuangzi," Paul Rakita Goldin brings to light the existence of an undis-
cussed presupposition in the *Zhuangzi* that runs counter to some of the
predominant claims of Western scholarship on early Chinese philosophy.
The *Zhuangzi* is well known for its position that our existence as human
beings is only a "temporary stage" in an endless process of cosmic transformations that will invariably lead our material to take on some new
form after we pass on. Yet many of the passages in which such a view is
expressed also speak of the "mind" (*xin* 心) as capable of remaining at
ease in the midst of such corporeal changes. Given the nearly inescapable
conclusion that the *Zhuangzi* conceives of the mind in such passages "as
an entity with no physical material at all," Goldin asks the question of
how the work "account[s] for intelligence within its theory of cosmically
recycling matter." The answer would seem to be that while our *material*
may get constantly recycled, our *"disembodied minds"* continue to live on
in some timeless existence—in short, a kind of mind-body dualism, and
one which, Goldin points out, is implied in other texts of the time as
well. In light of this, Goldin takes issue with such authoritative critics as
A. C. Graham and Herbert Fingarette, who have stated with conviction
that the conception of a mind-body dichotomy never existed in pre-
Han China. As Goldin shows, while the early Chinese philosophers may
not have problematized the issue in the way Western thinkers would, the
dichotomy was at the very least part of the unexpressed "folk psychology"

that lay at the basis of such texts as the *Zhuangzi* and informed the way in which they conceptualized certain philosophical issues central to them.

In his "'Nothing Can Overcome Heaven': The Notion of Spirit in the *Zhuangzi*," Michael J. Puett positions the *Zhuangzi*'s discourse on spiritual power within its fourth-century B.C. intellectual milieu. In the passages in which the term *spirit-man* (*shenren* 神人) occurs, the figure is contrasted with the ritual specialists (*wu* 巫) of the day; as Puett notes, the *Zhuangzi*'s critique of these latter and the positions they assumed concerning the relationship between humans and spirits is a theme it holds in common with other texts from the period. Texts such as the "Nei ye 內業" chapter of the *Guanzi* 管子, however, while critical of the ritual specialists, share with them emphasis on the goal of gaining knowledge of and power over things, claiming only that one can attain a more direct access to spiritual powers through the cultivation of *qi* 氣 rather than through divination and other magical arts. The *Zhuangzi*, on the other hand, counters both by claiming that the truly spiritual are those who are unaffected by such considerations in the first place, because, content to follow their Heavenly allotment and the fate of ceaseless transformation, they paradoxically liberate themselves and become no longer dependent upon any individual things. For Zhuangzi, then, the notion of "spirit" lay not in seeking to transcend one's humanity to become like either the controlling spirits or Heaven itself, but rather to accept the order of Heaven and thus gain access to "that point that nothing can overcome." As Puett shows, then, the *Zhuangzi* uses a terminology "very similar to [that used in] the self-cultivation literature," yet offers "a gnosis different both from that obtainable by spirit specialists and that described in the self-cultivation literature itself." And in the sense that he advocates conformity with Heavenly patterns, Puett argues, Zhuangzi is by no means a relativist, but instead "a cosmologist with a strong commitment to a certain definition of the proper place of humanity in the universe."

Finally, in "Transforming the Dao: A Critique of A. C. Graham's Translation of the Inner Chapters of the *Zhuangzi*," Shuen-fu Lin deals head-on with the issue of the nature of the *Zhuangzi* as a text and the nature of early Chinese texts in general, as well as the related problem of translating such texts into English. Lin begins with a review of some recent Western theories of translation and in this context notes how A. C. Graham comes close to the ideal, espoused by such people as Vladimir Nabokov and Walter Benjamin, of a "literal translator" who seeks to incorporate "the original's mode of signification"—an ideal that, of course, can only be approached and never fully attained. At the same time, however, Graham's achievements in recapturing the original sense of the text remain fundamentally marred by his problematic conception of precisely what the text is. Lin suggests that Graham's refusal to recognize the Inner Chapters as integral pieces of prose stems in part from his "lack of a clear notion of the development of ancient Chinese philosophical prose"; whereas in fact, Lin argues, these chapters may be considered as a kind of transitional type of philosophical essay—"a series of stories . . . intermixed with passages of discursive prose, designed for the articulation of philosophical ideas"—that would become precursor to the evolved argumentative essays of the later Warring States. Thus while Lin praises Graham for the remarkable job he does in both reproducing the precise sense of the text's conceptual terminology and in preserving its original forms of language, he calls into question Graham's habit of tampering with the *Zhuangzi* as a source text, of his "moving of passages and fragments into more suitable contexts" and "relegating occasional passages to Zhuangzi's afterthoughts or annotations by Zhuangzi himself." After citing several examples to point out the problematic nature of Graham's transpositions, Lin analyzes the structure of the "Xiaoyaoyou" chapter to demonstrate how the typical Inner Chapter does, after all, "have an intricate logic of its own in the unfolding of its ideas"—a conclusion that will no doubt rekindle the debate over just how early Chinese texts were composed and in what manner they should be read.

The nature of the early Chinese text is, indeed, a very thorny issue to deal with, and the *Zhuangzi* is certainly no exception in this regard. Questions on who authored which sections of the work, how the work was transmitted, what sorts or accretions or emendations took place during that process, and what is the nature of the philosophical affinities between the various sections of the composite work we know as the *Zhuangzi* are all exceedingly relevant to how we go about interpreting the text and the conclusions we can draw from textual examples that run across the work's three divisions, its various chapters, or even different sections within the same chapter. While there are a number of good arguments in support of the traditional view that the "Inner Chapters" were authored by Zhuang Zhou 莊周 himself,[5] the counter-evidence is by no means inconsequential, and in any event the "Outer" and "Miscellaneous" chapters of the work have a great intrinsic worth of their own as products of the philosophical lineage, regardless of which texts may or may not have been authored by its founder. Of no little importance, however, is that the "Inner Chapters" remain, arguably, among the very richest in the work, and whatever that may suggest in terms of authorship, it is certainly some justification for continuing to keep much of the focus on those chapters, as many (but not all) of the essays in this volume do. At any rate, this is not the place to review in detail the complex issues involved in the textual transmission of the *Zhuangzi*, nor to impose any particular perspective on how they should be resolved, but rather must we leave it up to each author of this volume to decide, implicitly or explicitly, how such issues might be implicated in the context of his arguments.[6]

The corpus of *Zhuangzi* interpretation forms an ongoing discourse that will certainly not achieve its final resolution with this volume, and before long a new group of worthies will come along to variously elaborate upon, take issue with, or forcefully overturn many of the views expressed therein. Unlike Hundun 渾沌, we are born too insufficiently ill-equipped to simply remain silent and wholly oblivious to the distinctions we seem so obstinately bent on perceiving. As scholars, staking claims and expressing opinions seems to be something we are almost compelled by nature to do—and if that is the case, is there any reason for us not to simply self-affirm and play our given roles? So long as we understand that ours is not, and can never, be the final answer, the ultimate perspective—so long as we recognize that we are each just one of many hollows through which the wind blows to produce its orchestra of tones—then we can scarcely go wrong. The *Zhuangzi*, of all texts, can never be tied down to a single interpretation, and the more angles from which we explore it, the closer we may get, perhaps, to that ever-elusive comprehensive vision of the work—or, failing that, the less we stand to lose in the process. For "if we hide the world in the world, so that nothing is able to escape," what more do we have to lose? Indeed, I suspect, we have much to gain. From the point of view of their differences, the scholarly perspectives expressed in this volume may be as divergent as Chu and Yue, but from the point of view of their sameness, they are all as one—it is precisely with such dual understanding, our dear reader, that we hope you will approach the essays of this volume and join us in the ongoing transformation of the *Zhuangzi*'s philosophy.

Notes

1. For those who may be coming to this volume uninitiated, the *Zhuangzi* is one of the unquestioned philosophical and literary gems of Warring States-period China (481–221 B.C.), the formative period of Chinese philosophy. Along with the *Laozi* 老子 (*Dao-De jing* 道德經), the *Zhuangzi*

constitutes one of the two works of that period that would later be labeled "Daoist" (*daojia* 道家), a style of thought which would come to represent, along with Confucianism and Buddhism (which would make its way into China a couple of centuries later), one of the three major philosophical traditions in Chinese history. Tradition has it that the Inner Chapters (*neipian* 內篇; chapters 1–7) of the *Zhuangzi* were written by the historical Zhuang Zhou 莊周 himself (ca. 365–ca. 285 B.C.), though this view has by no means gone unquestioned (for more on the work's division into Inner, Outer, and Miscellaneous chapters, see the note on this below). As to the philosophical content of the *Zhuangzi*, this will become apparent readily enough in the essays to follow, and there is thus little need to elaborate upon it any further here. On Zhuangzi's dates, see Ch'ien Mu 錢穆, Xian-Qin zhuzi xinian 先秦諸子繫年 (1935; 2d. ed., rev. and enl., 1956; Taipei: Dongda, 3d. ed., 1990), pp. 269–271.

2. Paul Kjellberg and Philip J. Ivanhoe, eds., *Essays on Skepticism, Relativism, and Ethics in the* Zhuangzi (Albany: State University of New York Press, 1996), p. xiv.

3. See especially in this volume the essays of Brook Ziporyn, Dan Lusthaus, and Chad Hansen.

4. Roger T. Ames, ed., *Wandering at Ease in the* Zhuangzi (Albany: State University of New York Press, 1998), p. 14.

5. The *Zhuangzi* was most likely divided into the arrangement of Inner 內, Outer 外, and Miscellaneous 雜 chapters 篇 when it was first collated by Liu Xiang 劉向 (77?–6 B.C.) in the Western Han dynasty (西漢 206 B.C.–A.D. 8). The text was later rearranged somewhat by Western Jin-dynasty (西晉 265–A.D. 316) annotator Guo Xiang 郭象 (252?–A.D. 312), on the basis of Sima Biao's 司馬彪 (???–A.D. 306) edition. While the "Yiwen zhi 藝文志" of the *Han Shu* 漢書 lists the *Zhuangzi* in fifty-two chapters (*pian* 篇), Guo Xiang's version—the only one now left to us—is in thirty-three chapters: seven inner, fifteen outer, and eleven miscellaneous. According to Tang-dynasty (唐 618–A.D. 907) scholar Lu Deming 陸德明, however, "the inner chapters of the various editions are all the same 內篇眾家並同." See Zhang Dainian, *Zhongguo zhexueshi shiliaoxue* (Taiwan reprint; Taipei, Songgao, 1985), p. 77. A Japanese manuscript of one of Guo's annotated editions preserves an afterword by Guo, in which he states that he discarded some thirteen chapters he thought to have been written by later followers who could not adequately comprehend their master's thought. See Wang Shu-min, *XianQin Dao-Fa sixiang jianggao* (Taipei: Zhongyang yanjiuyuan Wenzhe yanjiusuo, monograph no. 2, 1992), p. 64. The majority of scholars since the time of Wang Fuzhi 王夫之 (A.D. 1619–1692) have taken the view that the Inner chapters were written before the Outer and Miscellaneous chapters and were composed by Zhuang Zhou himself (for a list of variant opinions, see Liu Xiaogan, "Zhuangzi zhexue ji qi yanbian" [Beijing: Zhongguo shehui kexue,

1988], pp. 3–4; see also his work in English translation, *Classifying the Inner Chapters* [Ann Arbor: University of Michigan Center for Chinese Studies, 1994]). Wang Fuzhi's comments may be found in Zhang Dainian, *Zhongguo zhexueshi shiliaoxue*, p. 75. For more on the divisions of the *Zhuangzi* and its nature as a text in general, see the chapter by Shuen-fu Lin in this volume.

6. Archaeological discoveries may yet cause us to rethink some of our earlier assumptions about the *Zhuangzi* as a text. Still awaiting publication is an important set of Han-dynasty bamboo strips unearthed from Fuyang 阜陽漢簡, which, as disclosed at a recent conference in Beijing, is said to contain the following eight *Zhuangzi* chapters: "Dazongshi," "Yingdiwang," "Zai you," "Tian Di," "Zhi le," "Da sheng," "Tian Zifang," and "Zhi beiyou" —that is, the last two of the seven Inner chapters, six of the fifteen Outer chapters, and none of the eleven Miscellaneous chapters. The significance of this, of course, remains to be determined, and what further surprises may be lurking within the chapters themselves must for the present time remain unknown to us.

1

Bimodal Mystical Experience in the "Qiwulun 齊物論" Chapter of the *Zhuangzi* 莊子

HAROLD D. ROTH

Introduction

During the past two decades the text of the *Zhuangzi* has been placed into dialogue with Western philosophy through the analyses found in a number of books, including two excellent collections of essays, Victor Mair's *Experimental Essays on the Chuang Tzu* and Paul Kjellberg and P. J. Ivanhoe's *Essays on Skepticism, Relativism, and Ethics in the Zhuangzi.*[1] Among the significant issues raised therein are those of whether the author, Zhuangzi, expresses a viewpoint that can be identified as "skeptical" or "relativist," and the authors answer in a variety of interesting and sophisticated ways. However, with certain exceptions that I will indicate below, most of the authors included in these volumes either deny, neglect, or, at best, only point to the mystical dimension of the text. It is this dimension that I hope to demonstrate is critical to the understanding of its philosophy.

In recent research on the historical and textual origins of the several related lineages of master and disciples that were part of the Daoist tradition of the fourth through second centuries B.C., I have argued that the experiential basis of these lineages can be found in mystical praxis.[2] That is, the one element they share is a common basic practice of breathing meditation, a practice that led its adepts to profound mystical experiences that provided the insights into the nature of the world and of a fundamental moving power that infused it and everything within it, that they called the "Dao." This is not to say that only members of these lineages practiced breathing meditation, but only to say that it was these adherents who took

this practice to its farthest limits. Textual evidence for this breathing practice survives in the Duodecagonal Jade Tablet Inscription, the *Laozi* 老子,
several essays in the *Guanzi* 管子 ("Nei ye 內業" and "Xinshu, shang and
xia 心術上、下"), the Mawangdui "Huang-Lao" texts, the *Lüshi chunqiu*
呂氏春秋, and the *Huainanzi* 淮南子. Related practices are also found
in the *fangshu* 方術 texts from Mawangdui and Zhangjiashan, but these
finds cannot be classified as "Daoist," because they show no evidence of
the distinctive cosmology of the other sources and because they seem to
be part of their own distinctive medical tradition.[3]

In my research I have referred to this Daoist breathing practice as
"inner cultivation." It involves following or guiding the breath while one
is in a stable sitting position. As one does this the normal contents of consciousness gradually empty out, and one comes to experience a tranquillity
that, as one's practice develops, becomes quite profound. Eventually one
comes to fully empty out the contents of consciousness until a condition
of unity is achieved, which is spoken of with a number of related phrases,
such as "attaining the One," or "attaining the empty Way." After this experience one returns and lives again in the dualistic world in a profoundly
transformed fashion, often characterized by an unselfconscious ability
to spontaneously respond to whatever situation one is facing. This new
mode of being in the world is frequently characterized by the famous
phrase from *Laozi*, "doing nothing, yet leaving nothing undone" (*wuwei
er wu buwei* 無為而無不為). I will argue that there is concrete evidence
that the author of the Inner Chapters of the *Zhuangzi* was aware of—and
likely followed—such inner cultivation practice.

These two complementary results of the practice of inner cultivation show a noteworthy similarity with the two fundamental categories
of mystical experience that Walter Stace has seen in religious traditions
throughout the world: introvertive and extrovertive. He defines the former
as a "unitary" or "pure" consciousness that is nontemporal and nonspatial
and is experienced when the individual self loses its individuality in the
One; he defines the latter as "the unifying vision—all things are One"
coupled with "the more concrete apprehension of the One as an inner
subjectivity, or life, in all things."[4] For him, this unity is directly perceived
within the experience and will later be variously interpreted depending
on the "cultural environment and the prior beliefs of the mystic."[5]

I have recently argued that Stace's phenomenological model of what
I have called "bimodal" mystical experience can be fruitfully applied to
the case of early Chinese mysticism, though it needs certain modifica-
tions.[6] Stace strongly values the introvertive over the extrovertive, a bias

caused by his almost exclusive reliance on Indo-European textual sources for his theories and by his limited reading of these sources.[7] While this is a doubtful contention even among these sources, it is certainly not true of early Chinese mystical writings, especially the *Zhuangzi*. Indeed, Lee Yearley argues that with Zhuangzi we have neither the Christian "mysticism of union," in which a union occurs between an "unchanging Real and the changing but still real particular individual," nor the Indian (Hindu-Buddhist) "mysticism of unity," in which the mystic attains unity by uncovering an inherent identity with a monistic principle that is the sole reality of the universe.[8] Rather, Zhuangzi espouses what Yearley calls an "intraworldly mysticism," in which, "One neither obtains union with some higher being nor unification with the single reality. Rather, one goes through a discipline and has experiences that allow one to view the world in a new way."[9]

While embracing Yearley's insights into what he calls "intraworldly mysticism," I see them as a corrective rather than a replacement for Stace's phenomenological model. That is, what I hope to demonstrate in this chapter is that what he calls "intraworldly mysticism" is not an entirely new mode of mystical experience, but rather a uniquely "Zhuangzian" form of Stace's extrovertive mode. As such, it is integrally related to the introvertive mode, although I would most certainly concur with Yearley that the unity attained fits into neither of his two categories of Indo-European mystical experience. For Zhuangzi the Stacian "objective referent" of this introvertive mystical experience—the Way—is not a static metaphysical absolute (and Chad Hansen is most certainly correct in arguing that such a concept is not present in the *Zhuangzi*[10]), but rather a continuously moving unitive force that can be merged with when consciousness is completely emptied by inner cultivation practice and can then serve as a constant guiding power throughout the many activities and circumstances of daily life.

Mystical Praxis in the "Inner Chapters" of the *Zhuangzi*

Before analyzing the evidence for bimodal mystical experience in the "Qiwulun" of the *Zhuangzi*, I would like to briefly touch base with the evidence for inner cultivation practice in the Inner Chapters as a whole (of course I am assuming here a common authorial viewpoint in these seven initial chapters of the text). There are four passages that attest to

this, two of which I will only summarize, two of which I will analyze:
(1) The fasting of the mind dialogue in which Confucius teaches Yan Hui.
Here Hui is told that he must completely empty out his consciousness to
find the Way and then he will be able to act spontaneously in the world
and thereby "fly by being wingless" (*yi wu yi fei* 以無翼飛) and "know
by being ignorant" (*yi wu zhi zhi* 以無知知);[11] (2) The brief mention of
how the Genuine breathe from their heels while the Common breathe
from their throats, a passage that also implies that such breathing manifests a profound "mechanism of Heaven" (*tianji* 天機).[12] I have written
elsewhere how the latter key technical term demonstrates an awareness of
the breathing practice outlined in the oldest epigraphic source for inner
cultivation, the Duodecagonal Jade Tablet Inscription.[13]

The third passage is the famous dialogue in which Yan Hui ironically
"turns the tables" on his master by teaching *him* how to "sit and forget"
(*zuowang* 坐忘):

(Confucius:) "What do you mean, just sit and forget?"

(Yan Hui:) "I let organs and members drop away, dismiss eyesight and
hearing, part from the body and expel knowledge, and
merge with the Great Pervader. This is what I mean by 'just
sit and forget.'"[14]

To let "organs and members drop away" (*duo zhi ti* 墮肢體) means to lose
visceral awareness of the emotions and desires, which, for the early Daoists, have "physiological" bases in the various organs.[15] To "dismiss eyesight
and hearing" (*chu cong ming* 黜聰明) means to deliberately cut off sense
perception. To "part from the body and expel knowledge" (*li xing qu zhi*
離形去知) means to lose bodily awareness and remove all thoughts from
consciousness. These are all familiar as apophatic aspects of the breathing
meditation found in other sources of inner cultivation theory. To "merge
with the Great Pervader" (*tong yu datong* 同於大通) seems to imply that,
as a result of these practices, Yan Hui has become united with the Dao.
Notice here the antimetaphysical tendency of this final phrase: it implies
the reality of the Way without establishing it as any kind of abstract
metaphysical absolute.

There is another passage in the "Dazongshi" chapter that I think provides clear and incontrovertible evidence of the presence of a Stacian-type
introvertive mystical experience: the dialogue between the "Self-Reliant
Woman" (Nü Yu 女偊), who has "the Way of a sage but not the stuff of
a sage," and her disciple, Buliang Yi 卜梁倚, who has the reverse qualities.
While here we do not find concrete evidence of inner cultivation prac-

tice, we see its results in a series of stages: (1) After three days, he could put the human world (*tianxia* 天下) outside himself; (2) After seven days, he could put things outside himself; (3) After nine days, he could put life outside himself. And once he could do this, he could "break through to the Brightness of Dawn, see the Unique, be without past and present, and then enter into the unliving and undying. That which kills the living does not die, that which gives birth to the living does not live."[16] In early Daoism, there is only one power that is beyond living and dying in the cosmos, one power that generates life and brings about death: the Way. In this passage, Buliang Yi has gradually stripped away all the contents of consciousness until he has reached an experience of totally merging with the Way. This certainly qualifies as the penultimate introvertive mystical experience. Its presence here indicates the author's awareness of such an experience; in the "Qiwulun" we shall see further references to this experience and how it relates to the extrovertive mode that is spoken of much more frequently.

Skepticism in the "Qiwulun"

Most of the essays that discuss the related issues of skepticism, relativism, and perspectivism in the *Zhuangzi* center almost exclusively on the "Qiwulun." In general, most authors agree that all three are present but disagree about the extent to which they dominate the philosophical discourse and the degree of thoroughness with which they are applied. Hansen argues for a perspectival relativism in the text. In the "Qiwulun" we find that all the doctrines of the Confucians and Mohists that each school thinks are true have a truth only relative to the perspective and viewpoint of each of the schools themselves: "What is it is also other; what is other is also it. There they say 'that's it,' 'that's not' from one point of view. Here we say 'that's it,' 'that's not' from another point of view. Are there really it and other? Or really no it and other?[17]

"The strategy," Hansen argues, "is to show that all discrimination, evaluation, classification, and so forth, are relative to some changeable context of judgment."[18] This relativity of judgment implies that the knowledge it yields is likewise only relatively true and that there is, for Zhuangzi, no standpoint from which anything can be known to be objectively true. According to Hansen, this skepticism most certainly extends to the "mystical monist's" claim for a metaphysical, absolute One beyond the world of distinctions. He sees the parodying of Hui Shi's statement that "Heaven and Earth are born together with me and the myriad things and I are one" (天地與我並生，而萬物與我為一) to be a critique of precisely this position.[19]

Lisa Raphals argues that the "Qiwulun" demonstrates the use of skeptical methods but not the presence of skeptical doctrines.[20] That is because it emphasizes the distinction between small knowledge (*xiaozhi* 小知) and great knowledge (*dazhi* 大知). She equates the former with ordinary knowing, "with *shi-fei*, the language and practice of moral judgment," and the latter with illumination (*ming*), *dao,* and *jue* "awakening."[21] The presence of the latter notion shows that the author was *not* an adherent to skeptical doctrines because he asserts the existence of a greater form of knowledge, something a true skeptic would never do. A true skeptic would say that we cannot know whether or not there are greater or lesser forms of knowing because we cannot know for certain whether knowing really knows anything real. Raphals recognizes three possible ways to interpret this essay that include a skeptical reading (Zhuangzi seeks great knowing but questions whether it is possible) and a mystical reading, that "unitive" mystical experience is the source of the knowing Zhuangzi refers to as "great," which she says could be compatible with a skeptical reading but which she declines to pursue.[22] It is compatible with a skeptical reading only if that skepticism is applied to the knowing of mundane life. This is an important insight, and I shall be pursuing it in line with Raphals's unexplored mystical reading of the "Qiwulun."

Thus Raphals differs from Hansen on the issue of the thoroughness of Zhuangzi's skepticism: Hansen argues that it is applied to all forms of knowing; Raphals argues that there is a kind of knowing that is exempted from the skeptical critique, "illumination." I will argue that this represents a distinctive mode of knowing that arises in the sage after the penultimate introvertive mystical experience of merging with the Dao and that it represents Zhuangzi's understanding of the kind of cognition that occurs within what Yearley calls "intraworldly mysticism" and that I prefer to regard as a type of extrovertive mystical experience.

In his first of two articles on the philosophy of the *Zhuangzi,* Philip J. Ivanhoe also examines the question of whether Zhuangzi was a skeptic and in the process throws considerable light on this distinctive mode of knowing advocated in the text.[23] He provides a valuable definition of four kinds of skepticism and examines whether or not each can be found in the *Zhuangzi.*[24] He concludes:

> 1. that Zhuangzi was not a sense skeptic because the two dream passages

in "Qiwulun" imply that there is knowledge but that the problem is that we don't usually know how to reach it;[25]

2. that Zhuangzi was not an ethical skeptic because his skill passages present paradigms of persons who embody the Way;[26]

3. that Zhuangzi was an epistemological skeptic about intellectual knowledge but not about intuitive knowledge (he doubted, in Ryle's distinction, "knowing that," but not "knowing how");[27] and

4. that Zhuangzi was a language skeptic who mistrusted proposals about what is right and wrong (not that there are right and wrong actions) and who doubted the ability of words to express the Dao. Ivanhoe maintains that Zhuangzi used proposals that he constantly negated to therapeutically undermine our confidence in proposals which are the products of our scheming minds.[28]

Ivanhoe argues further that Zhuangzi uses a kind of perspectivism aimed at dismantling intellectual traditions and leading to a process of unlearning so that one can get back in tune with the Dao.[29] This is greatly aided by the processes of "sitting and forgetting" and "fasting of the heart and mind" by which we forget "the narrow and parochial views which society has inflicted upon us."[30] Thus Ivanhoe concurs in general with Raphals's argument that Zhuangzi excludes an important mode of knowing from his skeptical probing. For him it is the intuitive knowledge of the Dao; for her it is the great knowledge of illumination. In my analysis, these are simply two aspects of the same cognitive mode that arises within the extrovertive mystical experience.

Two Distinctive Modes of Consciousness in the "Qiwulun"

Angus Graham made an important breakthrough in translating and understanding the "Qiwulun" when he identified a number of key technical terms also found in the Mohist Canons.[31] Most important for this analysis are the contrasting demonstratives *shi* 是 and *fei* 非, which he renders as "that's it" and "that's not" and for the Mohists were judgments rendered about the truth or falseness of propositions about knowledge, and the contrasting pronouns *shi* 是 and *bi* 彼, which he renders as "It" and "Other." Both pairs are used in the text to represent the conflicting intellectual positions of the various philosophers:"And so we have the 'that's it,' 'that's not' of Confucians and Mohists, by which what is it for one of them for the other is not, what is not for one of them for the other is."[32]

In a more general sense, *shi* and *fei* also stand for basic positions or standpoints that individuals take in the world and for the conceptual categories and intellectual commitments that are associated with them, as Hansen accurately understands.[33] In this light, Zhuangzi differentiates between two modes of adherence to such viewpoints that are symbolized in the text as *weishi* 為是 (the "that's it" which deems, or the contrived "that's it") and *yinshi* 因是 (the "that's it" which goes by circumstance, or the adaptive "that's it").[34] In the former mode one rigidly applies a pre-established way of looking at the world to every situation in which one finds oneself; in the latter mode one lets the unique circumstances of the situation determine one's understanding and approach to it. The former involves a rigid attachment to oneself and one's intellectual commitments; the latter involves a complete freedom from such an attachment, a freedom to act spontaneously as the situation demands. From the psychological perspective, each represents a distinct mode of consciousness containing its own distinctive mode of knowing. The quintessential contrast between these two modes is found in the famous "three every morning" passage:

> A monkey keeper handing out nuts said, "Three every morning and four every evening." The monkeys were all in a rage. "All right," he said, "four every morning and three every evening." The monkeys were all delighted. Without anything being missed out either in name or in substance, their pleasure and anger were put to use; his too was the "that's it" which goes by circumstance. This is why the sage smoothes things out with his "that's it, that's not," and stays at the point of rest on the potter's wheel of Heaven.[35]

The monkeys are attached to one fixed way of seeing the underlying reality of the seven nuts; the keeper is not. They symbolize the *weishi* mode, a mode also characteristic not only of the Confucians and Mohists, but also of Zhao Wen 昭文 the zither virtuoso, music-master Kuang 師曠, and Zhuangzi's old friend Hui Shi 惠施.[36] "All illumined an It that they preferred without the Other being illumined" and "so the end of it all was the darkness of chop logic."[37] Each developed his own unique viewpoint on the world and came to prefer It and only It and thereby left no room to adopt any Other. They were therefore fixated in this position and, like the monkeys, could never set it aside to see another way. "Therefore the glitter of glib implausibilities is despised by the sage. The 'that's it' which deems he does not use, but finds for things lodging-places in the usual. It is this that is meant by 'using Illumination' (*yi ming* 以 明)."[38]

By contrast, the monkey keeper is able to shift his conceptual categories—his way of conceiving of the same underlying reality—to harmonize with that of the monkeys because he is not attached to any one particular way of seeing this reality. His is the *yinshi* mode of consciousness that adapts spontaneously to the situation, an "illumined" consciousness that exhibits an intuitive knowledge that knows *how* to act without even knowing *that* it is acting. That is, the sage acts without self-consciousness and without being governed by any directing principle. His consciousness knows spontaneously how to respond because it is not confined to any one particular perspective.

Zhuangzi seems to be operating from this mode of consciousness throughout the "Qiwulun." The language skepticism and therapeutic use of perspectivism that Ivanhoe has noted are possible because the author is unconfined by any one way of looking at things. For example, in the Gaptooth and Wang Ni dialogue, Zhuangzi says, "how do I know that what I call knowing is not ignorance? How do I know that what I call ignorance is not knowing?"[39] Or in the Lady Li story, "How do I know that to take pleasure in life is not a delusion? How do I know that we who hate death are not lost children who have forgotten the way home?"[40] Self-negating propositions and challenges to the culturally accepted ways of looking at the world abound in this chapter. They are examples of an illumined cognition that becomes possible when attachment to a rigid and fixed worldview is abandoned.

Furthermore, Zhuangzi makes it clear that abandoning a fixed viewpoint is concomitant with abandoning attachment to the self. For example, he seems to quote and largely approve of the saying "Without an Other, there is no Self; without Self, no choosing one thing rather than another."[41] That is, if you lose the distinction between self and other, then you lose the self and, with it, any bias towards choosing one thing rather than another. There is also another relevant argument: "No thing is not 'other;' no thing is not 'it.' If you treat yourself too as 'other,' they do not appear. If you know of yourself, you know them."[42] It and Other do not appear because "treating yourself as other" (*zibi* 自 彼) involves abandoning attachment to your self. That is, it involves having the same attachment to your self as you have to anything else. This lack of self-attachment is an essential characteristic of the free and spontaneously functioning consciousness that Zhuangzi is advocating.

Zhuangzi has several related metaphors for the unique type of cognition of this *yinshi* consciousness, which include staying "at the point of rest on the potter's wheel of Heaven" (*xiu hu tianjun* 休乎天均);[43] "using illumination" (*yi ming* 以明);[44] "opening things up to the light of Heaven" (*zhao zhi yu tian* 照之於天);[45] and, as Raphals has already pointed out, "great knowing," and "greatly awakened" knowing. All these imply a fundamental shift in perspective away from attachment to one's individual viewpoint and toward freedom from such attachment that involves going along with the responses that emerge spontaneously from the Heavenly within one. So far we find that this *yinshi* mode of consciousness fits well with Yearley's "intraworldly mysticism," Raphals's understanding of "great knowledge," and Ivanhoe's intuitive "knowing how." What I would like to argue here is that for Zhuangzi, this *yinshi* consciousness with its characteristic mode of knowing is not the sole result of mystical praxis: there is another equally important experience on which it rests.

Introvertive Mystical Experience in the "Qiwulun"

There are a series of passages in the "Qiwulun" that talk about the *yinshi* mode of consciousness coming to an end. Perhaps the most important one is the following:

> If being so is inherent in a thing, if being allowable is inherent in a thing, then from no perspective would it be not so, from no perspective would it be not allowable. Therefore when a "that's it" which deems picks out a stalk from a pillar, a hag from beautiful Xi Shi, things however peculiar and incongruous, the Way pervades and unifies them. As they divide they develop, as they develop they dissolve. All things whether developing or dissolving revert to being pervaded and unified. Only those who penetrate this know how to pervade and unify things. The "that's it" which deems they do not use, but find lodging-places in daily life. It is in daily life that they make use of this perspective. It is in making use of this perspective that they pervade things. It is in pervading things that they attain it. And when they attain it they are almost there. The "that's it" which goes by circumstance comes to an end. It ends and when it does, that of which we do not know what is so of it, we call the Way.[46]

This is an extremely rich passage that must be carefully analyzed. Zhuangzi begins the passage with a reiteration of what some scholars have called his relativism or perspectivism. There are no perspectives, no viewpoints from which a thing is always so, is always true. The normal mode of *wei-shi* consciousness clearly differentiates things such as a stalk and a pillar, a hag and a beauty, and simultaneously makes preferences based on these perceptual distinctions. However it is only the Way that can pervade these things and unify them. That is, it is the one and only perspective from which all things are seen just as they are, without bias, without preference, the only perspective from which "all things are seen to be equal," of equal value and worth (or lack thereof, as in the title of this chapter). It is just this kind of seeing that is the essential defining characteristic of the "great" or "awakened" knowing of the *yinshi* mode of consciousness that is developed by those rare people who can penetrate through (*da* 達) the common *weishi* mode. In this passage Zhuangzi clearly states that such people possess the exact same ability that the Way has to "pervade and unify" (*tong wei yi* 通為一) all things.

Using this ability, these sages find temporary lodging places, that is viewpoints to which they are completely unattached, within the common experience of everyday living. The passage then reiterates that in using this Way-like perspective, the sages pervade things just as the Way pervades them. And in pervading things like this, these sages attain the Way itself. It is at this point that their distinctive everyday mode of *yinshi* consciousness comes to an end and they have the experience of merging with the Way itself. This is symbolized by the phrase "that of which we do not know what is so of it, we call the Way." Knowing what is so of something implies a separation between the self that knows and the object that is known. But the Way can never be known as an object; it can only be "known" when the distinction between self and other, subject and object, dissolves in the introvertive mystical experience of uniting or merging with the Way. Thus the extrovertive mystical experience of "pervading and unifying things" must depend on the introvertive mystical experience of merging with the Way. Or, rather, there is a recursive relationship between the two modes of this bimodal mystical experience. In other words, once one loses the self temporarily by merging with the Way and then returns to the everyday dualistic world, one is no longer attached to oneself and then the *yinshi* consciousness arises.

This then is the way in which this bimodal mystical experience operates in the "Qiwulun" to generate the distinctive cognition that makes use of the skeptical methods that Hansen and Raphals identify and the distinctive form of linguistic skepticism that Ivanhoe identifies. These can be practiced because sages are not attached to their individual selves because they have already gone through the experience of total self-forgetting or total self-emptying in which they merge with the Way. But after this introvertive experience they return to the world of everyday living, while at the same time retaining their prior condition of contact with the Way, the "great pervader" and unifier of all things. This condition of simultaneously seeing unity within multiplicity (or to paraphrase Stace, of apprehending the One as an inner subjectivity in all things) is one of the significant characteristics of the extrovertive mystical experience. We might best describe it as a "Tao-centered" mode of being in contrast to the "ego-centered" mode of being that most of us are enmeshed in and that Zhuangzi symbolizes as the "that's it which deems."

There are other passages that speak of the intimate relationship between the introvertive and extrovertive modes of mystical experience in *Zhuangzi*. For example,

> What is It is also Other; what is Other is also It. There they say "that's it,"
> "that's not" from one point of view. Here we say "that's it," "that's not"
> from another point of view. Are there really It and Other? Or really no It
> and Other? Where neither It nor Other finds its opposite is called the axis
> of the Way. When once the axis is found at the center of the circle there
> is no limit to responding with either, on the one hand no limit to what is
> it, on the other no limit to what is not. Therefore I say: "The best means
> is Illumination."[47]

In other words, after the experience of merging with the Way, one has discovered the "axis at the center of the circle" within, and so when one carries this experience back into everyday life and naturally maintains a connection to the Way, one can always respond spontaneously and harmoniously to whatever the situation demands, to whatever set of "It"/ "Other" or "that's it"/"that's not" categories are found in the limited *weishi* viewpoints of those with whom one is interacting. This is the particular skill or knack of the monkey keeper and, in another passage, a similar circular metaphor is also used to characterize it, "staying at the point of rest on the potter's wheel of Heaven."[48] The Way is the very center within the sage from which the "great" or "awakened" knowing of the *yinshi* mode of consciousness operates. The metaphor of a center implies impartiality: the center is equally distant from—or close to—any point on the circle. Therefore there is no bias; no thing is only It and not Other.

It is from this "Way-centered" perspective that Zhuangzi rejects all forms of propositions that attempt to establish true knowledge from a limited perspective. For example, we find his rejection of a series of intentionally paradoxical propositions, including Hui Shi's famous "heaven and earth were born together with me and the myriad things and I are one," which looks, at first, to be a concise statement of an extrovertive mystical experience. Zhuangzi says:

> Now that we are one, can I still say something? Already having called us one, did I succeed in not saying something? One and the saying make two, two and one make three. Proceeding from there, even an expert calculator cannot get to the end of it, much less a plain man. Therefore if we take the step from nothing to something we arrive at three. How much worse if we take the step from something to something! Take no step at all, and the "that's it" which goes by circumstance will come to an end.[49]

Zhuangzi rejects Hui Shi's saying because it is made from a dualistic, *weishi*, standpoint. That is, when one is truly united with the myriad things one cannot say anything because in this experience of unity there is no self from which such a statement can be made. Only after one is separated, in his words, after one has "taken the step from nothing to something," can one even make such a statement. But what is the point of making such a statement? It cannot give one true knowledge of the condition of unity because one is already functioning in a dualistic consciousness when such a statement is made. The only way of "knowing" such a unity is to experience it in a nondual fashion. It can never be adequately described by propositional knowing, which simultaneously reifies the self that asserts the truth of the propositions ("Without Other there is no Self. Without self, no choice between alternatives"). Propositional knowing is, in Ryle's words, a "knowing that." Nondual knowing, however, is a "knowing how." Knowing *that* is the knowing of the *weishi* mode of consciousness. Knowing *how* is the knowing of the *yinshi* mode of consciousness and, as we shall see, is linked with the many skill passages in the text that are particularly collected in chapter 19, "Da sheng" 達生 (Fathoming life). Notice, too, that here again, in the last sentence, Zhuangzi mentions the unity that comes about after the *yinshi* mode comes to an end. This unity is spoken of in one final passage that I would like to analyze:

> The men of old, their knowledge had arrived at something: at what had it arrived? There were some who thought that there had not yet begun to be things—the utmost, the exhaustive, there is no more to add. The next thought there were things but there had not yet begun to be borders. The next thought there were borders to them but there had not yet begun to be "that's it," "that's not." The lighting up of "that's it," "that's not" is the reason why the Way is flawed. The reason why the Way is flawed is the reason why love becomes complete. It anything really complete or flawed? Or is nothing really complete or flawed?[50]

Lisa Raphals sees these as stages in the history of knowledge but also acknowledges the possibility of a mystical reading in which these stages represent the return from an undifferentiated mystical experience to the perceptual and linguistic distinctions of the phenomenal world, and I concur with the latter interpretation.[51] When one is merged with the Way in the introvertive mystical experience there are neither things nor a self which perceives them. When one emerges, one returns to a perceiving self and a perceived world of things, and such a return is inevitable. Establishing borders among things, I think, implies identifying them with words and ideas, and at this point one is living in the *yinshi* mode of consciousness. It is only when one begins to use these labels to establish propositional knowledge about these things and its concomitant preferences that one gets into trouble because one simultaneously reifies the self that knows and the objects known, giving both an ultimate truth that Zhuangzi thinks they do not have. One here ventures into the *weishi* mode of consciousness of the dream that Zhuangzi satirizes with such phrases as "Yet fools think they are awake, so confident that they know what they are, princes, herdsmen, incorrigible!"[52] It is in this mode that we are prevented from penetrating through to the Way that pervades and unifies. It is this mode that is the dream from which we must awaken and understand that the mode in which most of us function every day is really the "ultimate dream." How are we to accomplish this awakening? I would argue that it is by following the apophatic practice of breathing meditation that is mentioned elsewhere in the Inner Chapters and which, I think, formed the distinctive technique around which Zhuangzi and his community of early Daoists formed.

Great Knowledge

So what, then, for Zhuangzi, constitutes "great knowledge" or "awakened knowledge?" Great knowledge consists in knowing *how* dualistic cognition—in other words knowing *that*—and all forms of propositional knowledge that arise from it, are true only relative to the standpoint and the circumstances of the knower. This type of cognition entails directly experiencing how to take all things as equal by pervading and unifying them, just as the Way does. As I see it, *all things* refers not to just external phenomena but also to all aspects of one's own experience, including the very self we take to be our foundation. This is what Zhuangzi means when he says that one must treat oneself as other (*zi bi* 自 彼). This does not imply the total negation of dualistic cognition but the relativizing or perspectivizing of it. This is what is meant by "finding lodging-places in daily living." Dualistic cognition and propositional knowledge may be useful in certain specific circumstances, but when the circumstances change, as they inevitably do, one must abandon them and allow oneself to respond to the new situation without their determining influence. This yields an awareness that is able to focus completely on what is taking place in the present moment.

So when Zhuangzi dreams he is a butterfly in the famous story, he is totally experiencing being a butterfly, and he has none of the conceptual categories of Zhuangzi the man. Then when he wakes up he is again the man who remembers the sensation of being a butterfly. His question about his own identity arises from his total lack of attachment to any one way of looking at things, even to the standpoint of his own self. This is a perfect demonstration of the total fluidity of conceptual categories that is one of the essential defining characteristics of the *yinshi* mode of consciousness.

This distinct quality of psychological freedom and concomitant total concentration is at the heart of all the many skill passages throughout the text that Yearley, Ivanhoe, and others quite rightly point to as paradigmatic examples of the results of "intraworldly mysticism" and "intuitive knowing." These passages contain stories of masters of the *yinshi* consciousness, the "that's it" which goes by circumstance, who can totally concentrate on whatever task they are involved in, be it carving an ox, catching a cicada, plunging over the Spinebridge Falls,[53] carving a bell stand, or even serving in government—albeit reluctantly. Note that the last two "fast" in order to still their minds to prepare them for the tasks confronting them.[54]

Indeed, I would like to suggest that the cultivation of such a mode of consciousness—of a "Dao-centered" mode of being—was one of the central focuses within the community of Zhuangzi and his later disciples. Evidence of it can be seen scattered throughout the entire thirty-three-chapter work. The depiction of this mode of consciousness in the text of the *Zhuangzi* constitutes a major contribution to the cross-cultural study of extrovertive mystical experience that sets this mode squarely on a par with the introvertive, thereby helping to counteract the Stacian bias and clearly indicating the bimodal character of mystical experience in early China.

Notes

I wish to thank Professor Scott Cook of Grinnell College for organizing the Association for Asian Studies panel for which I initially wrote this
piece. I also wish to thank my colleagues and friends Sumner B. Twiss, Aaron
Stalnaker, Jung Lee, and Anne Heyrman-Hart for their valuable criticisms of
an earlier version of the work. [A revised version of this chapter has recently
been published in *Journal of Chinese Religions* 28 (2000), pp. 31–50. We are
grateful to the editors of *Journal of Chinese Religions* for agreeing to let us
reprint the chapter in the present volume.]

    1. Victor Mair, *Experimental Essays on the Chuang Tzu* (Honolulu: Uni-
versity of Hawaii Press, 1983); and Paul Kjellberg and P. J. Ivanhoe, *Essays on
Skepticism, Relativism, and Ethics in the* Zhuangzi (Albany: State University of
New York Press, 1996). I share the same assumptions as the scholars included
in these two volumes that there is one author to the Inner Chapters, and I
will follow existing conventions in referring to him as Zhuangzi.

    2. Harold D. Roth, "Redaction Criticism and the Early History of Tao-
ism," *Early China* 19 (1994), pp. 1–46; "Evidence for Stages of Meditation in
Early Taoism," *Bulletin of the School of Oriental and African Studies* 60:1 (June
1997); and "*Lao Tzu* in the Context of Early Daoist Mystical Practice," in
Religious and Philosophical Aspects of the Laozi, ed. Mark Csikszentmihalyi and
P. J. Ivanhoe (Stanford: Stanford University Press, 1999), pp. 59–96.

    3. Don Harper has accomplished seminal work in translating the texts
of this tradition. See his *Early Chinese Medical Literature: The Mawangdui Medical Manuscripts* (London: Royal Asiatic Society, 1997). He has also begun an
important analysis of how this tradition relates to the early texts of Daoism in
this book and in a new article: "The Bellows Analogy in *Laozi* V and Warring
States Macrobiotic Hygiene," *Early China* 20 (1995), pp. 381–92.

    4. Walter Stace, *Mysticism and Philosophy* (London: Macmillan, 1960;
repr. Los Angeles: Jeremy P. Tarcher, 1987), pp. 111, 131.

    5. Ibid., p. 66.

    6. Roth, "Some Issue in the Study of Chinese Mysticism: A Review
Essay," *China Review International* 2:1 (Spring, 1995), pp. 154–72.

    7. Stace, *Mysticism and Philosophy,* p. 132.

    8. Lee Yearley, "The Perfected Person in the Radical Chuang-tzu," in
Mair, pp. 130–31.

    9. Ibid.

    10. Chad Hansen, "A Tao of Tao in *Chuang Tzu*," in Mair, p. 37.

    11. ZZJS 146 ff.; HY 9/4/24ff. [Throughout this volume, all references to
the text of the *Zhuangzi* are to Guo Qingfan 郭慶藩, *Zhuangzi jishi* 莊子集
釋 (Wang Xiaoyu 王孝魚, ed.; Beijing: Zhonghua shuju, 1961); and *Zhuangzi
yinde* 莊子引得, Harvard-Yenching Institute Sinological Index Series no. 20
(Beijing, 1947).]

12. ZZJS 228; HY 15/6/6–7.

13. See, Harold D. Roth, "Evidence for Stages of Meditation in Early Taoism" and "*Lao Tzu* in the Context of Early Daoist Mystical Praxis."

14. ZZJS 284; HY 19/6/92–93. My translation is based on A.C. Graham, *Chuang-tzu:The Seven Inner Chapters and Other Writings from the Book Chuang-tzu* (London: George Allen & Unwin, 1981), p. 92. I deviate only in translating *tong* (通) as "merge" instead of "go along," and in translating *datong* as the "Great Pervader." [Whenever Graham's translation is used as a basis, the page number will be indicated after "Graham."]

15. I follow Graham in understanding *zhi ti* as the four limbs or members and the five orbs or visceral organs that are the physical manifestations of the five basic systems of vital energy in the human body. This is preferable to the alternative "drop off limbs and body" because two lines later, the text refers to parting from the body (*li xing*), which would be redundant if the second interpretation were taken. For the associations of the emotions with the various internal organs or "orbs," see Manfred Porkert, *The Theoretical Foundations of Chinese Medicine* (Cambridge: MIT Press, 1974), pp. 115–46.

16. ZZJS 252–53; HY 17/6/39–42; Graham 87.

17. ZZJS 66; HY 4/2/29–30; Graham 53.

18. Hansen, "A Tao of Tao," p. 45.

19. ZZJS 79; HY 5/2/52–53.

20. Lisa Raphals, "Skeptical Strategies in *Zhuangzi* and Theaetetus," in Kjellberg and Ivanhoe, 26–49.

21. Ibid, p. 30.

22. Ibid, pp. 30–31.

23. P. J. Ivanhoe, "Zhuangzi on Skepticism, Skill, and the Ineffable Dao," *Journal of the American Academy of Religion* 64.4 (1993), pp. 639–54.

24. Ibid, p. 641.

25. Ibid, p. 642.

26. Ibid, p. 643.

27. Ibid, p. 648.

28. Ibid, p. 649.

29. Ibid, p. 645.

30. Ibid, p. 653.

31. A.C. Graham, "*Chuang Tzu*'s Essay on Seeing All Things as Equal," *History of Religions* 9 (October, 1969–February, 1970), pp. 137–59.

32. ZZJS 63; HY 4/2/26; Graham 52.

33. Hansen, in Mair, *Experimental Essays*, p. 34.

34. The two pairs of Graham's English translations of *shi* and *fei* are from his book *Chuang Tzu: The Inner Chapters* and from the *History of Religions* article, respectively.

35. ZZJS 70; HY 5/2/38–40; Graham 54.

36. ZZJS 74; HY 5/2/43–44; Graham 54.

37. ZZJS 75; HY 5/2/45; Graham 55.
38. ZZJS 75; HY 5/2/47; Graham 55.
39. ZZJS 92; HY 6/2/66; Graham 58.
40. ZZJS 103; HY 6/2/78–9; Graham 59.
41. ZZJS 55; HY 4/2/14–15; Graham 51.
42. ZZJS 66; HY 4/2/27; Graham 52.
43. ZZJS 70; HY 5/2/39–40.
44. ZZJS 63, HY 4/2/27, Graham 52; ZZJS 66, HY 4/2/31, Graham 53; ZZJS 75, HY 5/2/47, Graham 55.
45. ZZJS 66; HY 4/2/29; Graham 52.
46. ZZJS 69–70; HY 4–5/2/34–37. My translation departs from Graham's (pp. 53–54). The key departure is my rendering of the verbal phrase *tong wei yi* as "to pervade and unify" rather than Graham's "interchange and deem to be one." I feel this better captures the activity of the Way and of the sages who identify completely with it: the Way pervades everything and in pervading them unifies them. They are unified to the extent that each and every thing contains the Way within it; and they are unified in that, from the perspective of the Way within, each thing is seen to be equal. Because they attain this Way, sages can have the exact same perspective.
47. ZZJS 66; HY 4/2/29–31; Graham 53.
48. ZZJS 70; HY 5/2/39–40; Graham 54.
49. ZZJS 79; HY 5/2/52–55; Graham 56.
50. ZZJS 74; HY 5/2/40–43.
51. Raphals, "Skeptical Strategies," p. 33 and p. 46, note 34, respectively.
52. ZZJS 104; HY 6/2/82–83; Graham 60.
53. I take the title of the waterfall from Victor Mair, *Wandering on the Way: Early Taoist Tales and Parables from Chuang Tzu* (New York: Bantam Books, 1994), p. 182. Mair's consistent translation of such names in order to give the reader a sense of their implications in Chinese is one of the strengths of his translation.
54. The bell carver (ZZJS 658 ff.; HY 50/19/54 ff.) and Yan Hui (ZZJS 146 ff.; HY 9/4/24 ff.) both practice a fasting of the mind in order to cultivate stillness and emptiness. This is another indication of the importance of inner cultivation practice in developing the *yinshi* mode of extrovertive mystical consciousness.

2

How Many Are the Ten Thousand Things and I? Relativism, Mysticism, and the Privileging of Oneness in the "Inner Chapters"

BROOK ZIPORYN 任博克

A fundamental tension has attached itself to attempts to read the "Inner Chapters" of the *Zhuangzi* as a coherent whole, which dates back, in one form or another, to the conflicting interpretations of Guo Xiang 郭象 and Zhi Daolin 支道林 seventeen centuries ago, and continues to this day. Its most recent form has come into particularly sharp focus quite recently in Western studies of the text, for example, as the question of how to square Zhuangzi's "perspectivism" (which seems to preclude privileging any particular truth claim over any other) with his apparent approval of one particular perspective (for example, that which sees that all things are one, or that all perspectives are equal), as is attested by the recent publication of the book *Essays on Skepticism, Relativism, and Ethics in the Zhuangzi.*[1] This chapter attempts a solution to this quandary, which, unlike all the essays in that volume, eschews the assumption that Zhuangzi must be *either* a relativistic perspectivist *or* privilege one particular perspective, but cannot do both. Under the auspices of that premise, various writers suggest either that Zhuangzi's skepticism and relativism are insincere, merely provocative rhetoric, or, more generously, therapeutic techniques meant to clear away all cognitive prejudices and pretensions of knowledge to open the mind up for true mystical intuition, which alone can provide true information about the way the world is—namely, that it is one, or that all its things and perspectives are equal, or that it is born from the Dao, or that it has its own natural laws, which can thus be apprehended and followed. Another suggestion (Robert Eno) is that Zhuangzi is a thoroughgoing relativist with respect to "discourse daos," that is any propositional assertion about what is right or wrong, about which practice has superior value, and thus is a hard skeptic concerning cognitive knowledge and the efficacy of debate. He is not, however, a relativist with respect to skill-*daos*; it is absolutely better to be a master of some *dao* than to have no mastery; it is just that it does not matter what *dao* it is, and there is no way to adjudicate the relative merits of *daos* by means of words. The skepticism is a therapy by which the attachment to cognitive views and argumentative positions is cleared away, opening one up for skill mastery in dealing with the world.

In contrast to all these views, which see the coexistence of the skeptical and relativist trends and the "mystical" trends as an irreconcilable problem, but somewhat in consonance with Eno's reading, I will argue that Zhuangzi, in the "Inner Chapters," is both uncompromising in rejecting the possibility of any unbiased or universal perspective providing uniquely accurate information about the world in anything like what we mean by an "objective" sense, *and* elaborates and privileges a particular perspective—the perspective that all things are one and that all perspectives are equal. This perspective is no more immune to Zhuangzi's skeptical objections than any other. But its self-referential nature and pragmatic nondiscomfirmability give it certain unique qualities, not the least of which is a kind of staying power in the midst of the transformation of perspectives, which amounts to a *performative* (tautological) demonstration of its "truth." That is, by assuming this perspective, and the standards of truth adjudication that come with it, one has *made* it nondisconfirmable, and in this sense universally applicable and, in this rather narrow sense, "true." It is precisely its ability to coexist in and as any other perspective, including its direct contradiction, that gives it the special skill-functions that Zhuangzi describes so enthusiastically.

My reading of the "Inner Chapters" will develop the position that this text is best interpreted as presenting an *omnicentric holism*. This term is to be understood in the following manner. *Whole* here refers to any group of mutually determining and dependent terms. *Center* is here used as a figurative term for the authoritative point in any *whole* in reference to which all other points derive their significance, value and identity, the master signifier or locus of ultimate value upon which the meaning of all other parts, as instrumental value, depend. This is the point from which the whole can be seen in its "true" aspect, as it "really is," from which the true value and nature of each of the parts can be validly assessed, as opposed to the distorted partial perspectives of the parts. It denotes the point or perspective that beholds the whole qua whole and to which all the points have a direct relation. Epistemologically, this would be the one perspective from which all things can be viewed accurately. Given this definition, *unicentric holism* will refer to any doctrine holding that there is indeed a perspective from which all things can be viewed aright, from which their connections may be comprehended in their true aspect; this would be the holistic view that the quiddities of all things are determined solely by their relations to other things, and thus the whole is more than the sum of its parts, but that a whole has only one center and hence one and only one true perspective that can validly determine the value and nature of the parts. The parts cannot be the locus of an accurate apprehension of the whole, on this view, since they are themselves separate and considered in themselves represent a distortion; they can only be properly understood in the perspective of the whole, that is, from the one center. In contrast, I will use the term *omnicentric holism* to refer to any doctrine that holds that, indeed, the quiddities of all things are determined solely by their relations to other things, and thus the whole is more than the sum of its parts (holism), but that this is true in so thorough a sense that each point in any whole is a center of that whole, such that each one adequately represents, perceives, includes the whole. This means that any part *is* the whole itself, and all the parts inherently include each other. This somewhat unusual view will hopefully become more lucid as we proceed.

My claim vis-à-vis the "Inner Chapters" is that we have here an omnicentric holism constructed through the premise that *a thing entails a perspective*, and closely connected to this is an extreme commitment to value paradox, since each perspective constitutes its own whole, is intrinsically correct, and includes its opposite. This paradoxical structure applies equally to natural, moral, and epistemological value; in all three cases, the negative is given a positive meaning and value, on an equal footing with the initially positive. This situation is crystallized in the images of "traveling two roads at once" (*liang xing* 兩行) and "the potter's wheel of heaven" (*tianjun* 天鈞) which "responds but does not store" (*ying er bu cang* 應而不藏):[2] the spinning periphery standing for the ever-shifting responsiveness, creative of rights and wrongs, that is, of viewpoints with a this and a that, comprehending and harmonizing with the standpoints of others, while the center of the spinning potter's wheel is still, "at rest" (*xiu* 休), "not storing" in the sense of not adhering to any *shi/fei* ("this/that") as fixed or universally justified.

Perspectives here means both emotional moods and philosophical positions, as well as identities as such. "This/that"s, as we shall see, apply to all of the following dyadic pairs: (1) emotional perspectives (joy/sorrow, etc.) (2) concepts of identity (self/other), (3) value concepts (right/wrong, benefit/harm) and (4) life and death (an extension of now/then). Hence the value paradox and omnicentrism of the *Zhuangzi* entails the claim that the true man has no fixed identity; he may have the ability to have emotions, to feel his way into various positions and perspectives as expressed by others or even himself, to live and die; on the other hand, he maintains a central point that is still, uninvolved, not fully absorbed into or committed to this perspective, which means, as the image of the pivot or hinge suggests especially, he retains the ability to jump back out of it when the situation changes, to identify equally with the opposite when the time comes, to know even now that it too will equally be a "this." This situation, again, is described as responding without storing, traveling two roads at once, knowing through not knowing (*yi wu zhi zhi* 以 無知知), words that are no words, the Dao that is not a Dao (*bu yan zhi bian, bu dao zhi dao* 不言之辯，不道之道). Epistemologically, this will allow Zhuangzi to avoid the usual quandary of the relativist, that is, the criticism of self-contradiction that comes with making the universally applicable claim that no claim can be universally applicable, the absolute truth that nothing is absolute. For Zhuangzi, the claim will amount rather to the suggestion that every claim is absolutely true and cannot be assailed from anywhere, since the only standards for judgment are internally posited—and this goes for Zhuangzi's own claim, this one, as well. By its own standards, namely, that "All positions are right," the position "All positions are right" is obviously right.

Are All Things One?

The view that "All things are one" has been attributed to the *Zhuangzi* since ancient times. Recently, both Graham and Hansen have made much of their interpretation that Zhuangzi never actually asserts that all things are one; he merely says repeatedly that the sage *treats* things as one.[3] Hansen goes even further, claiming that the view that all things are one is for Zhuangzi no different from any other view, even suggesting that Zhuangzi is ridiculing the sage for treating all things as one![4] In my view, there is an important insight here, which, in Hansen's case, is pushed much too far. Hansen represents the purest expression of the view that Zhuangzi is a "hard relativist," that by *dao* he means simply *any* guiding discourse, not a metaphysical entity called "the Dao," and that he cannot consistently privilege any particular perspective. I share Hansen's commitment to the thoroughgoingness of Zhuangzi's relativism and indeed, am willing to extend it not only to questions of value but also to questions of fact. However, as I wish to show here, I do not think this forces us to ignore the obvious fact that Zhuangzi privileges the perspective of oneness, or to charge Zhuangzi with carelessness or self-contradiction for this reason.

If we are to understand Zhuangzi correctly, it is indeed crucial to distinguish between the bare assertion of oneness and the sage's ability to regard as one, or as many. We see this clearly in the "Dechongfu" chapter: "*If* things are viewed from their differences, one's own liver and spleen are as different as Chu and Yue. But if viewed from their sameness, all things are one."[5] The ability to switch perspectives is what is crucial here so far. We will see below more concerning this ability to unobstructedly switch perspectives, as a function of the pivot of Dao, which responds without cease.

But it must be noted that as actually used by Zhuangzi, the view that "All things are one" is clearly not on a par with other views; not only in terms of sheer bulk of usage, but also in unmistakable rhetorical charging and, most important, in terms of the variety of uses to which it is put, the number of types of consequences and developments the text utilizes this premise to draw. This is not because it has some unique truth value, but because it proves more useful in achieving what Zhuangzi wants to achieve. That is, this perspective, that all things are one, is in fact ultimately privileged in the *Zhuangzi*, but for a very distinctive reason, as alluded to briefly above, having to do with this *performative* power of such a truth claim. Thus throughout the "Inner Chapters" we find assertions of this view used as premises for further, ethical, axiological conclusions, namely, for the sake of value paradox, as we shall see below (whereas the contrary view, of the multiplicity of things, tends to fall into the background as a rhetorical device, possibly because it is the common sense view already assumed by most readers). Thus Confucius, just after the above-quoted statement that things can be seen either as the same or different, praises a cripple for seeing all things as one, therefore not seeing anything as lost—such as his foot, or by an implication soon picked up, life itself. This "not seeing anything being lost" is echoed in the passage about hiding the world in the world in the "Dazongshi" chapter, the extreme rhetorical emphasis of which creates an impression that this is Zhuangzi's own position. This metaphor is structurally similar to two others of great importance: "riding on transformations of the six breaths" (*yu liuqi zhi bian* 御六氣

之辯) (it does not matter which ones are present at any time, the totality is the same, and one can ride on any arrangement, so there is no possibility of loss) and the "monkey keeper and his seven chestnuts" (it does not matter which way he presents them at what time, the totality is the same, and one can abide by any arrangement, so there is no possibility of loss).[6] Similarly, a state beyond the fear of death is described as "Wandering in the One Vital Force of heaven and earth . . . depending on the varying things to give oneself over to the one body [of all things]" (遊乎天地之一氣 . . . 假於異物，託於同體).[7] In all these cases and many others, the perspective that views all things as one is shown to have a very special efficacy in overcoming the problems of existence with which Zhuangzi is concerned.

But the theoretical derivation of the view that "all things are one" must be looked for elsewhere: given that Zhuangzi asserts that there is a sense in which all things are one, what exactly is this sense? For we must know this before we can understand what kind of holism, if any, we are dealing with here. There is another class of statements that asserts a stronger sense of what it means for all things to be one, for the universe to form some kind of whole. I am thinking here not so much of the assertions "Dao is everywhere" (wu suo bu zai 無所不在), which only become explicit as such in the Outer and Miscellaneous chapters, nor even of the famous "Heaven and earth were born together with me, and all things and I are one" (天地與我並生，萬物與我為一) passage, which, as Graham points out, is quickly called into question and which is part of an example concerning perspectives used in disputation, exemplifying the extremes of permissible paradox, and not forming the conclusion of the discussion.[8] A much more solid basis for discussion of Zhuangzi's holism is found in the less spectacular statements such as the following: "Dao has never begun to have divisions; words have never begun to have constancy; it is due to deeming assertions that there are borders between things,"[9] or a little more directly, the description of the perfect knowledge of the ancients (which therefore is of course still presented merely as one possible perspective, albeit one that is powerfully flagged): "They held that there had never yet begun to be anything . . . Thereafter they held that there was something, but it had no divisions to it; thereafter they held that there were divisions but no right and wrong."[10] Here we are merely being told what certain people, the ancients, thought; but the rhetorical approval of the first view is unmistakable. "Having no divisions" (feng 封) seems to describe a state of universal oneness, that there is no division between this and that, that all things are to be viewed as one thing, or better, no thing, since "one thing" is commonly defined in contradistinction to something else. In the "Dazongshi" chapter we have the powerful metaphor of the boat alluded to already in this chapter:

> The great mass burdens me with a form, labors me with life, eases me with old age, rests me with death. Thus that which makes my life good also makes my death good. A boat can be hid in a ravine, or a net[11] in a lake, and this is called safe. But in the night a powerful one may come along and bear them off, while the ignorant know nothing of it. So even when the small is hid in the large in so ingenious a way, it may still vanish. But if you were to hide the world in the world, there would be no such vanishing. This is the great trick for making things eternal. Now you happen to have taken on a human form, and you delight in it; but this human form is constantly undergoing thousands of changes—so there should be no limit to your joys. Thus the sage wanders in that in which nothing vanishes and all are preserved. Early death, old age, beginning, end—he considers them all good.[12]

It is crucial to note here that, if we go by only the passages cited so far, we have here what can superficially be read as a model *unicentric* holism. Indeed, if the above and what is immediately related to it were all there were, Zhuangzi would be a *unicentric* holist. The direct axiological result sought from this form of holism is clear: we are to become resigned to the so-called negative by seeing it as the work of the whole, the same whole that gives us the so-called positive. Thus everything is good. The way to see this is to "hide" the whole in the whole. That way nothing can fall out. If we place value in any part of the whole, in other words, we will be vulnerable to its loss. But if we place value in the whole as such, we will never be without it, for there is nowhere for it to go. The whole is always the whole. Or, in the imagery employed by the first part of this passage: "the same agent (the great clump, i.e., the whole, the primal all-together *hundun* 混沌) performs what I, from my limited perspective, call good and bad (life, death). Thus if one is good, all are good." The same sentiment, that apparent value contraries are in fact the work of a single entity, and hence cannot really be value contraries, appears many times in the Inner Chapters: we are told about being and nonbeing being parts of one "body" (*ti* 體),[13] about "acceptable" and "unacceptable" forming one thread,[14] about a single agent creating all and destroying all.[15] In between, we are told repeatedly to give ourselves over to the unavoidable (*bu de yi* 不得已, etc.) and repose in it as fate, the providence responsible for all these contrary changes.

Thus far, it sounds as if Zhuangzi is a typical unicentric fatalist, perhaps even a pious quasideist. No wonder those stories about "the Creator of Things" in the "Dazongshi" chapter sound so convincing and so easy to understand. The conclusion is always, "Where could it/he/they send me which would not be okay?"[16] This has led many to read Zhuangzi as if he were in fact a unicentrist, saying in effect, "All things are arranged by fate; you, from your limited small perspective, call some good and some bad, but really they are all equally the work of the whole, and thus all are equally good. Renounce your selfish individual perspective and adopt the perspective of the whole, and you will be able to affirm all things. Accept the work of providence." The prevalence of rhetoric emphasizing the big/small contrast, especially in the "Xiaoyaoyou" chapter, reinforces this impression. "Riding the rightness of heaven and earth, charioting on the changes of the six breaths"[17] is taken in this sense, as accepting that what is done is done by the whole, and if we take on its perspective instead of our own, then all is right and good, and we should go along with it.

But this is a very partial picture of Zhuangzi, one which, I hope to show, leaves out exactly the essential things. We will see it come apart in two places. First, on examining the "monkey keeper" metaphor we will come to see *what* the indifferent totality, in the paradigmatic case, is a totality *of:* namely, of *shi/fei.* The two parts that make up the whole, which one always has and can never lose, are right and wrong, defined perspectivally, as we shall see below. This will similarly unlock the other metaphors of the same structure (the boat, the six breaths), allowing us to see the same structure there—an *omnicentric* structure. Second, the passage last quoted concludes with two more phrases: "so as to wander without end—what would such a one have to wait for/depend on?"[18] This introduces an entirely new wrinkle: for an assertion seems to be being made here that in this submission to fate and subordination of the individual perspective to that of the whole, rather than being passive and dependent, one has suddenly become perfectly free and independent! This too subverts a unicentric reading, and it is with this point that we will start, allowing it to lead us to the other. The dependent, then, is the free. How so?

A Thing Is a Perspective

The "Xiaoyaoyou" seems to switch abruptly from the question of relativism (perspectivism, as of the differing views of things espoused by the little birds and the great Peng, or the relative ages and size of various creatures) to the question of dependence (i.e., Liezi still had to "depend on" [wait for] the six-month wind, like the Peng bird, but for one who rides on the rightness of heaven and earth and the changes of the six breaths, what would he have to depend on?), leaving the relation between them somewhat mysterious. This relation between perspectivism and dependence is the focus of the next chapter, the world-historical riddle, "Qiwulun." Nanguoziqi says, "I have lost me," after looking as if he had "lost his opposite" (*sang qi ou* 喪其耦).[19] "I have lost me" introduces a doubleness; for it implies both that I am still here and that I am gone. I am absent and present, both at once: "I" lost "me" (*wu sang wo* 吾喪我), I am both the loser who is left behind after the loss and that which is lost. This both/and equivocation on the question of the existence of the self (the "true lord," the "one who blows the breath," etc.) is a central theme of the chapter. Zhuangzi generally ends his discussions with a double-pronged question: "Is there really X? Or is there really no X?" In my view, this is meant to imply neither that there is X (a true ruler, etc.) nor that there is not, but simply to come to rest precisely at the uncertainty and the question itself. That in itself is his conclusion, that balanced teetering of yes and no. What is the basis of this ultimacy granted to teetering?

"Losing me" is paired with and indeed seems to be identical with "losing his opposite." Here the great question of the mutual definition of dyadic pairs makes its unmistakable appearance. It is here too that the decisive step toward omnicentrism is made. For here we begin to see concretely what a "whole" is for Zhuangzi. It is not an undifferentiated mass of indifferent matter or *qi*, as we might think from an unreflecting reading of some of the passages quoted above, and others. Instead, the primary idea of a whole is of a correlative pair, which Zhuangzi pares down to its purest and most abstract form: this and that, or self and not-self. Graham's work on the "Qiwulun" has shown the clever manner in which the punning of these terms (*bi, shi* 彼是) with those also meaning "right and wrong" (*shi, fei* 是非) is exploited, but the holism that emerges from Zhuangzi's consideration of correlative pairs, self and not-self, right and wrong, in connection with certain assumptions about intersubjectivity, is an omnicentric holism, not a unicentric one.

Let us briefly take it step by step. The question is, "What do you mean, you lost you?" The answer that is given seems unrelated; we are told about the piping of earth and heaven, that is the sounds that emerge from the hollows of trees and rocks as the wind passes through. This is not only a clever continuation of the wind imagery from the chapter before but a striking metaphor of the voices of philosophers arguing their rights and wrongs with each other from their various perspectives, as Wang Fuzhi 王夫之, Guo Xiang 郭象, and many others have noted.

They can all be perceived as a harmonious piping of the one blower, the wind; in the same way, perhaps, the philosophers' arguments can be heard as the pipings of Dao. This is a possible reading, but I prefer to take a more cautious interpretation. For what has this to do with the explanation of "I lost me?" Perhaps it can be construed to mean, "I no longer see my viewpoint as my own, but instead as that of the blower, the Dao, and the same goes for the viewpoints of others." This seems to be part of the answer, but it does not go far enough and leads us again too far in a unicentric direction. There is much evidence for another, more central reading. Nanguoziqi says, "Blowing through the ten thousand differences so that each puts forth from itself; they all take their individualities from it—but *who* is the blower?" (*nu zhe qi shei ye* 怒者其誰邪).[20] This "who," in my view, is a gloss on "I lost me." This question word is Zhuangzi's typical yes/no, the same yes/no we saw implied in the structure of "'I' lost 'me,'" the simultaneous presence and absence of the self, and Zhuangzi's insistence on ending all his discussions with a wavering pair of questions, rather than a conclusion. The blower, then, is the self, always both present and absent in the sounds. The true self, in short, is "Who?" Or, to put it otherwise, the true self is "Is there really a true self or not?"

What are the sounds then supposed to represent? A few lines later the answer is given explicitly: "Joy, anger, sadness, happiness, worry, regret, fickleness, inflexibility, modesty, willfulness, candor, insolence—music from empty holes, steam forming mushrooms!"[21] That is, all the states, conditions, moods, perspectives through which the self commonly transforms in manifesting itself, are the "music from empty holes." Note too that these perspectives are roughly grouped in opposite, polar pairs. This suggests that the primary referent of the metaphor of the music from holes is the emotional perspectives experienced by the individual subject; that is why Nanguoziqi lost "himself" in contemplating these pipings: he sees only the transformations, and no "true ruler" among them other than the posing of the question about the true ruler.

This point is made more forcefully a few lines farther, when the question of a true controller is raised explicitly. First we are told that "the self" as such is correlative with these, its objects (note that initially the "objects" are not things in the outside world, but the self's own emotional perspectives): "Without them there is no me, without me there is nothing to pick them out."[22] It seems as if there's some controller—but no sign of him can be found. It is like the body itself—do the parts rule each other in turn, or is there a real enduring ruler to them all? And again, we end up with the same deliberately ambiguous conclusion: it has no sign or form, is identified with no one part or stage in the transformations, and yet it has its unmistakable functions. These are the same words used later to describe Dao as such: "Dao has realness and reliability but no form or deliberate activity" (*you qing you xin, wu wei wu xing* 有情有信，無為無形).[23] We may perhaps infer from this that the Dao is to the world as the self is to the passing emotional perspectives. It is both present and absent—in other words, "I" have lost "me."[24]

What is contrasted to this losing of me is the forming of a completed mind (*cheng xin* 成心); put in the language of the large/small contrast, Zhuangzi later says: "Dao is obscured by small completions" (*Dao yin yu xiao cheng* 道隱於小成).[25] To become fixed in one perspective among these transformations and identify with it, take it as the true self or ruler, put all value in it, "follow it as master" (*shi* 師) produces a definite this/that or right/wrong perspective (*shifei* 是非)—that is, to stand in a single "self" and define it as "this" and "right" while any other perspective is "other" or "wrong." This would be to assert that the true ruler does (or does not) exist, is identifiable with some one set of contents, at whatever level of abstraction or subtlety, without the balancing "loss" or negation of this true ruler in the form of the constant question. The rule of the self or of the Dao is dependent on "not playing the ruler," as in the *Laozi*. If it does assert itself as ruler, if it manifests as definitively present and known, it ceases to be ruler, it ceases to be present as underlying controller or self. The rationale for this claim in the *Laozi* had to do with the dialectic of eminence and return; for Zhuangzi, on the other hand, it has to do with the unwarranted adoption of *any* perspective, entailing a neglect of the fundamental mutual penetration, transformation, and interdependence of all perspectives.

It is crucial to remember the paradigmatic example of transformation that is given right at the beginning of this discussion of correlative dependence: the fact that the perspectives or moods in one's concrete experience transform into one another. Dependence is conceived within the context of transformation. One person's perspective is constantly changing. So the "small completion" is a reference not only to getting fixated on only a part of the whole in a spatial sense, but more centrally in a temporal sense: it does not ask for one constant vision of the whole rather than the parts but rather to be open to the change through the whole spectrum, riding on all—or rather *any*—of the six breaths. We are told repeatedly that "knowledge" (*zhi* 知) cannot discern the origin of these changes—these seem phenomenologically to emerge from nowhere like mushrooms formed of steam, and it is fruitless to seek a definite origin, that is, a definitive self, a blower, a true master of all this. That is, unlike Spinoza, Zhuangzi does not implore us to recognize the cause of these transformations, the whole, comprehend it, and surrender to it. This would still be "taking a mind with some particular completed perspective (in this case, the perspective of the whole) as your master." This would be, in short, unicentrism. But Zhuangzi does not recommend this. What then does he recommend?

It is at this point in the text that the connection to the disputes of philosophers is explicitly made: "Words are not just blowings; words have something they refer to. It's just that what they refer to is not fixed."[26] This may be construed as a possible objection to what has been said so far from a theoretical interlocutor (or straw man), along the following lines: "Yes, maybe the fickle individual emotions are like music from empty holes, maybe in the personal sense no firm ground of a self can be either found or dismissed. But it is different with the words of us philosophers.[27] Words, unlike emotions, are not like wind, because they have something they refer to, and that gives them a more solid ground, so that arguments can have some efficacy." Zhuangzi's response is, in effect: "But really there is no difference, for this thing they refer to is just as unstable as the emotional perspectives—indeed, when you get right down to it, they're one and the same thing." Changing emotions are varying perspectives on the world; but various worldviews, as exemplified in the doctrines of philosophers (i.e., their unproven starting points), are also varying perspectives. What they depend on is a *shi/fei*, a standard of reference; this is unfixed, for everyone takes himself as *shi*/this/right and everyone else as *fei*/that/wrong. So are words arguing philosophical positions really any different from blowing breaths or chirping birds (perhaps the derisive little birds of "Xiaoyaoyou"), from the changing modes and emotions an individual goes through, or not? Again we end in a question—Zhuangzi is subtle enough to see that to conclude even that words can conclude nothing would make him a hypocrite.

Now just as "the wind" is something that is known and heard nowhere but in all the sounds, the "true self" is nowhere but in all the changing emotions, and the "truth" (Dao) nowhere but in all the different words, positions, and arguments of the philosophers. In this sense, they are all correct. For all are indeed "this, self, right"—from their own perspective. This is where things start to get interesting. For again, this is not to be construed unicentrically. They are not said to be correct *because* each is an expression of the universal Dao; that is, they are not just correct *subspecies aeternitas* or in the view of the Whole, to perceive which each must relinquish its own perspective. Rather, each one is "right" *precisely from his own petty limited partial perspective*, and this is affirmed as the truth, as what brings the "*shi*"-ness, or rightness, or *value*, into things at all. Their *shi* 是 comes from being a part, and seeing things from a partial angle, *not* from seeing things as from the perspective whole. "The Dao" is derived from this consideration, not vice versa.

Thus the Ruists and Mohists are equally partial, each *shi*-ing what the other *fei*s and vice versa. But if one really wanted to make sure that everything each affirms is negated and vice versa, as each side of the debate seems to do, the easiest way would be to use the *obvious* (*ming* 明) state of affairs, namely, this fact itself, the fact that they negate each other.[28] The obvious fact itself solves the problem and ironically achieves what they themselves wanted to do, namely, negate each other! They are negated by negating and they are affirmed by affirming, all from their own individual limited perspectives. The fact that everyone has a different perspective and view is obvious; that is why there is an argument in the first place. But that obvious fact is what solves the problem, settles the argument: you wanted to negate them? They are thereby negated! You wanted to negate both of the disputants of that other argument, or affirm both, or affirm one and negate the other? They are both negated, and both affirmed! Take your pick! Hence, "the sage steers by the light of chaos and doubt" (*hua yi zhi yao* 滑疑之耀).[29] As Zhuangzi says a little later, "Things are affirmed by affirming them, negated by negating them. Paths are formed by walking, things are so because they are called so. Why right? Because someone holds it to be right. Why wrong? Because someone holds it to be wrong. Everything has some perspectives which hold it to be right and some which hold it to be wrong, so there is nothing that is not right, nothing that is not acceptable."[30] It is not a question of digging down to the inner essence of things, or seeing the truth behind appearances, for example, seeing that in their ultimate essence all things are expressions of the whole or the Dao, the wind blowing through all the holes, which is Good, and therefore, despite appearances, all are really good. Instead, Zhuangzi redirects us to the appearances themselves: the obvious appearances are of all having their own views, the chaotic welter of all affirming themselves—and in this way all things are affirmed, the wind's "great harmony." The affirmation of everything comes then not from a unicentric penetration to the one true transcendental perspective, which can never be explicitly posited as anything more than a Who? but rather from a going along with the surface phenomenon where each thing affirms itself. Indeed, it is just this welter of contrasting and conflicting individual perspectives that itself produces this transcendental Who? this quality of Who-ness, which is nothing but the impossibility of settling into any definite identity or perspective as definitive. Who? is in effect a shorthand way of indicating the chaos and doubt of the shimmering unsettled surface, not a way of grounding, transcending, or going beneath it to a true knowledge of its real source.

Of course this language, "each thing affirms itself," is a dead giveaway referring back to one of the premises of early Chinese thought which deserves more extensive attention: the assumption that "things" are conceived on the model of animate, mutually aware social entities. A thing, for Zhuangzi, has a *perspective*. Perhaps we can even go so far as to say that, on the most crucial and paradigmatic level, a thing *is* a perspective. Each thing has a view of the world, a distinctive perspectival relationship to all other things. There is no concept here of an inanimate thing that is not also a perceiver in this broad sense; a thing takes in and responds to its particular context in a way roughly analogous to the way a perceiver in a social world feels and responds to that social environment. Moreover, as in the Ruist case, the argument rests on conceiving these perceivers as *social*, which is to say, as also being perceived by others. The world of others that each entity perceives consists also of not merely inanimate things, but perceiving entities; the presence of each one is felt by all the others, and vice versa.

The implications of this assumption become clearest in Zhuangzi's elaboration of his technique of "using the obvious" (*yiming*): "Nothing is not 'that,' nothing is not 'this.' What appears from 'that' [perspective] one does not see, but what is in one's own awareness is known to one.[31] Thus I say, that emerges from this, and this follows upon that."[32] Here we must pause to note that this "thus I say" makes absolutely no sense unless we assume an intersubjective concept of "things" here. For what went above, if situated in an ontology of insentience, would lead only to the conclusion that everything can be one person's this and another person's that, but not that these two somehow cause each other or arise mutually. The mutual arising is deduced here solely from the fact that, *since each perspective has not only a "this" but also a "that"* (that is, since each entails not only the affirmation of its own position but, what is really just the simultaneous flip side of the same act, the refutation of the opposite position), *and since by definition each one is only seeing everything from its own perspective*, since it would have no awareness of what lies outside of that perspective, the existence of any notion of "that" at all must mean that any "this"'s *own* perspective already includes a "that." For if it did not come from its own perspective, it could not come from anywhere—nothing can come from another perspective—and we know that it does come, that we have the concept "that" (i.e., "wrong," "other"). This only works because both "this" and "that" are implicitly assumed to be sentient perceivers, on a social model, who see each other from their own perspectives. Thus I see you, and you see me. My world includes only what exists from my perspective, and yet it includes a you, an other perspective, in contrast to which I define myself. Your world is defined by your perspective, and yet it includes a me. This fundamental enigma of sociality (together with the cluster of meanings that turn out to be implied in the terms *shi* and *fei* in the language Zhuangzi is using) is the basis of the mutual causation of self and other in Zhuangzi, and not at all the abstract linguistic considerations sometimes attributed to him (i.e., the differential nature of language, where each *word* has meaning only in contrast to its opposite and in difference from other words).

A metaphor may allow us to understand this situation more clearly. Imagine a large booth with a sliding door, such that there are two compartments, only one of which can be seen at any time. Inside each of the two compartments stands a human figure, of which only one is visible or audible at any given time, the other being sealed off in his compartment by the closing of the sliding door. Each of these figures insists that he alone is the real one and that the other is an android or imposter. The one you can see says, "I am the real one; you can tell if you compare us carefully. Look at me closely, and then take a look at him; that way, having the standard of my genuine appearance, you'll be able to determine that he is a fake." He then slides the door over, concealing himself to reveal the other, so that you may compare them. But of course as soon as the other appears and the first is hidden, this other says just the same thing, adducing himself as the standard by which to judge the falseness of the first one. This process goes on indefinitely. Whichever is present asserts itself as the real, the right, the true, the standard of value by deviation from which all others are to be judged as false and wrong, but inherent in this establishment of a standard is the revealing of the other to show the difference, which puts the other in the position to make the same claim, and so ad infinitum. The only thing that is agreed on, that is stated from both perspectives, is that one is real and the other is false. This is structurally necessary, even if this process continues forever or is carried to new orders of abstraction. Similarly, for Zhuangzi, all experiences entail the positing of a perspective that is an aggressive assertion of its own rightness and, simultaneously, the positing of an other to which it is to be compared, which is to be judged as false in accordance with itself as standard. But this very counterpositing necessarily gives that other a voice, as it were, for all positing and all perception structurally necessitates this self-assertion. To even mention this other, to even refer to it, to call it to awareness in any form, is to put it in the position of focus, which is necessarily the position of self-assertion, the establishment of itself as a standard of value. And since there is no other standard than the standard asserted by some focus, this process continues forever and can find no final resolution.

The value question then also hinges on this perspectivism, this assumption of sentient points of view that include each other. For their inclusion of each other is a form of negating each other; they include each other *as* their own "other" "that" "wrong" in contradistinction to their own "self" "this" and "right." Value paradox looms before us here. Moreover, once the opposition between "self" and "other" (this/that, right/wrong) proves to harbor this paradox, then everything flies toward paradox, for this is the most basic distinction we know of. Zhuangzi immediately applies the paradox at a metalevel to the paradox itself, again poking fun at Huizi by quoting his doctrine of "The thing born is the thing dying" (*fang sheng fang si* 方生方死); so if "this" and "that" "birth" each other, they also "die" each other, and vice versa, and if this is right it is also wrong, and if wrong also right.[33] Thus the sage does not pursue this or any other line or argument designed to get to the bottom of things—he just "reflects them in heaven" (*zhao zhi yu tian* 照之於天)[34]—which I take to be identical with using the manifest, the obvious (*ming*). This term is often taken to be the point at which Zhuangzi takes refuge in a kind of intuitionism, thereby discarding his therapeutic skepticism; that is, if this *ming* is translated to mean something like "illumination" or "enlightenment," we get the impression that Zhuangzi is telling us to forget all these logical disputes, which solve nothing, and rely instead on our language-transcending intuition, which alone will show us the truth, reveal the way things really are. My reading of this term yields almost precisely the opposite meaning. I take it to mean the obvious, what is self-evident and clear when confronted with the problem of a multitude of perspectives contradicting each other: namely, this fact that there are a bunch of perspectives contradicting each other. *Ming* then refers to the surface fact that they all affirm themselves and negate each other, that they appear as a complete confusion, an unstable mutual undermining—for after all, "if right were really right, its difference from not-right would be so clear that there would be no dispute at all."[35] This very unstable surface is what is referred to as the "Equalizing Heavenly Potter's Wheel," to be discussed below. Heaven then is not the secret hidden essence of things, the harmonious creator behind their present conflicting appearances, but rather that surface of obvious conflict itself, once we cease the futile attempt to try to get to the bottom of it or find out what harmony lies behind it. It is this feature, as we will see, that keeps Zhuangzi from asserting even that it is possible to know what is called "Heaven" and what is called "man," that this "reflection in Heaven" is to be understood as the acquisition of some kind of knowledge that reveals the truth about things and provides a kind of transrational certainty. Quite the contrary, it is the full acceptance of doubt and chaos, and the self-affirmations of whatever is encountered thereby revealed and then renounced.

This appeal to "obvious fact"—functionally similar to what ancient Skeptics called "the apparent" or "the evident," but with an emphasis not on the few perfectly stable and certain facts of experience but rather in the "torch of chaos and doubt," the very unceasing unstable surface shimmer itself—leads us directly into omnicentrism:

> This is also that, that is also this. This has its own this/that and that also has its own this/that. So is there really a this/that or isn't there? When this and that no longer find anything to be their opposites, (or do not see each other as opposites; cf., I lost me, he lost his opposite), this is called the Pivot of Dao. Once the Pivot finds the center, so that it can respond infinitely without obstruction, this/self/right is unobstructed and inexhaustible, and that/other/wrong is equally unobstructed and inexhaustible. This is why I said there's nothing better than using the obvious.[36]

I and you are not opposites when I see that the very opposition I/you, which I use to define myself as I and as right, is posited within myself, within my own perspective; "I/you" is a part of "I." I posit you as my own opposition; your wrongness and contradiction of me is my own doing, is part of my system of affirming myself, not its opposite. In this, a whole is indicated, consisting of two endpoints, this and that. But each half turns out to be the whole: each half constitutively includes the other half as well, and in that sense is unobstructed, infinite; *there is nothing outside either half taken in itself.* For this is this/that, and that is also this/that, and thus they are not opposites. This is omnicentrism. This is the key to understanding Zhuangzi's holism and his value theory. We must proceed slowly here.

Why are right and wrong each "inexhaustible"? Each one is in the center of its own circle, each one is a pivot or hinge of Dao, and each one "responds" without obstruction, and infinitely. We must first look into this expression *wuqiong* 無窮, which is usually translated as "infinite." But this can be misleading. The concept of 'linear extension without end,' or of 'numerical infinity' as such is perhaps less relevant here than the notion of 'infinity as circular.' As a later chapter of the *Zhuangzi* puts it, "Beginning and end oppose each other without start or finish, and none knows where it comes to an end (*qiong*)."[37] This word *qiong* is conventionally the opposite of terms such as *da* 達, meaning "reaching the goal, penetrating all the way through," or *tong* 通, meaning "unobstructed, successful." The latter term in particular is a central positive term for Zhuangzi, as we shall see below. *Qiong* thus means "obstructed," "failing to reach one's goal," "coming to the end of one's rope" or to a dead end. In the present case, this would seem to be equivalent to "not taking as opposite": *shi* is not exhausted by *fei*, does not see it as an other confronting, limiting, opposing it; it sees itself in its own *fei*. Likewise, *fei* sees itself in *shi*, sees that *shi* is a part of itself. Thus both are everywhere; they never reach an other that ends them; they are without limit or exhaustion. But this seeing of oneself in the other also allows for a practical change: it allows one to read and match up with the other and respond to him by assuming his *shi/fei* without losing one's own, for his *shi* also includes a *fei*, his self includes an other, which is oneself; thus I can be him (temporarily) without losing me. In this sense, to always be responsive is the same as being unobstructed, being inexhaustible The above passage would more correctly read: "responding without obstruction, without ever coming to something which it cannot see as part of itself, and also, on the contrary, which it cannot see itself as part of, and thus respond to sympathetically." In this sense, unobstructedness is synonymous with infinity and with freedom.[38]

This concept of "responding" is crucial here, and it will bring us back to the question of dependence (*dai* 待). The "Yingdiwang" chapter tells us, "Just be empty, that is all. The perfect man uses his mind like a mirror, responding but not storing, and thus he can overcome things without being harmed by them."[39] The "Renjianshi" chapter also glosses this concept of "emptiness" (*xu* 虛), saying not to listen with the ear or the mind, but rather with the vital force (*qi* 氣): "The vital force is empty and waits for things 虛而待物者也. Dao gathers in emptiness. This is called the fasting of the mind."[40] This emptiness, or fasting of the mind, turns out to be equivalent also to "I lost me," as Yan Hui's response shows.[41] It consists not of a blank void but rather of a responding to things, depending on things, riding things—of not holding to any one perspective as self, this, or right. In the "Xiaoyaoyou" chapter, dependence (*dai* 待) was transformed into freedom by *increasing* the scope of what was depended on, until it included the entire spectrum, until it was "unobstructed" and limitless (*wuqiong*), thus making space for *any* content; this "lost self," "mind fasted" emptiness does not store: it holds onto no completed or definitive perspective (*cheng xin* 成心), no particular identity or concept of "right" (*shi/fei*). But it is not emptiness in the sense of a constant or definitive blank; it is a space that is always being filled by one or another perspective but that is unobstructed (*tong*) to other perspectives by virtue of the fact that each perspective intrinsically contains its own *fei*, its own negation, which provides the passageway to any other perspective that comes along. This allows it to "respond" to any of the six breaths that happen to appear to it and thereby ride it unobstructedly where it may go, assuming whatever *shi* (identity—rat's liver, crossbow pellet, etc.) it may bring. This is both to depend (periphery: cast about on whatever wind appears) and not to depend (center: hiding the world in the world so that in spite of all "going away" it is never lost, shaking in the endless and *thus* being lodged in the endless [*zhen zhu wu jing, gu yu zhu wu jing* 振諸無竟，故寓諸無竟], turmoil-peace [*ying-ning* 攖寧]), unobstructed like the dimensionless blade through the sinews. To be both sides means to be the eternal "Who?" that blows these different transforming pipings forth—not to be any someone always, for that would be one of the different tones piped forth, but not to be no one either, for that would mean no piping. Rather to be "Who?"—responding to and depending on anything that comes along (a ceaseless question mark, with realness and reliability [*you qing you xin* 有情有信]) while not storing and not depending on anything (having no definite answer, without evaluative action or form [*wu wei wu xing* 無為無形]).[42]

This (never blank) "emptiness"—a particularly vivid and visceral form of *epoche*—is Zhuangzi's substitute for the "adequate ideas" of Spinoza—exactly the opposite strategy, it turns out. Rather than holding a comprehensive vision of the whole in one's mind, one keeps one's mind empty like a mirror, so that it may respond and "ride upon" whatever it encounters. This is to depend on whatever one encounters, to have no independent self, but also equally to be independent, since anything will do.

The doubleness of this formula is to be noted: on the one hand to respond, on the other hand not to store. These two sides correspond to the periphery and center (pivot, *dao shu* 道樞) of the circle, respectively. The two sides show up again in another decisive formula from the "Qi-wulun":"The sage harmonizes them with right/wrong and yet rests in the equalizing potter's wheel of heaven. This is called traveling two paths at once" 聖人和之以是非而休乎天鈞，是之謂兩行.[43] "Two paths" refers to both (1) resting in the equalizing potter's wheel (i.e., in the still center of the turning wheel, the interpenetration [mutual inclusion] of the opposites Self and Other, right and wrong) and (2) harmonizing with other perspectives by means of *their* perspectives of right and wrong. What is this equalizing potter's wheel of heaven? A passage from a later chapter, part of which I already quoted, and which Graham has argued convincingly may come from the hand of the same author as the Inner Chapters, puts it as follows: "All things are seeds [of one another], which yield to one another with their different forms. Their beginnings and endings are like a circle, and no beginning point can be found to it.[44] This is called the equalizing potter's wheel of heaven."[45] The image of the circle emerges again here, a circle which creates things: a potter's wheel.[46] It ties into the transformation of things, their circular beginnings and ends, which stand in a polar relationship to each other. Here we have a concrete image with which to think of what could be described as a "both 'both/and' and 'neither/nor'" structure. The center of the spinning potter's wheel is still, "at rest," the pivot of Dao; the periphery spins, and this spinning is responsive, creative of rights and wrongs, that is, of viewpoints with a this and a that. As we have seen above, *perspectives* here means both emotional moods and philosophical positions, as well as identities as such. "This/that"s apply to all of the following dyadic pairs: (1) emotional perspectives (joy/sorrow, etc.), (2) concepts of identity (self/other), (3) value concepts (right/wrong, benefit/harm), and (4) life and death (an extension of now/some other time). The recommendation then seems to be on the one hand to have the ability to have emotions, to feel your way into various positions and perspectives as expressed by others or even yourself, to live and die, and on the other hand, to maintain a central point that is still, uninvolved, not fully absorbed into or committed to this perspective, which means, as the image of the pivot or hinge suggests especially, the ability (*neng, tong*) to jump back out of it when the situation changes, to identify yourself equally with the opposite when the time comes, to know even now that it too will equally be a "this," and hence will be self, right, and life, since This includes That, and That includes This. This is to respond without storing, to travel two roads at once, knowing through not knowing,[47] words that are no words, the Dao that is not a Dao.[48]

Let us return to the question of the oneness of things; for now we can understand in what sense the claim "All things are one" is privileged in this text. It is not asserted that it is objectively true that all things are one—that they are all made of the same substance, or are produced by a single agent, and so on—and that the perspective that realizes this is uniquely right, while all others are wrong, being blinded by their merely partial vantage points; that would be a typical unicentric position. Rather, all perspectives equally come forward into experience, and all, including this one, are equally without any justification that lies outside themselves—any evidence that "all is one" is gathered from within this perspective itself, as is the case for any other perspective, and thus it has no more objective ground of rightness than any other. But this particular perspective, once it does happen to be the one that comes to the fore—and it will do this not because it has some special access to the truth, but for the same relativistic, perspectival reasons as any other position—it has a unique power to "stick," to confirm itself. Why? Because, as we have seen, for Zhuangzi, "things" means primarily "perspectives." Hence, to see all *things* as one is to see all *perspectives* as one. That means to see this perspective itself as interconnecting with all other perspectives, including its opposite, the perspective from which all things appear to be different. The perspective that all is one is privileged because it can embrace its other, the view that all is different, in a way that the latter cannot embrace and include it. This does not mean it is "true"—the objective claim is no more than that the universe of appearance *can be* seen as one, just as it can be seen as many. But once it is so seen, everything changes, for thereafter all ways of appearing can be experienced as being, as it were, internal to that perspective, rather than usurpations of it, as is the case for any other perspective. Once I have seen things *as* one, I can go ahead to see them as many without fearing that this will disconfirm or dissipate my view that they are one, for to see them as one is to see the transformations of perspectives with equanimity, as aspects of this oneness, or more strictly, since this "all is one" is for the Inner Chapters of the *Zhuangzi* more a question of "sharing the same trait" or "all affirming the same thing" than "being made of the same substance," as all being one in sharing the trait of being *shi*, of affirming themselves, of being a perspective that forms a center of all things and interpreting all in terms of itself. Thus when the "all things are different" comes to the fore, its very ability to see things as different is a confirmation of its sharing this trait of seeing things from its own perspective and hence a confirmation of the oneness of all perspectives, of all things. Hence Zhuangzi says, "Their oneness is one, their not-oneness is also one."[49] Once the view that all is one has happened to occur to one, all other views become viewable as merely confirmations and aspects of it. The unicentric viewpoint that all things are produced by one agent—the great clump, Heaven, Yin and Yang, the unknowable Laozian noneness from which moods and perspectives arise, and so on—gains its special place through its connection to the omnicentric perspectival point, that all things *can be seen as* affirming the same thing, namely, that they are *shi*, extending their own value perspective over all other things; this sort of oneness has the effect also of making the transformation between perspectives comprehensible and unobjectionable, while also bringing with it the value implications that everything is right and good. All perspectives posit their own criteria for right and wrong, always in terms of their own position; this is as completely true of the present perspective as of any other. However, in its own terms, the criterion for truth espoused by this view extends to all possible views; whatever asserts itself is right, including this view and also including any other view. Once this has been even experimentally accepted, it is logically impossible for this claim to be disconfirmed; no possible proof of any other position would succeed in disproving it, as it has already allowed that all other views are also right; indeed, the rightness of other views will only further confirm this view. The truth claim of the position that all is one is thus, depending on one's preferences, to be described as tautological, unverifiable, and thus meaningless, or as performative and thus necessary.

Application to the Recent Conflict of Interpretations

My view, then, is that the Inner Chapters are best read as a whole, that there is no insurmountable interpretative difficulty in doing so, and that such a reading suggests strongly that Zhuangzi *both* rejects the possibility that any perspective can have other than an internal justification, hence ruling out any appeal to a metaperspective that is objectively true, any literal true ruler that can be known or taken for guidance in any sense, *and* privileges one particular perspective among all these perspectives, namely, what we can call the view that "All things are one." We find the latter view explicitly adduced as one possible view that can be taken on all things,[50] and just as explicitly the claim that the opposite view (that liver and gall, if viewed from their differences, are as distant as Chu and Yue) is equally possible. Zhuangzi then *develops* the oneness view, not because he pretends to have grounds for knowing it is the objectively true of the two views, nor even that it is pragmatically "true"—instead, he merely describes the features that go with taking this view. It is simply one more view among all views, which comes about for unknown reasons and affirms what it affirms and negates what it negates. Once it does happen to occur to one, however, it has certain special characteristics that Zhuangzi is clearly interested in exploring. These characteristics have nothing to do with it being true or false. They include a number of things that Zhuangzi knows can be made to sound desirable also to inhabitants of other perspectives—skills, transcendence of loss and death, political acumen. It also includes an attitude toward all other perspectives that gives it, not a unique truth value, but a unique staying power. That is, this particular perspective is related to all other perspectives as a mirror (as the perfect man's mind is compared to[51]) is to all other determinate things, as the pivot of a revolving potter's wheel relates to all other points in the wheel. It is still one more point, one more determinate thing, one more view among all views, and just as unable to justify itself in any objective terms, by any criteria that are not wholly internal to itself. Nonetheless, like the mirror, because it can function not only as itself but also in and as any other view, it is not destroyed by the passage into another perspective, but instead confirmed and maintained. Put it this way: if the usual relativist runs into self-contradiction because he claims that "since all propositions are relative to some perspective, none can be true," thereby creating a paradoxical truth status for this claim itself, Zhuangzi has no such problem because he claims instead that "since all propositions are relative to some perspective, they are all necessarily true!" The criterion for truth *propounded by this view itself* is simply that whatever any view affirms is necessarily true to it. By its own standard, this must also be true of this view itself. All the fun-sounding stuff Zhuangzi then suggests one can do if one adopts this view—sail about on the changes without being dependent on any determinate conditions, soaring beyond life and death, and so on—are all consequences of this particular feature of this peculiar view. This entails no claim that it is true in any sense other than that in which any possible view is true—it affirms what it affirms. All that is maintained is that it is possible to adopt this view, it is available; it is one among the infinite number of possible perspectives. That being so, one is always at liberty to adopt it if one likes. Zhuangzi obviously enjoys making this sound like a fun thing to do, but he does not and cannot have any argument that it is the right thing to do.

I propound this view as a way of mediating the two sides, which are locked in combat in the debate. I think Hansen is eternally right that Zhuangzi cannot be just another mystic ignoring his own arguments for perspectivism by bringing his own in through the back door as objective. Indeed, I think I am just elaborating on Hansen's immortal early insight that Zhuangzi's central insight is simply that uncompromising skepticism and absolute mysticism are one and the same thing. That being the case,

it should not be necessary any more to argue against the mystical reading, except to the extent that it misunderstands itself. In this, by the way,
I am following Zhuangzi's own method of resolving debates—that is, by
using *ming*, which I have suggested should be read not as "illumination"
or "enlightenment" or anything else smacking of a privileged intuition
into a final truth, but rather, as a nominalization of the common usage of
this character to mean "what is obvious." That is, what is obvious in the
disputes between Mohists and Ruists is that they affirm what the other
denies and deny what the other affirms—period. That in itself is enough
to solve the problem; what is obvious or apparent is that there are apparently different and conflicting perspectives, and that is all Zhuangzi needs
to end the argument.

I also believe my remarks are more or less in keeping with Zhuangzi's
explicit formulation of his theory of knowledge at the beginning of the
"Dazongshi" chapter, where he states that even the recourse to Heaven
is not going to overturn the language skepticism of the "Qiwulun,"[52]
thereby retracting the previous provisional formulation which was itself
merely a way of saying, "Let's use the obvious—the fact that we don't
know what's going on; that emptiness, it turns out, functions like the view
that all perspectives are one, which in turn has a bunch of interesting
consequences." I assume that the same would be said for Dao or "true
ruler"—how do I know that what I call "Dao" is not really not Dao?
and so on. The solution Zhuangzi suggests is to abandon the project of
objective knowledge or cognitive knowledge of any kind, even intuitive knowledge if it is construed as knowledge of the way things really
are. Instead, "There is true knowledge only when there is the true man,"
which I take as a way of saying that "true knowledge" is only a way of
describing the state of mind of a particular type of person. That this type
of person is described as the "true man" presents no problem if construed
as legitimately internal to the perspective of this person himself—whose
perspective is distinctive in that he grants himself freedom to call anything
just what he likes.

Even more crucial is the assertion a few lines down that "his oneness
is one, his not-oneness is also one,"[53] which nicely crystallizes the ironic
attitude toward the perspective that affirms oneness; the whole point of
the oneness perspective is that for it, it is all the same whether things are
regarded as one or not one; compare the barb, presumably at Huizi, that
frames the "three in the morning story" about "wearing out one's spirit
to make things one without realizing the sameness," which I read to mean
the sameness whether one takes things as one or does not. In either case,

one is in one's own *shi/fei*, and the oneness Zhuangzi has in mind is just that of always seeing oneself at the *shi* of some *shi/fei* pair and thus forever situated at the *shi*-ness. This may be taken to rule out an acceptance of the view of oneness as a perspective that is uniquely right to the exclusion of its opposite, the view that things are many, for example.

It seems to me that this will also allow Zhuangzi to freely say whatever he likes about the oneness Dao—including all the metaphysical and mystical stuff that some find objectionable in the "Dazongshi" chapter.[54] He is just saying more about what this particular perspective is like. And I do not have any problem with calling it "mystical" indeed, as long as the peculiar nature of this particular mysticism, or perhaps insight into all mysticism, is recognized. The truth claim about this mystical view that all perspectives are equal and in that sense all things are one, however, is just that it is no more false than any other view and can prove no more or less about itself by appeal to extrinsic standards than any other view.

As for the "true ruler" I think Zhuangzi is consistent with the *Laozi*'s view of Dao: it guides if and only if it does not guide. The content of its guidance is indeed no more than that, as the useful knowledge is to pay attention to the "obvious" fact that everyone disagrees and no conclusion has been reached. In both cases, the empty nonknowing proves useful, and in that sense is one's proper guide. The true lord is our failure to find any true lord, and knowing that does not even help us know definitively that one exists or does not. Hansen is right to view all Zhuangzi's questions as questions; that is exactly where he wants to end up, and those are his only answers. But to be undecided about everything has a particular efficacy, he suggests. He cannot claim or argue it, just depict it, perhaps as an ad hoc response to the taunts from Huizi that end the "Xiaoyaoyou" chapter. I follow in this the interpretation of Dao that has been stated explicitly in a comment on the opening lines from the *Laozi* found in the (probably Tang forgery) *Guanyinzi* 關尹子, which more or less sums up my view: "It is not that there is a Dao which cannot be spoken; unspeakableness is the Dao. It is not that there is a Dao which cannot be thought; unthinkableness is the Dao." Dao, that is, in the full sense: a guiding orientation, the course and source of whatever things are encountered—to not have one is to have one, and this is indeed the only way to have one, and one always does. It should be noted here that, while this perspective cannot make any claim to proffer objective knowledge, it does perform many of the functions for which objectivity was perhaps sought in the first place: universal applicability, the power to withstand every empirical test, and intersubjectively agreeable self-evidence.

An extended metaphor may help to make this clearer, which I will offer here with the usual qualification that it is not to be taken too literally or as according perfectly with the case in hand; nonetheless, I think it will prove significantly useful in clarifying what is at issue here. Zhuangzi's view of experience is comparable to finding oneself in a card game, where cards are constantly being issued to one from an unknown source and one is constantly discarding but without ever having been explicitly told what the object of the game is. A certain set of rules might suggest that the best thing to do is maximize the high cards you hold while discarding the low cards as much as possible, but it is equally possible, for all you know, that the object is to have the lowest card, or the most cards of the same suit, or same number, or different suit or number. Both the source and the object of the game are unknown. You do not even know how large a deck it is or what the proportions of cards in it is. Occasionally an "instruction card" is issued, that is, a card with instructions printed on it, stating that the object of the game is in fact such and such—to collect high cards, for example. But other instruction cards are issued as well, with contradictory instructions and explanations of the makeup of the deck and the object of the game. Sometimes, after receiving such a card, a player might accept its claims and proceed to order his hand accordingly—having drawn "the object of the game is to collect high cards," he proceeds to do so. If he gets a card that states, "The object of the game is to collect low cards," he quickly discards it; for he already knows it is false, *fei*. There are even cards that suggest that the collection of instruction cards, or the absence of them, is the true object of the game, and so on.

Now given this scenario, Zhuangzi's "regarding all things as one" amounts to, not an instruction card that reveals the true state of the deck—namely, that all the differences in the cards are merely illusory (perhaps comparable to the Spinozistic or Advaita Vedanta conception of the One), or that the object of the game is simply to collect as many cards as possible and thus they are all of equal value, or that they all come from a single source and thus are to be valued equally without caring anymore about winning or losing—but rather *a wild card*. It reveals no information about the source of the cards, the makeup of the deck, or the object of the game. Nor is it, more to the point, an injunction to ignore all the instruction cards and instead pay attention to the actual makeup of the cards being issued, in the belief that this will reveal an unbiased picture of the true source and object of the game (comparable to the mystical view that, once reason has been abandoned, an intuitive regard for nature will reveal the truth). Rather, it stays with the "obvious" and inescapable state of things: we do not know the rules, the source, the object of the game, and in fact, every so often someone declares the object to be such and such, and we must tally our winnings according to this ad hoc temporary rule, which will be replaced by another in the next round. Given the unknowability of what cards are coming or what hand is better than what, the only thing that will be useful in *any possible case* is the wild card. Whether it is declared at a given time that the object is to collect high cards or low cards, whether there is one source or many, however many different objects of the game may be successively declared, the wild card will always be the best thing to be holding. Note that "best" here is no longer "best in terms of some given instruction card or concept of what the true object of the game is" but one that, due to its uniquely empty status, will be equally useful no matter what the object is *regarded to be* at any given time.

Why is the sage's "regarding things as one" equivalent to a wild card? It is not a claim about any truth or value, like an instruction card, nor the assertion of some intrinsic order to the cards missed by every instruction card, some alternate source of true knowledge. It is merely the acceptance of the apparent fact that new cards keep coming and new concepts of the object of the game keep getting declared and that the one thing every possible object of the game has in common is that it has something that is considered good in its view or context, and it is to this oneness that the wild card addresses itself. Whatever the particular content might be that is desired in any given case, there is always something or other that can fit into the presently prevailing scenario as desirable; the only thing that will always be desirable, "what all things agree in affirming," will be something that can be anything. It presupposes no knowledge about how things really are or what is really good; in fact, "oneness" here means precisely the same thing as "complete absence of any definite knowledge." The attainment of this view consists not in adding additional facts to our knowledge but in removing any and all claims to know how things are or are not, even, as Zhuangzi makes explicit, the claim that we do or can know nothing. In good Daoist fashion, it is this sort of a value emptiness in which all beings unite themselves. It is not a claim about the true reality that dwells beneath the flux of deceptive appearances; rather, it is that claim that every appearance so far makes some declaration about what is good and what is bad, on some level, and that we simply do not know what will or will not always be declared good, that apparently there are conflicting claims, and we have no perspective-independent means of adjudicating between them; and thus the only card that will survive all revolutions of perspective, that can persist whatever the appearances do, is not some unchanging truth underlying them, but rather the one thing that, like the mirror, can be anything and is not restricted to any given determinacy. Zhuangzi's "oneness" view persists and prevails not because it is uniquely true or undoubtable, nor that it escapes the critique of reliance on internal criteria that Zhuangzi applied to all other possible perspectives, but merely for the reason that no one ever discards a wild card.

Notes

1. Paul Kjellberg and Philip J. Ivanhoe, eds., *Essays on Skepticism, Relativism, and Ethics in the* Zhuangzi (Albany: State University of New York Press, 1996).
2. ZZJS 70, 307; HY 5/2/39–40, 21/7/33.
3. A. C. Graham, *Chuang-tzu: The Seven Inner Chapters and Other Writings from the Book of Chuang-tzu,* (London: George Allen & Unwin, 1981), p. 56: "It may be noticed that Zhuangzi never does say that everything is one (except as one side of a paradox . . .), always speaks subjectively of the sage treating as one."
4. Chad Hansen, *A Daoist Theory of Chinese Thought: A Philosophical Interpretation* (New York and Oxford: Oxford University Press, 1992), pp. 270, 410, 412, note 86.
5. ZZJS 190; HY 12/5/7.
6. See ZZJS 17, 70; HY 2/1/4, 5/2/38–39.
7. ZZJS 268; HY 18/6/68–69.
8. ZZJS 79; HY 5/2/52–53.
9. ZZJS 83; HY 5/2/55.
10. ZZJS 74; HY 5/2/42.
11. Following Yu Yue's suggestion, I read shan1 山 as shan4 汕. See Wang Shumin, *Zhuangzi jiaoquan*, pp. 226–27 (Wang himself rejects this reading).
12. ZZJS 242–44; HY 16/6/24–28.
13. ZZJS 258; HY 17/6/46.
14. ZZJS 205; HY 13/5/30–31.
15. ZZJS 212, 252–53, 281; 14/5/43–44, 17/6/41–43, 19/6/88–89.
16. ZZJS 262; HY 17/6/60.
17. ZZJS 17; HY 2/1/21.
18. Ibid.
19. ZZJS 43; HY 3/2/1–3.
20. ZZJS 50; HY 3/2/8–9.
21. ZZJS 51; HY 4/2/13.
22. ZZJS 55; HY 4/2/14–15. *Qu* 取 here echoes the "*xian qi zi qu*" 咸其

自取 of a few lines back, referring again to the wind sounds. The relation between the self and the passing moods is thus likened to that between the wind and the sounds from the various holes; to "pick themselves out" is perhaps a way of indicating the interdependence indicated by the citation to which this is a note. I pick them out, but the I who picks them out (distinguishes them, individuates them) is nothing but them, the passing moods, the sounds from the holes. Hence this line could perhaps also be translated, "Without them there is no me, without me they have nothing to pick themselves out from," that is, nothing from which they are distinguished, nothing to which they are related or the parts of which they are, but this sounds confusing in English.

23. ZZJS 264; HY 16/6/29.

24. As should be clear from the above, I regard this statement not as indicating that the "true self" has lost the "false self," but rather that the self, the ruler, is simultaneously present and absent, is indeterminable as either definitively present or definitively absent; this situation itself describes both the so-called false self and the so-called true self.

25. ZZJS 63; HY 4/2/25.

26. ZZJS 63; HY 4/2/23–24.

27. Once again we can perhaps hear Huizi speaking here.

28. ZZJS 63; HY 4/2/26–27. My interpretation of the infamous *yiming* 以 明 is, I realize, rather unusual. I take *ming* to mean, not "illumination" or "enlightenment" or anything like that, all of which seem to me vague and useless readings, which moreover have Zhuangzi suddenly begging the question in a weirdly emphatic way, but rather simply, "what is evident, clear, obvious." I hope the justification for this reading, and why I view it as superior to the other, will emerge in the following pages.

29. ZZJS 75; HY 5/2/47.

30. ZZJS 69; HY 4/2/33–34.

31. Or, following Chen Guying, who cites Yen Ling-feng and Chen Qitian, the first *zhi* 知 may be replaced with *shi* 是, resulting in: "what appears from one's own perspective alone is known to one." See Chen Guying, *Zhuangzi jinzhu jinyi* (Taipei: Shangwu yinshuguan, 1989), pp. 61–62.

32. ZZJS 66; HY 4/2/27–28.

33. ZZJS 66; HY 4/2/28–29. My construal of a jump in levels is based not only on the Huizi quote (see "Tian xia," ZZJS 1102; HY 93/33/71–72) but also on the *suiran* 雖然, "However," which otherwise seems quite superfluous.

34. ZZJS 66; HY 4/2/29.

35. ZZJS 108; HY 7/2/90–91.

36. ZZJS 66; HY 4/2/31.

37. "Tian Zifang," ZZJS 712; HY 55/21/29.

38. "*Shi yi yi wu qiong, fei yi yi wu qiong* 是亦一無窮，非亦一無窮"

could thus be read to mean either, "'Right/this' [responds] unobstructedly and 'wrong/that' also [responds] unobstructedly," implying that either this or that can be the pivot in the center of the circle, or "[The pivot's response to] 'right/this' is unobstructed, and [its response] to 'wrong/that' is also unobstructed." In the first case, we have an obvious omnicentrism: even the wrong (as defined by any given perspective, even that of the whole) is the center, even it is unobstructed and infinite, in the sense that what we call wrong is just another perspective, which views itself as right, and as such embraces all other perspectives as wrong, so that there is nothing that does not fall within its scope. On the second reading, we will also end up with an omnicentrism, albeit a subtler one. But context seems to push us toward the second interpretation, which I will now pursue.

39. ZZJS 307; HY 21/7/32–33.

40. ZZJS 147; HY 9/4/27–28.

41. "Before I heard this, I was Hui, but now that I've heard it, I have never begun to be Hui, can this be called emptiness?" Confucius answers, "You've got it!" ZZJS 148; HY 9/4/28–29.

42. As Zhuangzi is quoted as saying, strikingly, in a later chapter, "Without praise or blame, now a dragon, now a snake, changing together with the seasons and unwilling to be or do any one thing exclusively, now above, now below, taking harmony as the measure, floating along in the ancestor of all things, taking things as things without being taken as a thing by things." "Shan mu," ZZJS 668; HY 51/20/6–7.

43. ZZJS 70; HY 5/2/39–40. I take Graham's reading of *tianjun* 天鈞. See Graham 54: "stays at the point of rest on the potter's wheel of Heaven." I translate in a way that preserves both the sense of equalizing and the concrete image of the potter's wheel, to which I attach great importance.

44. Following Guo Songtao 郭嵩燾, as cited in Chen Guying, *Zhuangzi jinzhu jinyi*, p. 795.

45. "Yu yan," ZZJS 950; HY 75/27/9–10.

46. Ch'ien Mu quotes Cao Shoukun 曹受坤 as follows: "*Huainanzi*'s 'Yuan dao' says, 'The potter's wheel turns in circles, makes a full revolution and then starts again . . .' This corresponds with the sense of turning in circles.'To travel two roads' indicates that no matter how it rotates, to the right or to the left, it always returns to the one [central] point." Ch'ien Mu, *Zhuangzi zuanjian* (Taipei: Dongda tushu gongsi, 1989), p. 15. Elsewhere, Ch'ien Mu has this to say about the *Zhuangzi*'s heavenly potter's wheel and omnicentrism: "All phenomena in the world are spinning around, in constant motion, and all depend on having a center. But all things in the world are one center. Not understanding this, we want to make ourselves the center. [Thus far Ch'ien is speaking unicentrically, but he continues:] One's self is indeed a center, but we ought not to annul all the other centers by only acknowledging this one center. By the same token, we ought not to annul the center which is our self

just because of the presence of the many other centers. This is what Zhuangzi calls 'walking two.' Two means self and other. Walking two doesn't mean two forming opposites, which leads to contradiction and conflict. Rather, the two refer to a center and a periphery, which can rotate unimpededly. Each thing in the world is a center and each has a periphery, and all can rotate unimpededly." Ch'ien Mu, *Zhongguo sixiang shi* (Taipei: Xuesheng shuju, 1985), pp. 42–43.

47. ZZJS 150; HY 9/4/31–32.

48. ZZJS 83; HY 5/2/60–61.

49. ZZJS 234; HY 16/6/19–20.

50. ZZJS 190; HY 12/5/7.

51. ZZJS 307; HY 21/7/32.

52. ZZJS 225; HY15/6/3–4.

53. ZZJS 234; HY 16/6/19–20.

54. See especially ZZJS 246–247; HY 16/6/29–31.

3

Harmony and Cacophony in
the Panpipes of Heaven

SCOTT COOK 顧史考

"Now, tell me, have not you seen a play acted with Kings, Emperors and Popes, knights, ladies and various other personages brought on to the stage? One plays the ruffian, another the cheat; here is a merchant, there is a soldier; one is the wise fool, another the foolish lover. But when the play is over, and they have taken off their dresses, all the actors are equal . . . Now the same thing . . . happens in the comedy and traffic of this world, where some play Emperors, others Popes and, in fact, every part that can be introduced into a play. But when we come to the end, which is when life is over, Death strips them of all the robes that distinguished them, and they are all equals in the grave."

"A fine comparison," said Sancho, "although not so new that I haven't heard it on various occasions before—like the one of the game of chess, where each piece has its particular importance while the game lasts, but when it's over they're all mixed up, thrown together, jumbled, and shoved into a leather bag, which is much like shoveling life away into the grave."

"Every day, Sancho," said Don Quixote, "you grow less simple and wiser."
—Cervantes, *Don Quixote*

The vanity of life's claims upon individual status and position, wealth and power, talent or wisdom, in view of the overwhelming impermanence of it all in the face of Death, the great equalizer, is surely one of the most enduring and universal themes of human concern and its expression in literature, art, and philosophy throughout the ages. We spend the greater portion of our lives chasing after profit or fame, elusive riches or fleeting reputation, only to realize that no sooner have they come within our grasp than do they slip through our fingers as old age comes to summon us back to our ultimate place of origin. With this, too, comes the realization that, no matter how differentiated we have become from our fellow human beings in this life, no matter what sort of value distance we have been able to place between ourselves and others through the course of our momentary existence, we all at the end return to the same terrestrial abode, indistinguishable from each other in the black morass of primordial oblivion.

How does one come to terms with this dark realization? Some deny it altogether, burying their deceased parents with all the accoutrements befitting the position they held while still alive, expecting the departed will continue to enjoy their accustomed privileges in the afterlife, and fully anticipating that they, too, will receive similar treatment when their time has come. Others erect monuments to themselves or their ancestors in the form of writings, compositions, artwork, or institutions, hopeful that though their bodies and souls perish without a trace, their names and memories will live on throughout the course of human history. Still others, recognizing the folly of such futile striving, simply give themselves up to despair in the face of nature's unforgiving cruelty. Yet there are also those—perhaps rarest of all—who come to observe the process of life and death as one would a great spectacle: a performance to be lived, participated in, and celebrated—much, indeed, like some marvelous play staged for our benefit, or a great chess match in which we play our part until the conclusion is reached and we are shoved away into the indiscriminate leather bag of death . . . that is, at least, until it is time for the next round and the entirely new set of circumstances it brings with it.

That Warring States China was just such a heated chess match rife with its kings, knights, rooks, and pawns is certainly beyond all doubt. And the prevailing philosophies of the time—the Confucian and, to a lesser but not insignificant extent, the Mohist—steadfastly upheld that preservation of these hierarchically differentiated social roles was precisely the means by which harmony and order could be maintained in the chaos of the times: "with closeness between father and son, propriety between ruler and minister, distinction between husband and wife, order between old and young, and trust between friend and friend."[1] Mencius's picture here represents, of course, the ideal; the reality was that those sons and ministers were often subject to slander and execution, and the fathers and rulers to assassination and usurpation, and while the hierarchical distinctions themselves continued to be reinforced, the "closeness" and "propriety" that were supposed to accompany them were nowhere to be seen. Indeed, for philosophers such as Zhuangzi and, before him, the person or persons known as "Laozi," it was precisely the placement of value distinctions upon such hierarchical roles that led to such chaos in the first place. And yet, Zhuangzi asks, to what end? For when such distinctions are viewed from the standpoint of the ceaseless transformation of life and death, far from being eternal and of unchanging worth, they are seen as merely fleeting moments in the game of life that all come to naught once its players are "shoveled away into the grave."

Zhuangzi's most powerful formulation of this notion, along with his understanding of how best to live in this world in the face of it, comes at the outset of what is arguably the most seminal chapter of the *Zhuangzi*, the "Qiwulun 齊物論" (Discourse on the leveling of things),[2] and is expressed in the form of one of the most enduring images in pre-Qin Chinese literature: that of *Tian lai* 天籟, the "panpipes of Heaven." In this chapter, we shall attempt to unpack the implications of this complex and subtle passage and see what it might have to tell us about Zhuangzi's view of the emergence and inevitable mortality of life's differentiation and the aesthetics that lay behind our properly coming to terms with it.

The Harmony of Heaven and Earth

The passage takes the form of a dialogue between master and disciple, and begins with the idea of "losing myself" (*wu sang wo* 吾喪我).[3] Let us first quote the entire text of it below:

1. Nanguo Ziqi 南郭子綦[4] sat leaning on a table, breathing out as he looked up toward Heaven—there detached, it seemed as if he had lost his mate (*sang qi ou* 喪其耦).[5]

   Yancheng Ziyou 顏成子游,[6] standing in attendance before him, said, "What's going on?! Can the body actually be made to resemble dried-out wood, and the mind be made to resemble dead ashes?! Your table-leaning of today is not the table-leaning of before."[7]

2. Ziqi said, "Yan 偃,[8] is it not indeed wonderful—your asking of this?! Presently, I (*wu* 吾) have lost myself (*wo* 我). Do you understand this? You have heard of the panpipes of man (*renlai* 人籟), but have not yet heard the panpipes of Earth (*dilai* 地籟); [or you may have] heard of the panpipes of Earth, but not yet heard the panpipes of Heaven (*tianlai* 天籟)!"[9]

   "May I be so bold as to ask you what this means?" asked Ziyou.

3. Ziqi said, "Now the Great Clump[10] spits forth its breath and its name is 'the wind.' Now if only this would not arise![11]—for once it arises, then the 10,000 crevices howl angrily. Could you alone have never heard their [sounds of] 'breeeoo, breeeooo?!'[12] In the lofty peaks of mountain forests,[13] there are the holes and crevices of giant trees hundreds of yards round. Like noses, like mouths, like ears, like vases, like cups, like mortars, like mud-holes, like puddles. Murmurers,[14] whistlers, yellers, suckers, shouters, wailers, resonators, screamers. Those in front resound with a 'waaaaa,' and those that follow chime in with a 'ngroooong.'[15] With a light wind, there is a small harmony (*xiaohe* 小和); with a gale wind, there is a great harmony (*dahe* 大 和).[16] When the violent wind passes on by (*ji* 濟),[17] then the numerous crevices become silent (*xu* 虛, 'vacuous'). Have you alone never seen the wavering and quivering (of the trees)?"[18]

4. Ziyou said, "As for the panpipes of Earth—these are the numerous crevices. And as for the panpipes of man—these are aligned bamboo tubes. May I venture to ask about the 'panpipes of Heaven?'"

Ziqi said, "Now blowing forth the 10,000 differences and causing them to be themselves (*zi ji* 自己)[19]—they all take for themselves, [but] who is it that rouses (*nu* 怒) them forth?!"[20]

We have here the strikingly vivid image of a chorus of sounds produced through the course of a windstorm as it passes over crevices of myriad shapes and sizes located in the crags and trees of lofty mountain peaks. One of the first questions that comes to mind is this: what is the aesthetic nature of such an image? Is it a cacophony or a symphony?—a lament over the noise of the world or a celebration of sounds? Once we realize that there is probably no good answer to this question, we will have come one step closer to appreciating the profundity of Zhuangzi's philosophy. We could make arguments for either side. For the former, we note the phrase "now if only this would not arise" and how the myriad crevices would "howl angrily" were it to do so.[21] We could further note instances from later in the chapter, such as where man's "mutual cutting and scraping" (*xiang ren xiang mo* 相刃相靡) with things (stemming from his deeming his own individual perspective as "right"), and how he thereby needlessly wears himself out, "not knowing to where he returns" (*buzhi qi suo gui* 不知其所歸), are spoken of as "tragic" (*bei* 悲) and "sorrowful" (*ai* 哀).[22] Is it not such things that the image of myriad crevices each howling forth its unique brand of noise was meant to depict? On the other hand, the description itself of the chorus of sounds is not "noisy" at all; it seems rather a beautiful portrait of a natural phenomenon. The wording used to describe the chorus as a whole does in fact tell us so much: a light wind gives us a "small harmony" (xiaohe), and a gale wind performs a "great harmony" (dahe) (sec. 3). What are we to make of all this?

Perhaps the answer is whatever we want. That which sounds harmonious to humans may make birds fly off and fish submerge in fright.[23] Then again, the angry cries of a myriad clashing individual entities might annoy us only if we recognize ourselves as one of their number, as a competitor whose meager voice gets drowned out in all the racket. If, instead, we were to step back for a minute and listen to the chorus from the standpoint of its unity—as a naturally harmonious blending of diverse instruments performing a unified yet ever-changing piece of music—then we might come to see ourselves too playing whatever instrument is natural to us without trying to impose it upon others, reacting instead to the musical situation and taking delight in our role in the great improvisation of life.

Freedom and Dependency

The crux of this passage rests in the ambiguity of the final line, between the fact that the myriad crevices take the sounds they produce from the uniqueness of their own natures, and that they yet seem at the same time to depend upon the wind that rouses them forth before they can assert themselves. This issue—that of the relationships among freedom, individuality, and dependence—is an important and complex one for Zhuangzi; to better understand it, we must first examine the passages from the opening chapter, "Xiaoyaoyou 逍遙遊" (Far and leisurely roaming), where it is initially explored:

> In the Northern Darkness (beiming 北冥) there is a fish, and its name is Kun 鯤. The largeness of Kun is such that it is unknown how many thousands of li[24] it is. It transforms and becomes a bird, and its name is Peng 鵬. The back of Peng is [so large] that it is unknown how many thousands of li it is. With a violent surge (nu 怒, "angry") it flies, its wings resembling clouds that overhang Heaven. Now this bird, when the sea sets into motion, will journey to the Southern Darkness (nanming 南冥). The Southern Darkness is Heaven's Pool (tianchi 天池).
>
> ... In the Peng's journey to the Southern Darkness, the water is beaten up 3,000 li as it strikes itself upward upon a whirlwind to the distance of 90,000 li. It takes off by means of the six-month wind. . . .
>
> ... If the accumulation of wind is not thick, then there will not be the

power to support its great wings. Thus for 90,000 *li* in height this wind must be underneath—only then can there be this rising up upon the wind. With its back against the blue sky and nothing to cut off or obstruct its flight—only then can it make these plans to go southward. . . . and moreover journey to the Southern Darkness.

The marsh quail laughs at it: "And where might he be going? I take a leap upwards and come down again without going more than a dozen yards,[25] gliding about amidst the wild fields—this is indeed the ultimate in flying. And where might he be going?!" This is the debate (*bian* 辯) between small and great.

Thus those who have the knowledge to carry out the duties of an office, the conduct to oversee a village, the virtue to accord with a ruler, or the ability with which to win the trust of a state—the way they view themselves is also thus. Yet Song Rong Zi 宋榮子[26] gave them all a hearty laugh . . . he still had that which was not firmly rooted. Now Lie Zi 列子 moved about by riding upon the wind with a graceful beauty, travelling for all of half a month before returning . . . In this way, though he could avoid walking on foot, he still had that upon which he depended (*dai* 待, "to wait for").

Now as to he who mounts the axis of Heaven and Earth (*cheng tiandi zhi zheng* 乘天地之正), rides out the changes of the six energies (*yu liuqi zhi bian* 御六氣之辯),[27] so as to roam about in the limitless (*you wuqiong* 遊無窮)—upon what would he have to depend? Thus it is said: "The attained man has no self; the spiritual man has no merit; the sagely man has no fame."[28]

For brevity's sake, the passage cited here has been greatly truncated, but enough of its essential elements have been included to allow us an appreciation of the dilemma it poses. To start with, let us note the relevance it has to our interpretation of the *tianlai* passage. In both, the wind and the dependence of things upon it constitute one of the central themes. We may further observe that it is one and the same term, *nu* 怒, which both "rouses forth" the sounds of the myriad crevices (sec. 4) and gives the Peng flight with its "violent surge." This is probably not coincidental. Just what are the connections among wind, angry exertion, and dependence? To find out, let us follow the Peng on its southbound journey.

For the moment we might disregard any profound implications to be drawn from the fact that the great Peng is a transformation of a gigantic fish named Kun and that it travels at such great distances from the Northern to the Southern Darknesses only to end up in the same place from which it began its journey—Heaven's Pool.[29] Instead we shall concentrate on the Peng itself and on the images it gives us. We are, at first, led by Zhuangzi almost imperceptibly into an unreflective infatuation with the bird. It is portrayed in lofty, majestic terms: a huge creature that soars to great heights and vast distances after striking up whirlwinds and cascades of ocean water with its immense wings that overhang the heavens. It is a great bird with lofty aspirations, and it seems the very image of freedom as it soars across the ocean skies from one end of the world to the other.

But then we are reminded that the Peng is not free at all. In fact, precisely because of its sheer immensity it is subject to constraints creatures of ordinary size never know. To support its vast wings in flight, it requires the strength of a great wind beneath them, and such a wind, moreover, though it may carry them for six months at a time, comes about only once a year. Lesser creatures, by contrast, feel free to do as they please. The marsh quail, for one, darts about the fields as it feels fit, requiring little effort or preparation as it takes off at will on one of its dozen-yard flights. They may even laugh at the Peng—but what do such creatures know about greatness?

What kind of trick is Zhuangzi playing on us? The little creatures appear petty and insignificant in their overestimations of the preferability of their allotted fates. Like Hui Shi 惠施, they are narrow-minded and have no appreciation for the "great and useless." At the same time, however, they are clearly portrayed as much less dependent in their activities than the Peng. So which alternative is preferable? To search for an answer to this question may be futile, since Zhuangzi is always careful never to assert anything—except, perhaps, the assertion that assertions lead one into trouble. If, nonetheless, we continue our search, we may turn to the penultimate paragraph. There, at least, comes what appears to be a clear progression: first the state officials, who, like the little creatures, tragically view their lots as the ultimate standard for mankind. Next Song Rong Zi, who, thinking himself above all that, lets out a laugh at such men; but precisely because he laughs, is he really any better than the marsh quail? Then we are given Lie Zi, who seems the perfect human counterpart of the Peng, riding gracefully upon the wind for long periods of time. But once again we are reminded that Lie Zi, too, *depends* upon the wind. If any of these is better than the others, then this is only relatively so, for, as we are told in another part of this passage, though Peng Zu 彭祖 may be renowned for his longevity, there will always be the *mingling* 冥靈 tortoise, which takes five hundred years as one spring and five hundred years as one autumn; and though the tortoise may be thought the ultimate in long living, there will always be the great *chun* 椿 tree, which takes eight thousand years as one spring and eight thousand years as one autumn; and so on, ad infinitum. They all have to die sometime. And is it not *death*, ultimately, into which all distinctions are dissolved? It may be in this sense that the Peng, for all the greatness of its journey, arrives in the end right back where it started: to resubmerge in the indistinct darkness of Heaven's Pool.

The solution to this dilemma, if there is to be one, comes in the final paragraph. We are there given a way out of the circle of dependency; poetically, we simply "ride out the six energies," "roam about the limitless," and so on. No longer "waiting" for any specific "six-month" wind, we instead ride out all the atmospheric changes that come our way in turn. We are able to do so once we rid ourselves of self (*ji* 己), merit (*gong* 功), and fame (*ming* 名). In the terms of the "Renjianshi" chapter, this is the result of the "fasting of the mind" (*xinzhai* 心齋), in which the mind is made vacuous and one comes to respond to things spontaneously with one's vital energy (*qi* 氣).[30] There, the vital energy is described as "that which is vacuous and *awaits* things" (*xu er dai wu zhe* 虛而待物者). There is a sense, then, in which total *in*dependence is achieved only through total *de*pendence; one need not await for anything *in particular* by virtue of the fact that he instead awaits *everything* to come to him.[31] Like the mirror or the pool of still water, one actively seeks nothing while clearly reflecting all that happens his way. This is how the attained man roams about the world.

Self-Attainment and the Forgotten Self

Let us now return to the *tianlai* passage. To reiterate, Nanguo Ziqi has lost his "self" (*wo* 我); he has lost his "mate" (*ou* 耦); in other words, he has lost his notion of individuality and thus all sense of any distinction between "self and other" (*bishi* 彼是). Having lost and forgotten himself, Ziqi then seems to forget the fact that he has forgotten himself as he goes on to expound to his disciple the notion of the panpipes of Heaven. Why panpipes? Why was this musical instrument in particular chosen as the metaphor by which to express the central idea behind the "Qiwulun?" The answer to this question may very well tell us a great deal about the notion that stands behind the image.

Guo Xiang's 郭象 (A.D. 252?–312) analysis of these panpipes is particularly insightful:

> *Lai* 籟 are panpipes (*xiao* 簫). For the tubes of the panpipes are uneven, with *gong* 宮 and *shang* 商 tones of different pitch, and thus there are short

and long, high and low—a myriad of different sounds. Yet although the sounds have a myriad of differences, the standard (*du* 度) with which they are endowed is uniform, and thus [notions of] superior and inferior have no place among them. This is compared to the wind upon things: the different tones are all alike in their correctness, and each takes for itself (*ziqu* 自取) therein—the panpipes of Heaven and Earth are thus revealed.[32]

For Guo Xiang, human panpipes are the perfect metaphor for the "panpipes of Earth," or the diversification among the myriad things, in that they represent well the idea of equality through diversification, each producing a different pitch through a similar standard. This accords well with the view consistent throughout all of Guo's commentary: the equality or oneness of all things is achieved precisely by the fact that they all share the single standard of "self-attainment" (*zide* 自得). The numerous crevices and sounds of the earth described by Ziqi are celebrated for their diversity and for the fact that each does what is appropriate to itself.[33] Each one of the myriad crevices takes in precisely as much wind as it can allow and lets forth a corresponding sound exactly in accordance with its own capacities. The "panpipes of Heaven," then, might be explained as simply that by which the panpipes of Earth can produce such a symphony of diversification, and this, for Guo, amounts to nothing but the fact that each takes its own sound for itself. But what role does the wind play in all this? Do these myriad crevices not also have "that for which they wait?"

For Guo, the myriad sounds produced by the myriad crevices, we might add, differ fundamentally from the cacophonous voices of the Confucians, Mohists, and other schools in at least this respect: they are merely self-affirming and each expressive of its own particular voice; there is none that seeks to set the standard for all the other voices. For to seek such a standard, to give rise to judgments of right and wrong, is a way of thinking that violates the fundamental principle of nature: that diversification is at the fount of all existence, and it is sheer folly to expect that the wind would hold the same meaning for everything. But by simply self-attaining, by celebrating the distinctiveness of one's own particular self, one is ultimately celebrating the diversity of all creatures and things that exist in the world, and in this sense one has both captured and lost oneself simultaneously.

But what are the panpipes of Heaven? Is Ziqi's enigmatic question about "who" it is that "rouses forth" the differences of the world meant to have an answer? For Guo, the question is purely rhetorical—there are no external causes[34]—and the panpipes of Heaven is merely the general name for the self-so diversity of all the myriad things of existence.[35]

Guo's analysis is as a whole quite insightful and helps us to bring out many of the subtleties of the passage; its drawback, however, is that it is probably too uncompromising in its treatment of the chorus of Earth's panpipes as simply self-attained entities. The problem is that this does not go far enough in explaining how this passage relates to the remainder of the "Qiwulun" chapter, which seems to be centered around the theme of the worldly debate of the Confucians and Mohists and what the attained man's attitude should be toward such "righting" and "wronging": "The *Dao* gets hidden in minor accomplishments, and words get hidden in glory and eminence. Thus there is the righting and wronging of the Confucians and Mohists (*ru mo zhi shi fei* 儒墨之是非)—righting what [the other] wrongs and wronging what [the other] rights. If you want to right what is wronged and wrong what is righted, then there is nothing better than 'using illumination' (*yi ming* 以明)."[36] As we know from the "Renjianshi" chapter, Zhuangzi perceived knowledge and fame as the ill-boding vessels of one's downfall.[37] This being so, what attitude should be taken toward those who engage in such fare? For one cannot force an end to such debating by joining in the debate oneself, by trying to end such argumentation through argument; one must begin, instead, by changing one's own attitude. This is precisely the state achieved by Nanguo Ziqi and, indeed, the literary stance adopted by Zhuangzi himself.

Let us not forget how the passage opens: Nanguo Ziqi has lost his "mate"; he has "lost himself." Ceasing to see himself as an independent unit set in opposition to others, he can now embody the totality of the natural world within himself.[38] If Zhuangzi himself has achieved a similar state, then his "leveling" or "equalizing" of "things" or "discourses" must not take the form of a stance *against* such discourses; rather he must, in effect, allow them to cease of themselves. While he could have simply chosen not to speak, when he does so, he merely uses goblet words (*zhiyan* 卮言), which may extend forth endlessly and are of no harm to anyone.[39] That is why, we may say, the "Qiwulun" is so confusing and elusive and why Zhuangzi asks so many questions, each from two sides, yet gives answers to none of them.[40] And that is also why we encounter so much difficulty when trying to find definite conclusions or even preferences in the words that Zhuangzi writes.

But let us once again return to the imagery of the panpipes and this time enlist the help of the late-Ming/early-Qing commentator Wang Fuzhi 王夫之 (1619–1692), whose description of these pipes emphasizes a number of features different from those stressed by Guo Xiang:

All sounds are panpipes. Panpipes originally have no sound—the breath (*qi* 氣) stimulates them and there is sound. Sounds are originally undifferentiated—the mind causes the breath to let them loose, take them in, raise them up, or drop them down, and the variations of the twelve *gong*-tone [transpositions] and the seven modes infringe upon and rob each other—these are what is known as "transforming sounds" (*huasheng* 化聲).[41] If one listens to them with a mind having neither "myself" nor its "mate," then all the craftiness of a Ling Lun 伶倫[42] becomes nothing but a simple meandering "woo woo 嗚嗚."[43] The cleverness of the mind, the stimulation of the breath—why must these be taken as a matter of course?! In this way, then, the lips, teeth, throat, and tongue are [just] a [group of] gourd and bamboo instruments. Of that which the trigger of the breath drums up (*qiji zhi suo gu* 氣機之所鼓), the word is established on the basis of the sound; the meaning is established on the basis of the word; and "that" and "this," "right" and "wrong," are distinguished and analyzed to the minutest detail. Yet to be in ignorance as to whence they come forth—what, then, is the value of putting them in order (*wu zu ji hu* 惡足紀乎)?[44]

Thus it is that the panpipes represent an ordered group of sounds, to the extent that they are differentiated from one another through the cleverness of the mind. Yet the pipes have no sound until they are blown, and so before they are played, as when they cease, they are all even in their silence. It is important to note that for Wang all the differentiated sounds, and all the "this" and "that," "right" and "wrong," are not necessarily denied their place in the grand scheme of things, but rather must one *know how to listen to them*—one must be aware that all such differentiation ultimately arises from and constantly returns to a state of nondifferentiation.[45] It is this by which all that is uneven is naturally made even. It should be noted that Wang Fuzhi, in contrast to Guo Xiang, follows the Sima Biao version of a crucial textual variant at the end of the passage, where rather than the blowing wind causing the myriad crevices "to be themselves" (*shi qi zi ji* 使其自己), it causes them instead to "*cease* of themselves" (*shi qi zi yi* 使其自已) (par. 4).[46]

So given the description of the panpipes of Earth, Wang Fuzhi addresses a question that Guo Xiang had chosen to deemphasize, or, we may say, ignore altogether: what role does the wind play in the self-sounding—and, ultimately, self-ceasing—of the myriad crevices?[47] This is, to be sure, the central question of the passage, with which Nanguo Ziqi himself enigmatically concludes his brief lesson: "Who is it that rouses them forth?" Without necessarily having an answer in mind, the fact that Nanguo Ziqi understands the significance of the question to begin with is precisely what allows him to adopt a transcendent posture toward all the noise of the world of sectarian argument and debate.

We asked earlier the question of what the aesthetic nature of the *tianlai* image might be—a cacophony or harmony?—and suggested that the answer may lie in the attitude of the listener. If we want to hear a harmony, we should listen to the world the way we listen to a piece of music: from the standpoint of its unity. With music, we do not concentrate upon the individual notes one after the other or choose to listen to some instruments at the exclusion of others. Rather, we listen to the entire composition as a single, unbroken movement of sound, arising out of the silence that marks its beginning and returning to rest in silence once more as its progression of melodic themes finally draws it to a conclusion. Music is characterized by movement and rest, and like a storm that suddenly appears in the skies above us, a musical performance would mean nothing without the quiet tranquillity that both precedes its rise and follows its passing. Those who know how to listen to all of life's activity from the point of view of its inevitable return to the pool of transformation from which it first sprung are those who have finally awakened to become aware of the fact that all of this was just one great dream.

Such a state of mind is, in fact, a celebration of diversity, but it is a celebration that can only come from the recognition that all things are equal in their diversity, and this because they all arise from and return to the same source. We need not read *zi ji* 自己 as *zi yi* 自已 in order to arrive at this conclusion, for the text gives us other clues as well. There is even what may very well be an intentional play on words: the "evenness" (*qi* 齊) of things is achieved precisely by virtue of the fact that they all return to silent vacuity when the violent wind "passes on by" (*ji* 濟).[48] And this brings us back again to the question of dependency. The numerous crevices can assert themselves in sound only when the wind comes along to fill up their cavities; all individual perspectives thus invariably have "that for which they wait." Freedom, or independence, can be attained only through the loss of both self and other; losing the need for all self-assertion, one thereby loses all dependency—for one simply awaits everything and lets things transform of themselves. This was, indeed, the vision of Wang Tai 王駘, that crippled sage whom Confucius wanted to make his master:

Confucius said (of Wang Tai): "Death and life are great indeed, and yet he is incapable of changing with them; although Heaven and Earth were to overturn and crumble, he would not become lost along with them. He is manifestly without falsehood, and does not shift along with things; he allows things to transform and holds fast to his source (命物之化而守其宗也)."

    ..."Looked at from the standpoint of their differences, there are the liver and gall, Chu and Yue. Looked at from the standpoint of their sameness, the myriad things are all one (自其同者視之，萬物皆一也). Now as for someone like this [man], he is not even aware of what is appropriate to his ears and eyes, and instead roams his mind in the *harmony of virtues* (*you xin hu de zhi he* 遊心乎德之和). He looks at things from wherein they are one, and perceives not wherein they are lost—[thus] he looks upon losing his foot just as he would earth scattered upon the ground."[49]

It is, as Guo Xiang maintains, that all things are equal in their self-so-ness, but this holds true only for those who know how to listen to, or participate in, this symphony of life and death. Zhuangzi's philosophy offers us the chance to learn how to live our lives aesthetically, to appreciate that all we encounter are simply themes and variations upon the ever-changing melody of the Great Transformation. He teaches us how to hear and appreciate the Great Harmony, a harmony quite unlike that of the Confucians, which, marred as it is by hierarchical order, is wholly dependent upon finding the type of listener with ears and mind predisposed to accepting it as musically pleasing. The panpipes of Heaven may be enjoyed by all, for they exclude nothing and embrace all things as equal members of a diverse and intricate orchestra. Like Heaven's potter's wheel (*tianjun* 天均), it is that through which all opposing perspectives are brought into harmonious balance in a single "instrument": "Thus the sage harmonizes things through right and wrong, and brings them to rest upon Heaven's potter's wheel. This is what is known as 'walking two roads' 是以聖人和之以是非，而休乎天均，是之謂兩行."[50]

    Zhuangzi's sage is not one who, like the Confucian sage, has become his own master through a lengthy process of learning and the accumulation of proper action, but rather one who has mastered dependency precisely because he has forgotten himself, discarded all worldly learning, and through the attainment of a kind of dense vacuity merged himself with the great, pure unity of all existence: "The masses go about busily, while the sage remains in obtuse ignorance, joining up with the myriad years and achieving a unified purity (參萬歲而一成純)."[51] He is, in short, a man who has managed to "hide the world within the world" (*cang tianxia yu tianxia* 藏天下於天下), to "roam about where no thing can escape from" (*you yu wu zhi suo bu de dun* 遊於物之所不得遯), and emulate "that upon which all transformation awaits" (*yi hua zhi suo dai* 一化之所待).[52]

Conclusion

The realization, from the standpoint of inexorable nature and its ultimate reclamation of life's manifold differentiation, that "all things are one," that all the values to which we have become accustomed to clinging are, in the end, but relative, transient, and empty hollows that merely echo at the call of the wind, can be a difficult one with which to live. It challenges our entire mode of existence: to go about as we normally would in the face of such cognizance that all the "ought"s of conventional ethics are invalid, would only oblige us, as Nietzsche proclaims, to "consciously reside in untruth" or else grow "profoundly disillusioned" about our past, our present motives, and the promise we hold for the future. And yet there may be an alternative:

> Is it true, is all that remains a mode of thought whose outcome on a personal level is despair and on a theoretical level a philosophy of destruction?—I believe that the nature of the after-effect of knowledge is determined by a man's *temperament*: in addition to the after-effect described I could just as easily imagine a different one, quite possible in individual instances, by virtue of which a life could arise much simpler and emotionally cleaner than our present life is: so that, though the old motives of violent desire produced by inherited habit would still possess their strength, they would gradually grow weaker under the influence of purifying knowledge. In the end one would live among men and with oneself as in *nature*, without praising, blaming, contending, gazing contentedly, as though at a spectacle, upon many things for which one formerly felt only fear. One would be free of emphasis, and no longer prodded by the idea that one is only nature or more than nature.[53]

This is not far, to be sure, from the "temperament" of Wang Tai, who, "manifestly without falsehood," would simply "hold fast to the source" and contentedly allow his mind to "roam in the harmony of virtues" as the world changed, shifted, and even crumbled around him. And it is not unlike, certainly, the disposition of Nanguo Ziqi, who having "lost himself" would no longer hold any standpoint from which to "praise," "blame," or "contend," but rather, detached from it all, would "gaze" upon it "contentedly, as though it were a spectacle." Neither "only nature" nor "more than nature," he would become uniquely capable of listening to all the bluster of the world "free of emphasis" and thus hear it not as a cacophony but, rather, appreciate it as a unified yet ever-changing symphony of miraculous musical transformations. Such individuals are, indeed, rare; but this sort of aesthetic appreciation for life's diversity without evaluation is a state of mind we are clearly capable of approaching. The key lies in becoming aware that the life we are living is as if it were some grand play, an immense chess match, or a magnificent chorus of disparate instrumental players—in which we never lose sight of the fact that the roles and robes are temporary, winners and losers merge together, and all the tensions of life's ever-changing melodic theme and variations are ultimately resolved in a concluding silence once the final note is struck.

Notes

1. *Mengzi* 孟子 5.4 (3A.4); Jiao Xun 焦循, *Mengzi zhengyi* 孟子正義 (Shen Wenzhuo 沈文倬, col.; Beijing: Zhonghua shuju, 1987), p. 386. Mencius's formulation here is one of a number of similar examples that can be found through such works as the *Lun Yu* 論語 and the *Li Ji* 禮記.

2. Some, such as Wang Fuzhi 王夫之 (A.D. 1619–1692), group the three characters that make up this chapter's title differently, so that it would be rendered "Equalizing the Discourses of Things." This is an equally valid reading. For a summary of the positions taken in the debate over the correct reading of the title, see Wang Shu-min 王叔岷, *Zhuangzi jiaoquan* 莊子校詮 (Taipei: Zhongyang yanjiuyuan Lishi yuyan yanjiusuo, monograph no. 88, 1988), pp. 39–40; or Yen Ling-feng 嚴靈峰, "Zhuangzi Qiwulun pian zhi gaiding yu jiaoshi 莊子齊物論篇之改定與校釋, pt. 1" (*Dalu zazhi* 24:3), p. 69. I have argued elsewhere that the term *qi* 齊, "equalize," "even," "level," does not, generally, refer to a literal equalization or evening, but rather a proportionate one ("Unity and Diversity in the Musical Thought of Warring States China" [1995 Ph.D. dissertation, University of Michigan]. Ann Arbor: University Microfilms, 1996, pp. 67–68, 74–75). This is especially true in the *Zhuangzi*. On the authorship of the "Qiwulun" and other *Zhuangzi* chapters, see note 5 of my "Introduction." For convnience, I will refer to the author(s) of the chapters in question as "Zhuangzi."

3. Compare this also to the idea of *zuo wang* 坐忘, "sitting and forgetting," in the "Dazongshi" chapter, a state to which Yan Hui ultimately attains, at which point his teacher, Confucius, expresses a wish to become *his* disciple. See ZZJS, 284.

4. Nanguo Ziqi, given in the "Xuwugui" chapter as Nanbo (南伯) Ziqi, may have been an actual historical figure, utilized by Zhuangzi by imparting him with "entrusted words" (*yuyan* 寓言) much in the same way as he used Confucius and Lao Dan. Tang-dynasty commentator Cheng Xuanying 成玄英 identifies him simultaneously as a minister of King Zhuang of Chu 楚莊王 (r. 613–591 B.C.) and as a younger half-brother of King Zhao of Chu 楚昭王 (r. 514–488 B.C.), which makes little sense. Ch'ien Mu has him as a worthy esteemed by Tian He of Qi (who established himself as the first

Tian-family marquis of that state in 386 B.C.), who lived roughly the same time as Lie Yukou (列禦寇, Lie Zi). According to Ch'ien, all three references to him in the *Zhuangzi* have to do with self-forgetting. See Ch'ien Mu 錢 穆, *XianQin zhuzi xinian* 先秦諸子繫年 (1935; 2d ed., rev. and enl., 1956; Taipei: Dongda tushu gongsi, 3d ed., 1990), p. 178.

5. The rendering of *ou*—which in some editions is written 偶—as "mate" follows Guo Xiang's 郭象 (A.D. 252?–312) reading. Much of Wang Fuzhi's interpretation of this chapter hinges on this reading. Qing commentator Yu Yue 俞樾 reads the character as equivalent to *yu* 寓, "lodging," meaning the body (*shen* 身) into which the spirit (*shen* 神) is "lodged." Guo interprets *da* 荅 (= 嗒) as the appearance of being "dismembered" (*jieti* 解體). *Yan* 焉 may be interpreted as an adverb of manner, equivalent to *ran* 然, which several pre-Song sources quoting the passage have in its place. ZZJS 43–44; Wang Shu-min, *Zhuangzi jiaoquan* 41–42.

6. Said by Jin-dynasty commentator Li Yi 李頤 to be Nanguo Ziqi's disciple. As Wang Shu-min points out, with a surname containing the Yan 顏 of Yan Hui, and the name (Yan 偃) and style (Ziyou 子游) of Yan Yan 言偃, this person appears to be an amalgamation of these two Confucian disciples. ZZJS 44; Wang Shu-min, *Zhuangzi jiaoquan*, p. 42.

7. Or: "The one who is now leaning on the table is not the one who was leaning on the table before."

8. As mentioned in note 6 above, Yan is the given name of Yancheng Ziyou.

9. It is uncertain whether the term *wen* 聞 should be translated as "heard of" or simply "heard"; the two have different connotations. I thank Manyul Im for reminding me of the importance of this distinction. The latter makes for the more interesting reading.

10. The term *dakuai* 大塊, "Great Clump," has been interpreted variously as "the appearance of the great unhewn" (Sima Biao 司馬彪 [A.D. ???–306]: 大朴之貌), "non-entity" (Guo Xiang: 無物也), or "the name of the creator of things" (Cheng Xuanying: 造物之名). The best interpretation probably is that of Yu Yue, who, noting that the term *kuai* refers to a "handful of earth," takes *dakuai* to refer to Earth itself (地也) (Wang Shu-min locates a much earlier gloss of *dakuai* as Earth in Li Shan's 李善 [A.D. ???–689] commentary to the *Wenxuan* 文選. See *Zhuangzi jiaoquan*, p. 43). This works well, since it is currently *dilai*, the panpipes of Earth, of which Nanguo Ziqi is talking.

11. On the use of the term *weiwu* 唯無, see my translation of the *Mozi's* "Fei yue" (Denouncing music) in "Unity and Diversity," p. 187. Wang Shu-min believes the characters *zuo ze* 作則 had not been in the original text and were later added on the basis of Guo Xiang's annotation. He argues that that type of grammatical construction did not exist in pre-Han texts and cites a number of other examples from the *Zhuangzi* to prove his case (the *Mozi* examples also conform to Wang's theory). See Wang Shu-min, *Zhuangzi jiaoquan*, p. 44.

12. The actual Old Chinese reconstruction of *liao* 翏, in William H. Baxter's system, is (OC) *b-rjiw. See William H. Baxter, *A Handbook of Old Chinese Phonology* (Berlin and New York: Mouton de Gruyter, 1992).

13. I take 佳 as 崔, thus reading *weicui* in the sense of "lofty peaks," following Li Yi and Xi Tong 奚侗. See Wang Shu-min, *Zhuangzi jiaoquan*, p. 45.

14. The following describe the types of sounds produced by the wind passing over the various crevices and holes, the shapes of which were just enumerated. For details, see the notes to ZZJS 47–48 and Wang Shu-min, *Zhuangzi jiaoquan*, pp. 45–46.

15. 于 *wja and 喁 *ng(r)jowng.

16. *He* 和 may also have here the sense of "respond [in chorus]," "chime in," and thus form a counterpart to the *chang* 唱 "call out," "lead-sing," of the previous line.

17. The use of the character *ji* 濟 here is interesting because it is cognate with the *qi* 齊 ("even, proportioned; to even, to proportion") of the chapter title. I have elsewhere discussed the close relationship of the two in connection with a passage from the *Zuo zhuan*, Zhao 20; see "Unity and Diversity," p. 69. As noted there, *ji* has the basic sense of "to complete" (*cheng* 成), in the sense of "to have passed on by." (The term is also glossed as "to cease" [*zhi* 止], which is close in meaning). The term can thus more literally mean "to cross a river," or particularly with the rain radical (*ji* 霽), "(of weather) to clear up, blow over, pass on by." Combining these senses, we end up with the idea that the "evenness of things" (*wu zhi qi* 物之齊) is achieved by virtue of the fact that they all return to a unified silence (vacuity) after that which informs them with life and individuality finally passes on by (*ji* 濟). More on this shortly.

18. The characters are 調 *diw and 刁 *tiw (some suggest it should read 刀 *taw). They are visual, yet homophonic counterparts of the *b-rjiw 翏 sounds made by the crevices. As Guo Xiang says, they refer to the "appearance of movement and swaying 動搖貌": "This speaks of how the sounds of things already being different, their movement and swaying of their forms is further not the same 言物聲既異，而形之動搖亦又不同也."

19. It appears that in Sima Biao's edition the character *ji* 己 was given as the easily mistaken *yi* 已, which he glosses as "to cease" (*zhi ye* 止也). Guo Xiang interprets on the basis of an edition that obviously has the former, and I follow this reading in my translation. See ZZJS 50.

20. From "Qiwulun," ZZJS 43–51; HY 3/2/1–9.

21. This might, however, represent something of an overinterpretation of the phrase *wei wu* 唯無, although it does tend to carry something of this sense. Again, see the discussion of this term in the footnote to my translation of the "Fei yue" chapter of the *Mozi* in my "Unity and Diversity."

22. ZZJS 56; HY 4/2/18–19. 靡 is a loan for 磨.

23. As, for example, happened when the musics of Yao and Shun were played in the "fields of Dongting 洞庭之野." See "Zhi le," ZZJS 621–23;

HY 47/18/37–38. A similar thing happens later in the "Qiwulun" chapter, in response to the all-too-human beauty of such ladies as Mao Qiang 毛嬙 and Li Ji 麗姬; ZZJS 93–96, HY 6/2/68–70.

24. A *li* is a measure of length equivalent to approximately one-third of a mile.

25. More precisely, several *ren* 仞, each equivalent to several feet in length.

26. This figure is probably the same as the philosopher Song Xing 宋鈃 (ca. 360–ca. 290 B.C.).

27. 辯 is here equivalent to 變 ("changes"). In the *Zuo zhuan* (Zhao 1), the "six energies" are given as yin, yang, wind, rain, darkness, and light.

28. The text for the quoted passages may be found in ZZJS 2, 4, 7, 14, 16–17; HY 1/1/1–4, 6–8, 1–2/1/15–22.

29. One of the lines from the passage not cited here tells us that the Northern Darkness, too, is "Heaven's Pool." See ZZJS 14; HY 1/1/13.

30. For an analysis of this notion and its relation to Confucian thought, see my "Zhuang Zi and His Carving of the Confucian Ox," *Philosophy East and West*, 47:4 (October 1997), pp. 521–53.

31. I thank Brook Ziporyn for first putting it to me in precisely this way. Guo Xiang puts the same idea succinctly in another way: "If one rides upon whatever he encounters, then for what further would one have to wait." For Guo Xiang, even the hint of a favoring of the Peng bird over the other creatures goes out the window; they are all equally correct in their self-affirmation, or self-so-ness (*ziran* 自然), in that each does what is appropriate to its own nature. As stated elsewhere in the "Xiaoyaoyou" chapter, "the impersonator of the dead does not leap over the sacrificial utensils to replace the cook" (庖人雖不治庖，尸祝不越樽俎而代之矣; ZZJS 24–26; HY 2/1/26). Guo puts it the following way: "Thus the ability of the Great Peng to fly high, the ability of the marsh quail to fly low, the ability of the Chun tree to live long, and the ability of the morning mushroom to live briefly—all this is what they are able to do of their own self-so-ness (*ziran*), and not what they are able to do through purposive action (*wei* 為). . . . Thus he who 'mounts the axis of Heaven and Earth' is simply following along with the natures (*xing* 性) of the 10,000 things. He who 'drives the changes of the six energies' is merely roaming about the road of change and transformation. Going on in this way, to where could one go and meet with obstruction? If one rides upon whatever he encounters, then for what further would one have to wait (*dai*, 'depend')? This, then, is none other than the far and idle roaming of the man of utmost virtue who has merged notions of self and other into the darkness (*xuantong* 玄同). Had one had therein that for which he waited, then although he be as lithesome as Lie Zi, he would still not be able to travel without the wind. He would thus have to simply first obtain that for which he waited, and only then roam and idle far-away—not to mention the Great Peng! . . . Thus either having or not having that for which things wait (*youdai*

wudai 有待無待)—this is something I cannot make even (*qi* 齊). As far as they are each content in their natures, the natural trigger (*tianji* 天機) unfolding of itself, with them receiving it yet unaware—then this is something that I cannot make separate (*shu* 殊). For 'having no waiting' is still insufficient to distinguish from 'having that for which one waits'—let alone [the distinction between] the largeness or tininess of those who have to wait!" ZZJS 20.

Notice that Guo here borrows the language of the "Qiwulun": though all things and creatures are naturally different from one another, they are all ultimately "made even" (*qi* 齊) insofar as considered from the standpoint that they are all self-affirming. Commenting upon the reasons behind Nanguo Ziqi's detached appearance in the "Qiwulun," Guo uses similar language: "For he who lets things be self-so and forgets right and wrong, within his body he merely gives sole reign to natural trueness (*tianzhen* 天真)—what further does he have?! Thus at rest he is like the standing of a dried-out tree, and in movement like the motion of withered branches; sitting he is like dead ashes, and walking like wandering dust. The deportments of movement and rest are *things which I cannot make one.* As far as being of no [set-]mind and self-attained, these are *things of which I cannot make two*" ZZJS 44. More on Guo Xiang below. For a more general treatment of Guo's philosophy, see Brook Ziporyn, "The Self-so and Its Traces in the Thought of Guo Xiang," *Philosophy East & West* 43 (July, 1993), pp. 511–39, and his *The Penumbra Unbound: The Neo-Daoist Philosophy of Guo Xiang* (Albany: State University of New York Press, 2003).

32. ZZJS 45.

33. Guo: "Now although the sounds of the *gong* and *shang* tones go through thousands of changes and a myriad of transformations—singing and harmonizing; great and small—there is none that is not suited to what it receives, and each assumes its proper portion." ZZJS 48.

34. "Things all obtain it of themselves, and that is all. What master could have roused them forth and caused them to be thus?!" ZZJS 50.

35. "Now with the 'panpipes of Heaven,' how could it be that it further exists as some separate thing? It is simply that numerous crevices, the aligned bamboo tubes, and the like, connecting with the various living beings, gather to form together a single 'Heaven,' and that is all. Since non-being is already non-being, it cannot give birth to being; being having not yet arisen, it cannot further produce life. This being so, who is it that gives birth to the living? They spontaneously (*kuairan* 塊然, lit. 'clump-like') give birth to themselves, and that is all. They merely give birth to themselves—it is not that 'I' give birth to them. Since 'I' cannot give birth to things, neither can things give birth to 'myself'—thus 'I' am self-so. To be so of one's self—this is called 'naturally so' (*tianran* 天然, 'Heavenly so'). [Things are] just naturally so; it is not a matter of purposive action—thus they are spoken of in terms of 'Heaven.' It is by this [term] that their being self-so is made clear—how could it be that ['Heaven'] is referring to the 'blue skies'?! Yet some say that the 'panpipes of Heaven'

makes use of things and causes them to follow itself. Now Heaven cannot even possess itself—let alone possess things! Thus 'Heaven,' is the general name for the 10,000 things; there is none that is suited to be Heaven—[so] who would be in charge of making use of things?! Thus each thing gives birth to itself and has nowhere from which it comes out—this is the *Dao* of Heaven." ZZJS 50.

36. ZZJS 63; HY 4/2/25–27.

37. In the voice of Confucius instructing Yan Hui: "And are you indeed aware of wherein virtue is shaken up and of what sake knowledge comes forth? Virtue is shaken up through fame (*ming*), and knowledge comes forth of struggle. 'Fame' is reciprocal crushing, and 'knowledge' is the vessel of struggle. These two are ill-boding vessels (*xiong qi* 凶器), and not that whereby one may exhaust his conduct. And [though your own] virtue be earnest and your word sincere, [you] have still yet to arrive at the other man's vital energy (*qi*), and [though you yourself] strive not for fame and renown, [you] have still yet to arrive at the other man's mind (*xin*). And yet you forcefully make in front of the other man a showy display of your words of humanity, propriety, and the straight-lined—this is to peddle your beauty by way of the ugliness of the other man, and this is called 'to bring ruin upon others.' For those who bring ruin upon others, others will invariably bring ruin upon them in turn. Alas, you are bound to meet up with ruin at the hands of another!" ZZJS 136; HY 8/4/5–9.

38. Wang Fuzhi (see below) puts it in these terms: "For discourse arises from having 'mates': I see that 'that' [person] is different from myself, and it is as if an enemy is standing before me—not yielding to the other, one must respond to [the challenge]. Yet 'having a mate' arises from 'having a self': my knowledge and opinion is established in 'this,' and outside of 'this,' all is 'that'—'that' can then form a pair with 'myself' (*yu wo wei ou* 與我為偶). If one incorporates all discourses on things and knows whence they arise, and does not come out of the center of the ring and merely divide off a single corner, then there are no things that are not 'myself,' and 'myself' is not worthy of being established. That wherein there are no things that are not myself—only Heaven is thus. I being none other than Heaven, who would form a pair with myself?! Thus when myself is lost, [my] mate is lost; when [my] mate is lost, myself is lost. If [one] does not exist, then neither exists, and all that is uneven is made even" Wang Fuzhi, *Zhuangzi jie* 莊子解 (A.D. 1709) (Wang Xiaoyu 王孝魚, ed.; Beijing: Zhonghua shuju, 1964), p. 10. Or in the terminology of Xiong Shili 熊十力 (A.D. 1885–1968), a la Mencius, one may gain his "great self" (*daji* 大己), his "true nature" (*zhenxing* 真性), only by losing his "small self" (*xiaoji* 小己). Xiong Shili, *Yuan Ru* 原儒 (A.D. 1856) (Taipei: Mingwen shuju, 1988), p. 11.

39. This term appears in the "Yuyan" and "Tianxia" chapters. For a detailed explanation of *zhiyan* and related terms, see Shuen-fu Lin 林順夫, "The Lan-

guage of the 'Inner Chapters' of the Chuang Tzu," in *The Power of Culture: Studies in Chinese Cultural History*, ed. Peterson, Placks, and Yu (Hong Kong: Chinese University Press, 1994), pp. 14–21.

40. In the terms of the *Zhuangzi*, rather than making his own judgment (*weishi* 為是) and thereby merely adding his own "fledgling chirping" (*guyin* 穀音) to the chorus, the "attained man" is content to lean upon what is naturally correct (*yinshi* 因是), to use Heaven and nature as the true source from which to reflect all things, and to "walk two roads" (*liangxing* 兩行) at the same time. These terms all appear elsewhere in the chapter, and are all notoriously difficult to interpret. *Weishi* may very well not even constitute a set term; in its few appearances, as in *wei shi bu yong* 為是不用 (ZZJS 70; HY 4/2/36), it probably simply means "therefore." A. C. Graham translates *weishi* as the "'That's it' which deems" and *yinshi* as the "'That's it' which goes by circumstance" (See A. C. Graham, *Chuang-tzu: The Seven Inner Chapters and Other Writings from the Book of Chuang-tzu* [London: George Allen & Unwin, 1981], p. 11). As he puts it elsewhere: "*yin-shih* is . . . to make relative judgments according to changing conditions like the Taoist sage; *wei-shih* is . . . to judge between alternatives according to one's fixed preconceptions, like the Confucians and Mohists." "Chuang-tzu's Essay on Seeing Things as Equal," *History of Religions*, 9.2 (November, 1969), p. 143. *Yinshi* is a more likely candidate to constitute a set term, as it appears several times in the chapter, but some still argue that even this is in each case a contextually related phrase, meaning "because of this." Wang Shu-min, *Zhuangzi jiaoquan*, p. 60. Guo Xiang treats it as a set term, glossing it at one point with "going along with what they like and self-affirming 因其所好而自是也." ZZJS 73, note 19. We might also note that Graham takes the character *yi* 已, which follows *yin shi* at a couple of points in the chapter, in the sense of "to stop," rather than as a near-equivalent to the aspect particle *yi* 矣. That the former reading is unlikely can be demonstrated by comparing the wording of two passages in which the construction occurs:

《齊物論》：「適得而幾矣。因是已。已而不知其然，謂之道。」

《養生主》：「以有涯隨無涯，殆已！已而為知者，殆而已矣！」

In the second example, it seems clear that the *yi* 已 at the end of the first phrase cannot be taken as "to stop" (though Graham manages even that somehow), and the similarity of the grammatical pattern between the two (已 followed by 已而) suggests that the characters be read the same way for both. ZZJS 70, 115; HY 5/2/37, 7/3/1.

41. This is a term that comes up later in the "Qiwulun:" "The mutual dependence of transforming sounds (i.e., righting and wronging) seems as if it is mutual independence (*huasheng zhi xiangdai, ruo qi bu xiangdai* 化聲之相待，若其不相待.") ZZJS 108; HY 7/2/91. Guo Xiang glosses the term by

equating it with "the disputation of right and wrong" (是非之辯為化聲).
ZZJS 109, note 3.

42. Ling Lun was said to have been a music master at the time of the
legendary sage-ruler Huang Di and to be the first to have created the twelve
pitches and the five tones of the pentatonic scale. The story can be found in
the "Gu Yue 古樂" chapter of the *Lüshi chunqiu* 呂氏春秋.

43. This description would appear to be borrowed from Su Shi's 蘇軾
(A.D. 1036–1101) *Qian chibi fu* 前赤壁賦 (Former Rhymeprose of Red-cliff):
"One of the guests played a long vertical flute, harmonizing along with the
words of the song, and it sounded a meandering 'woo-woo': as if bitter, as
if covetous, as if crying, as if complaining. The tones left-over (*yuyin* 餘音)
hung in the air, like a continuous stream of silk thread. It could make the
submerged flood-dragon in a secluded ravine dance, or the widowed lady in
a solitary boat cry."

44. Wang Fuzhi, *Zhuangzi jie*, p. 11.

45. One should, in Wang's words, "Give reign to their unevenness, and
allow them to stop of themselves. Know that from which they arise and
that from which they cease, that they all borrow the breath of living men
to 'mutually blow about' and make clever variations. Then it will be seen
that they are not worth arguing distinctions with, and that all are enveloped
within the midst of 'not-yet-beginning-to-be'; so as to allow the wind of
'transforming sounds' to pass on by and [things to] return to vacuity. Then
there will be nothing that is not even." Wang Fuzhi, *Zhuangzi jie*, p. 10. In
the second sentence, Wang appears to borrow language from both the *tianlai*
passage (*xiang chui* 相吹) and the "Xiaoyaoyou" chapter (ZZJS 4; HY 1/1/4),
where mention is made of "living things being mutually blown about by the
wind" (*sheng wu zhi yi xi xiang chui* 生物之以息相吹). From this description,
rich in the language of the "Qiwulun," it is apparent that Wang Fuzhi puts the
emphasis on the "ceasing 已" and the "returning 反" of the myriad voices.
Naturally, once these voices have arisen, they are uneven, but when seen in
terms of their all having derived from a common source in the "vacuity" to
which they all ultimately return, then, both posterior to their existence and
prior to their beginnings, these voices cannot but be thought of as even.

46. For more on this variation see Wang Shu-min, *Zhuangzi jiaoquan*, p. 48.
Wang Shu-min argues in favor of Guo's reading, though most current editions of the text read *yi*. We might also note here that Wang Fuzhi reads the
title of this chapter as "Leveling-out the Discussions of Things," rather than
"A Discourse on the Leveling of Things," a fact consistent with his emphasis
on the centrality of the Confucian-Mohist dilemma in this chapter.

47. In Wang's interpretation, the wind and the crevices are equally dependent upon each other in their production of sounds, and the notion captured
in this image may be extended to the phenomenal world of men and things:
"The Earth originally has no sounds—it relies upon the wind to have sounds.

Neither can the wind produce sounds—it borrows the twists of the mountain
forest and the crevices of giant trees to have sounds. The two depend upon
each other; they stimulate each other and sounds come forth, and these sounds
have no inherently fixed forms. They resemble men (i.e., 'like mouths,' etc.)
and resemble things ('like vases,' etc.), and so the 'empty crevices' of [actual]
men and things, receiving the breath and being drummed into action, are also
simply thus. Murmurers, whistlers, yellers, suckers, shouters, wailers, resonators, screamers, singers, harmonizers—this is the utmost in unevenness. Yet
the wind passes on by, and they all return to vacuity. Although there are the
after-tones of wavering and quivering, they are yet all 'aging and deteriorating,' and 'nothing can revitalize them.' Thus that which arises and rouses them
into howling returns to its [state of] non-arising, and there is then nothing
that is not even." Wang Fuzhi, *Zhuangzi jie*, p. 12. Wang borrows here a line
from the next section of the "Qiwulun" chapter: "'They seal up like coffin
ropes—this speaks of their aging and deteriorating (*laoxu* 老洫); their minds
are close to death, and nothing can revitalize them" (*mo shi fu yang* 莫使復
陽). ZZJS 51; HY 3–4/2/12–13. The line describes the different mental states
of men wrapped up in the debates of right and wrong. Such men, like the
son of the *qin* master Zhao Wen (昭文, ZZJS 74–75; HY 5/2/43–46), devote
themselves to their positions until death without ever reaching completion.
Wang's point seems to be that while the diversification of the myriad voices
is a given, there is no sense in clinging to one's own particular view, because
all returns to vacuity in the end.

    48. As mentioned in a note to the translation above, this pun may also
have been operative in a reputed speech of Yanzi 晏子 (d. ca. 500 B.C.) given
in the *Zuo zhuan*, Zhao 20.

    49. "Dechongfu," ZZJS 189–92; HY 12/5/5–8. Passages such as this one
could be seen as argument against those who, like Chad Hansen, try to pro-
hibit us from thinking of Zhuangzi's thought in terms of what Hansen has
labeled "mystical monism" (something Hansen considers more a *Mencian*
trait). Hansen's prohibition seems to stem from an observation of A. C. Graham: aptly describing the "Qiwulun" as an essay which gives us "the sensation
of a man thinking aloud," Graham notes that Zhuangzi, after stating (perhaps
after Hui Shi) that "heaven and earth were born together with me and the
myriad things and I are one," "immediately proceeds to argue that the claim
that everything is one is self-contradictory." Graham, "On Seeing Things as
Equal," pp. 137–38. This is true enough, but the nature of the argument is
such that Zhuangzi has only discovered that he has frustrated his own desire
to merge into oneness with all things precisely because of the fact that he
has made a statement in the first place. It is not, as Hansen claims, that the
"monist" perspective is just that—one of many perspectives. It is clearly more
than that; if we want to view it as a perspective, then it is the perspective that
effaces all other perspectives, the guiding perspective from which to view the

relativism of all that is broken up from this "one." It is clear from the passage above that "looking at things from wherein they are one" is a good thing to do; it would require no small amount of ingenuity to come up with any other interpretation. Indeed, the assertion that the "monist perspective" was for Zhuangzi on equal footing with all others would demand a highly "selective" reading of the work. A great deal would have to be explained away, and one can only argue so many times that these are all "provisional formulations" that Zhuangzi eventually comes back to attack. Why did Hun Dun die if not for the fact that his unity was broken up? Hansen wishes to view Zhuangzi as the ultimate logician. Yet though we assume, as did Fung Yu-lan and A. C. Graham, that he mastered their forms of logical debate, he still perceived the absurdity of that debate in light of the ultimate unity of all things. [For the contrary view, of course, see Hansen's article in this volume. There, Hansen makes a distinction between "naturalistic" versus "Parmenidean" forms of monism; it thus becomes clearer that his objections to "mystical monism" lay not so much in the "monism" per se as they do in the "mystical." For yet another perspective on this whole issue, see the article by Brook Ziporyn in this volume.]

    50. "Qiwulun," ZZJS 70; HY 5/2/39–40.

    51. "Qiwulun," ZZJS 100; HY 6/2/78.

    52. "Dazongshi," ZZJS 243–44; HY 16/6/25–29.

    53. Friedrich Nietzsche, *Human, All Too Human: A Book For Free Spirits* (1878; R. J. Hollingdale, tr., Cambridge: Cambridge University Press, 1986), pp. 29–30.

4

From "Merging the Body with the Mind" to "Wandering in Unitary *Qi* 氣": A Discussion of Zhuangzi's Realm of the True Man and Its Corporeal Basis

RUR-BIN YANG 楊儒賓

Is there any relationship between Daoist metaphysics and cultivation practices? This is an old question with a long history of debate. From Heshang Gong's 河上公 annotations to the *Laozi* on down, it can be said that there has never been a lack of those who would affirm the connection. Yet while those among the intellectual class advocating this view certainly exist, opposing voices are also numerous, as when Ma Duanlin 馬端臨 once said,

> The pathways of Daoism are varied and manifold, as former scholars have discussed exhaustively. In general, there is the doctrine of pure tranquility (*qingjing* 清淨), and there is the doctrine of refining cultivation (*lianyang* 煉養); there are also the doctrine of substance intake (*fushi* 服食), the doctrine of talismans (*fulu* 符籙), and the doctrine of canonical instruction (*jingdian kejiao* 經典科教). In the works of Huang Di, Laozi, Lie Yukou, and Zhuang Zhou, what is discussed is simply pure tranquility and non-activity (*wuwei* 無為), with some slight attention to the affairs of refining

Translated by Scott Cook. [The original essay, "Cong 'yi ti he xin' dao 'you hu yi qi'—lun Zhuangzi zhenren jingjie de xingti jichu 從「以體合心」到「遊乎一氣」～論莊子真人境界的形體基礎," first appeared in *Diyijie Zhongguo sixiangshi yantaohui lunwenji—Xian-Qin Ru-Fa-Dao sixiang zhi jiaorong ji qi yingxiang* 第一屆中國思想史研討會論文集——先秦儒法道思想之交融及其影響 (Tai-chung: Donghai daxue wenxueyuan, 1989), pp. 185–212. Due to considerations of space, I have slightly abridged the article in certain places in the translation, and in each case have noted the content of anything omitted from the original essay. Except where otherwise noted, all translations of *Zhuangzi* quotations appearing in this article are taken from Watson, *The Complete Works of Chuang Tzu.*—tr.].

cultivation—substance intake and the others are never mentioned. When it comes to Chisongzi 赤松子, Wei Boyang 魏伯陽, and the like, they discuss refining cultivation, but not pure tranquility.[1]

Ma's essay goes on to infer that the doctrines of substance intake and talismans are perverse, absurd, and highly detrimental; as for the doctrine of canonical instruction, although it cannot be said to have an overly harmful influence, its central import on the whole never departs from "the vulgar and superficial." Thus, according to Ma, the two branches of "pure tranquility" and of "refining cultivation"—particularly the former—must count as the more orthodox sects, those more in keeping with the original meaning of Daoism.

Ma's categorization has a certain logic to it, and we can generally find sufficient documentary support for his judgments as to the influence that each of the Daoist sects held during the course of history.[2] However, this author has his doubts as to whether the "pure tranquility" and "refining cultivation" esteemed by the Daoists can be so sharply separated from each other, and especially as to whether the affairs of "refining cultivation" are merely a borderline component to which "slight attention" is given. In this chapter, although I will not explore the Daoist philosophy of cultivation directly, I will attempt to extract from the Dao-embodiment[3] (tidao 體道) experiences described by Zhuangzi the corporeal components hidden within them, which are directly related to cultivation; moreover, I will go on to point out the inseparable connection between Zhuangzi's view of the corporeal self and his metaphysics.

The Forgotten Self
(Zuowang zhi shen 坐忘之身)

Zhuangzi's writing style is carefree and unorthodox, and his arguments often ebb and flow with the pulse of his words, seemingly broken off and then reconnected, and thus it is difficult to determine their sense in any single passage or segment. For the moment, we might as well set aside any judgments and begin by phenomenologically observing a few of the more famous passages and sentences in the Zhuangzi that speak to the experience of Dao-embodiment. For convenience of discussion, let us list them side-by-side below:

I smash up my limbs and body, drive out acuity and perceptiveness (cong-ming 聰明), cast off form (xing 形), do away with understanding (zhi 知),

and make myself identical with the Great Thoroughfare (*tong yu tatong* 同於大通). This is what I mean by sitting down and forgetting everything (*zuowang* 坐忘) ("Dazongshi")

...mind-nourishment! You have only to rest in inaction and things will transform themselves. Smash your form and body, spit out acuity and perceptiveness, forget you are a thing among other things, and you may join in great unity with the deep and boundless. Undo the mind (*jie xin* 解心), slough off spirit (*shi shen* 釋神), be blank and soulless. ("Zai you")

Body like a withered corpse, mind like dead ashes, true in the realness of knowledge (*zhen qi shi zhi* 真其實知), not one to go searching for reasons, dim dim, dark dark, mindless, you cannot consult him. ("Zhi beiyou")

You must fast and practice austerities, cleanse and purge your mind, wash and purify your essential spirit (*jingshen* 精神), destroy and do away with your knowledge (*zhi* 知). ("Zhi beiyou")[4]

The above four quotations are among the more closely observed passages in the *Zhuangzi*, but the connotations they hold in fact pervade the entire *Zhuangzi* text, forming a central axis around which the basic thought of the work is framed.

Why does this keynote repeatedly appear in the Zhuangzi? What relationship does such a keynote have with the concept of 'body' (*shenti guan* 身體觀) I wish to explore in this chapter? Having read the above passages, we can analyze the shared implications they ultimately contain.

First of all, these words reveal the fact that in the process of seeking the Dao, one must go through a stage wherein perception and rationality disintegrate: perception and rationality are the most basic preconditions for the production of "objects," and the most fundamental premise by which "experience" can grow. Zhuangzi, however, believes that the "consciousness of unification with the Dao" stands in opposition to perception and rationality, and thus in order to empirically embody the Dao, one must first dissolve his "limbs and body," "perception and intellect," "form and understanding," "mind and spirit." One must incessantly cleanse and purge them, wash and purify them, destroy and do away with them.

Second, having gone through the stage of the disintegration of perception and rationality, the "personal identity of the empirical self" also reciprocally unravels along with them. When Zhuangzi makes mention of one attaining the Dao, he often portrays a scene of being "blank and soulless" (*moran wuhun* 莫然無魂), of being "dim dim, dark dark, mindless, and unconsultable." The former likely refers to the removal of biases, wherein the concept of 'self' is no longer present; the latter refers to the mind's submergence into the depths of undifferentiated consciousness, wherein one no longer has any clear and distinct perception. Zhuangzi sometimes talks directly of "forgetting self" (*wangji* 忘己) ("Tian di"), "losing myself" (*sangwo* 喪我) and "losing one's companion" (喪其耦) ("Qiwulun"), of there being "no more Hui" ("Renjianshi") and being "utterly motionless, as if not human" ("Tian Zifang"); or in a more roundabout manner Zhuangzi speaks of being "dim and dark" ("Zhi beiyou"), of "carving and polishing returning to plainness" ("Yingdiwang"), or of the sage being "stupid and blockish" ("Qiwulun").[5] No matter whether Zhuangzi is using declarative sentences or descriptive phrases, in each case he points to a kind of realm far removed from pragmatic self-identity.

Third, after the seeker of the Dao dissolves the "personal identity of his empirical self," although his consciousness no longer unfolds around his "individuality," his present consciousness is now, on the contrary, situated at a higher and more authentic level. "True in the realness of knowledge, not one to go searching for reasons"—this points to the fact that this type of authentic consciousness is no longer subject to the influence of the operational modes of one's former consciousness, but rather constitutes a kind of direct awareness that can thoroughly reflect the whole in a single moment. For this reason, a great contrast based on the distinction between reflecting the whole versus clinging to the part, or authentic knowledge versus petty recognition, causes Zhuangzi to adopt a critical and mocking commentary upon worldly knowledge—a writing tactic to be found often throughout the *Zhuangzi*.

Fourth, following the emergence of authentic knowledge, the assimilator and the things assimilated come forth simultaneously, inter-penetrating each other. "Become identical with the Great Thoroughfare," "join in great unity with the deep and boundless"—these all point out how within our experience of embodying the Dao, although our consciousness of individuality and differentiation has long since been swept out of existence, a more authentic consciousness has yet already filled up the entire realm of existence, with no distinction between subjective and objective, between the conscious and the unconscious (matter)— "the vast, indistinct identity of mind and body, naturally merged into a single entity."[6]

Although there are varying degrees of detail where Zhuangzi speaks of the relationship between Dao and mankind, the four above points can more or less be observed. They do not, to be sure, constitute events in our daily lived experience, but if we consider them in the context of the Daoist tradition, or more broadly in that of what Aldous Huxley terms "the perennial philosophy,"[7] the particular Dao-embodiment experiences of which Zhuangzi speaks do, in fact, carry a considerable amount of commonly shared features. Nearly all mystics from all cultural traditions and nationalities affirm that aside from the empirical self, there is also a higher-level self; and they likewise affirm that people can merge as one with a higher entity. At the same time, within this state of conjoinment, while the one experiencing it may well lose his ordinary consciousness, his mind-soul now dwells in a clearer and more complete noetic state.[8]

Naturally, the particular features of mysticism are not limited to the above four points, and the comparison of Zhuangzi and mysticism is not the focus of this chapter. What concerns us here, rather, is that from Zhuangzi's narrations and the reports of mystics, we can observe how aside from what we can attain via the experience of our sense organs or through rational inference, there is also a kind of higher-level, more authentic reality. In order to comprehend this more authentic reality, we must first dissolve the empirical self that is bounded by perception and rationality and allow a more authentic and deeper consciousness to manifest itself, only after which may the two merge as one.[9]

Listening with the Vital Energy
(*Ting zhi yi qi* 聽之以氣)

Having experienced the collapse of one's empirical self, one's authentic self is then able to emerge simultaneously with one's authentic substance. Such a process is depicted throughout the *Zhuangzi* as well as in the reports of many mystics, and thus in order to explain this unique experience, we must affirm that the structure of human life itself has a certain universality to it, such that no matter how great the cultural differences of those having such an experience, in each case what one gains through it is similar.[10] However, while the structure of the human body is certainly generally the same everywhere and does not vary according to time or place, it is nonetheless true that Zhuangzi lived in the southern Chinese cultural sphere, where mysticism had a long and deeply developed tradition.[11] He thus had a greater background for thorough observation and explanation of the difficult cultivation issues encountered in a person's elevation from the realm of experience to the transcendental realm. Let us now take the issue of perception and rationality raised in the previous section and explore it from another direction.

In the first section, perception and rationality were spoken of negatively, as a kind of obstruction and thus in need of disintegration. What I would like to discuss in this section, however, is the following: The ears, eyes, and other sense organs are viewed as channels leading to deep-level consciousness; while they may have distinctions of function between them, they are the same in terms of their essential qualities, all alike insofar as they can be transformed into a state identical in essence to deep-level consciousness.

In order to highlight the argument, let us cite one of the more famous parables in the *Zhuangzi*. The "Renjianshi" chapter records an anecdote wherein Yan Hui 顏回 asks for guidance from Confucius, and Confucius responds with "fasting of the mind" (*xinzhai* 心齋). Yan Hui mistakes this to mean vegetarian intake and abstinence from wine, but Confucius considers that to be just ordinary fasting, whereas true fasting of the mind should mean, "'Make your will one! Don't listen with your ears, listen with your mind (*xin* 心). No, don't listen with your mind, but listen with your vital energy (*qi* 氣). Listening stops with the ears, the mind stops with recognition, but vital energy is empty and waits on all things (*xu er dai wu* 虛而待物). The *Dao* gathers in emptiness alone. Emptiness is the fasting of the mind.'"[12] Yan Hui is greatly pleased upon hearing this, and immediately follows up by asking for details. Confucius continues to elaborate,

> You have heard of flying with wings, but you have never heard of flying without wings. You have heard of the knowledge that knows, but you have never heard of the knowledge that does not know. Look into that closed room, the empty chamber where brightness is born! Fortune and blessing gather where there is stillness . . . Let your ears and eyes communicate with what is inside, and put mind and knowledge on the outside. Then even gods and spirits will come to dwell, not to speak of men![13]

The "fasting of the mind," the "losing the companion" (*sang ou* 喪偶) of the "Qiwulun," the "sitting down and forgetting" (*zuowang* 坐忘) and "achieving the brightness of dawn/seeing one's own aloneness" (*zhaoche jiandu* 朝徹見獨) of the "Dazongshi," and the mind-nourishment of "Zai you"[14] are all important textual references depicting the experience of attaining Dao. Theoretically speaking, these passages should be mutually illuminating and form one complete network of significance. However, when we examine the narration of "fasting of the mind," we discover that while the issue of perception and rationality touched upon therein certainly carries the same notion of disintegration as discussed above, the *mode* of disintegration is in fact quite different. We might raise the following queries as reference points by which to ponder the issue:

1. "Let your ears and eyes communicate with what is inside, and put mind and knowledge on the outside"—by what means can the ears and eyes be made to communicate with the inside?

2. How is "listening with the vital energy" possible? Why is the term *listen* (*ting* 聽), which carries perceptual implications, used in this instance?

3. "Vital energy is empty and waits on things; Dao gathers in emptiness alone; emptiness is the fasting of the mind"—just what sort of essential connection do the vital energy, emptiness, and Dao have?

Are such queries valid? Zhuangzi is a master of playing with language, of deconstructing language, a common observation of most *Zhuangzi* readers; moreover, Zhuangzi has never hidden his attitude toward language, which is a combination of distrust mixed with playfulness. In that case, how can we apply our customary way of reading the works of Kant or Hume—analyzing every word or sentence and disputing every detail—when reading the absurd language of Zhuang Zhou? And yet, in this *Zhuangzi* parable given in the form of a Confucian master-disciple dialogue, is the theoretical understanding conveyed thereby really so insignificant as all that? Let us make reference to another statement: "What do I mean by a True Man? . . . The True Man of ancient times slept without dreaming and woke without care; he ate without savoring and his breath came from deep inside. The True Man breathes with his heels; the mass of men breathe with their throats ("Dazongshi")."[15] Why is it that, in the highest form of human character in Zhuangzi's thought, the cultivation of "spirit" (*jingshen* 精神) can actually have such an effect that one does not dream in his sleep, is unaware of flavors while eating, and can even breathe with his heels? Judging by the literal meaning of the words, the relationship of consciousness to the sense organs in the True Man at this time is no longer one of destruction and overcoming but rather of permeation and transformation.

This notion of the True Man's consciousness permeating and transforming his sense organs is difficult to understand, because if we accept a mind-body dualism, or believe that the function of each sense organ is separate without any overlap, then the effect of consciousness obviously cannot be exaggerated to the point of transforming the basic character of the sense organs. But in our understanding of the mind-body relationship, we should seriously consider some of the views of the Daoist tradition, rather than treating common sense as the unassailable standard.[16] Drawing on that tradition (along with the Confucian and Buddhist), the Ming-dynasty *Zhuangzi* commentator Lu Xixing 陸西星, for instance, makes the following two points in explaining the character of the True Man:[17]

1. The subtlest movements of the human body can unite with the deepest levels of human consciousness: the so-called "mutual reliance of mind and breath," "mutual preservation of spirit and vital energy," and "nourishing the soul and embracing the one" refer to none other than this.

2. When a person attains to the realm of "mutual reliance of energy and breath," his sense organs become fully permeated by the vital energy and thus lose their specific functions and move toward uniformity with deep-level human consciousness.

Looking back in this light at the issue of the theory implicit within the "fasting of the mind," we might answer the first question of how the ears and eyes can communicate with the inside as follows: because the ears and eyes at this time are no longer the "restricted sense organs of a perceptual person in the empirical world," but rather "interpenetrating channels permeated by and permeating the vital energy." Thus both permeated by and permeating into the vital energy, the ears and eyes are not only a receptive-reactive sensory system but also the channels through which the deep-level consciousness must pass in its outward movement and at the same time also a kind of path for the reflective looking and inward listening of human consciousness returning to its origins.[18]

Five Organs All Complete
(*Wuguan jie bei* 五官皆備)

The *Wenzi* 文子 states that "The highest learning listens with the spirit (*shen* 神), the middle learning listens with the mind, and the lowest learning listens with the ears."[19] This explanation is of great interest, and moreover, is mutually elucidating with Zhuangzi's three-stage doctrine of listening with the ears, the mind, and the vital energy. We must, however, still return to the same question: why do Zhuangzi and Wenzi use the term *listen* to describe the functions of the mind and vital energy? Is there a certain logic to the notion that "listening" runs through all three levels of learning and is used by the ears, mind, and vital energy alike? Or is this just an arbitrary application of a metaphorical means of expression?

When it comes to the transferred application of sense-organ terminology to the function of other forms of consciousness, we cannot but recall a story of profound significance from the *Liezi* 列子:

> Among Lao Dan's disciples was a certain Kangcangzi 亢倉子, who attained Dan's *Dao* and was able to look with his ears and listen with his eyes. The Marquis of Lu heard of this and was greatly astonished . . . Kangcangzi said, "The one who conveyed this to you was rashly misleading—I can look and listen without the use of my ears and eyes; I cannot switch the functions of my ears and eyes . . . My body (*ti* 體) merges with my mind, my mind merges with my vital energy, my vital energy merges with my spirit, and my spirit merges with nothingness (*wu* 無). If the slightest something or the smallest sound comes to disturb me—whether it be as far as outside the eight wilds or as close as between my eyebrows and lashes—I invariably perceive it. Yet I don't know whether it's felt through my seven apertures and four limbs, or perceived through my heart, gut, and six organs—I simply self-perceive it, and that is all."[20]

Another story describes how after Liezi "took Mr. Laoshang 老商氏 as his master, befriended Bogaozi 伯高子, advanced through the Dao of these two masters, and rode back home upon the wind," Yinsheng 尹生 heard about it and wished to study the Dao with him, but Liezi for a long time would not open his gate, and Yinsheng left disappointed, only to return later to express his grievances. Liezi then explained his former experiences to him, and when he came to describe the ultimate realm of embodied realization, said, "'Having advanced [beyond] inner and outer, my eyes were like my ears, my ears were like my nose, and my nose was like my mouth—none was not identical [with the others]. My mind consolidated and my form dispersed, and my bones and flesh all melded together . . . I was ultimately unaware: did the wind ride me, or did I ride the wind?'"[21]

Looking with the ears and listening with the eyes would truly be bizarre and in violation of common sense.[22] But if it is a matter of saying the human sense organs can blend—the "eyes like ears, ears like nose, nose like mouth"—or of "not knowing whether it's felt through the seven apertures and four limbs, or perceived through the heart, gut, and six organs," then it is not all that preposterous, and not necessarily in violation of "common sense."

We might begin with a discussion of "common sense." In the ordinary person, the consciousness of each sense organ has its own individual sphere of application, and it is difficult for them to overstep each other. As early as the time of Aristotle, however, it was already pointed out that we humans not only can discern considerable differences among the same type of sensation—such as the various colors of red, yellow, orange, and green that form the objects of our sense of sight—but we also can discern discrepancies between different types of sensation—such as the white of sight and sweet of taste, and so on. However, upon what basis is it that such discernment becomes possible? Aristotle believed that we should not imagine that this type of sense of discernment lies at the same level as the sense of sight and sense of taste, but rather there is a type of sense capability that unifies the various sense organs and is, moreover, original to them. This is the "general faculty of sense-perception," or we may say, a type of "common sense."[23]

This common sense can not only distinguish between the differences among different types of perception, but it can further understand the movements, states, numbers, unities, and other forms ungraspable by individual sensations. Thus, using our imagination, we can search for a type of connection among our different sense organs, such as when we apply the taste "sweet" to describe a "sweet sound" (hearing) or a "sweet smile" (sight), and so on. Yet this type of imagination results from its establishment upon the operations of this general faculty of sense perception.[24]

This kind of common sense perception is in fact quite close to the phenomenon of "synesthesia" commonly found in religious and artistic experiences. What the term *synesthesia* refers to is precisely the mutual communication and simultaneous emergence of the various types of sense perception. Artists and religious adepts often manifest this capability to an unusual degree through either innate talent or cultivation, but in actual fact it is something that everyone possesses, not just these two types of people. It is only that it remains latent in the ordinary person, who is unable to move about freely between one realm and the next.[25]

Is the meaning of 'synesthesia' limited only to the level of perception, or can it be applied more broadly? In light of goals I seek to demonstrate in this chapter, I believe that it can. It happens that Merleau-Ponty's views in this area can provide us with a good deal of useful information. According to Merleau-Ponty, the inter-communication of the various sense-perceptions was originally an extraordinarily common principle, but because we have been blinded by so-called scientific knowledge, we have actually broken with concrete experience. Our human existence (the human body), however, is by no means limited to this but has a much larger scope. That is, the human body is a "ready-made system" through which the ordinary experiences of the world assimilate and enter into one another; it incessantly transposes and translates all types of impressions, sensations, and concepts back and forth: "Man is a permanent *sensorium commune*."[26]

Merleau-Ponty's philosophy of body has many other significant points worth elaborating upon, but from the brief description above, we can affirm the fact that such notions as the mutual interpenetration of the sense organs, or the entire body being one common sense organ, have a physiological basis to them. The phenomenon of "vital-energization of the sense organs" (*ganguan qihua* 感官氣化) described by Zhuangzi and other Daoist philosophers, too, cannot escape this basis; yet because the Daoists had their own tradition of cultivation discourse, they did not treat such concrete empirical phenomena as synesthesia as the determinate and ultimate basis. They were, certainly, not like the Buddhists in viewing human life from birth to maturity as a course of obfuscation and pollution, which thus called for a long period of destructive cultivation before one could return to one's original state.[27] The Daoist philosophers did, however, share with them the affirmation that the ordinary "empirical self"—whether it be the "bodily self" or the "rational self"—was dependent and limited[28] and that if one wanted to attain to the realm of free-and-easy nondependence, it would only be possible by standing on the foundation of synesthesia and thoroughly breaking through the determinate functions of the sense organs, allowing all sensations to meld into one whole and be fully integrated by the vital energy. In a word, only after having going through the course of "I've lost myself" could there truly be an "I."

Considering it in the above context, we can understand the implicit meaning of "eyes like the ears, ears like the nose, nose like the mouth—none not identical." What Liezi describes here is none other than the realm of synesthesia. The eyes, ears, nose, and mouth each have their functions and can certainly not be the same, but after the functions of these sense organs are fully permeated with the vital energy and lose their determinate attachments, the vital-energized eyes are no longer the eyes of experience, the vital-energized ears are no longer the ears of experience, and so on with the nose and mouth. As the difference between the corresponding "empirical" and "vital-energized" "sense organs" grows ever wider, the vital-energized eyes, ears, nose, and mouth grow, on the contrary, more and more identical in essence to each other—thus the text says "there is none not identical."[29]

To return from the Liezi example to Zhuangzi, we may begin to recognize the meaning behind the phrase "let your ears and eyes communicate with what is inside." If we extend the scope of this recognition and apply it to an examination of Zhuangzi's ideal human characters, we discover that all these characters must possess such qualifications. Any remaining doubts about this may be dispelled by reference to the following passages:

> If you look at them from the point of view of their differences, then there is liver and gall, Chu and Yue. But if you look at them from the point of view of their sameness, then the ten thousand things are all one. A man like this *doesn't know what his ears or eyes should approve* (er mu zhi suo yi 耳目之所宜)—*he lets his mind play in the harmony of virtue* (de zhi he 德之和).[30]

> ... governs Heaven and Earth, stores up the ten thousand things, *lets the six parts of his body be only a dwelling, makes ornaments of his ears and eyes* (fu liu hai, xiang er mu 府六骸，象耳目).[31]

> They borrow the forms of different creatures and house them in the same body. *They forget liver and gall, cast aside ears and eyes* (yi qi er mu 遺其耳目), *turning and revolving, ending and beginning again, unaware of where they start or finish.*[32]

> The sage is the comprehender of true form and the completer of fate. *When the Heavenly mechanism is not put into action and yet the five vital organs are all complete* (wuguan jie bei 五官皆備)—this may be called the music of Heaven.[33]

The italicized phrases quoted above all implicitly contain the idea of synesthesia; given that their theoretical basis is on the whole identical with that discussed previously, I will not belabor the point here.[34]

The Full Mind and Full Form
(Xinquan yu xingquan 心全與形全)

The sense organs can be vital-energized, but is it only the sense organs that can be thus transformed? We cited Merleau-Ponty's explanation above that the *body* is a kind of "permanent *sensorium commune*" marked by mutual assimilation and interpenetration; if this is so, can there be any closer connection between the body and the common sense-organ? Below, we will examine this issue by further proposing that just as Daoist cultivation practice as applied to the sense organs cannot escape the basis of synesthesia, and yet the level it attains to is by no means limited to this; likewise, when such Daoist cultivation practice is applied to the *entire body*,

while it cannot depart from the "permanent *sensorium commune*," it is also
by no means restricted to this level. Such cultivation does not stop until
it has caused the entire body to become thoroughly run through by the
vital energy, to the point where there is nowhere it does not penetrate.

In the third section, we cited the words of Liezi, who after having
first "advanced beyond inner and outer," so that his "eyes were like ears,
and ears were like the nose," and so on, stated that his "mind consolidated
and form dispersed, and bones and flesh all melded together." How does
the form disperse? How do the bones and flesh meld together? Zhang
Zhan 張湛 states in his commentary, "The six internal organs and seven
apertures, four limbs and hundred joints, reside clump-like as a corpse, all
becoming the same thing" (*tong wei yi wu* 同為一物). Zhang's annotation
is quite good but is basically still an impressionistic description rather than
a theoretical interpretation. We must thus continue to ask the same question: the human body is a considerably complicated system—how could
it become one identical thing?

In order to dispel this doubt, let us first take note of an interesting
phenomenon: in Daoist thought, phrases such as *the four limbs and hundred
joints . . . all become the same thing* are not at all uncommon. Observe the
following examples:

> For [one with] the *Dao* stores his essence within, perches his spirit in
> his mind, is quiet, tranquil, and placid, and pleased and harmonious within
> his breast. Depraved energy (*xieqi* 邪氣) has nowhere to stick, and in the
> four limbs and many joints, sweats out through the pores and discharges
> within. Thus the triggers and pivots are smoothly well-tuned, and of the
> hundred vessels and nine apertures, none are not in balanced accord (*mo
> bu shun bi* 莫不順比). ("Taizu 泰族," *Huainanzi* 淮南子)[35]

> The fundamental requirement in all affairs is to first manage one's own
> body, to cherish one's great treasure. Using the new and discarding the
> old, the patterns of one's flesh interpenetrate, and one's essential energy
> (*jingqi* 精氣) renews daily, while the depraved energy thoroughly departs.
> Returning to his natural life-span, such a person is called a "True Man"
> (*zhenren* 真人). ("Xian ji 先己," *Lüshi Chunqiu* 呂氏春秋)[36]

> When the settled mind resides within, the ears and eyes are acute and
> perceptive, the four limbs are strong and firm; it can be a lodging place for
> the essence (*jing* 精). "Essence" is the most essential form of vital energy.
> When the vital energy follows the *Dao*, there is life; with life there is
> thought; with thought there is understanding—only with understanding
> does it come to rest! . . . The essence preserved, it spontaneously arises, and
> one's exterior is calm and radiant. Stored within, it serves as a fountainhead;

full-flowing and harmoniously balanced, it serves as the deep pool of vital energy. With a deep pool that does not dry up, the four limbs remain firm; with an inexhaustible fountain, the nine apertures interpenetrate . . . The mind is full (*xin quan* 心全) within, and the form is full without . . . For the *Dao* must be rounded and concentrated, broad and extending, strong and firm . . . when the full mind (*quanxin* 全心) resides within, it cannot remain hidden out of sight, but rather harmonizes with one's form and appearance, and manifests itself in one's color and complexion . . . The external form of the mind's vital energy (*xinqi* 心氣) is brighter than the sun and moon, and more discerning than one's father and mother. ("Nei ye 內業," *Guanzi* 管子)[37]

Thought, deliberation, acuity, perceptiveness, joy, and anger are the affections (*qing* 情) of humans. Thus by closing off the four passages, and halting the five [routes of] escape, one merges (*lun* 淪) with the *Dao*. Thus spirit and luminosity (*shenming* 神明) store up within the formless, and essential energy returns to utmost authenticity. ("Xia de 下德," *Wenzi*)

Thus when the spirit controls, the form follows; when the form conquers, the spirit is impoverished. Though acuity and perceptiveness may be used, they must return to the spirit—this is called the "great wash" (*taichong* 太沖). ("Quan yan 詮言," *Huainanzi*)[38]

Aside from the discussions of the philosophical texts listed above, we can also discover similar statements in the *Zhuangzi*: "He who follows along with it will be strong in his four limbs, keen and penetrating in thought and deliberation, acute in ear and perceptive in eye, and will wield his mind without wearying it, responding to things without prejudice" ("Zhi beiyou").[39] Though most of the passages cited above do not come from the *Zhuangzi*, they are not, after all, far removed from it in time. Given that, both in terminology and content, they can be said to be products of the same cultural milieu, certain of the doctrines they espouse can be used to corroborate each other in the absence of more sufficient textual sources.[40]

Although the language of the above passages is not identical, there is one point in which they affirm each other: all the wording affirms that the four limbs, flesh patterns, hundred vessels, and nine apertures of human beings can be altered and that the path along which this alteration heads is that of permeation and transformation by the vital energy. The "four limbs and many joints" "sweating" and "discharging," and the "hundred vessels and nine apertures" becoming "in balanced accord" in the *Huainanzi* "Tai zu" passage; the "interpenetrating" "patterns of flesh" and "daily renewal" of the "essential energy" in the *Lüshi Chunqiu*'s "Xian ji"; and the ears and eyes becoming "acute and perceptive," the four limbs "strong and firm," and the "nine apertures" "interpenetrating" and "manifesting in one's color and complexion" of the *Guanzi*'s "Nei ye" all express none other than the fact that the sage's cultivation does not take place simply at the "spiritual" (*jingshen*) level in the ordinary sense of the term but rather sets into motion physiological changes, causing the human body to become thoroughly remolded and transformatively renewed from the most fundamental ground upward.

The body, however, is still the body, after all. How can it be transformed? Even if we grant this transformation, what sort of special functions does this transformed body possess in comparison to those of its prior, untransformed state?

At this point, we must naturally bring into the discussion the concepts of 'vital energy' (*qi* 氣) and 'body' (*shenti* 身體) in Daoist thought. In Kangcangzi's own words, quoted in the third section above, he could not switch the functions of his ears and eyes, but because he could "merge" (*he* 合) his "body with mind," "mind with vital energy," "vital energy with spirit," and "spirit with nothingness," he could thus perceive even the slightest or most distant of things.[41] What Kangcangzi says here bears great interest and invariably causes us to think of a doctrine that the later-day adepts of internal *neidan* 內丹 cultivation so frequently loved to exaggerate: "refined (*lian* 鍊) essence transforms into vital energy; refined vital energy transforms into spirit; refined spirit returns to emptiness." The two are, in fact, quite closely related, whereas their understanding of the human body is widely disparate from that given by our own anatomical observation of the human organism. According to Kangcangzi, we can divide the structure of the human body (and, of course, the stages of cultivation) into the four levels of body merging with mind, mind merging with vital energy, vital energy merging with spirit, and spirit merging with nothingness.[42]

The third and fourth of Kangcangzi's points are hard to differentiate in theory; their differences certainly lie not at the theoretical level but rather in the degree of refinement achieved in cultivation. Thus what concerns us most are the first three, the first of which involves the issue of consciousness (mind, *xin* 心) and body (*shen* 身). According to Kangcangzi, the activity of the body can be transformed to a realm of mutual coordination with the consciousness. As to the notion of the "mind merging with vital energy," he then turns this on its head, advocating that the consciousness (mind) can be transformed to the point where it coordinates with the internal flow (*qi*) of human life; in other words, wherein consciousness can flow alongside the vital energy and become dispersed throughout the body.[43] The third, the "vital energy merging with spirit," then points to an even more advanced level, wherein, as Zhang Zhan puts it, "only the patterns of spirit are in motion, and no affecting movement does not penetrate"—a realm that one cannot hope to even fathom with rationality.

These three levels are linked up together, but we may first observe the first and second. The reason these two are worth discussing together is because they happen to form a mutually assimilating, reciprocally supporting relationship. To have the "body merge with mind" means to use the function of the conscious mind to transform the stubborn resistance of the body.[44] The main reason such transformation is possible is because the mind is "vital energy," and the body is also composed of "vital energy"; yet while the two are alike "vital energy," the latter is restricted by human physiological structure and thus can only work according to the operative rules of the body. The "mind," on the other hand, is certainly more agile, but if it cannot become more refined or exquisite—that is, if it cannot become vital-energized—it, too, will remain restricted. Yet in order to become thoroughly vital-energized, the "mind" can no longer be confined within the scope of the "mind," but must permeate into the "body" (*ti*) and flow together with its "vital energy."

Summing up the body/mind/vital-energy relationship, we discover a set of parallel phenomena:

1. The body merges with the mind: that is, the body loses its independent, perceptual significance and is completely transformed by the mind.

2. The mind merges with the vital energy: the mind loses its function as lord of the body; it is no longer the "heavenly ruler" (*tianjun* 天君),[45] but rather melds into the midst of the body's vital energy so that the entire mind becomes vital energy.

These two parallel phenomena arise simultaneously: once the first series of events start up, the second series will follow in its wake. Likewise, once the second series of events starts up, while it must certainly first go through the first series, it can, in turn, more deeply and thoroughly contribute to the first series.

The passages quoted above cannot be explained until they are established upon the basis of such a preliminary conclusion. The description given in the *Guanzi* "Nei ye" passage is particularly worth mulling over. "When the vital energy follows the *Dao*, there is life; with life there is thought; with thought there is understanding (*zhi* 知)—only with understanding does it come to rest!" This sentence points out that the vital energy is not, in fact, something readymade and given (Heidegger's "Present-at-hand")[46] but must be led forth, only after which can it possess a kind of capacity for efficacious perception,[47] a kind of capacity that is able to "understand"; and only after the level of "understanding" is reached can the practice of cultivation be considered to have completed a stage.

Even more worth noting is the "Nei ye" mention of the notions of the "mind's vital energy" (*xinqi* 心氣) and the "full mind" (*quanxin* 全心). It is also in this chapter that we get the *Guanzi*'s famous statement that "the mind is for harboring the mind; the mind has yet another mind within it" (*xin zhi zhong you you xin yan* 心之中又有心焉).[48] According to this statement, the mind can clearly be divided into two levels: empirical and transcendent. One level awaits transformation, whereas the other level can transform the first. The transcendental mind is without doubt the basis for human existence and both the start and return points for cultivation. There is a great difference, however, between these start and return points: at the start, the transcendental mind has a vast territory anxiously awaiting its subjugation and transformation; but by the time it reaches the return point, this vast territory will have already been tamed and come under the jurisdiction of the kingdom of this transcendental mind. It will, in fact, have turned into this transcendental mind. Given that the mind at this time will have thoroughly permeated the four limbs and nine apertures, holding nothing in reserve, the author(s) of the "Nei ye" chapter gave it the name of "full mind." That is to say, if the mind is unable to conquer and gain influence over that vast territory, it will simply not be complete.

The term "mind's vital energy" can also appear in place of the "full mind." While in the state of the "full mind" (or the state of the "mind being full" [*xin quan*], as it is given elsewhere in "Nei ye"), the mode in which one's mind unfolds is no longer one in which the intentions control the body but in which the intentions turn back inward and head in the direction of non-intentionalization, or, in the words of the *Huainanzi*'s "Quan yan" chapter, "Though acuity and perceptiveness may be used, they must return to the spirit." Thus their operations come and go simultaneously with the mode of human existence—that is, with the vital energy of the human body. For the full mind to be in the body is for the full mind to be in the vital energy, and thus the "Nei ye" author(s) can label the state of the mind at this time as the "mind's vital energy." In sum, once the concepts of "full mind" and "mind's vital energy" are established, we can immediately see that they implicitly contain the following two propositions:

1. The mind is no longer the empirical mind, but is dispersed throughout the structure of human existence and merges with the vital energy.

2. The body is no longer the body in the phenomenological sense, but rather is entirely run through by the "full mind," and thus carries the qualities of the "full mind."

Advancing from Skill to Dao
(*You ji jin dao* 由技進道)

If the body is run through by the full mind so that the entire body is the mind and the entire mind is vital energy, then the body should possess certain characteristics of the mind. Yet can the experience obtained through such rational inference be corroborated through experienced behavior? In particular, how can we imagine that consciousness can exist in other parts of the body aside from the brain? Before answering this query, let us first take a look at a well-admired parable from the "Yangshengzhu" chapter of the *Zhuangzi*:

> Cook Ding was cutting up an ox for Lord Wen-hui. At every touch of his hand, every heave of his shoulder, every move of his feet, every thrust of his knee—zip! zoop! He slithered the knife along with a zing, and all was in perfect rhythm, as though he were performing the dance of the Mulberry Grove or keeping time to the Jingshou music.
>
> "Ah, this is marvelous!" said Lord Wen-hui. "Imagine skill (*ji* 技) reaching such heights!"
>
> Cook Ding laid down his knife and replied, "What I care about is the *Dao*, which goes beyond skill. When I first began cutting up oxen, all I could see was the ox itself. After three years I no longer saw the whole ox. And now—now I go at it by spirit and don't look with my eyes. Sense-understanding has come to a stop and spiritual desire moves forward. I go along with the natural makeup, strike in the big hollows, guide the knife through the big openings, and follow things as they are."[49]

After Lord Wen-hui has finished listening to the words of Cook Ding, he exclaims in admiration, "Excellent! I have heard the words of Cook Ding and learned how to care for life!"[50]

Zhuangzi borrows the parable of Cook Ding carving the ox not, indeed, to tell us the story of a craftsman with marvelous skill, and also not merely to tell us how to fine tune our body. This parable clearly has a close connection to his discussion of the Dao/knowledge issue. Of even greater interest to us, however, is the mind-body concept upon which this narrative passage touches. Regarding Cook Ding's carving of the ox, we may find that the event is composed of three basic elements: (1) the initiator (subject) of the event, Cook Ding; (2) the recipient (object) of the event, the ox; (3) the intermediary that connects the two, the knife and the technique of carving. If we look generally at the technique itself, we might believe that as long as one obtains the intermediary and makes good use of it, one's skill can in principle become complete, the difference lying only in the degree to which one's workmanship matures.

However, as Zhuangzi sees it, the matter is by no means so simple. The perfection of a skill is not at all merely a matter of maturity of craft at the level of technique, but in fact it connects with the very issue of human existence. To put it simply, skill can be divided into two types: one is technique (*ji* 技), and one is Dao; one is wherein all one can see is the ox, and the other is wherein one no longer sees the whole ox; one is sense-understanding (*guanzhi* 官知), and the other is spiritual desire (*shenyu* 神欲).[51]

Why is it, then, that these two different types of skill represent two different levels of human existence? Because at the level of the "skill of the compass and T-square," what Cook Ding applied was a complicated set of discursive technical principles: what he faced was an object of distinct form and clear structure, and the subjective manner of operation through which he controlled this object was by way of the sense organs. At this time, no other parts of his body were involved in the action, and the true overseer was simply the intense consciousness of the actor. The sum of these several conditions shows that the existential state of the actor at this time is merely empirical and superficial, in which, that is, he resides merely at the stage of "things" and not at that of the application of "pure energy" (*chun qi* 純氣); or perhaps we might say that he can only "develop what is natural to man" (*kai ren zhi tian* 開人之天) and not "develop what is natural to Heaven" (*kai tian zhi tian* 開天之天).

The contrast between "things" and "pure energy," and between what is "natural to man" and "natural to Heaven," comes from the "Da sheng" chapter, in which Liezi asks Guan Yinzi 關尹子 how the Perfect Man (*zhiren* 至人) is able to "walk under water without choking, tread on fire without being burned, and travel above the ten thousand things without being frightened"—to which Guan Yin replies:"This is because he guards the pure energy—it has nothing to do with wisdom, skill, determination, or courage."[52] At the same time, it is something that cannot be reached from the level of (mere) "things" with "faces, forms, voices, and colors." In this response, Guan Yin also puts forth the proposition of "not developing what is natural to man, but rather developing what is natural to Heaven." According to Guo Xiang's 郭象 (252?–312) annotation, "to understand (zhi 知) without deliberation is to develop Heaven; to perceive (gan 感) only after understanding is to develop man. Thus developing Heaven is the movement of one's nature (xing zhi dong 性之動); developing man is the application of understanding."[53] Guo's annotation is right on: the distinction between technique and Dao is indeed the difference between what is "human" and what is "Heaven," or, more concretely, between the "application of understanding" and the "movement of one's nature." The "understanding" of which Guo Xiang speaks here is no doubt the "little understanding" (xiao zhi 小知), or the "offshoot of knowledge" (zhi wei nie 知為孽), attacked in the Daoist tradition—a kind of cognitive function restricted by the functions of the sense organs, or even by ideology.[54]

But what then is the "movement of one's nature?" Strictly speaking, the "nature" (xing 性) itself transcends movement and rest; it "moves without moving," and any notions of the operational states of movement and rest cannot be used to categorize it.[55] Yet if we allow a little leniency, we may conjecture that what the "movement of one's nature" or the "development of what is natural to Heaven" refers to is a kind of intuitive understanding that transcends perceptual boundaries; returning to the Cook Ding oxcarving example, we may say it is when "sense-understanding has come to a halt and spiritual desire moves forward." Because this type of intuitive understanding penetrates to the deepest levels of human existence and is not something the consciousness is capable of controlling, it thus belongs to the level of "Heaven" or "nature."

When analyzing this type of intuitive understanding deeply rooted in the basis of human existence, we discover a phenomenon worthy of our appreciation: accompanying this intuitive understanding comes the participation of the human body in the event. This is, perhaps, not easy to comprehend, but is in theory easily inferred: given that this knowledge comes from one's "nature" and not empirical consciousness, the vital energy, which forms the basic structure of the human body, is naturally guided forth to energize the four limbs and hundred bones and to merge with this understanding. Thus in this type of "skill of changing along with things," the entire human body participates in the action, and the four limbs and hundred bones are completely mobilized, drawn and incited by a kind of homogeneous trigger of vital energy (spirit), all creating the act of skill together. Let us recall Cook Ding's bearing at the time of his carving the ox: "At every touch of his hand, every heave of his shoulder, every move of his feet, every thrust of his knee—zip! zoop! He slithered the knife along with a zing, and all was in perfect rhythm, as though he were performing the dance of the Mulberry Grove or keeping time to the Jingshou music." It is deeply significant that in describing such superlative skill, what Zhuangzi borrows here is a musical image. This is because the meaning of music is whole and inseparable: only after a musical composition is performed from beginning to end, interconnected from start to finish, can we comprehend the subtleties of the entire piece. Similarly, if we want to understand the event of oxcarving, we can only begin to grasp the main idea if we figure in the entirety of Cook Ding's hands, shoulders, feet, and knees—in fact, the whole of his body—and recognize that there is a "spiritual desire" guiding and running through it all.

Because sense-understanding has come to a stop and spiritual desire moves forward, we can recognize the simultaneous operation of the "un-perceptualization of the sense organs" and the "perceptualization of the body." In another respect, the "un-objectification of objects" and the "mutual dissolution of object and subject" also emerge simultaneously. In the *Guanzi* "Nei ye" passage cited above, the vital energy was said to awaken ("think") after being led forth and to possess a certain sort of intuitive understanding upon awakening ("with thought there is understanding"); we can find corroboration for such a viewpoint in the "advancing from skill to Dao" passages of the *Zhuangzi*. For example, why would the grand marshal's buckle-maker of "Zhi Beiyou" consider his skill one of "using the method of deliberately *not* using other things" (*yong zhi zhe jia bu yong zhe* 用之者假不用者); or why would Bohun Wuren of "Tian Zifang" believe that only the "archery of a non-archer" (*bu she zhi she* 不射之射) represented true skill in archery?[56] All such passages can be explained to a certain extent from the perspective of the "un-perceptualization of the sense organs" and the "perceptualization of the body." Given that the focal point of this chapter is the mind-body issues touched upon in Zhuangzi's cultivation practices, I will set aside any discussion of theories implicit in his conception of artistry and turn the focus instead upon the "unobjectification of objects" and the "mutual dissolution of object and subject."[57]

Once there is no distinction between subject and object, or body and mind, we can see that the body at this point is thoroughly transformed and listens to the bidding of the vital energy. But the effect is not limited to this, because once "the body merges with the mind, the mind merges with the vital energy, and the vital energy merges with spirit," the various distinctions of ordinary experience have at this time been thoroughly dispersed, and thus the "body" (*shenti*) is no longer an "individual" (*geti* 個體), but rather the condensation point through which all the existential circulation[58] of the universe must pass when it turns back into the world of experience. Yet, to turn this around, in exactly what sense is it that the body heads toward the limitless circulation of vital energy?

Fully Embodying the Inexhaustible
(*Ti jin wuqiong* 體盡無窮)

In order to understand the final step in Zhuangzi's conception of the body, we must inevitably return to the notion of "vital energy" (*qi* 氣). In order to understand the vital energy, however, we must in turn first comprehend the basic presuppositions of Zhuangzi's metaphysics. Zhuangzi's metaphysics places particular emphasis on transformation and opposes static realist outlooks (as is commonly accepted by most Zhuangzi experts).[59] Many of Zhuangzi's famous propositions—such as "his life is the working of Heaven, his death the transformation of things" ("Ke yi"); "all creatures come out of the mysterious workings (*ji* 機) and go back into them again" ("Zhi le"); "climb up to Heaven and wander in the mists, roam the infinite, and forget life forever and ever without end! ("Dazongshi"); and "when the hinge is fitted into the socket, it can respond endlessly (*ying wuqiong* 應無窮)" ("Qiwulun")[60]—presuppose the outlook of a monism of vital energy. In other words, if we speak of it in terms of our individuality, we should agree in theory that man, in fundamental terms, cannot be an "individual" man, but is certainly a "cosmic man" that participates in the existential circulation.[61] To use Neuman's terms, man is in essence Mystic Man; all humans possess the capacity for mystical experience—it is certainly not the monopoly of a privileged few.[62] And yet, why is it that in reality so few people are capable of achieving it?

Zhuangzi's response was, "Now that we've already become 'things,' if we want to return again to the Root, I'm afraid we'll have a hard time of it!"[63] Once a man has become an individual, he has a hard time avoiding being restricted by the structure of this individuality (the body). However, the main preconditions forming the human individual—the sense organs and the body—are not, in fact, incapable of change. As mentioned earlier,

the sense organs and the body are not readymade and inalterable; fundamentally, they await the "implementation of the form" (*jianxing* 踐形)—
that is, vital-energization. Once the entire body is transformed by the
vital energy—that is, when the adept's body has become manifest to the
full—the sense organs and body that had originally been used to support
or restrain one into individuality have now become, on the contrary, the
channels through which the individual flows into and interconnects with
the outer world.[64]

If the sense organs and body no longer restrain the individual, so
that this individual can no longer be differentiated from all the things
and events outside it, then how can we demarcate the limit of "self" (*wo*
我)? Or, how can we delineate between "self" and "not-self?" Obviously,
if we follow along the lines of Zhuangzi's thinking, all bodies will ultimately not have the sense of body, and the meaning implicit in every
"self" will certainly self-disintegrate in the end. In the first section, we
already explained in brief the process of self-disintegration; in what follows, let us further observe how Zhuangzi demarcates the location of the
human body:

> Embody to the fullest what has no end (*ti jin wuqiong* 體盡無窮) and
> wander where there is no trail (*you wuzhen* 遊無朕). ("Yingdiwang")

> The sage penetrates bafflement and complication, rounding all into a
> single body (*zhou jin yi ti* 周盡一體). ("Zeyang")

> If he had only mounted on the truth of Heaven and Earth, ridden the
> changes of the six breaths (qi), and thus wandered through the bound-
> less (*you wuqiong* 遊無窮), then what would he have had to depend on?
> ("Xiaoyaoyou")[65]

How is it that the sage can round all into a single body? And if he has
already rounded all into a single body, why can such a term as *ren* 人
(person) (granted he is a *shengren* 聖人, sage-person) still be used? As Ming-
dynasty commentator Shen Yiguan 沈一貫 explains, having "taken
Heaven as his master" and thus attained to full universality, "although he
is still human in form and people refer to him as a person, he is in fact
Heaven."[66] The sage, that symbol of the perfection of human character,
has in fact already leapt beyond the scope of humankind and become, in
a certain sense, "Heaven," but because, in the eyes of observers, he still has
bodily existence, he is still referred to as a "person."

How, then, can the sage "round all into a single body?" The two
phrases from "Xiaoyaoyou" and "Yingdiwang" tell us quite clearly to

"wander through the boundless" and "wander where there is no trail."
"Wandering through the boundless" we can understand, because once
someone has dispersed his individuality and his body has been opened
up, his body's vital energy then participates in the circulation of the vital
energy of the universe, and there is no longer any self and other, subject
and object, to be distinguished. This is what is meant by "wandering in the
singular vital energy of Heaven and Earth." But why "wander where there
is no trail?" Worth noting here is that what one wanders through while
"wandering the trail-less" is certainly "vital energy," but this type of "vital
energy" can no longer be viewed as the energy of yin and yang, of wind
and rain, that fills up the space between Heaven and Earth. It cannot, in
other words, be seen as the "extrinsic *qi*" that human breath-organs take
in to breathe, but rather the "intrinsic *qi*" (or "mother of *qi*" [*qimu* 氣
母], "primordial *qi*" [*yuanqi* 元氣])[67] with which the "mind merges" and
which "merges with spirit." Within such a realm, man does not use the
functions of his sense organs, but rather participates in the circulation of
the universe with his full existence.

Actually, the word *participate* is not quite appropriate here, since
participation implies both the active intervention of a participant and
acceptance by that being participated in. But when the Perfect Man
"embodies the endless to the fullest and wanders where there is no
trail," he has no need of this effort to overcome subject and object; he
needs only to allow his human consciousness to submerge deeply into
his four limbs and many apertures and transform into the circulation of
a unitary vital energy. Once it is a singular vital energy that circulates, it
will naturally flow and connect both within and without the body. We
often see in the *Zhuangzi* that its images of the highest form of human
character always reside in a realm of silence and tranquility; this is because
only in such a realm can one's vital energy remain undisturbed, and one
will not be split up from the unitary state, in which the "workings of vital
energy are submerged into the ten thousand things," into different states
of consciousness. "Let your mind wander in simplicity, blend your spirit
with the vastness, follow along with things the way they are, and make
no room for personal views" ("Yingdiwang"); "withdrawn, he seemed to
prefer to cut himself off; bemused, he forgot what he was going to say"
("Dazongshi"); "a man of true brightness and purity who can enter into
simplicity, who can return to the primitive through inaction, give body to
his inborn nature, and embrace his spirit, and in this way wander through
the everyday world" ("Tian Di"); "Limpidity, silence, emptiness, inaction:
these are the level of Heaven and Earth, the substance of *Dao* and its

Virtue ... He who can embody purity and whiteness may be called the True Man" ("Ke yi")[68]—such limpidity, silence, emptiness, and inaction of the True Man refer not merely to the virtues of cultivation in the ordinary sense; they are, in fact, coexistent with the circulation of the universe,[69] and thus will invariably transform completely away his individual sense organs and his will, and meld them into the circulation of vital energy. Otherwise, once one has sense perception, this will immediately produce his separation from the circulating vital energy, and objects will arise from the midst of this transforming, circulating vital energy to condense into things absorbed by his sense organs.

After one merges the body with the mind, the mind with the vital energy, and the vital energy with the spirit, one's human consciousness and bodily energy will mix and flow together with the vital energy of the cosmos; the mind at such a time we may call the "wandering" (you 遊) mind. The term *wandering* is one very unique to Zhuangzi's thought. Sometimes we see him using it to describe certain True Men roaming the lands in all directions (the term *youxian* 遊仙 still preserves this sense); this concept, transmitted down from primitive religion, certainly has its reality within the cultural system, and Zhuangzi often makes use of this type of imagery. But on a more important level, Zhuangzi gives the term a new meaning:

> [T]he sage does not work at anything, does not pursue profit, does not dodge harm ... says nothing yet says something, says something yet says nothing, and wanders beyond the dust and grime. ("Qiwulun")

> Even now they have joined with the Creator as men to wander in the unitary energy (*yiqi* 一氣) of Heaven and Earth. ("Dazongshi")

> I'm just about to set off with the Creator. And if I get bored with that, then I'll ride on the Light-and-Lissome Bird out beyond the six directions, wandering in the village of Not-Even-Anything and living in the Broad-and-Borderless field. ("Yingdiwang")

> [E]nter the gate of the inexhaustible and wander in the limitless fields. ("Zai you")

> He will move in and out of the Six Realms, wander over the Nine Continents, going alone, coming alone. He may be called a Sole Possessor. ("Zai you")

> "It would be very different, though, if you were to climb up on the *Dao* and its Virtue and go drifting and wandering, neither praised or damned, now a dragon, now a snake, shifting with the times, never willing to hold

to one course only. . . drifting and wandering with the ancestor of the ten
thousand things, treating things as things but not letting them treat you as
a thing—then how could you get into any trouble? ("Shan mu")

[S]trip away your form, rid yourself of this fur, wash clean your mind,
be done with desire, and wander in the peopleless fields. ("Shan mu")

Why don't you try wandering with me to the Palace of Not-Even-
Anything—identity and concord will be the basis of our discussions
and they will never come to an end, never reach exhaustion! ("Zhi Beiyou")[70]

More examples could be cited, but their import is all the same. We might as
well, however, corroborate this with the description Zhuangzi's followers
give their own master: "Above he wandered with the Creator, below he
made friends with those who have gotten outside of life and death, who
know nothing of beginning or end" ("Tianxia").[71] How can a person
wander in the unitary vital-energy of Heaven and Earth? How can one
wander in the village of Not-Even-Anything; move in and out of the Six
Realms, wander over the Nine Continents; and wander with the ancestor
of the ten thousand things? How can one wander above with the Creator?
If Zhuangzi does not have in mind here the far and lithesome wandering
of transcendents or the agility of the imagination (as in Liu Xie's 劉勰
[d. 473] "spiritual imagination" [shensi 神思]),[72] then how should he be
interpreted? Zhuangzi has, in fact, already given us the answer: the real
meaning of "wandering in the unitary energy of Heaven and Earth" is
precisely to "let your mind wander in simplicity, blend your spirit with the
vastness" (you xin yu dan, he qi yu mo 遊心於淡，合氣於漠).[73] This type
of "wandering" is not, in fact, the traveling afar by means of the body, and
it is not the traversing of the six realms and four directions in thought, and
it is likewise not the wallowing indulgence of the ears and eyes. What it
refers to is the emergence and circulation of the spiritual energy (shenqi
神氣) together with the world in a kind of super-experiential state. Its
basis thus lies in the observer's elevation of himself to enter into a kind
of mystical state of coexistence with the existential basis of all things. This
type of "wandering" is not "external wandering," but rather a kind of
"internal view," and yet a view without a vista, without either the capacity
to view or the object of viewing, so that the "internal view" is simply the
circulation of singular vital-energy.

Once one has come to "wander in the unitary energy of Heaven and
Earth," his body has become thoroughly vital-energized and dispersed into
the circulation of existence. Certainly, if we observe his body from the

surface, we may still say the body remains the body, after all—the "they" (*das Man*) as determined and which can only exist within the form of the individual.[74] The body, however, should not be observed externally, but rather internally. Once viewed inwardly, to "wander in the unitary energy of Heaven and Earth" is clearly a phenomenological description of no gain; can Zhuangzi's concept of the body, however, not be sought after further?

It is clear that it can. We cited above the words of Kangcangzi: "the body merges with the mind, the mind merges with the vital energy, the vital energy merges with the spirit, and the spirit merges with nothingness." We mostly centered our discussion around the first three of these, barely touching upon the "spirit merges with nothingness." But if the connections among the body, mind, vital energy, spirit, and nothingness are unbroken, we have no reason to stop with the vital energy and spirit.

If we want to move further ahead, however, we will discover that the vista appearing before our eyes is not simple. Observe the following passages:

> Life and death are great affairs, and yet they are no change to him. Though Heaven and Earth flop over and fall down, it is no loss to him. He sees clearly into what has no falsehood and does not shift with things. He takes it as fate that things should change, and he holds fast to the source (*ming wu zhi hua er shou qi zong* 命物之化而守其宗) . . . In the way he goes about it, he uses his knowledge to get at his mind, and uses his mind to get at the constant mind (*changxin* 常心) . . . unifies the knowledge of what he knows, and in his mind never tastes death. ("Dechongfu")

> The men of old changed on the outside (*waihua* 外化) but not on the inside. The men of today change on the inside (*neihua* 內化) but not on the outside. He who changes along with things is one who uniformly does not change (*yi buhua* 一不化). ("Zhi beiyou")

> I will . . . form a triad with the light of the sun and moon, [and] partake in the constancy of Heaven and Earth. What stands before me I mingle with, what is far from me I leave in darkness. All other men may die; I alone will survive! ("Zai you")

> When he had put things outside himself (*wai wu* 外物), I kept at him for nine days more, and after that he was able to put life outside himself (*wai sheng* 外生). After he had put life outside himself, he was able to achieve the brightness of dawn (*zhaoche* 朝徹), and when he had achieved the brightness of dawn, he could see his own aloneness (*jian du* 見獨). After he had managed to see his own aloneness, he could do away with past and

present (*wu gujin* 無古今), and after he had done away with past and present, he was able to enter where there is no life and no death (*busi busheng* 不死不生). ("Dazongshi")[75]

These four passages bring us a view vastly different from that described above. To "take it as fate that things should change and hold fast to the source" is similar in meaning to "change on the outside but not on the inside," and what it describes appears to be a problem at the ontological level. If, however, to "wander in the unitary energy of Heaven and Earth" also involves the ontological relation between man and the myriad things, then there is an obvious contradiction between these two propositions.

That is, given that one does "not change (*hua*, "transform") on the inside," how can he still "wander?" And how *can* one "not change on the inside?" However, while there is certainly a distance between these two propositions, we need not go so far as to call it a contradiction. This is because when Zhuangzi mentions "holding fast to the source" and "not changing within," the realm he touches upon is already the ultimate, with no "one" or "many," no time or space, let alone, naturally, any notion of "individuality" to speak of. So long as one is an individual, one cannot transcend time and space ("put the world outside," "have no past or present"), cannot eternally remain unchanged ("uniformly not change," "constant mind"), and certainly cannot avoid destruction and death ("never taste death," "alone survive," "no life and no death"). In a word, there is absolutely no "self" to speak of at this time, for "I form a triad with the light of the sun and moon, and partake in the constancy of Heaven and Earth . . . All other men may die; I alone will survive!" This "I" (*wu* 吾), this "self" (*wo* 我), is by no means a "self" having any sense of individuality or individual consciousness.

What, then, is such a "self" all about? Zhuangzi has already told us that this is the ultimate entity, unique and unparalleled, eternal and unchanging, which he terms the "constant mind" or "solitary" (*du* 獨, "unique") entity. One can force a name on this ultimate entity and call it the "ultimate *Dao*" (*zhidao* 至道), "true nature" (*xing zhen* 性真), "true body of empty nature" (*xingkong zhenti* 性空真體), or "unity" (*yi* 一).[76] It may be convenient to borrow a theory employed in Vedic philosophy, which divides the human being into two parts: the individual self (Atman) and the impersonal self (Brahman). After the individual self is cleansed away, the impersonal self emerges. This impersonal self, however, is without sound or smell, without subject or object, and transcends absolutely all language.[77]

Since it transcends language and has no subject or object, we have
a hard time categorizing it in the domain of "self." We must, of course,
admit that Zhuangzi's thought has this side to it, but we should make
particular note of the fact that Zhuangzi never demanded the adept
to reside constantly within a mental state of "dwelling alone, peaceful
and placid, in spiritual brightness," nor is his doctrine "headed with the
concept of Great Unity."[78] He emphasizes in many places that men must
live in a vital-energized circulation that is concrete and with individual
consciousness; one wants to have unity in both unity and disunity and not
merely act upon the former while ignoring the latter. In a word, whether
or not the "constant mind" or "solitary entity" can be considered to fall
within the scope of "self" (wo 我) or "body" (shen 身) all depends on
whether we are willing to extend the meaning of these terms to the point
of transcending individuality. If I so extend them, then everything is my
self, everything is my body, and I am as great as the Dao (God, Buddhist
Heaven [fantian 梵天]); if I do not, then my self dissolves into the limitless, my body perishes, and a kind of solitary entity devoid of any sense
of individuality exists eternally.

The language of all Daoist figures is generally misty, indistinct, and
of hard-to-discern purport, and this is especially true of Zhuangzi. As a
major figure in the late-Zhou intellectual world, he could certainly not
have lacked any profound meaning to impart; but standing in the position
of advocating accommodation, elimination, and nonconstruction, he was
also unwilling to make use of a theoretical and systematic mode of discourse to promote his own views. To rake out Zhuangzi's meaning from
amidst his concentrated layers of "imputed words," "heavy words," and
"goblet words" is clearly no easy task. Nonetheless, while his expressive
techniques are certainly one of the major reasons why Zhuangzi's thought
is hard to grasp, another considerably crucial factor is doubtless the fact
that there is a vast discrepancy between ancient and modern philosophy
in respect to the concepts through which the body is understood, which
in turn has caused a shift in the whole model of explanation.

The "Tianxia" chapter of the Zhuangzi mentions that one of the
goals of Zhuangzi's philosophy was to "wander above with the Creator,
and make friends below with those who have gotten outside of life
and death, who know nothing of beginning or end." These phrases are
extremely eye-catching, and those who study the Zhuangzi often take
them as typical of Zhuangzi's style. How, though, may such a goal be
comprehended? If we believe that Zhuangzi's lament in "Qiwulun" that
"the hundred joints, the nine openings, the six organs, all come together

and exist here [as my body]—but which part should I feel closest to?"[79] is authentic; and if we also believe that his criticism of such figures as Hui Shi 惠施 (that it is fundamentally impossible to arrive at "Let love embrace the ten thousand things; Heaven and Earth are a single body"[80] through rational speculation) is defensible; and if at the same time we further believe that the substitute principle Zhuangzi proposes, that we can only have mystical union with the great Dao if we let the empirical self be cast off and thoroughly remolded, is reasonable—then I am afraid we cannot easily set aside, or even view as false propositions, the theoretical dilemmas tied up with Zhuangzi's doctrine of cultivation practice.[81]

This chapter is an attempt to take a more "positivist" position in discussing the mind-body conception involved in Zhuangzi's doctrine. We began by discussing Zhuangzi's doubts about, attacks on, and transformation of perception and rationality. Next, we saw how Zhuangzi's demands on the sense organs were mainly not about destroying the body and knowledge,[82] but rather having them meld into a single entity, the channel through which the mind's vital energy circulates. Next, we also discussed how not only the human sense organs, but even the entire body, needed to be permeated by the vital energy. Yet after the entire body is vital-energized, the distinction between subject and object, inner and outer, becomes extremely "dim and desolate" (danmo 淡漠); at this time, the circulation of the mind's vital energy has no inner or outer body to distinguish, and this is precisely a kind of spirit of "wandering." When one's cultivation practice has reached this point, he has already reached the highest limits the term *body* can bear. Beyond this point, when one enters the level of no death and no life, of solitary illumination by the light of the soul, no language whatsoever can be used any longer to describe it, let alone such terms as *self* and *body* that carry the sense of individuality.

Is the bodily transformation philosophy involved in Zhuangzi's doctrine of cultivation practice purely something that Zhuangzi came to realize for himself? This essay holds that, in part, it is not. There are some concepts, such as "wandering," that without doubt manifest a special brilliance in the *Zhuangzi*, while they are seldom encountered in other philosophical texts. But the body/mind/cultivation relationship in Zhuangzi's thought can also be found among other Daoist philosophers, and with rather similar demonstrations; it is only that they are not as detailed in content as what is recorded in the *Zhuangzi*. If we expand our scope and extend our exploratory antennae to Confucians such as Mencius—not to mention the neo-Confucian philosophers of later times—we may perhaps discover that once we come to talk about the body-mind-cultivation connection, they have a considerable number of points in common with Zhuangzi. After all, the structure of the human body is generally the same everywhere, and thus common points that transcend particular thought systems are more easily affirmed and accepted by each camp.

Looking at this from another viewpoint, however, though the structure of the human body is certainly largely the same everywhere, the position from which the various Confucian and Daoist masters deal with this issue arose from within a certain common cultural milieu. They believe the human body is not readymade and complete but rather a kind of starting point on the road toward perfection, capable of sublimation. One's actual body is taken as the starting point for sublimation, with the goal of achieving "the brightness of dawn" and "seeing one's own solitude" and ultimately arriving at its circulation back downward. This kind of bodily concept of full-course transformation is, however, not something commonly found in most cultural systems, whereas in China it is actually the order of the day. Viewed in this way, we cannot say that the metaphysics of bodily experience (or "bodily metaphysics") of the Confucians and Daoists was without its unique outlook.

Can the concept of body in Zhuangzi's thought be explored even further? The answer is clearly that it can. The present chapter has interpreted its way through the winding phrases of the *Zhuangzi*, seeking to shed light upon the factors involved in the transformation of physiological structure therein. Without doubt, however, the appearance of such notions in Zhuangzi's thought is not necessarily the result of his own creation but may very well be descriptive of the fact that there lay behind him an even more complete theory of the body to serve as his basis, which Zhuangzi could then select from according to his needs and apply with agility. In the process of self-cultivation, furthermore, transformation of the human bodily structure might produce certain physiological changes (such as radiance). In one respect, these changes can further be transformed into important symbols; in another, they afford us a more profound and thorough comprehension of such notions and cause us to understand that the Confucian and Daoist metaphysics of bodily experience is not at all misty and obscure but has within it only principles of inexhaustible complexity. All of this awaits deeper exploration.

Notes

1. *Wenxian tongkao* 文獻通考, *juan* 225, *jingji* 52, p. 1810 (Xinxing shuju facsimile of the Qianlong dian ben 乾隆殿本, 1965).

2. The "Daoism" (*daojia*) of which Ma Duanlin here speaks and the now-accepted notion of "religious Daoism" (*daojiao*) are in fact difficult to separate, and the changes these two terms have undergone historically are extremely complex. For more on the relationship between (philosophical) Daoism and religious Daoism, or between Lao/Zhuang and religious Daoism, see Sakai Tadao 酒井忠夫 and Fukui Fumimasa 福井文雅, "Dōkyō 道教 to wa nan 何 ka?," in *Dōkyō* 道教 *no sōgōteki* 總合的 *kenkyū* 研究 (Tosho kankōkai, Tokyo, 1977); Fukui Fumimasa, "'Dōkyō 道教' no teigi 定義 ni kan 關 suru ichini 一、二 no mondai 問題," *Waseda daigaku bunkenka kiyō* 早稻田大學文研科紀要 n. 23, 1978; Miyakawa Hisashi 宮川尚志, "Dōkyō 道教 no gainen 概念," *Tōhō shūkyō* 東方宗教 16 (1960); Fukunaga Kōji 福永光司, "Dōkyō 道教 to wa nan 何 ka?" *Shisō* 696 (1982); Kang Demo 康德謨, "Faguo liangwei xianzhe duiyu Zhongguo Daojia de kanfa 法國兩位先哲對於中國道家的看法," *Zhongguo xuezhi* 中國學誌 5 (1969); N. J. Girardot, "Part of the Way: Four Studies on Taoism," *History of Religion II* (1972) pp. 319–37; Nathan Sivin, "On the Word 'Taoist' as a Source of Perplexity," *History of Religion* (1978) pp. 303–30.

3. *Dao-embodiment* (*tidao* 體道) is a term well worth pondering; the term comes from the *Zhuangzi*, "Zhi beiyou": "He who embodies the *Dao* has all the gentlemen of the world flocking to him. As far as the *Dao* goes, [Lao Long] hadn't gotten hold of a piece as big as the tip of an autumn hair, hadn't found his way into one ten-thousandth of it—but even *he* knew enough to keep his wild words stored away and to die with them unspoken. How much more so, then, in the case of a man who embodies the Way!" (ZZJS 755; HY 59/22/54–56; Watson 242 [Here, as below, I have substituted *Dao* for *Way* and converted all romanization to Dalu pinyin—tr.]). "Dao" is self-embodied but can only take concrete form through its embodiment in people. The *ti* ("embody") here functions as a verb, and it could certainly be understood as a kind of metaphoric expression; yet as we shall make clear below, it might be more appropriate to take its meaning as a direct expression rather than as a metaphor.

4. These references may be found, respectively, on ZZJS 284, 390, 738, 741; HY 19/6/92–93, 28/11/53–55, 58/22/24, 58/22/29; and Watson 90, 122, 237, 238. [In the first two of these passages, I have changed Watson's translations of *congming* for purposes of consistency; in the last, I have changed *jingshen* from "inner" to "essential" spirit—tr.]

5. These references may be found, respectively, on ZZJS 428, 45, 43, 148, 711; 738, 306, 100; and HY 30/12/45, 3/2/3, 3/2/1, 9/4/28–29, 55/21/24, 58/22/24, 21/7/30, 6/2/78.

6. The phrase comes from Cheng Xuanying, *Zhuangzi jishi*, p. 391.

7. Aldous Huxley, *The Perennial Philosophy* (New York and London: Harper Brothers, 1945). The information that Huxley gathers from the great mystics around the world, both ancient and modern, reveals that all humans share certain unique experiences and a common life basis. If Huxley is correct, then we may need to reexamine whether the so-called outstanding feature of Chinese philosophy—the interpenetration of Heavenly Dao and human nature—does indeed appear only in China or the Eastern Pacific.

8. See William James, *The Varieties of Religious Experience* (New York: Longmans, Green, and Co., 1902), pp. 371–73; Richard M. Bucke, *Cosmic Consciousness* (New York), pp. 72–79; Walter T. Stace, *Mysticism and Philosophy* (Philadelphia: Lippincott, 1960), ch. 2, esp. pp. 131–33; Louis Dupre, *Ren de zongjiao xiangdu* 人的宗教向度 (Fu P'ei-jung 傅佩榮, tr.; Youshi, 1986), ch. 12; and Gao Tian'en, "Zhuisuo Xiyang wenmingli de shenmizhuyi 追索西洋文明裡的神秘主義," and Guan Yongzhong 關永中, "Shenmizhuyi ji qi sida xingtai 神秘主義及其四大形態," *Dangdai* 當代 n. 36 (April, 1989). The above works take different standpoints, and the degree of their concern for Daoist thought (especially that of Zhuangzi) is ultimately somewhat doubtful. Yet by the same token, if writings with no historical origins in Daoist thought can corroborate Zhuangzi's portrayal of the Dao-embodiment experience, it seems we should not neglect the information that this reveals.

9. [Yang's original essay (p. 188) contained another paragraph here describing some of the terms the *Zhuangzi* uses to stand for this deeper inner consciousness, or true original substance—such as *changxin* 常心, *lingfu* 靈府, *lingtai* 靈台, *zhenzai* 真宰, and *xushi* 虛室—through which it is portrayed as a realm of constancy, efficaciousness, purity, and emptiness, and yet with its own set of guiding principles.]

10. I agree with Stace's view (*Mysticism and Philosophy*, pp. 31–38) that the mutual discrepancies in many reports of mystical experiences stem not from the experience itself, but rather from their "explanations."

11. Meng Wentong 蒙文通, in his "Wan-Zhou xiandao fen sanpai kao 晚周僊道分三派考" (originally in *Tushu jikan* 圖書集刊, no. 8, Chengdu: 1948; later included in his *Guxue zhenwei* 古學甄微 [Chengdu: 1987]), argues that the "way of transcendents" (*xiandao* 仙道) in the late Zhou was divided into three sects, of which that of Wang Qiao 王喬 and Chisong 赤松 in the south, which emphasized *qi* circulation through breathing practices, was the most famous among the three. Meng's categorizations are very precise; however, I retain a cautious attitude toward his assertion that there was little connection between Zhuangzi and the practices of this sect.

12. ZZJS 147; HY 9/4/26–28; Watson 57–58 [I have emended "spirit" to "vital energy"—tr.]

13. ZZJS 150; HY 9/4/31–33; Watson 58.

14. For these last four references, see ZZJS 43, 284, 252, 390; HY 3/2/1, 19/6/92, 17/6/41, 28/11/53.

15. ZZJS 226–28; HY 15/6/4–7; Watson 77–78.

16. The mind-body relationship is an extremely complicated issue; for a concise argument, see T'ang Chün-yi 唐君毅, *Zhexue gailun* 哲學概論, *xia* (Taipei: Xuesheng, 1974), pp. 793–831. On the notion of "common sense," see section three of the present chapter.

17. [In the original essay (pp. 190–91), Yang quotes from Lu (*Nanhua zhen-jing fumo* 南華真經副墨, *juan* 2 *xia*, p. 3b) at greater length and also justifies the applicability of his comments to the present issue; I have omitted this paragraph here due to considerations of space.—tr.]

18. [In the original essay (p. 192), Yang concludes this section with a quo-tation from Chen Xiangdao 陳詳道 (quoted in Jiao Hong 焦竑, *Zhuangzi yi* 莊子翼, *juan* 4, p. 7a) that explains "fasting of the mind" in rather similar terms. The quotation begins with the *Wenzi* citation that Yang mentions at the beginning of the next section.—tr.]

19. This quotation appears near the beginning of the "Daode 道德" chapter.

20. From the "Zhongni 仲尼" chapter; See Yang Bojun 楊伯峻, *Liezi jishi* 列子集釋 (Beijing: Zhonghua, 1979), pp. 117–18.

21. "Huang Di" chapter; Yang Bojun, *Liezi jishi*, pp. 46–48. As Jin-dynasty commentator Zhang Zhan 張湛 explains these lines (p. 48), each of the various sense organs has its own function, but once the "spirit consolidates and the form is abandoned, and one awaits nothing from the outside," looking and listening are no longer dependent upon the ears and eyes, and all the various parts of the body merge as one.

22. Nonetheless, there have been those who held such a view. See, for example, Shen Yiguan's 沈一貫 comment on the "unaware of what is appropriate for the ears and eyes" line of the *Zhuangzi*'s "Dechongfu" chapter in his *Zhuangzi tong* 莊子通 (in *Wuqiubei zhai Zhuangzi jicheng* [Yiwen], v. 9), p. 169.

23. [See, e.g., Aristotle's *Sense and Sensibilia*, section 7.]

24. See Nakamura Yujiro 中村雄二郎, *Kyōtsū kankaku ron* 共通感覺論 (Iwanami: 1985), pp. 7–9.

25. Ibid., pp. 131–38. See also Joseph F. Donceel, *Philosophical Anthropology* (New York: Sheed and Ward, 1967), pp. 175–76; Naitō Kōjirō 內藤耕次郎, "Kyōkankaku teki shogenshō 共感覺的諸現象 ni kansuru kenkyūshi josetsu 研究史序説," in *Ritsumeikan bungaku* 立命館文學 (Kyoto), 1984.

26. *Phenomenology of Perception*, tr. Colin Smith (London: Routledge, 1962), p. 235. The quoted phrase, upon which Merleau-Ponty elaborates, is borrowed from Herder.

27. In later ages, there were many who advocated the convergence of Buddhism and Daoism, believing that with Laozi (or Daoists generally) there was also the theoretical issue of the return from and purification of worldly residue; see for example the chapter entitled "Lun zongqu 論宗趣" of Hanshan [Deqing]'s 憨山 [德清], *Guan Lao-Zhuang yingxiang lun* 觀老

莊影響論 (Taiwan Liulijingfang photocopy ed., 1972), p. 25, where the two are compared. Yet while Hanshan's theories of convergence have their own unique worth, they cannot necessarily be used to demonstrate that Laozi and Zhuangzi thought along similar lines.

28. Lao Ssu-kuang 勞思光 gives a very clear analysis of Zhuangzi's breakdown of the "bodily self" and the "cognitive self." However, his belief that Zhuangzi advocated a kind of viewing and admiring "affectionate self" (*qingyiwo* 情意我) can easily be misleading. The "*qing*" and "*yi*" of "*qingyi*" do not hold a particularly high place in Zhuangzi's thought, and even if we explain *qingyiwo* as "aesthetic self," it is doubtful whether this would clear up the issue. If the conceptions of vital energy and body cannot be brought in and discussed within the framework of "self," one will ultimately be unable to gain a full understanding of the *Zhuangzi*. See his *Zhongguo zhexueshi* 中國哲學史 (Taipei: Sanmin, 1981), *juan* 1, pp. 202–34.

29. The commonality of essence among the five sense organs can certainly be further distinguished, as with the phenomenon of "colored-hearing," which shows how the connections among sound, light, and color are much closer than those among other sense perceptions. See Naitō Kōjirō, "Kyōkankaku teki shogenshō," pp. 75–78.

30. "Dechongfu," ZZJS 190–91; HY 12/5/7–8; Watson 69.

31. "Dechongfu," ZZJS 193; HY 13/5/12; Watson 69.

32. "Dazongshi," ZZJS 268; HY 18/6/69; Watson 87.

33. "Tian yun," ZZJS 507; HY 37/14/26–27; Watson 158 [I have changed Watson's translation of *guan* 官 from "vital organs" to "sense organs"—tr.].

34. The reader may refer to the annotations to these passages in Lu Xixing, *Nanhua zhenjing fumo*; Shen Yiguan, *Zhuangzi tong*; and Jiao Hong 焦竑, *Zhuangzi yi* 莊子翼. [In his original essay (pp. 195–96), Yang concludes this section by noting how many traditional annotators, such as Hanshan and Lu Xixing, have often imported Buddhist notions to explain these passages. He notes that while this may be somewhat problematic, such Buddhist notions as the "full melding of the five sense organs and inter-application of the six indriyas" (*wuguan yuanrong, liu gen huyong* 五官圓融，六根互用)—expressed most clearly in the *Surangama* sutra (*Lengyan jing* 楞嚴經; see, e.g., the Dazhengzang 大正藏 ed. [Xinwenfeng reprint, v. 19], *juan* 8, p. 141; and *juan* 6, p. 131)—can indeed be said to reflect merely an alternate description of the same physiological phenomenon as that expressed in the *Zhuangzi* passages.—tr.]

35. Liu Wendian 劉文典, *Huainan Honglie jijie* 淮南鴻烈集解 (Feng Yi 馮逸 & Qiao Hua 喬華, collators; Beijing: Zhonghua, 1989), p. 668.

36. Chen Qiyou 陳奇猷, *Lüshi chunqiu jiaoshi* 呂氏春秋校釋 (Shanghai: Xuelin, 1984), p. 144.

37. Dai Wang 戴望, *Guanzi jiaozheng* 管子校正 (*Zhuzi jicheng* ed.), *juan* 16, pp. 270–71.

38. Liu Wendian, *Huainan Honglie jijie*, pp. 487–88.

39. ZZJS 741; HY 58/22/31–32; Watson 239 [I have altered Watson's translation slightly so that renderings of certain terms would agree with those in the above quotations.—tr.].

40. I agree with Benjamin Schwartz's view that *qi* (vital energy) was part of the "common discourse." See his *The World of Thought in Ancient China* (Cambridge: Harvard, 1985), pp. 179–84. Within the background of "common discourse," a number of viewpoints are shared, as they are constructions of the cultural system and not the "innovations" of philosophers.

41. Aside from the Kangcangzi passage, we might also observe the following words from the *Liezi*: "For the most sincere person can affect (*gan* 感) things, move (*dong* 動) Heaven and Earth, affect ghosts and spirits, and traverse the six directions" ("Huang Di"); and "The filling and emptying, growth and remission, of a single body all interpenetrate with Heaven and Earth, and respond empathetically with things" ("Zhou Mu Wang") (See Yang Bojun, *Liezi jishi*, pp. 57, 102). As to the causal relation between the vital energy and this almost "clairvoyant" or "telepathic" "affective interpenetration" (*gantong*), see below.

42. Zhang Zhan describes these in turn as "form and knowledge not going against each other"; "distancing oneself from the use of form and knowledge and simply relying on the undulating vital energy"; "quietly immobile, even knowledge is forgotten, and with only the patterns of spirit in motion, no affecting movement does not penetrate"; and "identical with nothingness, there is spirit, and identical with spirit, there is nothingness—how could these two have any form?!"

43. Although the "body" (*ti* 體) that merges with the mind and the "vital energy" (*qi* 氣) with which the mind merges both refer to the body, the former refers to the body in the anatomical sense, whereas the latter refers to the circulation and movement of energy within the body—the two reside at very different levels. See Ishida Hidemi 石田秀實, *Kiryū* 氣流 *reru shintai* 身體 (Tokyo: Heika, 1988), pp. 2–20.

44. This idea is similar to the "using intention to draw forth the vital energy" (*yi yi yin qi* 以意引氣) of later cultivation practitioners or the "using the mind's intent to command the vital energy" (*yi zhi shuai qi* 以志帥氣) of Mencius. The reason for this is that if the vital energy is not positively transformed, the ordinary intention/vital-energy relationship may become one of "the vital energy moving the mind's intent" (*yi qi dong zhi* 以氣動志) ("Gongsun Chou, *shang*," *Mencius* [3.2 (2A2)]) or one where "the mind dispatching the vital energy is called 'forced'" (*Laozi*, ch. 55).

45. Such texts as the "Jie bi 解蔽" chapter of the *Xunzi* 荀子 and the "Xin shu 心術" and "Nei ye" chapters of the *Guanzi* compare the "mind" to the "ruler." This type of comparison is, of course, used to emphasize the subjectivity and superiority of the mind. However, we could also use the

same metaphor in the following way: In the early stages of human spiritual development, the relationship between the mind and the four limbs and various other body parts may indeed be comparable to the ruler/minister model. After the spirit develops to a certain level, however, the "sovereignty" of subjectivity and superiority is thereupon displaced into the four limbs and body parts so that nowhere in the body are there servants, and the "heavenly ruler" is everywhere. All body parts converge into an equal field, all issue united commands and orders, and there is no longer any distinction between superiors and subordinates.

46. *"The 'essence' of Dasein lies in its existence,"* but "existence" cannot be ontologically confused with the traditional term *existentia*, which is "tantamount to *Being-present-at-hand*, a kind of Being which is essentially inappropriate to entities of Dasein's character." Martin Heidegger, *Being and Time*, tr. John Macquarrie and Edward Robinson (New York: Harper & Row, 1962), p. 67.

47. The term *thought* (*si* 思) here should read like that of *Mencius* "Gaozi, shang" (11.15 [6A15]): "the organ of the mind thinks." In both cases, *si* can be understood in the sense of *sikao* 思考 (to "think deeply," "reflect upon"), referring to the mind's capacity for a kind of self-awakening and self-exertion.

48. Dai Wang, *Guanzi jiaozheng*, p. 270.

49. ZZJS 117–19; HY 7/3/2–7; Watson 50–51 [I have modified Watson's translations of *guanzhi* (sense-understanding) and *shenyu* (spiritual desire) to conform with the discussion below.—tr.].

50. ZZJS 124; HY 8/3/11–12; Watson 51.

51. [Omitted from the translation here is a brief table contrasting these two realms. In the table (p. 201), Yang adds to this by categorizing the former type of skill, in which "the mind controls the vital energy," as the "skill of the compass and T-square" (*guiju zhi ji* 規矩之技); and the latter type, in which "the mind and vital energy merge together," as the "skill of changing along with things" (*wuhua zhi ji* 物化之技)—terms he borrows from the "Da sheng" chapter of the *Zhuangzi* (ZZJS 662; HY 50/19/62).—tr.]

52. ZZJS 633–34, 638; HY 48/19/7–9,16; Watson 198–99 [I have modified Watson's translation of *chunqi* from "pure breath" to "pure energy"—tr.].

53. *Zhuangzi jishi*, p. 638, note 1.

54. These terms come from the "Qiwulun" and "Dechongfu" chapters; see ZZJS 51, 217; HY 3/2/9, 14/5/52; Watson 37, 75. Lu Xixing, commenting on the former, describes "little understanding" as that which sets up boundaries and makes fine distinctions between self and others, whereas "great understanding" (*dazhi*) is the carefree knowledge that has forgotten both self and others. See *Nanhua zhenjing fumo, juan* 1b, pp. 4b–5a.

55. Although the phrase *movement of one's nature* comes from Guo Xiang's commentary, Zhuangzi himself indeed often uses the terms *mind* and *nature*

indiscriminately. As Shen Yiguan says, "Whenever Zhuangzi refers to the 'nature,' it is different from [that of] us [Confucians]. What we refer to as the 'nature' is goodness, the continuation of Heaven's goodness ... [whereas] when Zhuangzi speaks of the 'nature,' he is merely referring to the mind." "Du Zhuang gailun 讀莊概論," *Zhuangzi tong*, p. 7. Shen's explanation is correct, but it is not that "we Confucians" are immune to such indiscriminate use—as in Cheng Mingdao's 程明道 *Dingxing shu* 定性書, where he turns "settling the mind" into "settling the nature."

56. ZZJS 760–61, 724–25; HY 60/22/68–70, 56–57/21/57–61; Watson 244–45, 230–31.

57. [In his original essay (pp. 203–04), Yang does go on to give some discussion of Zhuangzi's artistic thought and its relation to such notions as 'changing along with things' and the 'archery of the non-archer.' He points out that in describing a consummate work of art, Zhuangzi invariably emphasizes how it transcends all limitations and enters directly into the deepest levels of one's perceptual energy, and that when completing the work of art, the mind both transcends self-consciousness and yet carries its creation in a definite direction, as it has already internalized the technical rules and thus paved the way for their subsequent effects. Thus breaking through the boundaries of subject-object and mind-body, the artist moves from his use of acuity and perceptiveness back to the realm of "spirit," wherein he "develops what is natural to Heaven." Yang then goes on to quote from the contemporary German Zen-inspired speculative philosopher Eugen Herrigel, who, in his practice of archery in Japan, became enlightened to the notion of the 'archery of the non-archer.' *Zen in the Art of Archery* (New York: Pantheon, 1953). As Yang points out, though the realm that Herrigel describes derives most directly from his study of Zen (Chan 禪) Buddhism, it of course made its way there, to large extent, from similar notions first set forth in the *Zhuangzi*.—tr.].

58. T'ang Chün-yi explains Zhuangzi's "vital energy" as the "circulatory existence" (*liuxing de cunzai* 流行的存在) or the "existential circulation" (*cunzai de liuxing*). See his *Zhongguo zhexue yuanlun* 中國哲學原論, *Yuan Dao pian* 原道篇, v. 2 (Xinya shuyuan, 1973), p. 786.

59. See Xiong Shili 熊十力, *Dujing shiyao* 讀經示要, *juan* 2 (Guangwen, 1972), pp. 77–79; T'ang Chün-yi, "Zhuangzi de bianhua de xing'ershangxue yu Heige'er de bianhua de xing'ershangxue zhi bijiao 莊子的變化的形而上學與黑格爾的變化的形而上學之比較," in *Zhong-Xi bijiao zhexue lunwenji* 中西比較哲學論文集 (Zongqing reprint, 1978).

60. ZZJS 539 (cf. "Tian Dao" 462), 625, 264, 66; HY 40/15/10 (34/13/14), 47–48/18/45–46, 18/6/61–62, 4/2/31; Watson 168 (144), 196, 86, 40 [I have modified Watson's translation of the "Dazongshi" line slightly for mutual consistency.—tr.].

61. The notion of a "cosmic man" is borrowed from R. M. Bucke's work, *Cosmic Consciousness*, pp. 61–80.

62. E. Neuman, "Mystical Man," in *Mystical Vision*, ed. J. Campbell (Princeton: Princeton University Press, 1982), pp. 375–415.

63. "Zhi beiyou," ZZJS 731; HY 57/22/10; Watson 235.

64. The term *xinshu* 心術 (pathways of the mind) often appears in philosophical texts from the late-Zhou onward. The meaning of *shu* here "refers to 'the path taken'" (Kong Yingda 孔穎達 [547–648], *Liji zhushu* 禮記注疏, *juan* 38 [Yiwen ed.], p. 6). The *Guiguzi* 鬼谷子 says *shu* "are the pathways through which the mind's vital energy comes to lodge, upon which the spirit does its bidding; the nine apertures and twelve lodging-places are the gateways of the vital energy" (*Guiguzi*, "Outer Chapters," "Benjing yinfu qipian 本經陰符七篇"; Zihui ed. [Shangwu, 1969], v. 4, p. 1a). Although the date of the *Guiguzi* is in doubt, its explanation here of the term *xinshu* happens to accord well with the conception of the body found in late-Zhou Confucian and Daoist philosophy. We can also trace the origins of Wang Yangming's 王陽明 later discussion of the relationship between *liangzhi* 良知 (innate knowledge) and the sense organs from such an angle. See Ishida Hidemi, *Kiryū reru shintai*, pp. 111–25.

65. ZZJS 307, 880, 17; HY 21/7/32, 70/25/9, 2/1/21–22; Watson 97, 281, 32.

66. Shen Yiguan, *Zhuangzi tong* (*juan* 9), pp. 729–30.

67. See Sima Biao's 司馬彪 (d. 306) annotation to the term *qimu* of "Dazongshi," cited in note 8 in *Zhuangzi jishi*, p. 249; and Lu Xixing, *Nanhua zhenjing fumo*, *juan* 2b, p. 13a.

68. ZZJS 294, 234, 438, 538–46; HY 20/7/10–11, 15–16/6/16–17, 31/12/68–69, 40–41/15/8–22; Watson 94, 79, 136, 168–70.

69. For further explanation, see Liu Wu 劉武, *Zhuangzi jijie neipian buzheng* 莊子集解內篇補正 (Taipei: Wenjin, 1988), pp. 14–17.

70. ZZJS 97, 268, 293, 384, 394, 668, 671, 752; HY 6/2/73–74, 18/6/67–68, 20/7/9–10, 27/11/42–43, 28/11/63, 51/20/6–7, 52/20/14, 59/22/47–48; Watson 46, 87, 93, 120, 124, 210, 211, 241 [I have slightly modified Watson's translation of the "Dazongshi" passage.—tr.].

71. ZZJS 1099; HY 93/33/67–68; Watson 373.

72. See Chou Chen-fu 周振甫, ann., *Wenxin diaolong zhushi* 文心雕龍注釋 (Taipei: Liren, 1984), pp. 515–17.

73. "Yingdiwang," ZZJS 294; HY 20/7/10–11; Watson 94.

74. Heidegger, *Being and Time*, pp. 166–67.

75. ZZJS 189–93, 765, 384, 252; HY 12–13/5/5–13, 60/22/77–78, 27/11/43–44, 17/6/40–41; Watson 68–69, 246, 120, 83 [I have changed the rendering of "*yi buhua zhe*," which Watson has as "is identical with him who does not change."—tr.].

76. For the first three of these, see, respectively, Cheng Xuanying's commentary in *Zhuangzi jishi*, p. 254, note 8; Hanshan, *Guan Lao-Zhuang yingxiang lun*, p. 32; and Lu Xixing, *Nanhua zhenjing fumo*, p. 201.

77. See Zimmer, *Philosophies of India* (Princeton: Princeton University Press, 1974), pp. 333–54.

78. Both of these phrases come from the description of the style of Laozi's Way in the "Tianxia" chapter of the *Zhuangzi*. ZZJS 1093; HY 92–93/33/55–56; Watson 371–72.

79. ZZJS 55–56; HY 4/2/16; Watson 38.

80. "Tianxia," ZZJS 1102, HY 93/33/73–74; Watson 375.

81. [At this point, Yang states, "Although the formation of the 'false-proposition' view stems from many causes, it is not without connection to the fact that certain recent interpreters of Zhuangzi's thought have either intentionally or accidentally ignored the mind-body conception found within it. One kind of oft-encountered viewpoint holds that Zhuangzi's thought is either mysticism, skepticism, or idealism, or else it is a complex mixture of all three." Leaving open the "relatively complicated" issue of mysticism, Yang goes onto criticize the critique common among certain mainland Chinese scholars in which Zhuangzi is viewed as primarily either an "idealist" or "skeptic," pointing out the great misunderstanding generated simply by explaining *qi* as "material" and *xin* as "ideal." Specifically cited in this regard are Guan Feng's 關鋒 "Zhuangzi zhexue pipan 莊子哲學批判"; Cao Dalin's 曹大林 "Luelun fandui jueduizhuyi de Zhuangxue renshilun 略論反對絕對主義的莊學認識論"; and Zhang Dainian's 張岱年 "Lun Zhuangzi 論莊子." By way of criticism of similar views, Yang goes on to quote a passage from Carl Jung's *Psychology and the East* (tr. R. F. C. Hull [Princeton: Princeton University Press, 1978], p. 53), in which Western psychologists are warned against understanding the soul in simply the spiritual sense and thereby falsely imposing a mind-body distinction upon it.—tr.]

82. We might look back upon the doctrines of the Peng Meng 彭蒙, Tian Pian 田駢, and Shen Dao 慎到 faction mentioned in the "Tianxia" chapter of the *Zhuangzi*: "A creature that is without knowledge does not face the perils that come from trying to set oneself up, the entanglements that come from relying upon knowledge. In motion or in stillness, he never departs from reason—in this way he lives out his years without winning praise. Therefore [Shen Dao] said, 'Let me become like those creatures without knowledge, that is enough. Such creatures have no use for the worthies or the sages. Clod-like, they never lose the Dao.'" Next, observe how Zhuangzi cites words of "great and eminent men" to express his own point: "'The teachings of Shen Dao are not rules for the living but ideals for a dead man.'" Such learning of "becoming like creatures without knowledge" is none other than what he refers to as the learning of "lopping away at the corners." See ZZJS 1088–1091; HY 92/33/49–53; Watson 370–71.

5

Guru or Skeptic? Relativistic Skepticism in the *Zhuangzi*

CHAD HANSEN

Recent years have witnessed a sea change in *Zhuangzi* interpretations. In 1983, I wrote, "The interpretation of Zhuangzi is a philosophical scandal." Today, it is more common for a work on Zhuangzi to discuss skepticism or relativism than mysticism. The roots lie in Wang Xianqian's 王先謙 recognition that the *Zhuangzi* was preoccupied with language and entered western sinology with Graham's discovery that the *Zhuangzi* used the technical vocabulary of ancient Chinese linguistic theory together with his breakthrough reading of the "Qiwulun" as an "inner dialogue" with positions posed, considered, and then subjected to doubt.

This view of the *Zhuangzi* undercuts the traditional, dismissive interpretation classically expressed by Schwartz: "We . . . begin our account of the historic Zhuangzi with the mystical vision which he shares with the *Laozi*. Zhuangzi's constant efforts to describe the indescribable in many ways simply amplify and enrich what we have already found in the *Laozi*."[1]

This philosophical shift in interpretive focus is remarkable. Traditional Zhuangzi interpretations, stemming from the missionary generations of sinologists, echo religious themes.[2] An aversion to "rigid" Western philosophy still draws many to the study of Chinese thought. They affectionately search the Chinese *dao* for a rebuke to Western reason. In sinological discourse, "analytic" is said with a sneer. "Relativist," "skeptic," "logic," and even "philosophy" fare little better. Traditionalists are loath to exchange the loveable, comic-strip religious mystic for a skeptical linguistic philosopher.

Recent discussion reflects this chronic nostalgia for the lost "guru," and several writers have challenged the characterization of Zhuangzi as a "relativist skeptic."[3] They typically pose skepticism and insight as an either-or choice. I try here to defend that interpretation of certain lines of thought in the *Zhuangzi* against these challenges. Further, I will explain how the *Zhuangzi* that emerges can still satisfy our nostalgic urge to find "guiding wisdom" in the text. The practical implications lie in its political anarchism—its aversion to things political. The Daoist text does contain political and personal wisdom via its relativist theory of language and skeptical epistemology.

After outlining the composite case these writers make against straightforward reading of the skeptical passages, I will first respond to this on methodological grounds and then clarify the conceptual background of the passages in question. Next, I will proceed to analyze the peculiar versions of monism, skepticism, and relativism implied therein. Finally, I will briefly address the political role that relativistic skepticism plays in the *Zhuangzi*.

The Case against Skepticism

I refrain here from spelling out the separate arguments of individual critics of skeptical interpretations. Instead, I set out the following line of thought that captures common threads in these arguments:

1. [Full text coherence] Start with an interpretive principle. A skeptical characterization must coherently explain the *entire* text of the *Zhuangzi* (or at least explain more of it than any rival view).

2. [Traditional tone] Then characterize the "overall tone" in traditional terms, for example, mystical, inspirational, credulous, and so on.

3. [Disabling definition] Offer an analysis of *skepticism, relativism,* or both that either shows them to be incoherent or that makes their joint use incoherent.[4]

4. [Therapeutic salvation] (Some versions only) Conclude that the skeptical (or relativist) passages are *really* only "therapeutic." Zhuangzi's skepticism buttresses the traditional view of the sage's claim to *supernatural* cognitive achievements. The passages recommend skeptical attitudes as a way to prepare our minds for a "spiritual transformation," peace of mind, or transcendent wisdom.

Steps 1 and 2 yield to the initial motivation to "disarm" the skeptical and relativist passages. Step 3 buttresses this initial motivation with a direct attack on the coherence of the alleged philosophical position(s), and step 4 completes the argument that the passages do not undermine the traditional picture of Zhuangzi as a mystical prophet.

In the second section, I will argue that step one's interpretive principle, full text coherence, is fallacious. The theoretically justifiable role of coherence in interpretation is holistic—it constrains how we interpret the entire linguistic community, not single authors or texts. Avoiding communal incoherence is the sound form of this interpretive injunction. A Chinese philosophical text, like a German, French, or English one, may contain inconsistencies and lack coherence.

If step 1 fails, step 2, the appeal to the traditional tone, only comes into play if step 3 succeeds. If the skeptical and relativist passages are coherent, then we simply conclude that they undercut the "dominant"[5] dogmatic religious themes.

For step 3's disabling definitions to show that skepticism and relativism are incoherent, the critics need to justify their disabling analyses as: (1) fitting in the conceptual and philosophical context of the *Zhuangzi* arguments and (2) consistent and competent philosophical explication of these positions. In the third section, I will argue that the disabling definitions fail on the first count, and in the fourth section, that they fail on the second. However, they do invite us to address the *kind* of skepticism implied by the various *Zhuangzi* passages, something I will do in the fifth section.

Coherence and Interpretation

Coherence is a formal principle guiding radical translation. As Quine puts it, we select among "translation manuals" for a language based on the effect the selection has on the total system of beliefs we attribute to the speakers.[6] The rival principles of interpretation (charity and humanity) tell us which *virtue* (truth or coherence) of the system of belief counts. I have argued[7] that *coherent* is preferable to the principle of charity's *true* as the virtue of another tradition's belief system since it preserves the possibility of intelligible disagreement between cultures.

The *full text coherence* objection (step 1 above) misapplies this coherence principle to a single philosopher (or text).[8] This invites the implausible conclusion that no individual can be committed to an incoherent philosophical position. That is clearly too strong a constraint on interpretation.

Interpretive coherence validly applies at the community level. The interpreter is an explanatory theorist and her theory, *qua* explanation, should be coherent. An interpreter's theory may attribute an incoherent theory to the author she interprets without herself becoming incoherent. That realization invites a reformulation of the principle of humanity that allows attributing incoherence to a text. Let us instead think of the principle of humanity as a principle of coherently explainable *access* to the belief system.[9] The interpreter's task is to attribute beliefs to which she can explain the community's access in ways that are coherent with everything else we know about them and their world.

Consider a scientific example. What should we make of the common ancient Chinese reference to ten thousand things (*wan wu* 萬物)? It must have been clear to Chinese thinkers that stars alone number more than ten thousand. Scholars may propose we modify our rendering of *wan* (ten thousand) so that it entails "many" or "all." Or we may modify our theory of *wu* (thing) to mean "thing-kind" rather than "particular object." Notice, however, that we do not attribute to Chinese thinkers the true (and fully coherent) astronomical belief in the approximately ten thousand things (galaxy clusters) that constitute the big-bang universe. Why not? Because we have no plausible explanation of ancient Chinese access to a theory of galaxy clusters.

We do not have such worries about anyone's access to beliefs about medium-sized mammals unless we know them to be extinct in China. The presence of the animals, normal light, and sensory capabilities is enough to justify access to beliefs about those objects.[10] The plausible access requirement poses a challenge analogous to galaxy clusters whenever we attribute a "theory-laden" concept. To credit the interpreted community with that concept is to credit it with a philosophical theory in which it plays a sufficiently similar role.

Since Sellars, philosophers have learned to include items such as *sense data, experience, truth, belief, reason,* and perhaps *morality, right, duty, justice,* and even *God* and *spirit* as theoretical terms.[11] We can take Chinese philosophers as advocating or opposing doctrines about *these* theoretical objects only if we provide a plausible argument that they had a theory enough like ours to underwrite the identification. We can take 天 *tian* (nature, sky) as "God" or "Heaven" only if we can plausibly explain how ancient Chinese thinkers would have come to a theology similar to our own.[12] Otherwise, we need some plausible alternative account of how ancient Chinese thinkers had epistemic access to these theoretical objects.

THE (PHILOSOPHICAL) COMMUNITY PERSPECTIVE

Interpretive coherence applies holistically to a linguistic community. We interpret the community's linguistic practices *as a whole* in ways that coherently make sense of their discourse (including their disagreements). We theorize about the norms enshrined in the community's linguistic practices. The norms govern how they should draw inferences from grammatical contexts using those terms.[13] We then interpret any particular sentence, chapter, or book the way (according to our theory) a representative member of that community should (as entailed by *its* norms). We combine the meanings of *these* terms and *these* structures to yield the inferential potential of a compositional sentence, paragraph, chapter, and so on. In principle, the inference from those strings should be accessible to any competent, informed reader in that original community.

Preserving coherence within a community's whole discourse should commit the interpreter to maximize the coherence of philosophical discourse, and not simply increase the truth or coherence of each separate text. A single sound objection can show that a widely believed and asserted view is wrong. Otherwise we might infer that by making or preserving overwhelmingly more texts than their opponents, one philosophical faction can make their views semantically true *or* consistent *in that language*. Coherence should instead take the form of making sense of the dispute, construing the terms and structures so that disputants do not "talk past" each other. Thus, I object to the proliferation of what I call "meaning-change" hypotheses in interpretive accounts of ancient Chinese philosophy. These hypotheses make the disputes empty.[14] They make the competing schools speak different languages, though they do not realize it. The disputants themselves believe falsely that they are disagreeing. A sound account of community coherence allows that two discussants can disagree about meaning, but that, in such a case, one of them is wrong. Neither faction can change the meaning of a term in its language by fiat, definition, intention, or sheer volume of babble.

Linguistic communities have a linguistic division of labor where the scorekeeping of "normally linguistically competent" speakers implicitly references the scorekeeping of experts—say for inferences involving "archaeopteryx" or "raptor." We hold speakers responsible for the inferential commitments that paleontologists should draw, not for those that "normal" speakers draw. Which inferences are licensed is independent of what individual speakers think. The norms may be controversial, subject to discussion and revision; the boundaries of linguistic communities may be variable and multiply overlapping.[15] But norms governing inferential licenses, prohibitions, and permissions are enshrined in the community's practices, not in individual intentions.[16]

So we can shift our interpretive focus from author to informed audience. What does the expression of this passage commit the writer to according to the norms of linguistic use of some philosophical community? What role do these passages play in the philosophical disagreements, given *these* concepts and background arguments? Our task is not to construct a theory of the mental states of a sage named Zhuangzi[17] but to interpret the sentences, arguments, and theories written in the text using the community's shared language. We will want to know what a competent ancient Chinese philosopher reading the passage would correctly take the passage to mean, that is, to what it would commit one who accepted it. The writer himself may or may not accept or appreciate those commitments.

We still reject the familiar claim that norms of discourse allow Chinese "logical errors" if contemporaneous Chinese thinkers recognize and conform to "valid" norms in reasoning. Even if a fallacious reasoning pattern is nearly universal in a group, as long as some school recognized and diagnosed an error, that bars the interpretive claim that the inference pattern is "correct in Chinese." It can be true that some school trained nearly everyone in the community to be indifferent to these norms, but the sheer popular weight of such indifference would not change the norms of the language.

The community I focus on here is the one engaged in philosophical discourse during the Warring States period. Hence, A. C. Graham's reconstruction of the Mohist dialectical works is important (along with his claim that the *Zhuangzi* shows signs of familiarity with these kinds of issues). Graham thus locates a relevant community of philosophically sophisticated inquiry. Given his friendship with Hui Shi 惠施, the link between a Zhuangzi persona and the community of linguistic theory is historically firmer than the fond and familiar religious Laozi-as-guru tradition.

That a community of careful, rigorous philosophy was thriving at the time of the text is enough to warrant calling a philosophical reading "authentic." Ancient Chinese literary, religious, historical, and philosophically inclined communities may all have read Daoists texts differently. The historical possibility of other readings does not require a special justification from a philosophical reading. I read these passages in the *Zhuangzi* as philosophical, in particular as informed by extensive contact with the school of Names and ancient Chinese semantic theory.[18]

Regardless of authorship, we should formulate *for ourselves* an account of what a representative, competent, thoughtful ancient Chinese philosopher (a contemporary with sound training) should have taken to be the implied commitments of a passage or argument. We would be judging as a contemporaneous (not contemporary) philosopher would. In effect, *philosophical* interpretation is joining with ancient philosophers in philosophizing.[19]

The Philosophical Context

I will summarize here some philosophically important differences in formulation and focus that distinguish ancient Chinese schools of linguistic thought from those most familiar in the Western tradition. These differences are relevant to the proper formulation of Chinese skepticism, relativism, and monism. My method below will be mainly analytical, not textual. I will focus on the analysis of the kind of relativism or skepticism implied in the passages in question. Readers interested in a more detailed account that stays closer to the text can consult my *Daoist Theory of Chinese Thought*. Please note that this analysis is controversial. I do not offer the following as observation reports, but as elements of my interpretive theory. With this warning, however, I will refrain from prefixing "according to the present interpretive hypothesis" repeatedly through the account.

First, I adapt Graham's metaphor for the "global" character of philosophical discourse in Classical China; that is, I understand it as "disputes about *dao*." I treat *dao* as a normative concept, a way to act. Ways are the subject of practical thought as facts are the subject matter of descriptive thought. The familiar translation of *dao* as "way" is satisfactory, though I sometimes use "guide" to stress the "normative" essence of *dao*-analysis.

One advantage of "way" in the present context is the rhetorical affinity of "way of life" with important Western notions; examples are Wittgenstein's "form of life" and Rawls's "comprehensive view," as well as his earlier "conception of a good life."[20] These all share important features with the Chinese conception of *dao*. They are wholesale guiding structures that include ways of describing and categorizing things for action. The norms of meaning and epistemic norms are included along with those of ethics. All such norms make up our comprehensive view or a "form of life."

I divide the concept of '*dao*' into "discourse" *dao* and "performance" *dao*. The former is paradigmatically verbal and written instructions. It embraces whatever *can* guide us—whatever conveys knowledge of "how to" or "what to" do. A "performance *dao*" is an interpretation into action, a *practical* interpretation. My use here borrows from a music model.[21] The score is the discourse *dao*, and a performance is a "practical" *interpretation*.

The test of being a discourse *dao* is its being subject to *normative practical* interpretation. Norm-guided, practical *interpretation* takes the form of an execution or performance. The test of a performance *dao*, then, is that it is subject to evaluation, that is, as a right or wrong *interpretation*. One can try to follow a *dao* and get it wrong.

Many *dao*s have both aspects. Discourse *dao*s range from explicit instructions and algorithms to gestures, examples, paths, maps, and descriptions of historical exemplars. Expressing, showing, and gesturing are themselves performances, subject to evaluation. Each is also a mode of discourse, subject to practical interpretation. An example or model may be both performance and discourse. To follow the example, we have to extrapolate it to our situation and correctly identify the relevant similarities. We can go wrong following an example as surely as we can following an instruction book.

A path can count as discourse *dao* (something we may "wander off" or "stay on") or as performance *dao* (a "trace" of actual past "walkings"). A road is a *dao*, but we should not think of it as *just* a physical object like the grass, lakes, and trees surrounding it. A road guides; that is, it counts as a road (way) when regarded as something we *should* stay on, though we *can* wander off.[22]

My distinction between discourse and performance is interpretive, not a distinction made explicitly in Chinese texts. Examples of dual-aspect *dao* are common in the texts, and even the best analyses blur correct interpretation and correct choice of discourse *dao*.[23] "Disputing the *dao*" neatly captures how easy it is to slide between the two. What I find most interesting is that ancient Chinese thinkers formulated and focused on the problems of interpretation first, and the model of interpretation provided the main form for discussing which discourse *dao* to choose. Choice of a *dao* is a performance interpretation of a "higher order" guiding *dao*—one for deciding which *dao* to follow here.

Confucius's *Analects* 13:3 states the interpretive problem in the form of a doctrine of "rectifying names." If names are not rectified, language, social affairs, ritual and music, and edict and punishment all go wrong and "people will not know how to move hand or foot." Mohists first raised the *selection* problem. The traditional 禮 *li* (ritual) might be the wrong guide.

Mohists proposed utility (the benefit-harm distinction) as the guiding higher standard and used it to solve the problems of both the interpretation and selection.

Paradigm discourse *daos* consist of words. To follow a *dao*, we must correctly assign the words used in it to things in the context of action. This rests on our ability to distinguish *bian* 辯, and all distinguishing can be viewed as using the *shi-fei* 是非 (this [right]-not this [wrong]) of objects following the norms implicit in the word—the *dao* of the word or the *way* the word is used in the relevant community. The Mohists speak of the *dao* of particular distinction pairs such as *you-wu* (being-nonbeing). So choosing a discourse *dao* is applying *shi-fei* (this-not this) to *daos*. The Mohist ur-norm is the distinction between *li-hai* 利害 (benefit-harm).

Mohists treat their disagreement with Confucians as showing the latter to be confused about how to distinguish between 義 "moral" and 不義 "immoral."[24] This way of formulating disputes about *dao* made philosophy of language immediately relevant to ancient accounts of moral disputes. The disputes are about distinctions, and Mohists called such disputes "distinction disputes" (*bian* 辯). The normative notion of a *dao* comprehends aspects of the Western concept of 'meaning.' A normative *dao* fixes the right use of a guiding term, the right way to distinguish (*bian*) using that term *and* its opposite.

With this background, we can preview Zhuangzi's skeptical position. Choosing and interpreting a *dao* are themselves performances. They presuppose some norm, standard, distinction, or *dao*. The *Zhuangzi* raises the obvious question: What is the correct standard (*dao*) to use in choosing and interpreting a *dao*? This question begins the relativistic regress that informs Daoist skepticism.

POLITICAL THEORY

Confucians and Mohists shared a view of the role of government ensuring broad compliance with a common conception of the moral life—unifying the *dao* of the social world. For Confucius, the ruler was like the father in inculcating and reinforcing a conception of morality by example. A Mohist discourse *dao* would have more emphasis on language. However, the Mohist conception of the moral education role of government was largely congruent with that of the Confucians. The political mechanism for harmonizing *yi* (morality) does start with everyone "reporting" their evaluative judgments to their superior, but it then gives the *superior* the performative authority to declare which *shi-fei* reports all should accept.

The goal is a leader-guided acceptance of a single social *dao*. It has little relation to what Rawls would characterize as the institutional structure of ongoing neutrality among comprehensive views (*daos*).

The quasihistorical account of philosophy in the "Tianxia" chapter of the *Zhuangzi*[25] suggests a similar analysis. Disorder follows on the loss of a common traditional ethical conception. This internal *Zhuangzi* account explicitly identifies the other stages leading to the *Zhuangzi* as endorsing impartiality or doctrinal bias in some way. Let us call them (1) the "few-real-desires" group, (2) the "can't-miss-*dao*" group, and (3) the "reversibility" group.

The few-real-desires group treats most of our desires as the product of our accepting a certain conception of the good life. Particularly, it thinks of insults and shame as harms only for those who accept an "optional," evaluative point of view. We could choose not to take that point of view that values status or social honor.

The can't-miss-*dao* group,[26] in effect, undermines the appeal to naturalness (or *tian* 天; "nature, sky") in selecting one way of life over another. If following *the* natural *dao* is the goal, you do not need to work at it—you simply *will*. There is no such thing as getting nature wrong. All "live options" for us now are equally natural; any we choose will amount to following the Great Dao. A negative way of putting the point is: *tian* (nature, sky) gives us no basis for selecting among rival ways of life.

The reversibility group suggests that we can take any existing guidance scheme of concepts and get an equally compelling *dao* by reversing all its values. Thus, Laozi values passivity, submission, and other female values over their Confucian-Mohist counterparts. The distinctions and names that constitute our ways of life are not attached in any constant way to correct guidance. This exercise, presumably, should undermine our attachment to any particular *dao*.

Zhuangzi's relativistic skepticism emerges in the context of this broad social-political movement toward impartiality, and it implicitly supports that trend. The *Zhuangzi's* skepticism lends support to ancient Chinese political advocacy of neutrality among conceptions of the good life.

THE LACK OF SENTENTIAL CONTEXT

Before elaborating on this political point, let us look at a major contrast in the structure we have been elaborating for disputing *dao*. When Chinese thinkers elaborate on normative *dao*, they focus on words, which mark distinctions. Western discussions of morality center on the role of

sentences—particularly the universal normative sentences called "rules,"
"laws," "principles," or "maxims." Western moral theory comes to focus
on finding some universal "ought" sentence—the first premise in moral
reasoning. Normative correctness is understood mainly in terms of sound
normative inference. A central puzzle of Western ethical theory is what is
the "axiom" or "first premise" of moral deduction.

Ancient Chinese thinkers, while correctly noticing the normative
and integrated character of language, reference, knowledge, and ways of
life, did not develop this insight using sentential concepts, nor did they
have any clear notion of sentential inference. They theorized about *daos*
of *daos* rather than *norms* of sentential inference.[27] The Chinese conception of 知 *zhi* (know) was, thus, non-propositional.

Chinese discourse about *xin* 心 (heart-mind) uses a belief context
(S *yi* 以 [with] T *wei* 為 [deem; do] P¹) that invites term rather than sentential analysis. Where Western accounts would have a person as believing
that S is P, ancient Chinese wrote of a person as tending to treat S as P
or to (say) "P" of S.[28] They linked this pragmatic attitude to their scheme
of *dao*, *shi-fei* (this-not this), and *bian* (distinction). To *wei* 為 (deem; do)
an object is to assign it some term in a discourse *dao*—rectifying a name.
"Dispositions to act" toward (to treat) a thing in a certain way replaces
Western propositional attitudes.

Chinese "knowing" follows on their counterpart of believing—*zhi*
(know) is a success verb. Knowing is *wei*-ing correctly.[29] One knows to
(say) P in the presence of S or knows to treat S as P. These features of *wei*
(deem) and *zhi* (know) give a distinctive character to Chinese skepticism
and relativism.

Monism, Skepticism, and Relativism in the *Zhuangzi*

I shall treat monism as a metaphysical posture,[30] skepticism as an epistemological one,[31] and relativism as a posture about standards of *shi-fei*
(this-not this) and *bian* (distinction; dispute).

METAPHYSICS: MONISM AND REALISM

Skeptical and relativist attitudes apply mainly to normative contexts.
However, a norm analysis implicitly presupposes a context (realities to
which we assign terms from our *daos*). We can loosely describe some

Daoist views as metaphysically naturalist. Our conceptions of that real world may be relative to our comprehensive views or ways of life, but the argument proceeds against a background assumption of a nature independent of our rival conceptions. We can call this Daoist view "monism" in a naturalistic sense.

Naturalistic versus Parmenidean Monism

The dominant Western sense of "monism" is a denial of dualisms. Robert Brandom (*Making It Explicit*) makes a helpful distinction between 'distinctions' and 'dualisms.' A distinction becomes a dualism when it entails deep puzzles about the relation of the two elements. Classical mind-body metaphysics is a dualism, as are transcendent supernaturalism, Plato's theory of forms, and Kantian noumena-phenomena. Common-sense divisions, however, such as male/female, old/young, living/nonliving, and so on are distinctions, not dualisms.

Notoriously, Chinese metaphysics lacks much evidence of the Indo-European mind-body dualism and (somewhat more controversially) has little or no transcendent supernaturalism.[32] If these antidualist characterizations are correct, then we can describe Daoist metaphysics as "monist" while accepting that it is committed to many ordinary distinctions. Daoists are naturalists. They accept natural differences in things, but no dualisms.

Naturalistic monism envisions a continuity of nature. Like the notorious butterfly that, by flapping its wings in Beijing, causes a blizzard in New York,[33] our actions causally ripple throughout the universe. This Chinese view of the continuity of the human social world and nature is a characteristic of Daoist reasoning that we can take as background in reading these *Zhuangzi* passages and of Daoist references to "one-ness" and "unity." This view has much of the flavor of modern physicalist monism—for example, when Zhuangzi describes his wife's death as merely a "transformation" of the same sort that gave her birth.[34] Of course, it is not materialist or physicalist in the sense of *denying* a mind-body dualism. It is naturalistic monism in virtue of neither presenting nor presupposing such a dualism.

Parmenidean monism, by contrast, is the denial not merely of dualisms but of distinctions. It commits one to a peculiarly strong version of one-ness, that is, not merely of some underlying natural continuity. Parmenidean monism denies all qualitative and quantitative difference. Besides Parmenides, Neo-Platonism, Spinoza, and *some* idealist views of "the absolute" may approach this kind of Monism about absolute reality. It seems to find expression in Indian Upanishadic and Buddhist metaphysics as well. It tends to be associated with mystical epistemic doctrines and semantics because, typically, it is hard to prove or to state without paradox. I see no prima facie reason to read references to unity or oneness in the *Zhuangzi* as Parmenidean rather than naturalistic monism or to link them to the mystical epistemology of Indo-European traditions.

China does offer *some* candidates for rough[35] counterparts of this stronger kind of Monism. Something like this may be the conclusion of Zhuangzi's philosophical companion, Hui Shi.[36] The metaphysics of what I called the "can't-miss-*dao*" group also suggests an intermediate kind of monism. Its core is continuity-of-nature monism, but they may try to derive from it a prohibition on making *any* distinction between *shi-fei* (this-not this).

I have argued that a philosophical reader could reasonably take passages in the *Zhuangzi* to reject both views. Graham first drew our attention to the fact that Zhuangzi seems to formulate and then reject Hui Shi's position on the notion that "all is one."[37] Zhuangzi's reasons follow lines of argument we find in the Mohist dialectical chapters. These point out that eschewing distinctions is unacceptable: "Denying denial is perverse" (Canon B79). The Mohists also rebutted, on coherence grounds, the closely related antilanguage view: "To take language as exhaustively perverse is perverse" (Canon B71; see Graham, *Later Mohist Logic*, pp. 445–46). Their acceptance of the then-common analysis of language as consisting in distinctions unites these two paradoxes. Rejecting all distinctions is tantamount to rejecting language and vice-versa. Hui Shi, from the fragments available, seemed to argue from the relativity of distinctions to the perspective that no distinctions were real. A Chinese reader familiar with linguistics would have good grounds for rejecting this inference. The *Zhuangzi* critique of Hui Shi's monism suggests that rejecting distinctions is implicit in the claim that "all is one." We cannot formulate it without making a distinction.

The *Zhuangzi* writer(s) show no signs of being relativist or pluralist about the world (i.e., committed to many metaphysically real worlds). The text, however, expresses a *descriptive* norm-pluralism (many norms systems exist, including higher-level norms for choosing/interpreting lower-level norms). Moreover, it is *skeptical* (agnostic) about normative realism. It is unsure if one and only one of the existing norm systems is correct.

The *Zhuangzi* shares with many writers of the period an implicitly naturalistic-monist conception of the world. However, it resists the temptation to slide into Hui Shi's Parmenidean monism—a blanket denial of distinctions. Speculation about what is ultimately real is not its central philosophical project.[38] The *Zhuangzi* aims its skeptical attitude at conceptions of the world that inform our rival views of what counts as the good life—*dao*.

SKEPTICISM: THEME, SCOPE, AND STRENGTH

Skepticism is an epistemological stance with many variations.[39] Following Goldman, we can distinguish among varieties of skepticism by focusing on its themes, its scope, and its strength.[40] To use his distinctions in the different conceptual context of Chinese thought, we must reformulate them in terms of distinctions or dispositions to treat as *shi-fei* (this-not this). These concepts underlie ancient accounts of knowing-to, knowing how-to, and contact-knowing (acquaintance), and thus Chinese skepticism. We avoid sententials such as *truth* or *belief*.

> Gaptooth asked Wang Ni. "Do you know what all things treat as 是 *shi* (this:right)?" "How could I know that?" "Do you know what it is you do not know?" "How could I know that?" "So in that case, does no one know anything?" "How could I know that? Still, let me try to state it—How do I know that what I call knowing is not non-knowing? How do I know that what I call non-knowing is not knowing?"[41]

Theme: Nonepistemic Goals versus Doubt about Epistemic Achievement

Several writers deny that Zhuangzi's is direct skepticism about our epistemic achievements—whether we have knowledge. They draw parallels to ancient Greek Pyrrhonian skepticism and construe Zhuangzi's theme as nonepistemic. They aver that Zhuangzi's apparent skepticism is really an attitude we *ought* to adopt (suspension of judgment) to get peace of mind. They justify this reinterpretation as a way to avoid an inconsistency in skepticism—the skeptic cannot know that he does not know.[42] If one claimed to *know* that no one knew, inconsistency would arise, but skepticism itself is not inconsistent. Does a problem arise when the skeptic asserts the doubt in the form of a skeptical conclusion "no one knows anything?" Indirectly it might if we combine it with a norm of asserting that licenses the familiar challenge "how do you know that?" If we conclude that any assertion entails a claim to knowledge, we get inconsistency. By itself, however, the *content* of the assertion is consistent.

But notice that the doubt expressed in the Gaptooth passage entails no such inconsistency and, arguably, is carefully drawn to avoid it. At its root is the worry that the standards for using terms such as *know* and *not know* could be other than they are. The "irony" is that the "therapeutic" strategy starts with a bogus accusation of the incoherence of ordinary philosophical skepticism and then accepts an alternative that is blatantly incoherent. The content of the recommendation is the judgment "we should not make *any* judgment." The recommendation condemns itself! Further, the incoherence of the therapeutic form is precisely the kind of incoherence to which ancient Chinese thinkers demonstratively had access. The ancient Mohists identified and criticized it, as does the *Zhuangzi* passage referred to above. Both would easily spot the "perversity" in *recommending* that we not make judgments.

While I reject the "therapeutic" strategy, I certainly accept the value of examining the practical significance of the skepticism in the *Zhuangzi*. However, I do not accept that a wider theme and significance for skeptical lines of reasoning rules out that the text also expresses skepticism about distinctions and *shi-fei* (this-not this) in the familiar sense of straightforward doubt of our epistemic achievements. It seems to me obvious that it does. Second, I conclude that a representative philosophical reader/writer should find this significance in the political implications, rather than in some recipe for spiritual edification.

Doubts about Knowing and the Basis of Knowing. While accepting the value of giving the wider implications of skepticism, I will not *call* those implications "skepticism." I restrict that term, as contemporary philosophical usage does, to philosophical doubts about cognitive achievement—*knowing* or *justifying.* We should bear in mind, however, that in the Chinese contexts, the "knowing" is practical, not descriptive, and "justifying" is not propositional inference but deriving distinctions from a standard. The doubt is about whether we do know the correct way to make the distinctions that underlie our action choices. The conception of knowing is normative and centers on interpretation more than on picturing or representing.

As I noted above, we can draw broad parallels between Chinese and Western conceptual structures for epistemic discussion. The rough counterpart of "belief" would be *de re wei*-ing (為, i.e., deeming-for-action) attitudes. That is to say, skeptical doubt centers on the normative assumption that we have *wei*-ed correctly when we distinguish between things particularly as they are relevant to our action.

Chinese thinkers of the period did not distinguish questions about causation and warrant of commitments. The Mohists recognize that we appeal to standards for applying guiding distinctions in the course of *dao*-ing—giving guidance. The *Zhuangzi* often presents such considerations in terms of an ambiguous *dependence*.[43] One *shi-fei* (this–not this) depends on a prior *shi-fei* (this–not this). The view I defend is that the *Zhuangzi* passages express skepticism in the context of their awareness that our judgments always have this dependence (causal or rational) on other *shi-fei* (this–not this) judgments. The skeptical theme focuses on relativity of justification. "Not yet to have it grown in the heart-mind and yet to have *shi-fei* (this–not this) is like going to Yue today and arriving yesterday."[44]

The *Zhuangzi* passages play on the view that people use many norms or standards of what would be correct *wei*-ing. The clearest case is *Mozi's* famous "three-standards":[45] (1) conformity to traditional *shi-fei* (this–not this) assignments, (2) measurable, empirical standards for word use, and (3) moral and utilitarian considerations. The plurality means possible conflict and entails that we will draw on some higher standard to tell us which to use in cases of conflict.[46]

We do not know which *wei*-ing is correct unless we know which standard to use. However, knowing that is another "knowing-to." Claims to know, thus, face a regress of norm guidance. Whenever we interpret or select a *dao*, we presuppose some further *dao*. The regress of implicit *daos* on which our judgments depend lies behind the *Zhuangzi's* expression of skepticism. We do not sense the pervasiveness of our reliance on *dao*. Humans forget they live in *dao* as fish forget they live in water.[47]

Scope

The scope of a skeptical attitude refers to the areas of knowledge it calls into question. Thus, one may be a religious skeptic or a skeptic about other minds, sense data, physical objects, or ethics.[48] One's skepticism may be narrow (e.g., skepticism about reconstructions of "the sounds of classical Chinese") or broad (e.g., skepticism of the external world). Most recognizable skepticism has some implicitly limited scope that it contrasts with paradigms of what we *can* know.

The *Zhuangzi* skeptical passages suggest a rather broad scope. While the skepticism resembles ethical skepticism in revolving around the regress of norms, it implicitly embraces all linguistic classification. A *dao*, a comprehensive view, includes "right" ways of classifying things. In China, doubt focused on norms of distinguishing more than on sense experience, other minds, and physical or theoretical objects. The scope of that doubt affects the whole scheme of "knowing what to do." The thing doubted is our comprehensive, guiding "form of life."

Stories of surprises, gestalt shifts, and dreams all play a role in this kind of skepticism.[49] These are familiar themes in the *Zhuangzi*, as in the following example:

> [Zhuang Zhou was hunting a strange magpie in a preserve and prepared to shoot it with his crossbow.] He noticed a cicada finding such lovely shade that it forgot itself. A mantis poised itself to strike at it, but was so taken with the vision of opportunity that it forgot its own situation. The strange magpie was then ready to take it in, but on seeing gain forgot its own authenticity. Zhuang Zhou said, "Eee! Things are inherently connected and different kinds call each other forth!" As he threw down his bow to leave, a game warden caught up and accosted him.[50]

The hunting story nicely embeds the theme of suddenly seeing things differently in a regress of conceptions. Each actor in the chain forgets the "escape" perspective when focusing on the "catch" perspective. When the "keeper" surprises Zhuangzi and chases him from the grove, Zhuangzi sees his confidence in his status as foolishness. An unappreciated feature of the context made him suddenly reclassify himself and other things differently for purposes of guiding action.

The *Zhuangzi* also targets norms of judgment that seem beyond challenge. We normally "know to do" things that keep us alive, but some ways of life (conceptions of the good life) treat accepting death as rational. Is this an objection to them? The *Zhuangzi* asks, "How do I know that avoiding death is not a similar mistake?"[51] Without knowing that I *should* value life, I cannot claim to *know to do* any of the things in which pragmatic survival (individual or social) is a motivating standard. Zhuangzi's conversation with the skull illustrates the possibility that something we do not "see" could make our common-sense judgment seem foolish:

> When Zhuangzi went to Chu, he saw an old skull, all dry and parched. He poked it with his carriage whip and then asked, "Sir, were you greedy for life and forgetful of reason, and so came to this? . . ."
> In the middle of the night, the skull came to him in a dream and said, ". . . Among the dead there are no rulers above, no subjects below, and no chores of the four seasons. With nothing to do, our springs and autumns are as endless as heaven and earth. A king facing south on his throne could have no more happiness than this! . . . Why would I throw away more happiness than that of a king on a throne and take on the troubles of a human being again?" ("Zhi le," [Watson 193–94]; ZZJS 617–619; HY 46/18/22–29)[52]

Dream passages illustrate the theme by showing how, in dreams, we classify others and ourselves in one way with little hesitation, then, on awakening, abandon that classification instantly. Am I Zhuangzi dreaming being a butterfly or a butterfly dreaming Zhuangzi?[53] Are we right merely to dismiss what we "knew" during the dream?

The main target of doubt in these passages is conventional wisdom, especially of our shared, conventional patterns of discrimination or distinction making. A key claim is that any time we make a discrimination, we fail to see something.

That the scope is broad, however, does not mean that it is total. It does not, as we noted above, signal any doubt about the natural-world context in which our ways of life operate, nor that the alternate "ways" operate in the same world.

Besides reminders of how we can go wrong, the stories mainly underline the irresolvability of our disputes about different ways of life and the difficulty of appreciating alternatives. They remind us that our confidence in our own comprehensive view is neither reliable nor unique to us. The text naturally implies that we are to learn (come to know) something from these stories. This knowing about knowing is valuable. Ignoring it would be bad from many, if not all, points of view.

Broad but not total skepticism of this type can support a normative conclusion, as it does for modern liberalism. The conclusion would be that we ought not to participate in social structures designed to oppress, mutilate, or kill those who do not share our way of life. Engaging in coercive activities to impose a single way of life on people requires a level of confidence that we have identified the correct comprehensive vision to which we are not entitled. The *Zhuangzi* stories remind us how frequently we have been wrong in our classifications and attitudes toward things.

Strength

The strength of a skeptical doubt is independent of its scope. A very broad skepticism might still be weak and a narrow skepticism might be quite strong. The stronger the demand the skeptic requires to justify a claim to knowledge, the weaker the skeptical considerations have to be to support the judgment that we do not or cannot have it. There are various dimensions of strength.

Doubt of Perfect *Knowledge or* Any *Knowledge?* Denying that we can be *certain* of something is a weak version of skepticism because "certainty" is a strong demand. Similarly, denying that we now know X is weaker than modal versions, which deny any *possibility* of knowing X. The Gaptooth discussion (cited above) suggests that the *Zhuangzi* position is weak in that it allows we *might in fact* know something but do not know that we know it.[54] Thus, it does not commit us to the claim that knowledge is impossible.

The passages we cited suggest that skepticism about how to act is comparative. We may know a way to do a thing, but can we claim to know the best way to do it? There are always possibilities we have not yet even contemplated. From our experiences of coming to realize better ways to view and act on things, we learn that our confidence is typically deceptive.

The dream sequences make a similar point. We learn that one way of life is not correct when we "awaken" to one that seems better. Each such "awakening" is a kind of knowing—that our past confidence was misleading about our epistemic status. We know then that we did not know before what we thought we knew. The repeated experience of coming to know should make us cautious or modest about our present state of knowledge even when it is a product of such "awakening." Even when our prior ways have seemed to work fine, they have turned out to come to seem inferior to some alternative. Typically, we had not even imagined the alternative. The regress of norms carries with it a regress of unimagined possibilities of alternatives.

The guidance-skepticism is weak in that it denies mainly that we can ever have *perfect, ultimate,* the *highest,* or *best* knowledge. Many other passages argue that we cannot even comprehend what perfection is and that it would appear to us as its opposite.[55] The demand is a strong one, so the skepticism is weak. This is, of course, precisely the kind of *dao* skepticism that justifies neutrality among comprehensive views and encourages the spread of different *dao*s. However, in making this point, the skeptic acknowledges that we can come to realize (know) that one *dao* is better than another. We simply cannot conclude that with this realization we have found the ultimate way.

Again, notice that this skepticism does not arise from any analysis of our perception or memory of some reality. It implicitly takes both for granted. It recalls common past experiences of coming to see as dubious what we had thought obvious.

One may object that the skepticism is so weak that it really has no opponents. However, the tradition defends us from accusations of triviality.

We find many claims in Confucian[56] and other authoritarian (proto-Legalist) writings that "sages" are capable of transcending the ordinary limited perspectives and achieving a "god's-eye" view or the ideal-observer's practical knowledge.[57]

Skill stories illustrate another feature of the *Zhuangzi's* skepticism. The texts note that skillful performers are all limited to their skill. Inevitably, they cannot do other things as well. Typically, the stories note that the skillful practitioner cannot convey his skill. A musician cannot play all notes at once, a debater cannot convince everyone, and so on. Zhuangzi sums up by noting that 成 *cheng* (completion) always entails 虧 *kui* (defect): "May men like this be said to be complete? Then so am I. Or may they not be said to be complete? Then neither am I, nor is anything else."[58]

The no-completion-without-defect insight reminds us that no matter how much we perfect our skill, we will be unable to do other things. This is rooted in the linguistic point. Anytime we learn to make and follow a distinction, there will be things we miss or are unable to appreciate. To make a distinction is to choose not to make other possible distinctions in the context: "Hence, divisions have that which they do not divide; distinctions have that they do not distinguish. You say, 'What does this mean?' Sages embrace things; ordinary people distinguish things so they can show them in relation to each other. So I say, those who distinguish have that which they do not see."[59]

Normally, we regard our own way of life as better than the ways of others. The skeptical passages warn us that our evaluation is not only suspect but argumentatively question-begging, since others have different standards of evaluation. We might *accidentally* be right, but we cannot conclude that we are so merely from the strength of our conviction, nor can we merely because we appeal to higher standards. Rival *daos* come complete with their own different norms of warrant: "Is man's life really as stupid as this? Or is it that I am the only stupid one, and there are others not so stupid? But if you go by the completed heart and take it as your authority, who is without such an authority? Why should it be only the man who knows how things alternate and whose heart approves its own judgments who has such an authority?"[60]

We would be unwise to ignore that the person with the rival form of life probably finds hers superior on functionally similar grounds. That is, though she does not appeal to the *same* norms, she does appeal to norms of warrant. She does recite justifications that convince her in as complex and complete a way. She may equally cite her *dao's* success in the actual world as judged by her norms. She too will have a skill, albeit not the same as ours. The crucial skeptical realization is that we can no more easily convince her that our way of life is better than she can us.

I referred to how dream passages illustrate the effect of conversion from one comprehensive view to another. When we are "within" one way of life, we find it obviously correct. When we have awakened to a different way, we equally clearly realize how we were wrong before. We instantly become as strongly convinced of our new view.[61] That we can so easily come to see things "in a new light" should lead us to realize how real the danger is that we may be misled merely by the iterative elaboration of a *dao* we accept.

How should the philosophically alert reader then make sense of the interspersing of these skeptical passages with talk about "perfected" people and absolutes? What they might find striking about such passages is that they often suggest that such perfection is unintelligible and irrelevant to us.[62] Typically, this kind of text makes its point by asserting a kind of reversal. Perfection may be the very opposite of what we now take it to be. Perfection from one perspective may appear as stupidity from another! The perfect musician may be one who does not play a note![63] The judgments and behavior of a perfect man are just irrelevant, incomprehensible, and of no use to ordinary people thinking about what to do.

We can also read passages such as "A man like this rides the clouds and mist"[64] as contemplating what might be possible with different *daos*. Some comprehensive way of life that is possible for us might give us powers over nature and our lives that we can now barely imagine. That is another sense that should lead us to doubt that we *now* know how to live. There almost certainly are far better possible ways to organize our lives, some whose superiority we could not now appreciate.

Arguments

Besides theme, scope, and strength, we can classify arguments for skepticism. The two most relevant to skepticism in the *Zhuangzi* are: (1) the fallibility of human cognitive faculties and (2) the question of dependency (grounds or warrant) for *shi-fei* (this–not this) distinctions. The core arguments for skepticism in the *Zhuangzi* are of the latter kind. Skepticism flows mainly from the dependency of knowing-to on presupposed standards. This opens up a regress of knowing-to or -how to use certain standards.

Many assume the Zhuangzi's skepticism is based, like Western skepticism, on human fallibility—particularly the unreliability of the senses. Little in the passages we have cited suggests any such analysis. Aside from the above insight that judgments of a perfect being are irrelevant to us, little stress is placed on any negative account of *human* cognitive psychology.[65] Our essential limitation is simply that we will die before we get all knowledge.

The *Zhuangzi* occasionally makes its skeptical point in physiological terms. It treats 成心 *cheng xin* as a natural organ that responds to things with *shi-fei*. These "grow" in the heart just as the heart grows in the body. The point there, however, simply recapitulates the regress-of-norms argument and points again to the inevitability of death. All *shi-fei* emerging from the heart rely on having some other *shi-fei* already present there. As I have argued (*Daoist Theory*), the discussion of the heart approximates the Humean skeptical conclusion that "you can't get an ought from an is." The heart-mind's judgments are dependent in its having already absorbed *shi-fei* presuppositions.

The *Zhuangzi* does express skepticism of claims to transcendental access to knowledge. Other thinkers claimed such epistemic access, and some attribute the access to a regimen, such as breath control or self-cultivation. Scholars have recently begun to highlight accounts drawn from the *Guanzi* and the *Xunzi*.[66] Because they are logical, rather than physiological, the *Zhuangzi's* "dependency" arguments still block these claims to perfect knowledge whether via innate, cultivated, physical, or religiously transcendent transformation—since we require both a norm to justify our reliance on the intuitive capacity and a norm to guide our use of it before we can vouchsafe that we have used it correctly or followed the right intuition.

Of course, the *Zhuangzi* is skeptical of these organ-based claims to innate, self-warranting knowledge. And it sometimes puts the point in physiological terms—that the 心 *xin* (heart-mind) is a product of its conditions of growth. It does not have innate or direct (intuitive) access to the correct answer to a know-to question. Graham identified the most obvious example of such an epistemological claim—Mencian intuitionism—but the argument refutes any such claim.[67]

I do not mean that no value can be derived from the relativistic skeptical insights. This strategy of reading leaves room for goals of personal or social transformation but not for peculiarly *religious*, *spiritual*, or *transcendent* knowledge. Common-sense practical implications abound, including tolerance, flexibility, and open-mindedness about other *daos* and their possible value in adapting our own.[68] This underwrites the famous *Zhuangzi* willingness to listen respectfully to freaks, convicted criminals, seemingly insane philosophers, centipedes, and skulls. The practical implication of this kind of skepticism is that we (socially or individually) should not waste *daos*.

PLURALISM (RELATIVISM, PERSPECTIVISM)

The term *relativism* has such a bad press among nonphilosophers that some avoid it in preference to terms such as *pluralism*, *perspectivism*, and so on. I find all three terms helpful in bringing out different aspects of the position enunciated in the *Zhuangzi*. One advantage of 'pluralism' and 'perspectivism' is that they draw attention away from truth and direct it to warrant or justification. 'Pluralism' emphasizes the multiplicity of *warranted* answers. 'Perspectivism' implicitly fills out the relativist formula with a broadly epistemic and conceptual context. Broadly speaking, a *relativist* analysis of a subject matter implies the correct answer to a question that begins with "it depends on . . ." Relativist analyses loosely contrast with *absolutist* or context-free answers.

Relativism does not imply that all views are warranted, justified, or rational.[69] If we fill the above ellipsis with something like "some perspective," relativism *may* allow that, for a rational view, there is a perspective from which it is rational. However, no perspective need warrant all views. Relativism is consistent with some views being unwarranted (e.g., logical contradictions and counter-intuitives).

The *Zhuangzi* uses relativism to support skepticism. Relativism illustrates how our confidence in our know-how depends on a regress of norms and context. Zhuangzi reminds us that others have *equal* confidence in their different contexts. The dependency relativism fuels the skepticism.[70]

Distinctions like those we used to pinpoint the skepticism can also help us locate what is distinctive about the *Zhuangzi*'s relativist arguments. The caveats about the changed philosophical context all apply here as well.

Theme

As with skepticism, we should not treat Zhuangzi's relativism as explicating the nature of truth, nor as a claim about meaning. The formulations in the *Zhuangzi* deal with indexical perspective (the way reference is indexed), value perspective that arises from being raised in or committed to one scheme of *shi-fei* (this-not this) (one *dao* [guide]) rather than another. The theme is the relativity of the *obviousness* of our action-guiding distinctions.

As in the case of skepticism, we can ask what the broader political, ethical, or spiritual point is of answering "it depends" to a question. Our answer, again, is to locate it in the political realm—an argument for political neutrality, toleration of different ways of living. More directly, the relativism motivates the skepticism, which, in turn, motivates the liberal political stance.[71]

Scope

The relativism, like the skepticism, is broad in scope. One target of relativist analysis is the dependency of our *dao* and our practical interpretation of it on accidental facts of our upbringing and past. To decide what a term should "pick out" when executing a *dao*, we appeal to our past training and practice. The linguistic focus of the *Zhuangzi's* relativism of reference derives from the indexical analysis of *shi-fei*, which figures so centrally in the account of *dao* (guide) and from Zhuangzi's appeal to the relativism of acceptability (*ke* 可 [assertible]). The *Zhuangzi* observes that any existing linguistic practice creates its own assertability conditions: "*Daos*: where can we go and they not be? Language: where can it exist and not be acceptable?"[72]

The focus on linguistic practices, acceptable ways to deploy distinctions, and so on nicely illustrates the *Zhuangzi's* characteristic analysis of ethical disputes in ancient China. Mohists and Confucians dispute about burial practices. Zhuangzi sees them as relying on different standards governing their use of "good" or "not-good." One *dao's* standards dictate using the term *good* of such practices, and the other does not. This linguistic analysis of the issue links the *Zhuangzi* passages to later-Mohist linguistics and to Hui Shi's paradoxes and theses.

Hui Shi's relativist analyses of comparative terms (*before/after, yesterday/today, high/low, large/small, useful/useless*, and so forth) stimulated the relativist lines of thinking in the *Zhuangzi*, but the "Qiwulun" arguments broaden that focus dramatically. They place Hui Shi's relativism of comparison alongside the relativism of reference of indexicals—particularly *this* (*shi*; this; right) and *that*. The indexical aspect of *shi-fei* (this-not this) thus broadens the scope of the relativist orientation.

Strength

Relativist postures can also vary along a vague strength dimension. Strong relativism would imply that the applicability of the term or the correctness of the judgment depended *entirely* on that to which it was relative. Pure subjectivism would be a strong kind of relativism.[73] Weak relativism would allow that the norm conditions *contribute* to a classification or evaluation. Clearly, the relativism in these Chinese terms is weak in this sense—judgments of large and small clearly have *something* to do with the world as well as our standards of comparison. Judgments about the reference of indexicals depend partly on where we are, and partly on where things are.

The Zhuangzi text draws in weak relativism. It would accept our making judgments and deeming ourselves right. We simply acknowledge that in our deeming, we depend on some other norm. The potential regress restricts our confidence, so we continue to listen to and discuss with others. We do not use coercion to eliminate rival *daos*. We accept that someone may be right (metaphysical realism), that if two views conflict, not both are right. And, trivially, we accept the answer we in fact accept. However, in acknowledging the relativity (dependency) of accidental or arbitrary historical causal grounds, we adopt a more modest epistemic posture—mild skepticism. We continue to discuss things and either seek to persuade (or be persuaded) from some common basis or agree to tolerantly disagree:

> Suppose you and I have a dispute about a distinction (*bian* 辯). If you win and not I, are you really *shi* [this:right] and am I *fei* [not-this:wrong]? If I win and you not, am I really *shi* and are you *fei*? Is one *shi* and one *fei*? Are both *shi* and both *fei*? If we cannot know this between us, isn't everyone similarly in this kind of darkness? . . . Therefore, neither you nor I nor other humans can resolve our dispute. Could we find anything else to depend on?[74]

What the relativism in the *Zhuangzi* explicitly denies is the Confucian-Mohist assumption that the appeal to norms can come to an end at *tian* (nature; sky). To borrow a modern formula, no fact of the matter settles our disputes about ways of life. There may be facts of the matter about whether *historically* the dispute simmers down, reaches a synthesis, or just disappears as the ways of life evolve within extant populations. No such fact, however, makes the surviving one correct. *Correct* is an irreducibly normative matter. That judgment can only be made by appeal to some norm—and *tian* is not a norm authority. Only a *dao* can play that role. This is the sound sense in which Daoism privileges *dao* over *tian*.

Conclusion: The Political Bite

The way in which relativism and skepticism are combined then schematically follows its pattern in the West. We are skeptical about our judgments because we appreciate the relativity of the grounds on which they depend. In the Chinese case, the judgments are the *bian* (distinction; dispute) and *shi-fei* (this-not this) assignments. The set of those judgments and the norms presupposed by them make up our rival *dao* (guides). Our experience of awakening or insight is typically accompanied by a sense of confidence relative to what we "knew" before. Given, however, the repetition of that kind of "waking" and our awareness that others (including those who disagree with us) have gone through a similar series of illuminations should give us epistemic pause. Many or most schemes of norms are the products of "emerging" from such insights stored up in our 成 *cheng* (prejudiced) 心 *xin* (heart-mind).

Political philosophers will find the rest familiar turf. Liberal justice addresses how we structure society's basic institutions (the constitution) in a way that is *neutral* among differing conceptions of the good life, different comprehensive guiding views (religious, moral, or philosophical), and ways of life. Liberal theorists argue that societies should adopt institutional structures that maximize freedom and allow, and even encourage, tolerance of different ways of life.

One attitude that supports this modern political theory is this kind of *mild* skepticism.[75] While not implying that we abandon or stop advocating our own conception of the good. it acknowledges that we have little confidence that we can rationally convince those with different comprehensive views starting *from their norms*. We cannot marshal arguments that should convince all others. At the same time, their arguments will not convince us. The skepticism does not rest on discovering anything *wrong* about our way of life.

The politically motivated doubt is weak in the way Zhuangzi's is. We doubt provability-to-the-other, but that gives us no reason to abandon our own way of life. Nor do we have reason to generate a gnawing, recurrent doubt about how we live. We need not keep ourselves only weakly committed to it or be on the verge of giving it up.[76] We need not cease caring about or advocating it. Nor need we passively accept, based on this weak skepticism, the elimination of our way of life by others. We do not face any obvious Hitler counter-example. When we reflect correctly on relativistic skepticism, we should risk no undermining of commitment other than agreeing to abandon prejudice, intolerance, and repression.

We cannot fully extrapolate this modern theory of justice to ancient China. Along with "sentences" and "truth," any neat counterpart of "justice" is hard to find in ancient Chinese political theory. Confucianism, Mohism, and Legalism typically do not address constitutional structure at any deeper level than Mozi's justification of the wise ruling elder. The chief task of political theory, in the time of Zhuangzi, was to identify the wise leader who would choose to impose a single way of life on everyone.

The contextual point of the *Zhuangzi's* skepticism is precisely that we should not attempt to do any such thing. No such person exists, and we should give up acting as if he/she does. *There are no sages* in the Confucian sense. Skepticism about ways of life *in the context of ancient Chinese political theory* is skepticism of government—an argument for anarchy.[77] The delivered conception of government in ancient China is intrinsically hostile to liberal neutrality and intolerant of diversity in ways of life (*dao*). If the purpose of government is to pick and impose a *dao* on the whole society, then, Zhuangzi correctly concludes, government has no value—"I will drag my tail in the mud."[78]

Notes

1. Benjamin Schwartz, *The World of Thought in Ancient China* (Cambridge: Harvard University Press, 1985), pp. 216–17.
2. One obvious example is the quest by Graham, Nivison, and Ivanhoe to identify Zhuangzi's "conversion experience." See A. C. Graham, *Chuang-tzu: the Seven Inner Chapters and Other Writings from the Book of Chuang-tzu* (London: Allen & Unwin, 1981); David Nivison, "Hsün Tzu and Chuang Tzu," in *Chinese Texts and Philosophical Contexts: Essays Dedicated to A. C. Graham*, ed. Henry Rosemont, Jr. (La Salle: Open Court, 1991), pp. 129–42; and Philip J. Ivanhoe, "Zhuangzi's Conversion Experience," *Journal of Chinese Religions*, 19 (1991), pp. 13–25. Ivanhoe traces the theme back to Maspero (Henri Maspero, *Le Taoisme et les religions chinoises* [Paris: Gallimard, 1971]).
3. These include Lisa Raphals, "Skeptical Strategies in *Zhuangzi* and Theaetetus," Paul Kjellberg and Philip J. Ivanhoe, eds., *Essays on Skepticism, Relativism and Ethics in the Zhuangzi* (Albany: State University of New York Press, 1996), pp. 26–49; Ewing Y. Chinn, "Zhuangzi and Relativistic Scepticism," *Asian Philosophy* 7:3 (1997), pp. 207–21, and "The Natural Equality of All Things," *Journal of Chinese Philosophy* 25:4 (1998), pp. 471–82; Paul Kjellberg, "Skepticism, Truth and the Good Life: A Comparison of Zhuangzi and Sextus Empiricus," *Philosophy East and West* 44:1 (1994), pp. 111–33, and

"Sextus Empiricus, Zhuangzi and Xunzi on 'Why be Skeptical,'" in Kjellberg and Ivanhoe, pp. 1–25; Bryan W. Van Norden, "Competing Interpretations of the Inner Chapters of the 'Zhuangzi,'" *Philosophy East and West* 46: 2 (1996), pp. 247–69; Philip J. Ivanhoe, "Skepticism, Skill and the Ineffable Tao," *Journal of the American Academy of Religion* 61:4 (1993), pp. 639–54, and "Was Zhuangzi a Relativist?" in Kjellberg and Ivanhoe, pp. 197–214; Robert Allinson, "On the Origin of the Relativistic Thesis for Interpretations of the Chuang-tzu," *Hanxue yanjiu* (1988), pp. 275–98 and "On the Question of Relativism in the Chuang-tzu," *Philosophy East and West* 39:1 (1989), pp. 13–26; and Eric Schwitzgebel, "Zhuangzi's Attitude toward Language and His Skepticism," in Kjellberg and Ivanhoe, pp. 68–96. Ivanhoe and Kjellberg's *Essays on Skepticism, Relativism and Ethics in the Zhuangzi* is a helpful collection of objections to skeptical or relativist interpretations. Schwitzgebel expresses in strongest language a common theme in these articles when he says that "although Zhuangzi argues for radical skepticism, he does not sincerely subscribe to it." Kjellberg and Ivanhoe propose the helpful notion of "therapeutic" skepticism (relativism) to describe the common interpretive theme that recurs throughout their edited collection.

4. Raphals argues that skepticism per se is incoherent, and Kjellberg and Ivanhoe appear to endorse that in their introduction as they say [strong] skepticism "is generally acknowledged as self-refuting since . . . we cannot know even that we know nothing" ("Skeptical Strategies in *Zhuangzi* and Theaetetus"). Stroud is widely acknowledged as having shown that past attempts to defeat the skeptic on purely analytic (logical or conceptual) grounds failed. Others (Van Norden, Chinn, and Ivanhoe) claim that the combination of relativism and skepticism is incoherent. Van Norden and Ivanhoe give definitions of relativism that virtually entail that relativism is self-refuting. Most of these accounts distinguish between what they consider "good" or "common-sense" versions and "radical," "strong," "extreme," or "philosophical" versions—to which they assign the self-refuting formulae.

5. I doubt that such themes are in any sense "dominant," but I will not pursue that question here.

6. W. V. O. Quine, *Word and Object* (Cambridge: MIT Press, 1960).

7. See Chad Hansen, *A Daoist Theory of Chinese Thought* (New York: Oxford University Press, 1992).

8. Some of my own interpretive prior formulations may have invited this mistake. In my *Language and Logic in Ancient China* (Ann Arbor: University of Michigan Press, 1983), I formulated humanity ambiguously as a principle preferring the more rationally coherent interpretation and compounded it by noting that coherence helps us explain a person's beliefs. However, I did broaden it in arguing that we should explain a sentence by showing its coherence in the context of a section, the section in a book, the book in the writer's work, the writer's work in a school's development, and the school in

a philosophical tradition. That formulation, though holistic in spirit, was unfortunate. It did not separate the semantic or language-interpretive principle from the epistemic one.

9. Grandy's formulation is that the imputed pattern of relations among beliefs, desires, and the world be as similar to our own as possible (Richard Grandy, "Reference Meaning and Belief," *Journal of Philosophy* [1973], pp. 439–52). We would want the pattern of relations to include those to our sensory apparatus, childhood training, and so on. What should be "like our own" would include the tendency to believe and utter incoherent things that we learn in Sunday school and the like. We can explain access to certain beliefs on perception grounds and others as natural or obvious inferences from other beliefs we attribute to them. Coherence thus becomes a part of the explanation of access to beliefs. See Simon Blackburn, *Spreading the Word: Groundings in the Philosophy of Language* (Oxford: Clarendon Press, 1984) for an extended account of the "virtues" appropriate for the principle of humanity.

10. Here I leave aside, of course, Quinian worries about the metaphysical shape our awareness of such animals takes. It is possible to argue that a community accesses cows as temporal slices or masses, but a theory that does not needs no elaborate justification.

11. See Wilfred Sellars, "Empiricism and the Philosophy of Mind," in *Science, Perception and Reality*, ed. Wilfred Sellars (London: Routledge & Kegan Paul, 1963).

12. The plausibility of a "story" may, of course, depend on what the interpreter or her audience takes to be true about these objects, human psychology, historical facts, and so forth. If one believes the Western "folk theory of ideas" or that God "contacts" humans regularly in some way and would similarly have "contacted" ancient Chinese thinkers, then a different story about the use of terms such as *belief*, or reference of 天 *tian* (nature, sky) would seem plausible to them. Arguments for innate conceptual structures or religious "instinct" in humans would work for those who accept them. The first interpreters in China assumed God's existence was rationally inescapable. This solved, for them, the problem of access to the same God as long as they credited Chinese philosophers with full rationality. (Thanks to Lauren Pfister, who makes this point about James Legge. See Lauren Pfister, "Clues to the Life and Academic Achievements of One of the Most Famous Nineteenth Century European Sinologists," *Journal of the Hong Kong British Royal Asiatic Society* 30 (1990), pp. 180–218, and "New Dimensions in the Study of the Works of James Legge (1815–1897): parts I and II," *Sino-Western Cultural Relations Journal* (1991), pp. 29–50.

13. I am drawing heavily here on Robert B. Brandom, *Making It Explicit* (Cambridge: Harvard University Press, 1994).

14. See Hansen, *A Daoist Theory of Chinese Thought.* It is commonplace among

sinologists to refer to words as "Confucian terms" or "Daoist terms," implying that anyone else who uses the terms "borrows" them, as if factions could own bits of Chinese language. Alternately, they speak of writers giving Confucian, Daoist, or Mohist "meanings" to the terms they borrow from each other.

15. "Competence" may include having relevant specialized knowledge, and most languages have a degree of linguistic division of labor. People who can read but do not know the field may not understand certain passages. Thus, the competent reader, on the present assumptions, should be philosophically informed. On other assumptions, he may need religious training, and so on. In principle, readers with different competencies could read the same essay differently. This leads to interpretive relativism: There could be more than one correct, historically authentic interpretation of a phrase.

16. I do not deny that the *Zhuangzi* might have been read differently by people without philosophical training in ancient China, just as it is today. If there was a sect of Huang-Lao worship, it may well have read this text in ways that lacked philosophical insight and subtlety. That is an insufficient reason for us to adopt such norms in our interpretation.

17. I hope the "informed-audience" focus will deter interpreters from the interpretive assertion I call "psychic-identification." "Although Zhuangzi says X, he really wants us to believe Y." Such judgments should follow from a plausible account of illocutionary force, not from independent access to Zhuangzi's mind.

18. Particularly the "Qiwulun." I need not deny that there is less evidence of such contact in other parts of the book. I accept the current textual theories of multiple authorship of this text. I would claim, however, that much of the rest of the book could have been read in ways consistent with the arguments in "Qiwulun" by informed philosophers. Few, if any, of them force a mystical or religious reading on us.

19. Sinologists chuckle at us when they suspect that philosophically inclined interpreters are more interested in what Zhuangzi *should* have said than what he did say. Our point here is more subtle than they think—having said what he did say, we explain its meaning by theorizing about what else he should accept in virtue of having said it—what saying it commits him to given the meaning norms of ancient Chinese language. We do not make the judgment simply by imposing our view of what is true.

20. See John Rawls, *Political Liberalism* (New York: Columbia University Press, 1993), and *A Theory of Justice* (Cambridge: Harvard University Press, 1971), respectively.

21. I note here the tendency in Confucius's *Analects* to refer to "ritual" and "music" together as models of action guidance. The implicit emphasis on aesthetic features of action judgment and its relation to guidance is a common theme in discussions of Confucius; see, for example, Roger Ames

and David Hall, *Thinking through Confucius* (Albany: State University of New York Press, 1987); and Robert Eno, *The Confucian Creation of Heaven* (Albany: State University of New York Press, 1990).

22. These different aspects of *dao* account for the alleged change of meaning that tradition associates with Daoism. Shen Dao 慎到 seems to have envisioned the actual course of action of the entire world and called that "The Great Dao." He then denied that it is normative; even a clod of earth cannot miss it! I have questioned the assumption that other alleged Daoists follow him in talking this way. Most seem to retain a normative use of the term.

23. For details, see the chapter on Mozi in my *Daoist Theory of Chinese Thought*, especially pages 115–21 and 124–28.

24. Mozi, "Against Aggressive Warfare" (17); Harvard-Yenching 28/17/11–12.

25. Chapter 33 "Tianxia" (The Social World) is found in the "miscellaneous" chapters. It has a markedly more political orientation than most of the inner chapter texts in which we find clear statements of skepticism and relativism.

26. See note 22.

27. They sometimes talked about compound terms, modification, and the effect on 説 *shuo* (explanation) and *dao* (discourse). In my view, the closest they came to sentential inference was in the Mohist "Xiao qu." See Chad Hansen, *Language and Logic in Ancient China*; for a contrary view, see A. C. Graham, *Later Mohist Logic, Ethics and Science* (Hong Kong and London: Chinese University Press, 1978).

28. This is what I take to be the correct analysis of the 以 ... 為 ... pattern in classical Chinese and the related use of one-place predicates as transitive verbs—to "white" something is to treat it as "white" in attitude and action. See my more complete analysis in Hansen, *A Daoist Theory of Chinese Thought*.

29. There are sentential contexts in ancient Chinese. Visual verbs (*see, observe*, etc.) and speaking verbs (*says, quotes*, etc.) introduce sentences.

30. I propose to detach mysticism from monism. Mysticism is a combination of an epistemological and a linguistic thesis. Mystics typically allege that they have found a special epistemological access to some incommunicable content. Most assume the content is monist, but that is not *entailed* by either the epistemic or the linguistic claims.

31. I reject mysticism while embracing a form of monism. The *Zhuangzi* expresses skepticism about its own *monistic* conception of the real world.

32. Noumenon-phenomenon parallels are more frequently alleged. I am skeptical of these as well, and align myself with the antidualist analysis of Chinese thought, for example, Ames and Hall, *Thinking through Confucius*.

33. This is a familiar illustration of chaos theory as applied to meteorology.

34. "Zhi le," ZZJS 614–15; HY 46/18/15–19.

35. I say only "rough" counterparts because I see little hint of the kinds of logical-semantic and grammatical considerations that inspired Parmenides and in turn Plato and his successors among Western mystics and idealists.

36. I am thinking of the "ten theses" quoted in the *Zhuangzi* "Tianxia" history of philosophy. The final one is "love all thing-kinds pervasively; the cosmos is one *ti* (body)" (氾愛萬物，天地一體也) ZZJS 1102; HY 93/33/73–74. Hui Shi's reasoning seems to rest on the relativist analysis of terms and the illegitimate inference from the premise that our distinctions between things are relative to our perspective to a conclusion that there are no distinctions in reality. See my discussion in Hansen, *A Daoist Theory of Chinese Thought*, pp. 269–72.

37. "Qiwulun," ZZJS 79; HY 5/2/51–54; Graham 56.

38. In a sense, Zhuangzi would not be skeptical about contact knowledge ("knowing of"). His skepticism applies to how we distinguish, classify and react to it but not that it is there and that we are in contact with it in the course of our thinking and acting.

39. I owe my classifications here to Alvin Goldman, *Epistemology and Cognition* (Cambridge: Harvard University Press, 1986). He is, of course, not responsible for my adaptation and application of them to the quite different context of Chinese thought.

40. In this division, I follow the helpful models of Raphals, Kjellberg, and Ivanhoe but with a more complex classification. My main reservation about their approach apart from the difference in treating the theme (see below), is that they tend to blur *scope* and *strength* into a single classification like "extreme" or "radical" skepticism.

41. "Qiwulun," ZZJS 91–92; HY 6/2/64–66.

42. The most prominent examples, I think, are Raphals ("Skeptical Strategies in *Zhuangzi* and Theaetetus"), who distinguishes between skeptical recommendations, skeptical doctrines, and skeptical methods; and Kjellberg ("Skepticism, Truth and the Good Life" and "Sextus Empiricus, Zhuangzi and Xunzi"). They both draw on the ancient Greek form of skepticism.

43. A theoretical discussion is in the "Qiwulun" chapter. ZZJS 66–70; HY 4–5/2/32–38. Graham treats 因 *yin* (because) as "criterion," which indeed captures one side of the ambiguity. The "shadow" passage also has a dependency theme and uses 待 *dai* (depend). ZZJS 110–11; HY 7/2/92–94.

44. "Qiwulun," ZZJS 56; HY 4/2/22.

45. "Against Fatalism," *Mozi*.

46. The *Mozi* discussions typically assume that all three standards support their conclusions.

47. ZZJS 272; HY 18/6/72–73.

48. Ivanhoe may have scope in mind when he gives his account of four "forms" of skepticism. See his "Skepticism, Skill, and the Ineffable Tao."

49. Yearley discusses this feature of skepticism in the *Zhuangzi* using the familiar story of the lucky-unlucky horse; see Lee Yearley, "Zhuangzi's Understanding of Skillfulness and the Ultimate Spiritual State," in *Essays on Skepticism, Relativism and Ethics in the Zhuangzi*, ed. Kjellberg and Ivanhoe, pp. 127–51.

50. "Shan mu," ZZJS 695; HY 54/20/61–4. Other examples include the story of Lin Hui discarding a priceless treasure to carry his infant child to safety ("Shan mu," ZZJS 685; HY 53/20/38–43), Zhuangzi's exposition of the "use of the useless" to Huizi in connection with the "useless" ailanthus tree ("Xiaoyaoyou," ZZJS 39–40; HY 3/1/42–47) and the overgrown gourd ("Xiaoyaoyou," ZZJS 36–37; HY 2–3/1/35–42), and the story about the butterfly dream (see below).

51. This comes from the story of Lady Li, who, after discovering the comforts of the palace after being taken captive to Jin, came to "wonder why she had ever wept." "Qiwulun," ZZJS 103; HY 6/2/78–81.

52. Species-based doubt expands on the theme. Clearly, the extinction of humans would to threatened species appear not to be such a bad thing: "Mao Qiang and Lady Li were beautiful in the eyes of men; but when the fish saw them they plunged deep, when the birds saw them they flew high, when the deer saw them they broke into a run. Which of these four knows what is truly beautiful in the world? In my judgment the principles of Goodwill and Duty, the paths of 'That's it, that's not,' are inextricably confused; how could I know how to discriminate between them?" Graham 58; "Qiwulun," ZZJS 93; HY 6/2/69–70.

53. See "Qiwulun," ZZJS 112; HY 7/2/94–96.

54. This is not what Goldman calls "iterative skepticism," which rests on a requirement that to know, one must know that she knows. This passage, however, does not put such a requirement on knowledge. It implicitly allows that we might know something without knowing that we know it. It is still a weak version, therefore, but for a different reason. It is technically not denying that we have knowledge. It suggests only that our having knowledge is "accidental" from our present perspective. The accidental element is not our coming to believe X, but our having acquired one of several available conceptions of knowledge. We might have been initiated into the right one, for all we know.

55. See, for example, the conversation between Nie Que 齧缺 and Wang Ni 王倪 in "Qiwulun"; ZZJS 91–97; HY 6/2/64–73.

56. Confucius was, famously, the most modest of the triumvirate of classical Confucians. Mencius and Xunzi both developed extended accounts of how perspective-transcending knowledge was available to well-cultivated Confucians. This informs their shared view that ordinary people can become sages and their authoritarian political stance that those who have should rule the rest of us.

57. In any case, the interpretative claim is not trivial because the dominant rival interpretation is that Zhuangzi *himself* claims "mystical" epistemic access to perfect knowledge. Examples include Cook (Scott Cook, "Zhuang Zi and his Carving of the Confucian Ox," *Philosophy East and West* 47:4, pp. 521–54), following Eno ("Cook Ding's Dao and the Limits of Philosophy," in Kjellberg and Ivanhoe, pp. 127–51);Van Norden ("Competing Interpretations of the Inner Chapters"), who credits Ivanhoe ("Skepticism, Skill and the Ineffable Tao"); and Yearley ("Zhuangzi's Understanding of Skillfulness and the Ultimate Spiritual State"). I deny that a competent philosopher among Zhuangzi's contemporaries would be justified in using supernaturalism to state the implications of such stories. Both Eno and Cook also express reservations about supernatural implications.

58. Graham 55; "Qiwulun," ZZJS 75; HY 5/2/46–47.

59. "Qiwulun," ZZJS 83; HY 5/2/57–58.

60. Graham 51; "Qiwulun," ZZJS 56; HY 4/2/20–22.

61. The stories seldom illustrate reconversion to one's original position. That is not because the new perspective is absolutely better. We simply adopt a new perspective, and from it we judge the old one wrong.

62. What is also striking about the narrative context of such references in the "Qiwulun" at least is that they all seem to be introduced by a "student" question following directly on some skeptical denial of the possibility of perfection. The Zenlike response of the "Qiwulun" invites him to reflect on the question: "how could you possibly recognize 'perfect' if you saw it?"

63. Graham's translation captures the point nicely: "To recognize as complete or flawed is to have as model the Zhao when they play the zither; to recognize as neither complete nor flawed is to have as a model the Zhao when they don't play the zither." Graham 54; "Qiwulun"; ZZJS 74; HY 5/2/43.

64. "Qiwulun," ZZJS 96; HY 6/2/72. The "Dazongshi" chapter has many examples of these themes.

65. There is more, for example, in the *Xunzi* "Rectifying Names" chapter, where we find a sketchy and troublesome account of the roles of the sense organs and the *xin* 心 (heart-mind). Notice that even if interpreted as motivating sense skepticism (see my denial in Hansen, *A Daoist Theory of Chinese Thought*), passages such as the butterfly dream do not work like appeals to illusion to show the fallibility of the senses.

66. Especially the "Xinshu" (chs. 36–37) and "Nei ye" (ch. 49) of the *Guanzi* and the more "absolutist" sections of the *Xunzi*, such as "Dispelling Obsessions" (ch. 21).

67. Mencius implied that all human hearts are born with a naturally accurate inclination to *shi-fei* (this-not this). This formulation is deliberately ambiguous. See my explanation in Hansen, *A Daoist Theory of Chinese Thought*.

68. Some critics object to the extreme toleration implied by this approach. I am not sure it validly implies toleration of, say Hitler, but it is true that the

Zhuangzi does not appear to address (or even worry about) such examples of human evil.

69. See Ivanhoe ("Was Zhuangzi a Relativist?" p. 198), Van Norden ("Competing Interpretations of the Inner Chapters"), and Chinn ("Zhuangzi and Relativistic Scepticism," p. 209). Others take the traditional reading of Daoism to entail that everything is right; see Eno, "Cook Ding's Dao and the Limits of Philosophy," p. 133.

70. We see a similar pattern in Western skepticism where skepticism of the senses is motivated by examples of the relativity of sense perception.

71. David Wong offers a closely related argument deriving norms of equal respect more directly from the relativism implicit in Daoism (David Wong, "Taoism and the Problem of Equal Respect," *Journal of Chinese Philosophy* 11 [1984], pp. 165–83). I agree with Barry (Brian Barry, *Justice as Impartiality* [New York: Oxford University Press, 1995]) that we need some skepticism to finally justify neutrality among ways of life in political matters, but I agree with Wong that the "thought experiments" in Daoism where we learn to view things from the other's point of view do help motivate treating others as equals when we disagree fundamentally with their comprehensive views.

72. "Qiwulun," ZZJS 63; HY 4/2/25.

73. Van Norden ("Competing Interpretations of the Inner Chapters," pp. 249–50) confuses relativism and subjectivism in his formulations.

74. "Qiwulun," ZZJS 107; HY 7/2/84–90.

75. See Barry, *Justice as Impartiality*. Chinn ("Zhuangzi and Relativistic Scepticism" and "The Natural Equality of All Things") notices this implication.

76. I have been stimulated by reading David Wong's "Zhuangzi on the Dilemma of Value Pluralism" (forthcoming) concerning the problem of maintaining our moral balance when cognizant of the kind of relativism to which Zhuangzi points. He powerfully and evocatively presents what he calls "the problem of commitment." In effect, I am suggesting here that the problem is an illusion that comes from confusing Zhuangzi's relativistic skepticism with a positive undermining of our beliefs about our way of life (i.e., by positively showing something wrong with them or positively demonstrating the superiority of something else).

77. Implicitly, here, I agree with Wong ("Taoism and the Problem of Equal Respect"; see note 71) that the Daoists' justification of anarchy is a reflection of their weakness as political philosophers. They did not envision any structural alternative to Confucian authoritarianism.

78. Arguably, Xunzi's response in his "Rectifying Names" (ch. 22) is equally forced on him. If anarchy is intolerable, as most Confucians feel, then the ruler must outlaw philosophy—because it leads to relativism and skepticism of the purpose of government.

6

Aporetics Ethics in the *Zhuangzi*

DAN LUSTHAUS

Hence would you say:
   "Now, Right is my master (shi shi 師是), so that I may be without wrong" or "Control is my master, so that I may be without disorder?"
   If that's right (shi 是), then you are not yet clear (ming 明) on the patterns (li 理) of Heaven and Earth, or the basic-drives (qing 情) of the 10,000 things.

   Whether strolling or limping, bent over or stretched out, [the one who knows inhabits] the basic between reverting-contraries and yet discourses on the extremes (fan-yao er yu ji 反要而語極)

—"Qiushui," *Zhuangzi*

Zhuangzi is commonly mislabeled a skeptic and an enemy of reason. Though he is often portrayed in the secondary literature as antilogical and antithetical to rational enterprises, the fact is that amid his startling and complex stories, many rational arguments occur. These arguments frequently employ a careful logical structure and are often logically compelling. Though his arguments do sometimes incorporate skeptical elements, these skeptical moments are either framed in irony or they mark transitional phases that are invariably superseded by either fresh logical arguments or, most often, exhortations to adopt certain attitudes or orientations. These prescriptive exhortations are invariably ethical, since they recommend how one should look and act henceforth. Far from his being a skeptic or mere relativist, I will argue that Zhuangzi is both an epistemic ethicist and a proclaimer of certain unavoidable limits. Thus it becomes highly reductionistic—and perhaps an outright falsehood—to characterize Zhuangzi either as a skeptic or a mere relativist.[1]

Zhuangzi's[2] approach to ethics is quite intriguing. While he rejects
the sort of norms and invariant criteria that his contemporaries—such as
Mohists and Confucians—adopted as stable foundations for their ethical
and political systems, in their place Zhuangzi offers an aporetic stance
that (1) relativizes extremes (preventing them from becoming invariant standards) and (2) then locates the limits of epistemological aporia
in order to develop an ethical orientation *using these aporetic limits as its
foundation*. One acts on the basis of what one does not know, what one
cannot control, what one cannot contain, rather than according to fixed
rules, determinate principles, or clear imperatives. It is a rare move in
the history of philosophy,[3] but one that is currently being attempted
again—this time by French thinkers (primarily Derrida and Lyotard). It
might be interesting to compare their efforts with Zhuangzi's, but that is
beyond the scope of the present chapter.[4]

In this chapter several passages from the two most popular and important chapters of the *Zhuangzi*, "Qiushui" (Autumn Floods; chapter 17)
and "Qiwulun" (Discourse on leveling things; chapter 2), will be examined. Zhuangzi's butterfly dream, possibly the most famous passage in the
text, will be examined to illustrate in what ways Zhuangzi uses skepticism
without being a skeptic. I first discuss the sense of "skepticism" being assumed here, with an eye to distinguishing between *skepticism* and *critical
thinking*. It is my contention that Zhuangzi is more justly approximated by
the latter label than by the former. The butterfly dream is widely cited as a
prime example of skeptical thinking; I will attempt to demonstrate that it
is not. Elsewhere I have provided a detailed analysis of the full argument of
the "Qiushui" chapter, the longest sustained argument in the entire work.[5]
The present chapter will reexamine the parts of that argument in which
Zhuangzi uses aporetic limits as the touchstone of his ethical philosophy.
Two models in particular, developed in that analysis, have great bearing
on the present topic. These models, which I have labeled the "Temporality Knowledge" model and the "Perspectival" model, are interesting for
another reason as well: they appear to imply a chart, similar in style to the
magic number charts popular in China since ancient times.[6] To further
illustrate that such charts can be found elsewhere in the text, including
in the Inner Chapters (the section of the text to which the attribution
of authorship to Zhuangzi is least challenged), I will also present another
version from the "Qiwulun" chapter. The model from "Qiwulun," which
Zhuangzi labels the "Eight Virtues," also illustrates Zhuangzi's approach
to ethics.

What Is *Not* Skepticism: Transforming the Skeptical Reading of the Butterfly Dream

A thoroughgoing skeptic would be one who rejects the very possibility of any sort of valid claim. However, resisting *certain* knowledge claims while accepting others is *not* skepticism, but rather *critical thinking*. This is especially the case when (1) cogent and reasonable arguments are being offered for rejecting resistible claims, that is, one demonstrates that it is reasonable to reject such claims while unreasonable to accept them, coinciding with (2) affirmative, positive claims being made in their stead. After all, the very essence of logic is the dyad acceptance/rejection, that is, affirming/denying, or as Frege put it, the referent (*Bedeutung*) of any proposition is "true" or "false."

For instance, medieval Indian philosophers entertained six or more *pramāṇas*, that is, valid means of knowledge, including perception, inference, scriptural testimony, analogy, and negation. When the fifth-century Indian Buddhist logician Dignāga rejected *śabda-pramāṇa* (scripture and testimony) as a valid means of knowledge, while accepting both perception and inference as valid, he was not a skeptic, no matter what form his arguments for such a rejection assume, even if they might bear some stylistic similarities to Greek skeptical arguments, especially if his positions remain consistent with each other. For Dignāga, scripture does not produce knowledge independent of perception or inference, since its claims can only be verified if proven empirically or substantiated by inferences. Since he accepts some means of knowledge as valid, he is not a skeptic simply because he rejects *some* other means of knowledge that others may deem acceptable.[7] Honest admission of the limits of one's knowledge—if accompanied by firm claims to some sort of knowledge (and Zhuangzi never says that he does not know anything)—*should not be characterized as skepticism*, even if it incorporates argumentative modes reminiscent of the classic skeptical tropes and modes along the way.

A skeptic not only questions (a certain type of) knowledge and even the possibility of such knowledge, but *concludes* that such knowledge is impossible, or indeterminable (which is a soft form of impossibility). In other words, a skeptic refuses to go beyond the impossibility or indeterminability of a knowledge claim. The skeptic's thinking concludes here. If pressed for a further conclusion, the skeptic must say not only that s/he does not know, but that X is unknowable (skeptics are no less prone to universalize their positions than others are). The more sophisticated the skeptic, the more the very criteria through which knowledge is generated will become problematized under his or her skeptical gaze.

But to pass through this open, indeterminate, inconclusive conclusion is to pass beyond skepticism. To reach any conclusion other than the impossibility of knowing *X* (in hard or soft forms) is to no longer be a skeptic. A skeptic *concludes* skeptically; one who concludes elsewhere is not a skeptic.

Zhuangzi is a *critical thinker* who uses skeptical rhetoric as a transitional phase in his arguments. Zhuangzi makes numerous claims and employs a variety of strategies to validate or authenticate them. His skeptical moments are correctly identified by Chad Hansen as "skepticism of evaluative distinctions made in prescriptive discourse."[8] However, this skeptical phase is not Zhuangzi's final move or ultimate position but part of a critical exploration of the foundations of "evaluative distinctions." The skepticism gives way to Zhuangzi's own "prescriptive discourse," a discourse whose prescriptive nature is frequently camouflaged in other sorts of rhetorical modes and tropes.

A prime example of this is the famous butterfly story at the end of the "Qiwulun" chapter. It is frequently offered as an example of a skeptic who cannot tell the difference between the "real" world and a dream world. The analysis of this story that follows is inspired by Kuang-ming Wu, who also insisted that the butterfly story remains misunderstood whenever we stop reading after the third sentence.[9] I have numbered the sentences for easy referral; the story in full reads as follows:

1. Previously, Zhuang Zhou dreamt he had become a carefree butterfly, a happily flittering butterfly, who himself experienced such a fit[10] between his intents and his surroundings (*yu* 與),[11] that he didn't know he was [Zhuang] Zhou.

2. Suddenly he awoke and was unmistakably, undeniably[12] Zhou.

3. He didn't know if he was Zhou who had dreamt he had been a carefree butterfly (*yu*), or a carefree butterfly dreaming that he had become Zhou (*yu*).

4. [Between] Zhou and (*yu*) the carefree butterfly there must (*bi* 必) be a distinction!

5. This is called "the transformation of things."[13]

Sentences 1 and 2 create a dissonance resulting in the skepticism of sentence 3. But the story does not end there. Sentence 4 begins to reason through the skepticism, utilizing the notion of logical (or quasilogical) necessity (*bi*) to establish and acknowledge real differences. The fifth sentence pronounces the conclusion, namely, shifting from dream to waking is an example of "transformation." Skepticism is a *passing phase* in this passage, used to arrive at the conclusion, which, for Zhuangzi, is the important point. This may be clearer if we convert the sentences into symbols (losing the wordplays but highlighting the logical relations).[14] X=butterfly; Y=Zhuang Zhou:

1. $X (-Y)$.

2. $(-X) Y$.

3. $(X \rightarrow Y) + (Y \rightarrow X) = -X-Y$

4. $X + Y$ (but $X \neq Y$)

5. $A \rightarrow B \rightarrow C \ldots$

Sentence 1 describes a situation in which a butterfly becomes so enthralled with his activity that he forgets he is Zhuangzi dreaming. Thus, experientially, the butterfly is present, and Zhuangzi is absent. In 2, the inverse is the case: Zhuangzi is unmistakably present, and the butterfly has momentarily disappeared. In 3, due to memory, a dilemma arises. For the question to arise Zhuangzi must remember what he was just dreaming; he must be aware of something that is no longer the case (viz., the butterfly in the dream). The dilemma arises from an apparent undecidability: If Zhuangzi can dream he is a butterfly such that the butterfly believes he is a butterfly with no awareness of Zhuangzi, why cannot that butterfly now be dreaming he is Zhuangzi such that Zhuangzi is unaware he is really a dream of the butterfly? How can one know which is true, which is a dream, and which is not? Zhuangzi supplies several implicit answers that can easily be made explicit.

First, the very first sentence states explicitly that it is Zhuangzi who is dreaming he has become a butterfly. The Zhuangzi of sentence 3 may be confused, but Zhuangzi the storyteller is not. *Contextually* Zhuangzi knows which is which. Second, the problem arises from a trick of memory, something not insignificant given Zhuangzi's emphasis on achieving forgetfulness (*wang* 忘). The butterfly forgot he is Zhuangzi, but Zhuangzi has not forgotten the butterfly. This reminds us that the parity presupposed in the dilemma is a false parity. And yet the butterfly *is* Zhuangzi in more than one sense. The first chapter of the text, "Xiaoyaoyou" (Free and easy meandering), extols a carefree attitude that always finds a way to enjoy circumstances, precisely the ideal the butterfly embodies. Some have taken that attitude to be the essence of Zhuangzi's philosophy. Unfortunately, Zhuangzi shows us here that that philosophy, as usually understood, is inadequate, or more bluntly put, it is a *dream*. The butterfly happily losing him-self (i.e., Zhuang Zhou) in his surroundings—an apt depiction of Zhuangzi's "carefree, meandering sage"—does not override or prevent Zhuangzi from waking up as Zhuangzi. Had he forgotten the dream on awakening, the dilemma, with its associated anxiety and doubt, would not have arisen.

Second, since the butterfly felt assured that it was indeed a butter-fly[15] without any awareness of Zhuangzi, Zhuangzi's own certainty about his genuine self-existence may be no more than a vertiginous mirror reflecting the same delusion. Of course, this sense of mirroring or parity between the two options is only an illusion, not least because the butterfly was entirely unaware of Zhuangzi, while Zhuangzi is entertaining this entertaining doubt precisely because he *is* aware of the butterfly. It is a question only he, not the butterfly, could raise and a question that can be raised only *after* having awoken, though, obviously without having fully separated from (i.e., forgotten) the prior dream state. Like many of us who at times have been caught in the transition from dream to waking during the immediate moments following our waking up, unsure whether the dream was real or not, Zhuangzi doubts his transitional waking doubt, a doubt that itself serves as a signpost for the transition. To blithely go through such transitions, oblivious to the transformation, would be to merely move from one dream to another. That he notices the transition and finds it perplexing is the sign that Zhuangzi is truly awakening.

The doubt of sentence 3 follows—logically as well as chronologi-cally—from the overdetermined certainty ("unmistakably, undeniably") of sentence 2. One's natural *non*skeptical *tendency* is to want to solve the dilemma by affirming 2 and denying the "butterfly as dreamer."[16] That tendency is precisely what Zhuangzi is trying to disrupt. What we think from the natural naïve viewpoint appears, from that perspective and by definition, to be indubitable. Waking requires waking from careless inat-tention and the naïve perspective.

The apparent dilemma of sentence 3 poses itself as a problem of mutual exclusion. If it is Zhuangzi who dreamt he was a butterfly, then it cannot be a butterfly who is dreaming he is Zhuangzi, and vice versa. If both possibilities are given equal weight and plausibility, then *neither* can be the case, at least not at the same time. So the temptation is to take sides, holding one option as the right option while rejecting the alterna-tive. The story, and much of the rest of Zhuangzi's text, is designed to discourage us from falling to that temptation. The options in sentence 3 are not equal or "equalized"—despite what translators and commentators commonly assert when "translating" the title of the second chapter, "*qi wu lun* 齊物論" (e.g., Discussion on making all things equal—Watson). The penultimate sentence of this chapter insists that between these two things, Zhuangzi and the butterfly (or each dreaming it is the other), there must certainly (*bi*) be a distinction. The point for Zhuangzi is not which of the two to choose as right. Since a case can be made for either, we will eternally be fighting whoever takes the other side. Nor are they the same thing because as formulated in sentence 3, they are mutually exclusive. The dilemma has arisen because of an undecidability, an aporia, between 1 and 2, i.e., between "Zhuangzi as dreamer" (X^1) excluding "butterfly as dreamer" (Y^1), and Y^1 excluding X^1. Positing "both X^1 and Y^1" is not a solution, however, since, by definition, they are mutually exclusive and thus incommensurate and incompatible. "Neither X^1 nor Y^1" is a rhetorical way of highlighting the dilemma but is neither a solution nor an avoidance of the problem, because Zhuangzi *has had* and *continues to have* experiences while waking or dreaming. How these different experiential contexts *relate* to each other is the question.

The question is not one of presence, since clearly while the question is being asked and considered, the butterfly is not present except perhaps as a memory of the questioner who himself is unmistakably present. It is a question about *priority*, that is, which is prior to which, Zhuangzi or the butterfly? Which has primacy? Primacy confers value and status. So the question is one of relative value, and it is the grasping after those values—values constructed by insisting on one part of a dyad while rejecting its contrary—that compels one to produce and confront the dilemma.

For Zhuangzi, the resolution comes by dropping the issue of primacy and instead facing the import of the experience itself. The "transformation of things" is one of his pivotal notions. Transformation, for Zhuangzi, means a change of context, such that the organizing criteria of one *Lebenswelt* are replaced in a subsequent *Lebenswelt* by new criteria. Zhuangzi becomes (*wei* 為) a butterfly, and a butterfly lives in and enjoys its *Lebenswelt*. The butterfly in his world was one Lived-world, one which arose through a transformation of Zhuangzi, a transformation from waking to dreaming. It was not irreversible, but some transformations (such as death) are. The transformation from dreaming to waking ironically brings only momentary clarity. For it is when awake that the dilemma arises. The relation between Zhuangzi and butterfly is not simply one of priority—at least not for Zhuangzi. Rather it is one of succession, in which the entire phenomenological horizon has radically shifted and will continue to shift.

Awakening is a transformation of Lived-worlds, one which may or may not carry memories of previous Lived-worlds. Each Lived-world is a situation framed by its own horizon. Situations carry their own rules—as situations change, new rules shape them. Transformation involves radical novelty, such that it is not that a self-same object goes from situation^a to situation^b, but that person^a in situation^a becomes something else (butterfly, natural phenomenon, etc.) in situation^b. The essence of the story is therefore beautifully captured by the image of the butterfly, which goes through a total life change when transforming from a caterpillar. This story is more about transformation than it is about dreams or doubts or primacies. Zhuangzi goes through five "transformations" as "himself" during the story, in at least one of which he is literally present in name only:

1. He is a dreamer absent from his own dream, i.e., an alter ego;

2. a suddenly awakened man fully imbued with the certainty of his own self-presence;

3. a doubter unsure of the line between waking and dreaming, self-presence and memory;

4. a rational, phenomenological discriminator; and finally

5. a voice disappearing into its own pronouncement.

The butterfly is *not* Zhuangzi, any more than Zhuangzi is really the butterfly. That despite the nontransference of identity from one transformation to another, nonetheless, the butterfly possesses a certain recognizable Zhuangzian personality—in fact it exemplifies it—makes the story that much more poignant. The fact that the butterfly seems to embody all the idealized values that readers attribute to Zhuangzi (carefree meandering, "fitting" circumstances, forgetfulness, etc.) and yet is only a transient dream (butterflies also represent the ephemeral), one from which Zhuangzi awakens only to be gripped by doubt, should perhaps caution us not to idealize those values more than did Zhuangzi himself. This story treats the "philosophy" usually attributed to Zhuangzi with deep irony.

For Zhuangzi transformation may be envisioned on major or minor scales. Small situation shifts might include the different ways one feels, thinks, behaves, and so on while in a classroom versus visiting one's parents versus visiting one's grandchildren versus partying with friends, etc. In each situation we are different people, shaped by the shifting horizons and context. The *Zhuangzi* text is replete with accounts of major shifts in *Lebenswelt*, such as the transformation from dream to waking, life to death, the recognition by Lady Li that her existence after being abducted is an improvement over her pre-abducted life,[17] and so on. The book begins with the giant Kun fish transforming into the giant Peng bird, and the scene itself soon shifts to the envious eyes of tiny onlookers disparaging the giant. These are all transformative shifts.

Then there is Master Yu in the "Dazongshi" chapter, who undergoes another sort of transformation:

> The Creator is making me all crookedy like this! My back sticks up like a hunchback and my vital organs are on top of me. My chin is hidden in my navel, my shoulders are up above my head, and my pigtail points at the sky. It must be some dislocation of the *yin* and *yang* . . . If the process continues, perhaps in time he'll transform my left arm into a rooster. In that case I'll keep watch on the night. Or perhaps in time he'll transform my right arm into a crossbow pellet and I'll shoot down an owl for roasting. Or perhaps in time he'll transform my buttocks into cartwheels. Then, with my spirit for a horse, I'll climb up and go for a ride. What need will I ever have for a carriage again?[18]

So in the butterfly dream we see skepticism used as a passing phase. The story goes through an aporia to a definitive (*bi*) distinction that is itself open-ended. One cannot predict the transformations to come. Zhuangzi makes this even more explicit in another Inner Chapters account of transformation as "Dream shifting:"

> Meng-sun does not know what he depended on to be born, does not know what he will depend on to die, does not know how to be nearer to the time before than the time after. If in transforming he has become one thing instead of another, is it required that what he does not know terminated in being transformed? Besides, at the stage of being transformed how would he know about the untransformed? At the stage of being untransformed, how would he know about the transformed? Is it just that you and I are the ones who have not yet begun to wake from our dream?
>
> But in his case, though something may startle his body, it won't injure his mind; he has abodes for no longer than a morning but no true death. It's just that Meng-sun has come awake . . . What's more, we go around telling each other, I do this, I do that—but how do we know this "I" we talk about has any "I" to it?
>
> You dream that you are a bird and fly away in the sky, dream that you are a fish and plunge into the deep. There's no telling whether the man who speaks now is the waker or the dreamer. Rather than trying to make

things "fit," laugh: rather than acknowledge them with your laughter, settle [things].[19] Peacefully settle [things] and let go of [your anxiety about] transformation; then you will enter into the One Vacant Sky.[20]

Here again we see a transition, or transformation (I have omitted the pre-aporetic statements of this passage in the interest of space) through the aporetic toward a more definitive conclusion, in this case Zhuangzi's own prescriptive discourse. Here we are advised how to come to terms with transformation. The butterfly story only implied these conclusions in that one assumes that the anxiety caused by the uncertainty of sentence 3 dissipated with sentence 5. The certainty of sentence 2 that was lost in sentence 3 returns with sentence 4's "necessary distinction." The naïve one-sided certainty of 2 is replaced by balanced, phenomenological reasoning, reasoning that produces a calm assuredness. Space limitations preclude further citing of these sorts of stories, but this structure—statements opening to an aporetic dilemma leading to a resolution that is either declarative or prescriptive—permeates the *Zhuangzi*.

Dissipating the Overflow: Horizons of Experience

The "Qiushui" chapter (Autumn floods)[21] begins with a conversation between the Lord of the Yellow River and Ruo, God of the North Sea. Due to the rising and convergence of the "one hundred streams" that flow into the Yellow River during the autumn floods, the River overflows and surges with pride and exhilaration (=flood) until it meets the Sea, whose vast expanse awes and humbles it. No matter how great the River becomes, the Sea is always greater. The River is made to feel larger or smaller depending on the fluctuations of external circumstances (seasonal effects on its tributaries), but the Sea remains undisturbed by such fluctuations. During floods the Sea does not fill up; during droughts it does not empty. Though the River swells with pride due to temporary gains, the Sea takes no pride in its own greatness, recognizing that the world is still greater than it. The Sea acts as a humbling context for the River, and, in turn, the world acts as a humbling context for the Sea. The River comes to this realization after encountering the Sea, while the Sea had already understood and accepted its own place in the larger sphere of things.

The second sentence of this chapter is itself quite interesting and deserving of comment. Describing the extent of the River's flooding it says, "Its current was greatly swollen (*da* 大), so that across its channel from bank to bank one could not distinguish an ox from a horse."[22] This enlargement of the River, by which he en-larges (*da*) himself and his importance in his own eyes, reflects that rivers are "above" sea level and thus flow down into it. The River's rapidly *rising* self-esteem propels him *downward* toward the level and leveling Sea. A mysticism that provokes the arrogant self-elevation that is unable to distinguish one side from another must necessarily plummet downward from its exhilarating, rushing heights, down into the humility of a "sea" that lies below it, and, as we shall see, a sea that understands itself and its relation to things precisely because it is able to make distinctions.

Zhuangzi is ridiculing the sort of mysticism that obscures oppositional distinctions, filling the space between opposing sides by thinking that what is on one side cannot or should not be clearly distinguished from what is on the other. We are warned at the beginning that the point of this exercise is not to think ourselves great if we fail to make distinctions. Zhuangzi is not advocating a cheap form of "nondualism," nor does he valorize fuzzy thinking. Rather, he leads the reader through a series of crucial, finely cut distinctions, while constantly reminding us to question the grounding standards from which they issue, especially if we construe such standards to be invariant, necessary, and absolute. The rigidity and universality of these standards will not be overcome by obscuring differences; that only serves to make the established standards invisible and possibly tyrannical. Nor does Zhuangzi propose absolute standardlessness as a cure (to what standard could he appeal for that?). Rather, he seeks to uncover the conditions by which standards emerge, namely the limiting factors of a particular situation as encountered by a "valuating perspective." This will be fleshed out later when we take up Zhuangzi's notion of a "Dao standard."

The River thought he was large, powerful, the biggest thing around, until he crossed over the threshold of the Sea. He thought he was big; now he realizes he is small. What ensues is a long discussion between the Sea and his new disciple, the River. Through a variety of arguments, initially focused on the problem of big and small, the River learns that merely determining something is larger or smaller than another is not sufficient for understanding big and small. Big and small are not merely physical dimensions, but *values*: major and minor, greater and lesser, grand and pittance, and so on. He has assumed that "bigger is better" and that being able to sort out things according to absolute standards of "size" would be sufficient to prioritize the world. The Sea will not let matters be settled so simply.

At issue are perspectives. Zhuangzi offers some analogies to illustrate this:

> You can't discuss the ocean with a well frog—he's limited by the space he lives in. You can't discuss ice with a summer insect—he's bound to a single season. You can't discuss the Way with a cramped scholar—he's shackled by his doctrines. Now you have come out beyond your banks and borders and have seen the great sea—so you realize your own pettiness. From now on it will be possible to discourse about the Great Principle.[23]

The central theme of the discourse between the Sea and the River is a common theme in early Chinese works: Which standard(s) should we live by? The Sea's response includes epistemological, ethical, psychological, and ontological discussions. She deals with the question of evaluating things in terms of bifurcation: big and small, worthy and worthless, right and wrong, and so on. Zhuangzi argues that between all opposites is a pivot, which in effect is a standpoint (*yi guan* 以 觀), and there are many such pivots. Unlike the surging "in-between" of the River that is incapable of making proper distinctions, this pivot is the hinge that supports the door, which both (1) divides one side from the other and (2) can freely swing back and forth between both sides.[24] These pivots are not strung out neutrally on a single line but are related to specific existential horizons. These horizons and their constitution occupy the bulk of the discourse.

Framing Dialectics in Axiomatics: Living within One's Limits

The River has come to believe that the correction for over- or underestimation is accurate estimation, that is, seeing things as neither greater nor lesser than they are.[25] He asks: "'If that is so, then if I [accept] that Heaven and Earth are large (*da* 大) and the tip of a hair is little (*xiao* 小), is that right?'"[26]

This question has several layers.[27] If what is big is identified as big, and what is small is identified as small, then is everything properly sorted out? Heaven and Earth stand for the largest imaginable extension, and the tip of a hair stands for the smallest discernible point. So the question is also asking about the utmost extents of large and small, their liminal defining boundaries. Knowing what is larger and smaller than oneself should give one an accurate sense of where one fits in in the greater (and lesser) scheme of things.

The Sea replies with an emphatic "No!" and immediately offers four statements about what cannot be controlled or altered, four influential framers of the human condition that are incapable of being fixed or canonized as stable standards, formulae, or maxims. These instabilities nonetheless constitute the foundations of an ethical orientation.

1. Measuring (lit. "weighing, evaluating") things is without end (*liang wuqiong* 量無窮).[28]

2. Time is without stopping (*shi wuzhi* 時無止).

3. Apportionment is without permanence (*fen wuchang* 分無常).

4. Ends and beginnings are without [necessary, predictable] reasons/ causes (*zhong shi wugu* 終始無故).[29]

These pronouncements assert that there is no end to measurement or evaluation; time never stops; what someone or something has or does not have—what one is apportioned, or one's portion—is not a permanent possession or loss, but only a temporary happenstance; and the ultimate beginning or end of someone (or something) is unpredictable.

All are stated in negative terms (*no* end, *no* stop, *no* permanence, *no* reason/cause); that is, these are four statements about the absence of certain constants or fixable standards. They could be rephrased in positive terms (measurement has infinite possibilities; time keeps moving; one's fortunes are always in flux; when and by what something begins or ends is open-ended) and thus taken as affirmative axioms. But the negative form places the emphasis on the lack of constancy.

These statements assert four existential limits or horizons that act as limitations not because of what they "are," but because of what they lack (*wu* 無). Or again, each is a nonlimit, which—precisely to the degree that it refuses to become a fixed constant—acts as a limiting horizon, a blatant reminder of what we cannot do (such as make time stop, predict the time of death, etc.). In fact, it is not exactly the absence of limits that is limiting, but rather it is the uncertainty, bred from a lack of comforting fixed rubrics with which to control outcomes, that people find emotionally limiting. "If there is no rule or formula to tell me how to do something, how am I supposed to do it, and what am I supposed to do?" At least since the time of Confucius, the Chinese had tirelessly sought to establish secure and immutable standards by which to evaluate their condition and formulate ethical guidelines. In response Zhuangzi presents a way to figure out what to do in harmony with the fact that there are no immutable rules. In the delicate balance between Zhuangzi's "skeptical mode" and what might be seen as his "insight mode," he offers ethical guidelines bereft of moral or fixed standards.

As if anticipating that the River will then ask "What do these statements mean?" or "How do you know that these four are in fact the case?" the text expands on them in the following way:

> For this reason, [one with] great knowledge:
> Observes (*guan* 觀) the far-away and the nearby, and hence [recognizes] that the little is not a pittance and the large is not much.
> [This is] knowing measurement (=evaluation) is without end.
> He fully-realizes (*zheng* 證) the past and present, and hence he is unworried about what is far off, and does not anxiously go on tiptoes to pluck [what the present puts just out of reach].[30]
> [This is] knowing that time is without stopping.
> He examines (*cha* 察) full and empty [or ample and lacking], and thus he does not delight in what he attains, nor grieve for what he loses.
> [This is] knowing the impermanence of apportionment.
> He comprehends (*ming* 明) the "pacific erasure"[31] [of oppositional extremism] and thus he doesn't rejoice at birth nor [consider] death a calamity.
> [This is] knowing the impossibility of [predicting necessary] causes/reasons of ends and beginnings.[32]

This can be recast as in Table 6.1.

This is really quite a remarkable little scheme, very deftly thought out and constructed, and it will take us some time to properly unpack it. We will do this by first identifying various structural elements of this model and their interplay.

Structure of the Table: Levels and Steps

We notice first that the four earlier pronouncements should not be taken as independent, self-evident axioms but are actually derived, or better put, they are labels for the outcomes or "conclusions" of epistemic procedures. Four conclusions are stated as axioms (A), followed by a "proof" for each (B–D), each concluding with a reiteration of the initial conclusion (E).

Two aspects of this model are immediately striking: Knowledge and temporality. The description of the epistemic activities of the one of Great Knowledge (*dazhi* 大知) shows how he learns to deal with time and the effects (or limitations) that time inscribes into his possibilities. Note the word for "great" is again *da*, "large." Using *da* to characterize "knowledge" signals that the term carries deeper implications than mere value-neutral "size": *da* also powerfully evokes positive values. If the River thinks that *da*

Table 6.1 Temporality–Knowledge Model

	1	2	3	4
A	Evaluating is without end	Time is without stopping	Apportionment is without permanence	Ends and beginnings are without reasons/causes
B	Observe 觀 far and near	Realize 證 past and present	Examine 察 full and empty	Comprehend 明 "pacific erasure"
C	little and large	far off and "pluck[able]"	attain and lose	birth and death
D	not pittance not much	not worried not expectant	no delight no grieving	no rejoicing no calamity
E	Knowing evaluation is without end	Knowing time is without stopping	Knowing the impermanence of apportionment	Knowing the impossibility of [predicting necessary] causes/reasons of ends and beginnings

is a value-free spatial term to be used for measuring or sizing up the vastness of Heaven and Earth, "*da* knowledge" reminds him that neither size
nor vastness is the true measure of *da* at all, since the type of knowledge
described here has nothing to do with vast erudition or wide learning, but
rather enables insight into life's uncertainties without denying, suppress-
ing, or obscuring them. "Great knowledge" means being smart enough
to not get unnecessarily entangled in debilitating, biased value judgments,
because one knows how to react with equanimity (walk the "level road"
or "keep an even keel") to whatever life (or death) throws at one.

Measuring size also involves temporality, while time both limits and
frees us. Thus, going from column 1 to column 2, Zhuangzi makes a transition from space to time. This is not an arbitrary transition but follows from
the logic developed in column 1. We will return to this in a moment.

We shall call the vertical structure (A → E) "levels" and the horizontal structure (1 → 4) "steps." The narrative order of progression goes
from level A to level E of step 1, then level A to level E of step 2, and so
on, until reaching step 4 level E. However, the table can offer other insights
if read in differing orders.

Another striking feature is the use of bifurcation, or oppositional
dyads. Reading down from B to D, we see that by way of an epistemic
grappling with one bifurcated pair (B), one acquires insight into another
bifurcated pair (C), which then neutralizes or negates the affective fallout
of a third bifurcated pair (D). This third pair signifies the problematic bifurcations, the sorts of values or value-driven reactions that tend to pose
or represent life's "problems." Also note a telling reversal in 4: while for 1
through 3 the oppositional dyads begin at B—with A merely stating the
absence of invariance in a single thing—4 presents the dyad ("beginnings
and ends") at A, and no dyad at all appears in 4B. In fact, with this reversal,
4 marks the culmination of the first three, and the "pacific erasure" (or
"level road") signals the culmination of the previous three lessons (we
will return to this shortly). Thus we see that the "table" is meant to be
read across as well as vertically.

Epistemology without Invariants:
The Temporality of Knowledge

Let us begin with an attempt to characterize the vertical aspects of this
model. The four statements of level A announce arenas lacking determinate invariant finite standards, arenas fundamentally subtended by uncer-

tainty, things over which we have no control, things which we can do nothing about, and hence things which limit our range of possibilities.

Level B combines two aspects: (1) an epistemic verb ("observe, realize, examine, comprehend") and (2) a dyadic opposition under scrutiny by the epistemic verb. Hence these are epistemological bifurcations, ways of viewing or examining certain oppositions. Methodologically speaking, the "levels" really begin here, that is, the model and its resulting insights are initiated by the application of these epistemological moves.

Level C introduces four new oppositional dyads, derived from the epistemic activities on level B. These oppositions mark situational parameters, that is, contrasting poles between which things can be evaluated or measured. The C dyads are oppositional fluctuations generated by our ways of measuring or evaluating things and circumstances. The opposing terms in each dyad are not permanent or invariant, and for people generally that lack of invariance or stability is both the problem and the solution: when we have what we want, we do not want to lose it; yet when we do not have it, we hope to acquire it. Level C can be understood as a limitation to the extent that we lack the ability to make the present moment be otherwise than it is, yet it provides freedom to the degree that we (a) realize it is only a measuring device and (b) react to it with the insights obtained at B rather than letting the values or parameters themselves determine our reactions.

Level D marks the affective, psychological, and cognitive distance between ordinary people and the one of Great Knowledge. This level "corrects" the usual realm of human existence that is shaped and twisted by how we react to the satisfactions or disappointments of our expectations or idealized values. These "problems" are negated (*bu* 不), which is to say that for the one of Great Knowledge the sorts of bedeviling bifurcations by which we gauge whether we are happy or sad, successful or disappointed, do not arise in the first place. Bigger is not better, nor is scarcity or rarity a sign of higher value. How these dyads arise, and whether they bind us or not is completely within our control. Thus these dyads are only limitations when they are *not* negated.

The final level, level E, reiterates level A, with the addition of the word *zhi* 知 (knowing), thus indicating (a) that an epistemic lesson has been learned, and (b) that the four pronouncements are neither simply axiomatic nor a priori assertions, but labels for the outcome of an epistemic procedure.

Reinforcing the point that Zhuangzi is not offering invariant epistemic formulae, 4E neatly sums up the crux of the whole model: *The*

one of Great Knowledge knows that it is impossible to know! Zhuangzi offers
guidelines in spite of the fact that there are no stable invariants upon
which to build ethical standards. Rather, one "builds" them on variable
uncertainties! Put more strongly, one gets one's ethical bearings *because
of* uncertainty.

We may now take a look at some of the horizontal "steps." But before we examine them, we should first take notice of the four epistemic
terms occurring in B. The first, *guan* 觀, means "observe," " contemplate,"
and in "Qiushui" seems specifically to denote seeing from a standpoint,
having a perspective. A standpoint is never neutral but rather constitutes a
locus from which and by which things are viewed, evaluated, and judged.
The values we see in things and ourselves are determined by where we
take our stand, how and from where we look at them. The second is *zheng*
證, which means "realize," "witness." The manner by which one witnesses
the "past and present" influences one's stance toward the future—whether
one looks forward to it with anxiety or eager anticipation. One thereby
realizes the significance of the movement of time. The third, *cha* 察, means
"examine," "investigate," "look into"; it is to detect the relations between
things so as to reach conclusions implied but not initially obvious prior
to the investigating. By examining such fullness/emptiness alternations
as breathing, digestion, or the cyclical patterns of the seasonal year, one
understands that whatever one is apportioned at any given moment will
not last forever. The final term is *ming* 明, "comprehension," written as a
combination of sun 日 and moon 月 and thus implying their combined
brightness. It denotes a type of understanding that sees things from both
sides, in their brighter *yang* aspects as well as their darker *yin* aspects—a
totalizing knowledge, or comprehensive comprehending, rooted in a
dialectical vision. One comprehends the pacific erasure (or level road),
which is to say, one overcomes the emotional turmoil that comes from
separating life from death by valuing one over the other.

Reading across: we observe, then witness/realize, then examine
more carefully, and finally clearly comprehend things from both sides. Or
rephrased, we take a view on things, watch what happens, examine the
results, and arrive at a complete understanding. Rather than impose or
impute values, we live by the world as we see it and learn multiple ways of
observing (*guan*). What do we observe by this four-step epistemology?

On encountering the Sea, the River *guan*s its size, its scope. The
remainder of the dialogue illustrates how to develop the other three epistemic attitudes from *guan*. To deepen his understanding, the River must
also *zheng, cha*, and reach *ming*. But the *explicit* instructions and ensuing

discussion focus almost exclusively on *guan*, implicitly—precisely because they are elliptical—inviting readers to trace out and develop the remaining three epistemic activities on their own.[33] The story in "Qiushui" that immediately follows the autumn floods story shares the same "elliptical invitation."[34]

Step 1 takes up the question of large and little—a dyad consistently used by Zhuangzi as the paradigmatic case of how values are assigned. More attention is given to the play between large and little, both as quantity and as value, than to any other issue in the autumn floods discourse. We are the size we are; taking our size as the criterion of measurement, there is that which is larger and that which is smaller. To us a five-hundred-year-old Redwood tree is large, and a slice of bread is small. To a mountain the tree is but a dot (but the continent is large); to an ant the bread slice is a gigantic world of nutrients (but a microbe is small). We may be able to get the mountain and tree to agree with us that the ant is little, but would the microbe agree?

Step 1, then, is a lesson in how, on the basis of being located in a particular point of view, we project the values by which we evaluate and measure the worth of things. One observes what is far and what is near. What is far away will look small, certainly smaller than it will appear when up close. What is near will look larger than something of comparable size that is distant. But this is only so because we are standing where we are standing. Small and large switch places as soon as we switch places! More important, we hold what is close to us, near to us, what we "hold near and dear," as more valuable than things, ideas, beliefs that are distant or remote from where we stand. We evaluate according to proximity. Our "values" reveal more about where we stand than they do about the things to which we attribute those values. Because (*gu* 故) large and small are relative to where we stand, imputing worth to things on the basis of how we quantify them becomes a matter of our own projection, a statement about the place on which we stand from which we view things, and not a true measure of the value of the thing itself ("the little is not a pittance, the large is not much").

Measuring/evaluating is interminable. *Liang* 量 is a broad term, involving such things as measuring the size, weight, shape, and so on of things, as well as "evaluating" them as better or worse, and so on. Measurements are interminable because there are infinite ways of measuring something, by infinite standards and from infinitely different starting points. More significant, as our perspective and/or situation changes, our consequent "evaluation" will also be different. Furthermore, to change

what is near into what is far (and thus the large into the little), or vice
versa, requires time. We have to travel from here to there, to go somewhere
else than where we are. Hence by means of changes through time we
understand the value of space! And it is in terms of, as well as by means of,
temporality that we learn how to change or shift perspectives. Initially we
have to travel from one standpoint to another; eventually, Zhuangzi hopes,
we will be able to think alternative viewpoints, take alternate standpoints
spontaneously. This is the foundation of Zhuangzi's "transformation of
things" (*hua-wu* 化物). In short, based on his understanding of what is
near and far, the one of Great Knowledge knows that big and small can
be applied to things interminably, and that the size of something—both
physically and in terms of its value—is determined by how and from
where one looks at it.[35]

With this changing of perspectives over time as a starting point, we
move to step 2. Here we face time directly and learn how to accept change
rather than become discontent with wherever one finds oneself. One does
not lament one's distance from (and thus inability to lay one's hands on
or directly participate in) the legendary and long-gone Golden Age—the
ideal and supposed source of the Norms promoted by the Confucians.
While we may grow angry or depressed or expectant and anticipatory
at the passage of time and what it brings or takes away, time just keeps
moving. That movement is value neutral, though we constantly react to
it by evaluating it (it is "good" to be young, it is taking "too" long, it happened "too" fast, those were the "good" old days, etc.). Because time never
stops and keeps on moving, the one of Great Knowledge takes things as
they come, neither pining for the past nor overly drawn to the novel, nor
overlooking what is present out of anticipation for what has not been.

Note that Zhuangzi explicitly mentions only the past and present.
The reason for this is that he is talking about knowledge: we can have
knowledge of the past and the present, but there is no true knowledge
of the future—even though knowledge of the former two may engender
attitudes toward the latter. As we will see at step 4, our desire to predict
what has not happened yet is symptomatic of our deepest problem and
fear—the uncertainty of death. Because one cannot stop the ongoing of
time, one perceives time's limitlessness as limiting one's efforts to hold
certain things indefinitely; what we try to delimit is limitless. Whatever we
set up, establish, systematize, order, and so on, will pass on, just as what we
reject and suppress eventually comes to be. By understanding the meaning
of past and present, the one of Great Knowledge has no anxiety about
what is or is not (presently or imminently) available. He is not anxious or

upset about what is temporally "far off" (*yao* 遙), nor does he overextend himself, grabbing at things that lie just beyond his grasp. He takes things as they come, leaves things as they go, and uses them while around. The movement of time is beyond his control, but how he "spends" it is not.

Since things come and go, sometimes we possess them, and sometimes we lose them. These fluctuations and our reactions to them are addressed in step 3. Whereas step 1 focuses on the projection of value, and step 2 teaches how to react to change in general, at step 3 the problem becomes more specific and more internal. Sometimes we view what the changes of time bring us as ample and sufficient, and sometimes they seem lacking and inadequate. We again impute values to those changes (it is better to have enough; poverty and renunciation are virtues, etc.), and these values become further sources for our discontent. We believe that gain is success, while loss is failure; accomplishment, winning, achieving are "good," while losing, quitting, failing are "bad." But the success of a farmer's crop, getting a promotion at work, finding an appreciative audience, and all the other sorts of things we count as success happen only sometimes, and only mean something to us because we know they are not inevitable. Meaning is grounded in the open possibilities of a perpetual "otherwise." Success is built on failure, and failure is always hot on the heels of success. Like the River's arrogance, success and failure, gain and loss, are ephemeral, passing changes conditioned by fluctuating external factors. Take what you get, don't grieve for what you lose. With time, all changes.

Our most prized possession is our life. Who does not believe that the best life is the "full" life? Who does not regret that the "emptying" of life is death, the "loss" of life? Our most feared and dreaded nemesis is death. The limits of life and death seem to be the most certain and unavoidable. Zhuangzi reminds us that while the inevitability of death is certain, the when and the wherefore are not. Death is both a symbol for limits in general and the most profound and limiting limit we can face—because death involves a transformation or passing through a limit the other side of which is so radically and utterly Other and nonobservable that we can scarcely even guess—much less know—what awaits. We do not know our living future; how much less do we know our dead future.

Still implicit in step 4 is the lesson of step 1, not just in terms of the projection of values and their affective consequences, but the valuing of "big and small" or "greater and lesser." Will we be "great" enough to be remembered (like Confucius and Bo Yi—and as Zhuangzi might say, if so, so what?)?[36] Or are we meaningless "little" insignificant ephemera crazed by the possibility of our own self-importance? By erasing oppositional extremism, one reaches a quietude, a peaceful, level way of balancing the dyads. It is not bifurcation or opposition per se that is erased, but the evaluative baggage—the extremism of clinging to one side while denigrating or opposing the other—that distorts our reactions, understanding, feelings, actions, and so on. Motives for forging such extremist standards abound: to justify our prejudices (derived from where we stand); to silence the screaming vertigo of limitlessness; to find comfort from the uncertainties and misfortunes that afflict us; to pretend there are invariants, subtending stabilities where there are none; to elevate our importance (in our own eyes as well as those of others); to "distinguish" and define ourselves so as to appear distinguished; and so on. When the baggage disappears, one still sees larger and smaller, past and present, empty and full, life and death, and all the other dyads mentioned in B and C, but the positive versions of the dyads in D are neutralized (demeaning/inflating, worry/anticipation, etc.).

Since such things as delight, grieving, and rejoicing, are also listed in D, does that mean that the one of Great Knowledge is a feelingless automaton, incapable of feeling happy or sad, joyous or depressed, and so on? I do not think so. The model does not posit the absolute absence of these feelings but only that these feelings do not arise as reactions to fluctuations in those specific circumstances. For instance, one can feel delighted or saddened, but not because of gain or loss. What else, someone may ask, would spur those emotions? The obvious answer is almost anything: a good book, a friend, plaintive music. For Zhuangzi, that signals a deeper and truer sense of enjoyment. The transformative power of humor exemplifies this for Zhuangzi.

By treading a balanced path, one tips neither toward life nor away from death. This does not involve fabricating an artificial parity aimed at obliterating all contraries but an ability to see that bifurcations derive from other bifurcations and that these ultimately are grounded in the standpoint from which we begin to view anything. As Zhuangzi indicates, as soon as one indicates a "this," there is already a "that." As Laozi (chapter 1) already said, "these pairs emerge together, but are differently named." Some things, such the size of a human body, time's movement, we can do little about, but, in spite of these apparent perspectival limitations, we can implement a fuller, more liberating range of perspectives than might at first seem available. The dialogue will continue by addressing precisely that issue.

Summary of the
Temporality-Knowledge Model

For Zhuangzi there are real limits that initially seem to restrict what we can do, feel, think, know. And yet the picture is more complex. Limits are not absolute but rather are characterized by an inability to determine and fix something unequivocally. This unfixability is precisely what functions as a limit—an invariant condition of variability about which we can do nothing, fate (*ming* 命), and, as such, it shapes or circumscribes the way we live, is our very life and death (*ming* 命). Thus what limits us is ironically the very absence of limits! The initial affective correlate to this lack of fixation and fixability is doubt and uncertainty. Zhuangzi offers ethical advice about how to come to terms with such limits. We cannot invariably choose our limits—any more than we can simply choose the direction of the flow of time—but we can choose how to view them, how to react to them. And through those choices, we open up our possibilities; the more possibilities we open, the more we have to play with, the more flexible and resilient we will be. To live we need not eliminate or banish doubt and uncertainty, but on the contrary, they become our teachers and liberators.

In the first step one learns to overcome the relativity of perspectives that invisibly impute values expressing the standpoint from which they are projected by noting their variability, how they change over time with changes of position. The second step reminds us that time is ongoing, that it never stops. Whereas the first step initially addressed spatial limitlessness, this step primarily focuses on temporal limitlessness. Dealing with the movement of time, coming to terms with its vagaries, informs our most basic human attitudes and concerns. This offers another way of looking at impermanence, drawing different implications than Indian Buddhists of that time drew, but equally as profound. The third step combines space and time, in that what one attains, obtains, or achieves, as well as what one loses or what passes away, is not permanent. This pertains as much to ideas, insights, reputation, and accomplishments as it does to concrete items that "occupy space." These are "*apportioned*" (*fen* 分): sometimes you get, sometimes you do not; sometimes you have something, sometimes someone else does. Whether ahead or behind at any given moment, it will be otherwise at some other time in some other situation.

The fourth step culminates and collectivizes the previous three, fully existentializing them in terms of the terminal limits of one's own life. Thus this step addresses the question of the parameters of perspectival horizons directly. The start and end of a life (as well as a situation, a perspective, a dream, whatever) is always contingent, never necessary, and thus uncertain and indeterminate. We do not choose our birth, nor is the moment of our death certain—even at the moment we may attempt suicide. There are no ultimate formulae by which such things can be planned or predicted with complete certainty (despite the common religious impulse to invent or valorize such foretellings). Just as a farmer plants his seeds hoping that the seasonal changes will allow his crop to grow well, so we too may act on probabilities but never with certainty. Because one never knows what will be with any degree of certitude, the one of Great Knowledge calmly and fully engages each moment. Zhuangzi adds:

> Calculate what is known by someone; it doesn't compare to what he doesn't know.
> [Calculate] the time he's been alive; it doesn't compare to the time he wasn't yet born.
> Using the extent of the little, one seeks to exhaust the scope of the extent of the large.[37]

The process of establishing and implementing ethical (or metaphysical) norms produces confusion, because the lack of invariance in reality will always challenge their purported invariability. As Zhuangzi says in the "Qiwulun" chapter: "If right were really right, it would differ so clearly from not right that there would be no need for argument. If so were really so, it would differ so clearly from not so that there would be no need for argument."[38]

Accepting the aporetic deconstruction of such norms itself becomes a different sort of norm, a norm not grounded in an uncertain invariant, but instead grounded in a deep uncertainty that is based on the lack of determinate invariants. Since rock-solid foundations ultimately fail to provide the invariant security they are installed to guarantee, relinquishing the need for such normative foundations offers a different sort of security, one predicated on the acceptance of uncertainty—and therefore unshakable. This reversal highlights Zhuangzi's unusual solution to the problem of ethical foundations.[39]

The Great Man: The Ethics of Aporia

How we see determines how we act. Zhuangzi's epistemological exercise yields practical consequences. It necessarily carries ethical implications.

The Sea makes this apparent by turning to a description of the Great Person's "activities" (*daren zhi xing* 大人之行), activities shaped by the epistemological considerations thus far elucidated.

> For this reason, as to the Great Man's actions:
> Though he would never harm another person, he doesn't make a lot out of (*duo* 多) humankind-ness or compassion.
> Though not motivated by pursuit of profit, he doesn't despise the porter at the gate [who only helps others for profit].
> Though he doesn't compete for goods and riches, he doesn't make a lot out of (*duo*) refusing or abandoning [them].
> Though he works (*shi* 事) unsupported by others, he doesn't make a lot out of being self-supporting (lit., the power to nourish [himself]) and he doesn't demean (*jian* 賤) the greedy or dirty.
> Though his activities are unlike (*shu* 殊) those of common people (*su* 俗), he doesn't make a lot out of being unique or eccentric.
> Though he lives as one of the [common] multitude, he doesn't despise [those who try to get ahead by] fawning and flattery.
> The titles and salaries of the age are insufficient to incite him, punishments and disgraces are insufficient to shame him.
> He knows right and wrong (*shi fei* 是非) cannot be separated, tiny and large cannot be cut-off (*ni* 倪) [from each other, or beyond liminality].
> I've heard it said:
> "The man of Dao isn't heard of (i.e., anonymous), fulfilling *de* 德 doesn't attain [anything] (*bu de* 不得) [or reaching *de* is no attainment], the Great man has no self (*ji* 己)."[40]

Quite a remarkable person indeed! Unlike Confucians who preach the importance of striving for and maintaining ethical norms such as humankind-ness (*ren* 仁)—and yet may not live up to them in their daily lives—the Great Man is impeccably ethical in his actions while unconcerned with norms. Unswayed by reward or punishment, praise or blame, he avoids the traps of oppositional extremism. He is independent and self-sufficient without paying homage to the cult of individuality. He is noncompetitive and does not seek advancement; he is just one of the crowd, and yet he thoroughly lacks that skewered spitefulness that Nietzsche called "ressentiment" with all its self-destructive consequences. The Great Man is so not because of an ethical formula or rubric, but because he embodies the aporetic vision that frees him from the tugging influence of oppositional extremism (right and wrong, tiny and large, etc.).

Some Perspectives on Value:
Positional Determinism

Somewhat later in the dialogue, the River poses a question that is both
shrewd and perplexed. He is puzzled about how the Sea could so easily
make a transition from epistemological discourse to ethical discourse (a
transition that continues to pose problems for philosophers, even today).
From where does the Great Man get his guiding values, such that he
acts and thinks as he does, once the apparent basis for valuation has been
thrown into the aporetic abyss? How are we to even value the Great Man
and what he embodies? By what can we decide or judge that his way is
better (*gui* 貴) than another's? The River asks: "Whether it is extrinsic to
things or intrinsic to things, how does there come to be a cut-off-point
(*ni*) between 'worthwhile' (*gui*) and 'worthless' (*jian*)? Or a cut-off-point
between little and large?"[41]

The River wants to know:

1. How did the Sea make the leap from epistemology to ethics?

2. How are we to properly distinguish between things (whether in
   terms of size or value)?

3. How do we know that what the Great Man does is worthwhile,
   valuable?

4. What, if anything, serves as a criterion for evaluation, whether we
   impose it or whether it is intrinsic to the things themselves?

5. And, as a corollary, what is intrinsic to things, and what do we
   impose?

He is still begging for a formula, a rubric, a constant rule—and asking
the most natural of questions. We would feel cheated if these questions
were not addressed by Zhuangzi. They go to the heart of everything the
Sea has been saying thus far. Is it even worthwhile (*gui*) to be concerned
with all this? Is the Sea just a skeptic, or does the critique offer any positive value—and if so, how are we to judge and apply its value? The question of value—implicit in distinguishing large and little—now becomes
explicit in the sine qua non of ethical questions: by what criteria can we
differentiate better (*gui*) from worse (*jian*) so that we may know which
courses of action are better or worse?

The Sea immediately offers three criteria, each suggesting a different answer to the River's questions. The answers are given in a syntactic

formula: *yi* X *guan-zhi* (以 X 觀之), "observing them by way of X." In the first three criteria the X indicates a perspectival standpoint. The formula will be used three additional times, in which X will denote a valuative criterion.

> Observing (things) by way of Dao, things have no "worthwhile" (*gui*) or "worthless" (*jian*).

> Observing them by way of things, each considers itself (*zi*) "important" (*gui*) while all consider others "less important" (*jian*).

> Observing them by way of common-convention (*su*), "honorable" (*gui*) and "contemptible" (*jian*) are not defined by individuals, [but communally].[42]

There is no *criterion*; there are criteria that are incommensurate with each other, each starting from a different standpoint and thus each providing a different answer to the River's question.

The first criterion does not apply the bifurcation between *gui* (positive value) and *jian* (negative value) at all. The second criterion applies a centrist principle, such that each thing elevates itself and demeans the other, as a self-justification that makes one superior by denigrating what is different or otherwise as inferior. This judgmental attitude—which Nietzsche has pointed out is one of *ressentiment's* major weapons against the feeling of self-impotency—is explicitly contentious. The third criterion applies the standard impartially. But Daoists (cf. *Laozi*, chapter 38) argue that this sort of "impartiality" is also implicitly contentious, since (1) it is a general rule for holding someone or something to be better than something else, and (2) rules are made to be enforced. When someone does not respond properly, an enforcer "rolls up his sleeves and forces him." Though Zhuangzi does not announce it explicitly, these three criteria are being implicitly judged according to Laozi's motto of "non-contention" (*buzheng* 不爭).

Note that Dao (the first criterion) is not even impartial; it takes no stock in such evaluative endeavors whatsoever. Serving as a "standard" or criterion for the absence of a standard or criterion, the measurement-values "worthy and worthless," when measured by the standard of Dao, simply do not obtain. Zhuangzi does not present Dao as a meta-criterion, but as one criterion among three, though one that simultaneously subsumes and opens the possibility for the other two.[43] In fact, all three operate by means of universalization. Though each criterion, or perspective, is particular, each can be universalized. (It is in the nature of a closed perspective to universalize itself while failing to recognize that such universalization is precluded—or at least relativized—by the fact that it is mutually exclusive from other universalizing perspectives, such as the three standards Zhuangzi has just given.) The first asserts the universal absence of *gui-jian*. The second treats the self and its values as universally *gui*, while what is other to it as universally *jian*. The third assumes that its consensual determinations of what is *gui jian* are universally applicable and universally definitive.

Which of the three is "best?" We miss the point if we declare the Dao-standard as superior to the others. We lack any criterion for doing so, especially if we adopt the Dao-standard as our criterion. The seemingly negative centristic standard is not entirely negative. Zhuangzi, after all, does accept some of Yang Zhu's 楊朱 centrism into his own thinking. When he refuses to accept an official post offered by the ruler, he does so by means of this second criterion, not the Dao-standard. As for the third standard, communal consensus (*su*), we have just seen the Great Man described as "one of the [common] multitude," even "though his activities are unlike those of common people (*su*)." Elsewhere in the text, when Zhuangzi describes his use of language, he calls the second type of language he uses "heavy words," words weighted with the heaviness of traditional authority: "A man without the Way of man is to be called an obsolete man."[44] All three standards have their appropriate uses; they are all to be used at one time or another. But by what criteria does one decide when to use which?

These three criteria are followed by three more criteria, offered with the same formula (*yi* X *guan zhi*), though the precise relationship between the first three and the next three is not clear. Are they simply further elaborations, such that we should understand Zhuangzi as offering six distinct criteria? Or do they unpack one or more of the first three criteria? The second three follow:

> Observing them by way of differentiation (*cha* 察):
>
> "If, because of something's being large we enlarge it (*da zhi* 大之), then among the 10,000 things none are not large. If, because of its being little we belittle it (*xiao zhi* 小之), then among the 10,000 things none are not little.
>
> If you know that Heaven and Earth may be considered minuscule grains and know that the tip of a hair may be considered a mountain range, then you have discerned [how] differentiations are quantified (*shu* 數)."
>
> Observing them by way of utility (*gong* 功):[45]

"If, because of something having [usefulness] (*you* 有) we have [use] (*you*) for it, then among the 10,000 things none do not have [use]. If, because of its being without [usefulness] (*wu* 無) we have no [use] (*wu*) for it, then among the 10,000 things none are not [use]less (*wu*).

If you know that East and West oppose each other, and yet they are impossible to use without each other, then you have determined [how] utility is apportioned."

Observing them by way of prejudice (*qu* 趣):[46]

"If, because of what's right (*ran* 然) in it we grant it right(s), then among the 10,000 things none are not right. If, because of what's false (*fei* 非) in it we falsify it, then among the 10,000 things none are not false.

If you know that Yao and Jie (paradigmatic good and evil rulers, respectively) each considered himself right and the other wrong, then you have discerned [what is involved in] clinging to prejudice."[47]

These six perspectival criteria can be schematized as in Table 6.2.

All six perspectival criteria explain what follows from the acceptance of certain perspectives. The formula literally means "take X to observe them/it." Let's take A2 as an example. Scanning it we see that "large and little" are again being taken as a paradigmatic case (though by no means should we restrict "differentiation" to size). By the rubric at A2e we see that the issue here has to do with quantification, correlating value with quantity. How does it work?

If one takes "differentiation" as the standard by which to observe things, then we must view things through bifurcations, dichotomies, oppositions. For instance, to differentiate size, we must distinguish between large and small. Now if we look at X and discern that in some way it is large (relative to Y and/or Z which are smaller), then two things follow: (1) We "enlarge" it, that is, we take something that finally is just what it is and assign a value to it based on its relative size, that is, extrinsic factors. (2) Because the value of relative size derives from *our* way of observing something, in principle it is something we can do to anything. There is always something smaller or larger than what we examine. Thus we can "enlarge" or "belittle" anything. Since the ten thousand things are all equally capable of being enlarged or belittled, depending on how we choose to apply our differentiations at any given moment, all things are both "large" and "little," which is to say, the values "large" and "little," once again, say quite a bit about how we look at things, but nothing intrinsic to things themselves. Recognizing this, we see the sheer arbitrariness of using our own size as an absolute criterion. Our size is only

Table 6.2 Perspectival–Criteria Model

	A	B	C
1a	Observing (things) by way of Dao	Observing them by way of things	Observing them by way of common convention
1b	things have no "worthwhile" (*gui*) or "worthless" (*jian*)	each considers itself "important" (*gui*) while they all consider others "less important" (*jian*)	"honorable" (*gui*) and "contemptible" (*jian*) are not defined by individuals [but communally]
2a	Observing them by way of differentiation:	Observing them by way of utility:	Observing them by way of prejudice:
2b	If, because of something's being large we enlarge it, then among the ten thousand things none are not large	If, because of something having (use) we have (use) for it, then among the ten thousand things none do not have (utility)	If, because of what's right in it we grant it rights, then among the ten thousand things none are not right
2c	If, because of its being little we belittle it, then among the ten thousand things none are not little	If, because of its being without (use) we have no (use) for it, then among the ten thousand things none are not (use)less	If, because of what is false in it we falsify it, then among the ten thousand things none are not false
2d	If you know that Heaven and Earth may be thought minuscule grains and know that the tip of a hair may be thought a mountain range . . .	If you know that East and West oppose each other and yet cannot be used without each other . . .	If you know that Yao and Jie each considered himself right and the other wrong . . .
2e	then you have discerned [how] differentiations are quantified	then you have determined [how] utility is apportioned	then you have discerned [what is involved in] clinging to prejudice

one more relative value. Thus what appears large to us—such as Heaven and Earth—can be belittled just as minuscule grains are. Likewise, a tip of hair can be enlarged just as a mountain range can. It all depends on what we use for the "standard" size; or put another way, it depends on where we decide to inscribe the cut-off-point (*ni*) between large and little. Since "large" always implies "larger than," and "little" always implies "smaller than," size measurements—and by extension, all valuative judgments—are relative. Understanding this, we "discern" what quantifying differentiations involves.

Similarly for B2 (utility), if we examine something in terms of its usefulness, we seek in it that which we can use, that which is exploitable in it. Once that is found, we can use it. In principle we can do that with anything. As Zhuangzi points out several times in the text, including later in "Qiushui," everything has a special use and is useful for some things while useless for others. A battering ram is useful for breaking down a door but useless as a toothpick. A horse is useful for transportation but useless for catching rats. Whether we find something useful or useless depends on us and our desires rather than strictly on a thing. By making oneself useful, one invites exploitation, and others will try to find ways to use one up. There is therefore also a use to uselessness; it helps one preserve oneself. A country that offers no "resources," that is, things which are useful that can be exploited, will be left alone by bigger countries, while one with valuable resources will be eyed hungrily by other nations and businesses eager to exploit it.

Similarly, if we judge the worth of something in terms of how it is not useful for a particular task, then everything can be so judged. Everything is useless in some situation or for some purpose. The Sea elaborates on this a little later in the text during her discussion of specializations. B2b and B2c each take one extreme of the bifurcated perspective of B2a and universalize that extreme, such that its opposite becomes eclipsed in the operation. When we see everything as useful, then uselessness disappears, and vice versa.

For A, B, and C, 2b and 2c show that bifurcated values can become disjuncted, and each can seem to operate independently of its opposite. That, for Zhuangzi, is the "delusion and confusion" that lurk if we lose sight of how valuations are derived from perspectives. Thus 2d is the reminder that both extremes share a common undergirding perspective and can never be ultimately separated such that one may operate or function without its opposite. For instance, East and West are opposites, yet each becomes meaningless without its opposite. They oppose-yet-revert

(*fan* 反) to each other. Thus utility, usefulness, is something we apportion
to things, something by which we partition (*fen* 分) things. Everything
is simultaneously useful and useless, which means that a thing's intrinsic
value is determined neither by utility nor its absence, since everything is
both. It is determined by how we look at it; if we seek to find a use for
it, it will be judged and evaluated according to the degree to which *we*
find it (in-)adequate for that use.

As for C, if we take a perspective on something in terms of whether
it confirms or denies what we already believe is right (*ran*), then we can
invariably find a way to make things fit our position or find some reason
for rejecting them. *Ran* literally means "so" but was used by Mohists and
others to indicate what was permissible or acceptable to assert, that is, to
take as being so. Neo-Mohist logic concerned itself with constructing a
rigorous method for determining what is or is not "so," that is, tenable,
or true. In "Qiwulun," Zhuangzi parodies their efforts, asking, "What
makes things so? Making them so makes them so. What makes things not
so? Making them not so makes them not so."[48] Thus while we pretend
to accept or reject something ostensibly on the merits of the thing itself,
ultimately we use things as pretexts to reconfirm our own prejudices. C2d
reminds us that "right and wrong" are matters of self-justification (Yao
was considered a paradigmatic wise and kind ruler, Jie was a paradigmatic
shrewd and murderous ruler).

C2e sums up the point of the whole table: our claim to objective
standards is a self-deception in which we indulge in order to disguise
the fact that we are merely clinging to our prejudices (pre-judged, pre-
decided), whether those are centric or communal. In either case, objective standards mask self-justification and self-confirmation. We invest our
world and the things within it with the bifurcational values of *gui-jian*, but
such investments have nothing to do with the intrinsic value of things.
Rather, they disclose the theoretical standpoints from which we view the
world, if we own up to our projections rather than making other things
wear them. As long as values are attributed to things in such a way that
the actual source of attribution is ignored—and these attributions then
become universalized or absolutized—differentiation, separating extremes,
assigning values, and so on, amount to little more than unconscious acts
of self-aggrandizement (*da*).

These perspectival criteria all operate by universalizing a standard,
applying it to everything, excluding nothing. Zhuangzi seems to be arguing that once one sets a standard, it becomes a criterion that may be
universally applied, though it is only universal in virtue of the fact that it
ignores opposing criteria, which too may be universally applied. In fact,

those opposing criteria are the dialectical twins of the criteria they oppose. Both twins derive from the same differentializing standard. In Zhuangzi's language, once one takes on "smallness" as the criterion, nothing is not small, that is, "small/little" is a relative judgment applicable to anything. Though universally applicable, it functions only insofar as we momentarily ignore the fact that everything is also "big/large." Hence, as he stated: "If we know Heaven and Earth as a minuscule grain and know a tip of hair as a mountain range, then we have discerned [what's involved in] quantifiable discriminations." If we take either "big" or "small" as exclusive universal criteria, they cancel each other out; each becomes meaningless. To say everything is big is to make "big" a meaningless term; to say everything is both big and small is to say nothing about things but rather much about the relativity and limitations of the notions of big and small. Zhuangzi also argues that values, not just descriptive predicates, operate in the same way. Worthy and worthless, right and wrong, and so on, are only universalized standards.

His critique is fundamentally rooted in an appeal to the notion of the excluded middle, namely, the mutual incompatibility of smallness and bigness as simultaneously descriptive of an X. Yet the excluded middle is not ratified, because these opposing claims can be and often are made about the self-same thing. Zhuangzi consistently suggests that the very nature of dispute (*bian* 辯) is to impute mutually opposed predicates to the same locus, since (1) dispute requires opposing assertions about the same thing (attributing opposing properties to the same locus); (2) no locus is ever reducible to a single predicate; and (3) predicates are never independent values but always arise in relation to their opposites from which they receive their relative value. Thus everything is both large and little, both useful and useless, both right and wrong, and so on—depending on how one looks at it. "Value," to be value, requires such opposition.

Zhuangzi has moved from epistemology to ethics by showing that epistemic distinctions invariably become valuational. When we declare something is "large," we "enlarge it," we "aggrandize" it, we impute a "value" to it based on its being larger than something else. We are perpetually "sizing up" the world around us: people, ideas, things, ideologies, methods, ad infinitum. To think is to evaluate, to compare by way of contrast (oppositions) and similarity (universal applicability). To think about thinking is to evaluate and assign values to various types of thinking: What sort of thinking yields "valid" knowledge? What sort yields "invalid" knowledge? How *ought* we to think? How *ought* we *not* to think? and so forth. Why ought one adopt *this* epistemological standard rather than *that* one?

Ethics and epistemology become two sides of the same coin. Epistemology gives us the tools for justifying our ethics, and ethics (thinking in terms of "better or worse") organizes the way we do epistemology (it is better to think this way than that way, etc.). Both create and are victims of "value."

The "Eight-*De*" Model

In the "Qiwulun" chapter, Zhuangzi presents a rich, suggestive model with many possible applications. In the space remaining I will quickly introduce the model and indicate briefly how it bears on the question of Zhuangzi's skeptical ethics. Zhuangzi writes:[49]

> Now Dao has never had boundaries, words have never had permanence. Consider "this is right" (*shi*) and then there are borders. Allow me to offer a word about these borders.
> There is Left, there is Right. There are discussions (*lun* 倫),[50] there are debates (*yi* 義).[51] There are divisions (*fen* 分), there are disputes (*bian* 辯). There are emulations (*jing* 競), there are contentions (*zheng* 爭). These are called "the Eight *De* 德"
> Beyond the six realms the sage exists but doesn't discuss. Within the six realms the sage discusses but doesn't debate. [In times like those described in] *The Spring and Autumn Classic*'s generations of former kings at [crossed] purposes,[52] the sage debates but he doesn't dispute.
> Thus, those who divide have not [really] divided, those who discriminate have not [really] discriminated. You say, How is that? The sage cherishes it [i.e., *Dao*, in his heart], and the multitudes dispute it, trying to display [and foist their own understanding] on each other. Hence it is said: "Those who dispute have not seen (*bujian* 不見)."[53]

The following table can help clarify the model:

Table 6.3   Eight–*De* Model

	A	B
1	LEFT	RIGHT
2	Discussions	Debates
3	Divisions	Disputes
4	Emulations	Contentions

Briefly, the trajectory runs from 1A to 1B to 2A to 2B and so on until 4B, in a descending spiral from the boundariless Dao.[54] How does it work? There are a variety of ways to approach this model, but I will only address one here, as an "orientation" model.

For the boundariless, there are no distinctions, no directions, nothing cut off from anything else. Elsewhere Zhuangzi reminds us that this does not mean that things are indiscriminately merged into an undifferentiated amorphous blob but rather that things remain always in dependent relations with other things and all things are the same as everything else precisely to the extent that each thing is itself, because each thing is above all else itself. Recognizing this commonality forged out of each thing's uniqueness is to see the "unity" or "oneness" of all things. With no reference points against which to measure, the sage just exists. Beyond the six realms (north, south, east, west, up, and down), which is to say, in the boundless, the sage just is. There is no grid by which his position can be fixed. And yet wherever he is, there is also his right and left.

My primary orientation to my surroundings is in terms of my body. I am located where my body is, and the world relates to me in terms of where it is in relation to my body, my reference point. My right side is always on my right, and my left side, on my left, no matter which way I face. My body is "one," and it does not come apart by distinguishing one side from another; yet in terms of orientation, for convenience and practicality, I can orient things to myself dyadically, by my right and left. I can wander throughout the world getting my bearings from myself, from my own center, always knowing what is to the right and left of that center.

But suppose we are facing each other, having a conversation. What is to my right will be to your left and vice versa. And as we move around, right and left will change relative to external things even while remaining constant in terms of each person's own body. Suppose you ask me for directions to a local coffee house. If I say go left, then right, then left, and so on, you will not know on whose right and left the directions rely, yours or mine. In order to not get in a fight with you over where right and left are if we face each other, we can select a neutral code for describing directions, one which fixes space "absolutely" so that our movements can be described relative to it. We call one direction east, its opposite west; one of its perpendiculars north, and its opposite south. Hence, when facing each other, we avoid a dispute over basic directional orientation by replacing the vocabulary of right and left—which is only absolute to my own body but relative to everything else—with the intersubjective, conventionalized (*su*) vocabulary of the cardinal directions. This is "discussing," or as the text literally puts it, setting "norms" (*lun*). Once a directional grid is established by convention, we can communicate, discuss, plan journeys, and draw elaborate maps with many destinations, including ones neither of us has ever visited. We can stand in different viewpoints and still agree about locations and directions because we use directions that are not centered in either one of us, being rather mere conventions to facilitate communication. That we "don't debate" means we agree to call east "east" and west "west," without trying to argue that one is "better" than the other, or more intrinsically "right" (*shi*) than the other. As Zhuangzi says: "If you know that East and West oppose each other, and yet they are impossible to use without each other, then you have determined how utility is apportioned."

"Apportioned" in this passage is another way of translating *fen* (rendered "divisions" in the Eight *De* model), which means to "cut with a knife, divide up, separate one thing from another." For Zhuangzi the sage does not divide or "cut up." The sage never thinks in terms of separating one thing from another, isolating east from west, right from wrong, and so on. To name or indicate one thing instantaneously invokes its opposite, as chapter 2 of the *Laozi* makes explicit. To indicate a left side, there must be also be a right. As Daoists say, in order to go left one must go right. This is not as paradoxical as it sounds. In order to take a step with one's left foot, one must first place all one's weight on one's right foot, and vice versa. When a person distinguishes her right side from her left, an imaginary border appears distinguishing one side from the other; *fen* (dividing) would mean to take out a knife and actually cut the body in two or to treat the two sides as truly separable—which they are not unless one kills the body.

Debates, which precede "dividing" in this model, are friendly exercises in which one makes a case for a position while an opponent makes the opposite case for an opposite position. As debating clubs know, one's effectiveness at debate has nothing to do with whether one actually holds the position one is arguing. In general, the sage will discuss (draw maps, plan journeys, communicate about the surroundings, etc.) but does not debate. He takes no sides. But during bad times—as when Chinese society was breaking down during the Spring and Autumn period—when those institutions that not only govern but also set standards, public taste, communication codes, societal theories by which the population lives, and so on, have run afoul, in short, when the culture is losing its Way, *then*, in an effort to correct the imbalances and bring people back to a level course, the sage will debate. He will take a contrary position to his opponent (the creator, defender, or believer of the socially damaging theory) and argue it. And yet he does not "dispute."

This is the ethical turn. The sage minds his own business when on his own. When he enters the realm of social interaction (within the six directions), he engages in conventional discourse, conventional understandings. When situations are bad enough to merit it, he will debate, take counterpoint positions and actions as antidotes for specific wrongs. He never descends lower where the processes producing bifurcations are forgotten while the aftereffects of bifurcations are adhered to and championed.

Undoubtedly Graham had this and similar passages in mind when he wrote that Zhuangzi accepts *lun* (discussion, sorting things out) but rejects *bian* (dispute). *Bian* indicates quarrelsome, divisive disputes in which holders of the respective sides take their positions in earnest and mean to vanquish their opponents at all costs, attempting to declare one direction, or one theory, group, institution, party, or religion, and so on, the only "direction" while trying to discard or eliminate its opposite. *Bian* is not simply generating or choosing alternatives; that already occurs in "debate." Debates involve using positions to redress something leaning too far in one direction; but one debates without attachment to the position, and once the debate is over or the reason for the debate has disappeared, the debater discards the position. *Bian* becomes problematic because the alternative or side that one chooses becomes exclusivistic, isolated, value-laden, extreme; the position one adopts is not a mere expedient, but *the* Truth; not just a "this is" opposed to a "that," but a "this and only this is right, good, etc." opposed to all else, especially the complimentary opposite that makes the "this" a "this" by providing its border, its boundaries, its cut-off point ("that" becomes the "evil" that must be opposed and eliminated).

The model operates by a progression. *Discussion*—talking about, theorizing about, imagining—by indicating and distinguishing distinct things ("consider 'this is right'") establishes the ground for *debates*. Denoting any X instantaneously generates a non-X, and once X and non-X are made explicit, they can be debated against each other. On the basis of such debates, if the debaters get carried away, complimentary opposites such as right and wrong, east and west, can become separated from each other, "divided." Then "disputes" emerge wherein people latch onto one side and try to completely eradicate the other, failing to recognize the inseparability of opposites. One becomes, for instance, pro-life, forgetting that life subsists on death: we kill to eat; each breath kills thousands of microbes; and so on. Life cannot survive without death, nor can death exist without life, since the number one cause of death is birth. The sage never indulges in such ideological extremism.

As for *emulation* and *contention*, these are the byproducts of disputes. As sides are more distinctly etched and highlighted, each becomes a position that others either idolize and seek to emulate ("I want to be like him") or spurn and denigrate ("those wicked heathens!").

The "discussants" *theorize*, playing with one way after another of looking at the world. The "debaters" take the theories generated by the discussants seriously, bringing the oppositions entailed in those theories into relief and arguing them out without becoming attached to either side. The "dividers" rend apart complimentary pairs formulated by the debaters, thinking that good can exist without evil, and so on. The "disputants" latch onto the positions isolated by the dividers, make their home in one, and devote their energy to snuffing out all contrary views. "Emulators" chase after the disputants' crumbs, imitating their ideas, actions, fashions. They no longer are thinking or theorizing or even seriously discussing; they parrot the ideas provided by the dividers, who also had ceased to creatively think but were merely taking too seriously the distinctions argued by the debaters. Dividers divide between Us and Them. Disputers discriminate and actively pursue the perpetuation of the Dividers' Us/Them. Imitators emulate their preferred Disputers and contend against those the disputers disapprove of, by reflex, by inheritance, by thoughtlessness. Imitators and contenders like or dislike, approve or disapprove, not through rational consideration, but reflexively, derivatively, according to standards and assumptions inherited and adopted from those before them, standards and assumptions that they never question.

Dividers do not really divide (1) because they cannot separate the inseparable and (2) because the separations that they think they author are only the byproducts of the theories and debates that preceded them. The disputers are even more derivative; they do not really dispute since—in the mind of the disputants—nothing is really in question, each disputer is only trying to make the opponents change their position. Everyone speaks, but no one listens to anyone else.[55] The derivative positions have become intransigent; they have become ideologies.

Zhuangzi's skepticism is one of the tools he uses to "debate"; it is a therapeutic device that in better times or under other conditions (viz., a world devoid of ideologues and their disciples) would be unnecessary. I close with the same quote that opened this chapter, this time adding the next few lines.[56]

Hence would you say:

"Now, Right is my master (*shi shi*), so that I may be without wrong" or "Control is my master, so that I may be without disorder?"

If that's right (*shi*), then you are not yet clear (*ming*) on the patterns (*li*) of Heaven and Earth, or the basic-drives (*qing*) of the 10,000 things.

This would be like taking Heaven as one's master so as to do without Earth; or taking *yin* as master so as to do without *yang*. Clearly, that's impossible to do.

Moreover, if [you] don't desist from such discourse, if you are not an idiot, you are a liar!

Notes

My translations and paraphrases in this chapter are based on the *Harvard-Yenching Concordance to Chuang Tzu* (Cambridge, MA: Harvard University Press, 1956), pp. 42–44, unless otherwise specified. I have also profitably consulted the following translations, but have frequently diverged from them: Burton Watson, *The Complete Works of Chuang Tzu* (New York: Columbia University Press, 1968); A. C. Graham, *Chuang Tzu: The Inner Chapters* (London: George Allen & Unwin, 1981); Herbert Giles, *Chuang Tzu: Taoist Philosopher and Chinese Mystic* (London: George Allen & Unwin, 1889); James Legge, *The Divine Classics of Chuang-Tze* (London: Oxford, Sacred Books of the East, 12, 1917). All translations will be my own unless otherwise stated.

1. *Essays on Skepticism, Relativism, and Ethics in the Zhuangzi*, ed. Paul Kjellberg and Phillip J. Ivanhoe (Albany: State University of New York Press, 1996), addresses some of these issues. The present chapter complements some of the essays there but offers a different viewpoint.

2. I will use this name as a synonym for the entire book bearing this name as its title, and not differentiate between the person or the book by way of italics because I am less convinced than many of my colleagues about where to draw that line.

3. The early Greek skeptics in the Western philosophical tradition also drew ethical conclusions from their epistemological aporetics, holding the pursuit of "cheerfulness" as exemplary. That the transition *from* skeptical epistemology *to* positive ethics might involve anything more than an arbitrary relation has rarely been questioned by Western thinkers, possibly because the skeptics themselves did not make the necessity of the connection as clear and compelling as they might have. In any event, unlike the skeptics who resist claiming they know anything and hold skepticism as their final epistemic stance, Zhuangzi's skeptical moments invariably lead beyond skepticism. Zhuangzi eventually reaches nonskeptical conclusions that become the basis for actions and attitudes, that is, ethics.

4. For an example of such a comparison, see Mark Berkson, "Language: The Guest of Reality—Zhuangzi and Derrida on Language, Reality, and Skillfulness," in *Essays on Skepticism, Relativism, and Ethics in the Zhuangzi*, ed. Kjellberg and Ivanhoe, pp. 97–126.

5. "The Overflowing of Oppositions (*Fan-yen*): The Structures of Zhuangzi's Arguments in 'Autumn Floods,'" delivered at the Eastern Division Meeting of the American Philosophical Association, Washington, D.C., December 1992.

6. The most basic version of the magic number chart is a set of nine boxes, set in three rows by three columns, containing numbers that, if added horizontally, vertically, or diagonally, always total fifteen. More complex versions of these charts totaling higher sums were also developed, and they were often conflated with the Luo tu and He shu, well-known popular Daoist cosmological charts. On these charts, see John Henderson, *The Development and Decline of Chinese Cosmology* (New York: Columbia University Press, 1984), pp. 82–87 and passim. "Reasoning" by charts is still a very common method among East Asian scholars. I have not seen these particular charts attested to in the secondary literature on Zhuangzi, so one of the aims of this chapter is to bring them to wider attention.

7. If his arguments were more sophistic than valid, he would be a sophist, not a skeptic. As it turns out, Dignāga was no sophist, but one of India's sharpest and most innovative logicians.

8. "A Tao of Tao in *Chuang Tzu*," in *Experimental Essays on Chuang-tzu*, ed. Victor Mair (Honolulu: University of Hawaii Press, 1983), p. 33. Note that four of the contributors to Mair's volume (Graham, Hansen, Crandell, and Yearley) explicitly classify Zhuangzi as a skeptic. Mair himself is the most striking exception; he calls Zhuangzi a *Homo ludens* (man the player).

9. In a paper delivered at the American Philosophical Association, Baltimore, 1982.

10. On "the fit" (*shi* 適) see "Da sheng" (ZZJS 662; HY 50/19/62–64) and Kuang-ming Wu's discussion in his *Chuang Tzu: World Philosopher at Play* (Chico, CA: Scholars Press, 1982, pp. 72–76). The butterfly does not ask any questions or feel any anxiety because everything "fits." He is so comfortable he becomes complacent; no problems, no questions arise. "The fit" plays a subtle but important role in many passages in the *Zhuangzi*, occurring seven times in "Xiaoyaoyou," seven in "Qiwulun," at least once in all the remaining Inner Chapters, and frequently throughout the rest of the text.

11. *Zi yu shi zhi yu, buzhi zhou ye* 自喻適志與，不知周也. The first phrase on its surface could be read "he enjoys himself" or "[everything] suits his purposes," but the terms that make up the phrase also can be read in a more technical way: *zi* (self) *yu* (metaphor, is like; to experience, perceive as) *shi* (the fit; cf. previous note) *zhi* (will, purpose, what one wants to do) *yu*

(a particle that can express doubt, an interrogative sense implying a positive response, etc.). Thus I have translated it to reflect these technical possibilities. The final *yu* 與 can be used to express "being *with*," "doubt," as well as a conjunction joining two things. I have rendered *yu* here as "surroundings" in the sense of what the butterfly "is with." One possible reading of the full story is to see *yu* as marking where the story turns from "being with" or comfortably blending with one's circumstances, to doubt, to conjunction of di-lemmas or seemingly incommensurate lived worlds. To indicate this I have marked in the translation where *yu* occurs.

12. Following the suggestion in the Harvard-Yenching concordance, reading *ququ* 蘧蘧 as *juju* 據據 (from the Cui 崔 edition), which means "strong evidence."

13. "Qiwulun," ZZJS 112; HY 7/2/94–96.

14. Students of Skepticism will notice that the structure of the sequence corresponds (slightly out of order) to the four alternatives commonly used by skeptics: X is (Y is not), Y is (X is not), Both X and Y are, and Neither X nor Y is. These alternatives can be found in Greek thought as early as Gorgias (who preceded the Skeptics); cf. Kathleen Freeman, *Ancilla to the Pre-Socratic Philosophers* (Cambridge: Harvard University Press, 1977), pp. 127ff. It also occurs in early Buddhist and Indian literature probably prior to direct contact between India and Greece; is featured in Nāgārjuna's thought (1st century) and William of Ockkam's "razor"; and is finally tamed and made reasonable by Leibniz in the form of his "truth tables."

15. The *zi* in the phrase *zi yu shi zhi yu* (see note 11 above) is intended to emphasize this.

16. Countless passages in Zhuangzi illustrate this. Cf. "Gengsang Chu" (ZZJS 802 ff.; HY 63–64/23/58–66; Graham 104) where this is discussed in the context of "shifting."

17. "Qiwulun," ZZJS 103; HY 6/2/79–81. Cf. Watson, 47, and Graham, 59.

18. Watson 84; ZZJS 258–60; HY 17/6/47–52.

19. The term *pai* 排 can mean "set up in rows," "arrange in order," "push," "clear up" or "settle difficulties." *Pai* is followed here by the phrase *an pai*, which I take as a cue to read *pai* as to "make peace with," "settle things up."

20. "Dazongshi," ZZJS 274–75; HY 18/6/76–82. I have combined Graham's translation (pp. 90 f) with Watson's (p. 88) and altered several phrases.

21. For comparison with my translations below, see also those of Watson, 175–82, and Graham, 144–49.

22. Translation from Legge; ZZJS 561; HY 42/17/1.

23. Watson 175–76; ZZJS 563; HY 42/17/5–7.

24. The pivot (*shu* 樞) is discussed in "Qiwulun" (ZZJS 66; HY 4/2/30

ff.). "Zhi beiyou" (ZZJS 752; HY 59/22/50–52) gives a good description of how this is to be understood. See Graham 162 or Watson 241–42 for a translation of this passage.

25. As others have already observed, the Confucian theory of "rectification of names" presupposes just such a correspondence theory.

26. ZZJS 568; HY 42/17/14–15.

27. One layer that I will only mention at this point but not explore until later is a syntactic ambivalence that will be brought into play soon. The syntax of the question allows it to be read as I have translated it above, but there is a more compelling reading. Note that I had to provide the verb ("accept"). The words for "large" and "little" are syntactically placed as verbs, thus giving the reading: "If so, then [if] I enlarge Heaven and Earth and belittle the tip of a hair, is that it?"

28. It is interesting to note that Zhuangzi's word for measuring, *liang*, was the term adopted by the Buddhists for *pramāṇa*, the means by which one acquires valid knowledge.

29. ZZJS 568; HY 42/17/15. The term *gu* 故 literally means "cause, reason." Ancient Chinese logicians and thinkers did not distinguish logical from causal relations, and the language embodies this bivocality. Near the end of the dialogue the term recurs, and by its usage there we can determine that the basic sense implied here is "formula," that is, abstracting a constant rule or formula from a set of data to be used for evaluating present situations as well as providing a rubric for future actions. Watson's translation of it as "fixed rule" (p. 177) seems closest to the mark.

30. *Duo* 掇 means "to pluck, to gather." *Qi* 跂 means "to eagerly stand on tiptoe for, to expect, anticipate." Thus in Chinese the image is rather clear: someone standing on tiptoes eagerly grasping at and plucking the fruit that harvest time has made available, that is, the fruits of the past that become available in the present; or someone on the lookout for the opportunity to do so. Literally the phrase reads: "[he] plucks and yet doesn't stand on tiptoes," so Zhuangzi is not saying that one should reject what is available or refuse to "pluck" it, but only that one does not overreach.

31. This translates *tantu* 坦塗. *Tan* means "level, smooth; quiet, peaceful; an open place." *Tu* may mean "road, what's happening in the streets," but it also means "smear, erase, blot out." It sometimes is used for its homonym *tu* 途, which means "road, path, journey, career, pursuit." The compound *tantu* can thus mean "a level road," on which there are no extremes, no drastic ups or downs, one that does not (prejudiciously) slant one way or the other, one that is ultimately the easiest to tread. Or we can bring the other senses of *tan* (peaceful, quiet, a broad opening) and *tu* (erasing) into play and thus get "pacific erasure" (punning [in English] on quiet, peaceful, and the open expanse of the Pacific Ocean, our largest sea), the quieting of oppositional extremism.

32. ZZJS 568; HY 42/17/15–18.

33. One additional clue: The epistemic term in step 4, *ming*, is used throughout the Zhuangzi as its most idealized way of knowing, including in "Qiwulun," where *ming* occurs five times, each time at a critical point. It occurs ten more times in the Inner Chapters (not counting compounds), and roughly one hundred times throughout the rest of the text (esp. chs. 13 ["Tian Dao"] and 33 ["Tianxia"]). See HY 705–06, V/88824.

34. The story following the autumn floods dialogue in the "Qiushui" chapter (ZZJS 591–95; HY 44/17/53–60) is one of Zhuangzi's most blatant examples of beginning a point and elliptically leaving it to the reader to complete the movement. A list of things (the Kui, a millipede, a snake, etc.) are given at the beginning of the story, which then proceeds through a chain of one-to-one exchanges, the first talking to the second one, the second talking to the third, and so on, each one marveling at how much quicker the next one is compared to it. However, the story ends before we meet the last two items on the initial list—the eye and the mind—though the reader should be able to provide the missing moves. Clearly the reader is expected to continue the trajectory of the argument. The editors may have put this story here because they recognized that both the autumn floods and the "Quickness" story share the same type of "elliptical invitation."

35. Graham sees this as the point of the famous exchange between Hui Shi and Zhuangzi on how Zhuangzi can know that the fish the two of them are watching from a bridge are happy. "Qiushui"; ZZJS 606–07; HY 45/17/87–91. Cf. Graham 123 and his "Chuang-tzu's Essay on Seeing Things as Equal," *History of Religions* 9 (1969/70), pp. 137–59.

36. Zhuangzi sarcastically mentions both earlier in the "Qiushui" chapter as people who are remembered for their sagacity, undeservedly.

37. ZZJS 568; HY 42/17/18–19.

38. Watson 48–49; ZZJS 108; HY 7/2/90–91.

39. [Or, as Guo Xiang 郭象 (252?–312) puts it, "If one rides upon whatever one encounters, then on what further would one have to depend (*dai* 待)?" ZZJS 20—ed.]

40. ZZJS 574; HY 43/17/24–28.

41. ZZJS 577; HY 43/17/28–29.

42. ZZJS 577; HY 43/17/29–30.

43. The "Dao-standard" does not efface other standards. It constitutes and relativizes them. The standardlessness of the Dao-standard is the very condition through which the others can occur in the first place, because it allows any and all bifurcations without allowing any of them to become absolute or fixed. It is the sine qua non of all oppositions. For Zhuangzi, expressions such as "all things are one" do not mean a merging of distinct entities into an indistinct effusion, but rather that things are united by a commonality; namely, each and every thing is doing what it does the Way it does. Their

commonality is based on each being true to itself, not on losing individual differences or blurring each thing's distinctness.

44. Graham 107; "Yuyan," ZZJS 949; HY 75/27/4.

45. *Gong* has a range of meanings, including "merits," "achievements," "accomplishments," "efficacy," "successful task." Its basic sense as used here seems to be "the successful use to which something can be put."

46. The term *qu* literally means to "lean toward one side," one-sidedness being the standard Chinese expression for "bias," "prejudice," that is, taking sides. It also implies leaning toward something, hence preference, what attracts one, what is pleasant, amusing, nice, and so on. It includes both our leaning toward something as well as the pull of attraction that thing has toward us.

47. ZZJS 577–78; HY 43/17/30–34.

48. ZZJS 69; HY 4/2/33–34.

49. In the interest of brevity I will forgo discussion of the numerous technical and textual problems contained in this short passage. I hope to return to it and do it justice on another occasion.

50. Most translators and commentators read *lun* 倫 as 論. An important exception is the commentary on the Inner Chapters by the Ming Dynasty Buddhist monk Hanshan Deqing 憨山德清, who reads *lun* as signifying "Confucian Norms." *Laozi Daodejing Hanshan zhu, Zhuangzi neipian Hanshan zhu* 老子道德經憨山註，莊子內篇憨山註 (Taipei: Xinwenfeng chuban gongsi, 1994), p. 245.

51. Most read 議 for 義.

52. The *Spring and Autumn Annals* purport to be chronicles during a time of great conflict between various Chinese states. Zhuangzi apparently means this phrase to indicate "in bad times, particularly those brought on by political mismanagement and conflict."

53. ZZJS 83; HY 5/2/55–58. *Bujian* is a pun since *jian* means both "to see" and "to be seen or show." Hence, the more they show off, the more they do not see *and* are not really showing themselves.

54. Cf. *Laozi* 17–19 and 38.

55. Hanshan Deqing's commentary explains this well: "Humans have never been far from the original Great Dao, but not knowing that, they pretend to know. Becoming attached to their own views, [each] thinking that s/he is right, they quarrel and dispute, arrogantly displaying [their view] to others, thereby concealing the Great Dao." Hanshan Deqing, *Laozi Daodejing Hanshan zhu*, p. 247.

56. "Qiushui," ZZJS 580; HY 43/17/37–39.

7

Reflex and Reflectivity:
Wuwei 無為 in the *Zhuangzi*

ALAN FOX 狐安南

Introduction

It is impossible to understand philosophical Daoism, that is, Daoism as found in the writings attributed to Laozi 老子 and Zhuangzi, without understanding the central practical principle of *wuwei*, or "nonaction." There are many different interpretations of this idea, many of which seem to overlook both the overall coherence of the *Zhuangzi* and its many subtle nuances. I propose to offer a different interpretation of this crucial notion, one that differs on some key points from the prevailing interpretation and arguably acknowledges some deeper dimensions of the text and its overall coherence.

The notion of *wuwei* arises earlier and in other contexts within Chinese thought. For instance, the term is used in the *Lunyu* (2.1) to describe the efficiency of excellence—the fact that the superior person needs to do little to be maximally effective because of the gravitational radiance of his charismatic virtuosity, his *de* 德. In the *Laozi*, *wuwei* appears numerous times and generally seems to refer to the avoidance of interference with the natural tendencies of events, which is one way of understanding the notion of *dao*. In this sense, cooperation or concordance with the natural course of events results in a sort of effortless grace, which requires both physical and mental agility and flexibility. Politically, this manifests as a kind of unobtrusiveness, an ability to function effectively but not prominently, which culminates in a kind of invisibility.

In approaching the *Zhuangzi*, however, which seems to build on Laozi's conception, we also need to keep in mind its characteristic and well-documented resistance to formulaic or forced behavior. Rather than discovering a new or better formula for behavior, the *Zhuangzi* emphasizes the benefits of becoming sensitive to a broader and finer range of the subtle demands, constraints, and inevitabilities of unique situations. This sensitivity allows us to respond most appropriately to every unique situation in the way that most or best respects subtleties of novelty and necessity.

Therefore the most effective and efficient mode of human experience is to blend or "fit" (*shi* 適) into our surroundings in such a way as to allow ourselves to respond effortlessly and spontaneously to any situation or circumstance, which is simultaneously affected by our presence within it. I suggest that this mode of reflective and unobtrusive activity is what Zhuangzi refers to as "*wuwei.*"

I propose to explicate Zhuangzi's conception of *wuwei* as it is articulated in the image of the "hinge of *dao.*" This image illustrates several key features of the mode of action of Zhuangzi's ideal person, namely, (1) effortlessness, (2) responsiveness, and (3) unobtrusiveness. First, I will look at and discuss the few actual instances of the term *wuwei* in the *Zhuangzi.*[1] Second, I will point out that the imagery used by the text to suggest this privileged mode of conduct frequently takes the form of some sort of adaptation or reflection.

Third, I will analyze the metaphor of the hinge and show how centralizing this metaphor can illuminate Zhuangzi's notion of *wuwei* and the realized person who acts according to this principle. It will be seen that the image of the hinge is used in the *Zhuangzi* to represent the way in which the ideal person responds to inevitability. In this way, I will argue that Zhuangzi's ideal person could be described as "perfectly well-adjusted."

Finally, I will demonstrate that this reading of the text offers new meanings and textures to materials that have for so long been read in only certain ways. Most of the translators and commentators who have brought the text to our attention have characterized it, somewhat unfairly, as "mystical," "skeptical," "escapist," "purposeless," and so on. I will show that this kind of reading, to a certain extent, misses the point of the text, so its truly unique contributions are overlooked.

Wuwei in the *Zhuangzi*

It must be noted from the outset that the actual phrase *wuwei* shows up only three times in the inner chapters. Of these, one instance seems to refer to *dao* 道 and the other two to the attitude of what Zhuangzi evidently sees as the "ideal person." In both of those latter two occurrences, we find *wuwei* used to describe the rambling/meandering/transparent/effortless activity of the sage. The first instance of the term occurs in the "Xiao-yaoyou" chapter. The text reads, "*panghuang hu wuwei qi ce* 彷徨乎無為其側."Various translations appear below:

Mair (p. 9)	"There you can roam in nonaction by its side"
Watson (p. 35)	"relax and do nothing by its side"
Wu (p. 55)	"Rambling-ly, there-exists-no making beside it"
Fung (p. 35)	"By its side you may wander in nonaction"
Graham (p. 47)	"go roaming away to do nothing at its side"[2]

The crucial term seems to be *panghuang*. The term implies something restless, not fixed, mobile, and in this sense to "roam in nonaction (*wuwei*)" suggests a kind of flitting about like a butterfly, at the mercy of the breeze and yet still somehow managing to travel from flower to flower, effectively arriving at its natural destination. As Roger Ames says, "[In the *Zhuangzi*,] *wuwei* is associated with the 'spiritual rambling' quality of the enlightened person who has overcome the distorting influence of ego-self and is able to experience the totality of things."[3]

The second occurrence of *wuwei* used to refer to the ideal person can be found in the "Dazongshi" chapter. The passage reads: "*xiaoyao hu wuwei zhi ye* 逍遙乎無為之業." A variety of translations are provided below:

Mair (p. 61)	"carefree in the karma of nonaction"
Watson (p. 87)	"they wander free and easy in the service of inaction"
Fung (p. 101)	"they wander in the realm of nonaction"
Chan (p. 198)	"they wander in the original state of having no (un-natural) action"
Graham (p. 90)	"they go rambling through the lore in which there's nothing to do."[4]

The term *xiaoyao* suggests an easygoing, carefree quality. This term is also used by the text's editor Guo Xiang 郭象 (252?–312) as part of the title of the first chapter, whose complete title, "Xiaoyaoyou," means something like "carefree meandering." The term *you* means to travel, saunter, roam, or wander. It is convenient, then, to render *you* as "meandering," since this evokes the image of a river that takes the path of least resistance and does not rush or confront. Its avoidance of resistance causes it to take a roundabout route, yet it ultimately arrives at its destination, the sea. As previously described, the butterfly is also a creature that meanders, at least in this sense. The syntax of the sentence seems extremely straightforward: it equates *xiaoyao* 逍遙 and *wuwei* by suggesting that by being *xiaoyao* one is engaging in *wuwei*. Therefore it seems reasonable to understand *wuwei* as a kind of "carefree meandering," effortlessly navigating the contours of inevitability while arriving inevitably at one's destination.[5] It is not necessarily purposeless, but its purpose is perhaps accomplished indirectly.

This also implies a certain degree of flexibility. But we must be careful not to reduce *wuwei* to "mere" flexibility. As Kuang-ming Wu suggests: "Zhuangzi wants us to adopt a flexible 'attitude' that best fits our disposition *and* the disposition of the situation in which we are at the moment."[6] The kind of flexibility involved here might be described as a metaphysical flexibility. *Wuwei* is not merely a way of *acting*; it is a way of approaching the world, of matching attitude to circumstance. This requires a willingness to shift contexts and see things from novel or different perspectives, continuously finding new possibilities in things. A good example of this principle in the text is found, in the "Xiaoyaoyou" chapter, in the story of Huizi:

> Huizi said to Zhuangzi, "The king of Wei gave me some seeds of a huge gourd. I planted them, and when they grew up, the fruit was big enough to hold five piculs. I tried using it for a water container, but it was so heavy I couldn't lift it. I split it in half to make dippers, but they were so large and unwieldy that I couldn't dip them into anything. It's not that the gourds weren't fantastically big—but I decided they were of no use and so I smashed them to pieces."
>
> Zhuangzi said, ". . . Now you had a gourd big enough to hold five piculs. Why didn't you think of making it into a great tub so you could go floating around the rivers and lakes, instead of worrying because it was too big and unwieldy to dip into things!"[7]

This story is reminiscent of the classic situation encountered by all parents at some point or another. The parent spends all week putting together an elaborate and extremely expensive toy, only to find that the child prefers the box that it came in. Why is this the case? Because the toy can only be what it was intended to be, but the box can be anything. This childlike (though not emotionally childish) sense of wonder,[8] this ability to see diverse, perhaps infinite, possibilities in things, is an aspect of *wuwei* in that it only becomes possible once we overcome our insistence on having the world conform to our own preferences. Instead of obstinately and vainly persisting against the tide of inevitability, which will only wear us out, Zhuangzi's ideal person adapts and conforms, reflectively and reflexively, operating in an effortless, responsive, unobtrusive fashion, by finding the fit (*shi* 適).

Reflex and Reflectivity: Finding the Fit

Although it rejects formulaic thinking, the *Zhuangzi* cannot correctly be described as completely relativistic, because, even though different concerns arise in different situations, each unique situation carries with it its own limitations and inevitabilities that need to be accommodated. This means that there are real constraints presented to us, which cannot be resolved away simply by denying their ultimate validity. So even though there are no single right or wrong ethical stances in general, there are ones that are *most* right and wrong given particular situational constraints. This ethical stance, then, is not entirely relativistic, nor is it entirely absolutistic.

In light of this reciprocity between ourselves and the world and the fact that our experience somehow represents the reconciliation of the two, the most efficient mode of action will be the one that follows the "path of least resistance," as we find in the story of Cook Ding. According to Watson's translation, the story goes like this:

> Cook Ding was cutting up an ox for Lord Wen-hui. At every touch of his hand, every heave of his shoulder, every move of his feet, every thrust of his knee—zip! zoop! He slithered the knife along with a zing, and all was in perfect rhythm, as though he were performing the dance of the Mulberry Grove or keeping time to the Jingshou music . . .
>
> Cook Ding laid down his knife and [said], "What I care about is the Way, which goes beyond all skill. When I first began cutting up oxen, all I could see was the ox itself. After three years I no longer saw the whole ox. And now—now I go at it by spirit and don't look with my eyes. Perception and

understanding have come to a stop and spirit moves where it wants. I go along with the natural makeup, strike in the big hollows, guide the knife through the big openings, and follow things as they are. So I never touch the smallest ligament or tendon, much less a main joint.

"A good cook changes his knife once a year—because he cuts. A mediocre cook changes his knife once a month—because he hacks. I've had this knife of mine for nineteen years and I've cut up thousands of oxen with it, and yet the blade is as good as though it had just come from the grindstone. There are spaces between the joints, and the blade of the knife has really no thickness. If you insert what has no thickness into such spaces, then there's plenty of room—more than enough for the blade to play about in. That's why after nineteen years the blade of my knife is still as good as when it first came from the grindstone."[9]

Of course, the dignitary for whose benefit the good cook explains his skill immediately sees the broader implications of "go[ing] along with the natural makeup" and concludes, "I have heard the words of Cook Ding and learned how to care for life!"[10]

What Wenhui learns is that true mastery and skill, in life as well as in cooking, involve a *knack*, not a *formula*. The ideal is to "follow things as they are" and therefore never confront obstacles, just as water flows around a rock in the stream. The "spirit" or "daemonic" (*shen* 神) to which Cook Ding refers can be seen as the "autopilot" that guides us in the absence of conscious intention. A mundane example of this would be walking through a crowd of people without noticing the many various adjustments our bodies make to avoid hitting anyone. But this kind of response can hardly be planned. It must occur spontaneously and completely integrated into whatever situation is at hand. As A. C. Graham says: "People who really know what they are doing, such as cooks, carpenters, swimmers, boatmen, cicada-catchers, do not go in much for analysing, posing alternatives and reasoning from first principles, they no longer even bear in mind any rules they were taught as apprentices; they attend to the total situation and respond."[11]

This mode of action is made available to us in a certain way, namely, by finding the "fit" (*shi* 適). Those who have found this fit remain, for the most part, invisible or inconspicuous by virtue of their perfect integration into their surroundings, like a chameleon. The word *shi* ranges in meaning, but generally refers to something that matches up or meets its match, such as in the context of marriage or referring to fulfilling some criteria or mandate. In this sense, for instance, it appears in the "Renjianshi" chapter, where the phrase *shizu* 適足 is used to refer to the extent to which someone's understanding is "sufficient for knowing the faults of others, but not his own."[12] The "sufficiency" in question refers to *shizu* or the extent to which his capabilities match up to what is necessary to accomplish the goal. In the Outer Chapters, the notion of the fit is explained in this way:"If the feet are forgotten (*wang* 忘), then the shoes fit (*shi*). If the waist is forgotten, the belt fits. If awareness of right and wrong is forgotten, the mind fits. If there is no internal change nor external influence, one's response fits the circumstances (*shihui* 事會). When one fits from the start, and there is never lack of fit, then there is the fit of forgetting all about fitting."[13] A perfect fit, then is transparent or unobtrusive.[14]

To be sure, for most of us, this "fit" needs to be found, because we have lost our knack for natural action, so our action is ill-at-ease or dysfunctional. Zhuangzi puts it this way in the "Qiwulun" chapter:

When [most] people sleep, their souls are confused; when they awake, their bodies feel all out of joint. Their contacts turn into conflicts, each day involves them in mental strife. They become indecisive, dissembling, secretive. Small fears disturb them; Great fears incapacitate them.

Some there are who express themselves as swiftly as the release of the crossbow mechanism, which is to say that they arbitrate right and wrong. Others hold fast as though to a sworn covenant, which is to say they are waiting for victory. Some there are whose decline is like autumn and winter, which describes their dissolution day by day. Others are so immersed in activity that they cannot be revitalized. Some become so weary that they are as though sealed up in an envelope, which describes their senility. Their minds are so near death that they cannot be rejuvenated.[15]

The dysfunctional attitude, then, is one in which response is impulsive, judgmental, stubborn, manic-depressive, and in conflict with the rest of the world. Contributing to our dis-ease is the fact that we blindly and obstinately insist on applying our values, outlooks, and perspectives without question in all situations, whether or not they are appropriate, and accepting them as beyond our control. This formulaic, rule-based approach to experience will often confront situations for which the rule is not exactly appropriate, and consequently dysfunction and conflict or "friction" will result from trying to jam the square peg into the round hole. However, finding the fit or "fitting in" requires the ability to adapt and change with the circumstances, rather than beating our heads against the wall of inevitability in a form of what psychologists call "obstinate progression."[16]

Finding this "fit" involves a kind of blending in with the circumstances, but it is crucially important to emphasize that this is not simply a matter of conforming to society and other forms of human contrivance. It is in fact accomplished by stripping away the artificial and arbitrary conventions of thought and behavior that are the result of social indoctrination and that only serve to impede spontaneous response.

The *Zhuangzi* describes this process of eliminating artificial and narrow constraints as "mind fasting" (*xinzhai* 心齋), a process that leaves one more "open-minded," more sensitive and responsive to genuine, inevitable constraints. As we will emphasize shortly, Zhuangzi's notion of the "hinge of *dao*" (*daoshu* 道樞) enables us to compare this process to clearing out a socket so that a hinge might move more freely in it. Such a process requires conforming to a broader array of situational variables, of which the conventions of human contrivance (*wei* 為/*wei* 偽) are only one small part. One is fitting into the world as a whole, as in the example of Cook Ding, not just the narrow band of reality circumscribed by the limits of social existence. The attitude becomes what might be described as "open-minded," and action becomes noncontrived (*wuwei*), effortless, and unobtrusive. Kuang-ming Wu says: "[Sages] know how to fit into nature, and so they are fit and do not suffer, and can help others without helping them."[17]

For Zhuangzi, freedom is the result of this "fit" (*shi*). But this kind of freedom is perhaps best understood as freedom *from* slavish, obstinate commitment to behavioral and evaluative formulae that force us to act inappropriately, rather than freedom to act inappropriately if we so choose. Cook Ding does not decide where he *wants to* cut; he *finds* the spaces between the bones. Or to return to the hinge image, freedom in this sense is what the hinge experiences when it is situated properly in the socket. It can be said to "move freely" in that, within the limits of its possible motion, it experiences no obstruction or friction that might impede its motion. In this sense, the sage serves as a kind of "human superconductor."[18]

Zhuangzi's privileging of the unobtrusive allows us to conclude that, for him, *inappropriate action* might be defined as that which is unnatural and "sticks out," that which leads to conflict, friction, frustration, and "disease"; while appropriate, natural, or spontaneous (*ziran* 自然) action leads to a condition of ease and contentment. Such "frictionless activity" (*wuwei*) leads to greatest contentment.

The Hinge of Dao 道樞

Zhuangzi describes the *daoshu* or "hinge of Dao" as a fulcrum that balances distinctions. Zhuangzi says: "A state in which 'this' and 'that' no longer find their opposites is called the hinge of the Way. When the hinge is fitted into the socket, it can respond endlessly. Its right then is a single endlessness and its wrong too is a single endlessness. So, I say, the best thing to use is clarity."[19] This condition is one of open-mindedness, which does not obstinately insist on the world conforming to our preconceived preferences. The hinge serves as a standpoint or fulcrum according to which various distinctions are enabled. Seeing dichotomies in this way shows them to be complements, not opposites. To insist on preferring one alternative to another is to establish evaluations, which we subsequently tend to apply dogmatically, arbitrarily, and indiscriminately.

Kuang-ming Wu rightfully suggests a parallel between Zhuangzi's idea of the hinge and the idea of *axis mundi*.[20] In the sense explicated by Mircea Eliade,[21] the axis establishes a reference point that provides orientation. This orientation subsequently enables and promotes the constitution of distinctions and evaluations. This heterogeneity characterizes what Eliade calls "sacred space." But although it is useful to recognize distinctions, Zhuangzi seems to suggest that it is unnecessary and in fact somewhat dysfunctional to systematically, categorically, and unreflectively prefer one pole of a dichotomy to another. To return to our guiding metaphor, a door can swing open or closed, but it is all the same to the hinge. The movement possesses an "absolute value," as the mathematician would say.[22] Zhuangzi encourages us to accurately perceive distinctions, not to allow them to become blurred in a condition of mystical transcendence. Clarity (*ming* 明), not obscurity, is the privileged state of mind. But what is revealed in the light of this clarity is the mutuality of distinctions, their paradoxical dependence on one another, represented elsewhere in the Daoist tradition as *taiji* 太極, or the unity of yin and yang.

This dynamically balanced approach to life shows us the relativity of perspective. Zhuangzi criticizes the Confucians and the Mohists both for their contentious, polemical philosophizing, and concludes: "What one calls right the other calls wrong; what one calls wrong the other calls right. But if we want to right their wrongs and wrong their rights, then the best thing to use is clarity."[23] This clarity can be seen, then, as just that vision or insight that remains aware of the complementarity of opposites. This can also be described in some sense as seeing the "big picture," in which all contradictions are located and resolved. In other words, it characterizes any perspective that includes an awareness of the relativity of all perspectives.

So then, in the light of this clarity, the genuine person does not identify with his evaluations, but simply watches as all distinctions revolve around a central standpoint—a standpoint that is located at the *daoshu* and serves as the pivot, the fulcrum. This permits effective and effortless adaptation to circumstances and conditions. As A.C. Graham points out in quoting from the "Ke yi" chapter: "Only when stirred will he respond, only when pressed will he move, only when it is inevitable will he rise up."[24] Graham further says: "The man who reacts with pure spontaneity can do so only at one moment and in one way; by attending to the situation until it moves him, he discovers the move which is "inevitable" (*budeyi* 不得已, the one in which he "has no alternative") like a physical reflex. But he hits on it only if he perceives with perfect clarity, as though in a mirror."[25]

This kind of inevitability, furthermore, does not imply any kind of determinism. This is because the genuine person is not rigidly constrained to a single response, but rather inevitably slips into the most natural (comfortable: *shi* 適), most effortless groove. The grooves in this case are not the ruts of repetitive and habitual activity. They instead represent the limitations and inevitabilities one encounters in the world, such that effortless activity follows the trajectory of the groove just as a surfer follows the motion of the wave or Cook Ding finds the spaces between the bones.[26] Zhuangzi says: "Only a person of integrity can recognize the inevitable and accept it as his destiny."[27]

This, of course, is why I emphasized earlier that Zhuangzi's understanding of freedom does not suggest the freedom to act inappropriately. The fact is that even though in any particular instance there may not be *only one* appropriate response, there is almost always, whether we recognize it or not, a *most* appropriate response. For Zhuangzi, this would seem to be the one that leads on the one hand to the least conflict, or dis-ease, and on the other hand to the most efficient and effortless experience, or ease, as seen again in the story of Cook Ding. Besides, to describe the activity of the genuine person in terms of the free will/determinism paradigm would be to commit to one side of a polar dichotomy, and since the sage occupies the socket of the hinge, such descriptions are themselves inappropriate, simplistic, and unhelpful.

The process by which the socket is cleared out so as to accommodate the hinge in this sense is described by Zhuangzi as self-forgetting (*xinzhai*

心齋,"mind-fasting").[28] Watson translates the relevant passage as follows: "'May I ask what the fasting of the mind is?' Confucius said, 'Make your will one! Don't listen with your ears, listen with your mind. No, don't listen with your mind, but listen with your spirit. Listening stops with the ears, the mind stops with recognition, but spirit is empty and waits on all things. The Way gathers in emptiness alone. Emptiness is the fasting of the mind.'"[29]

The word that Watson translates as "spirit" here is *qi* 氣 or "vital energy," which is described in the text as "vacuous" (*xu* 虛) and yet "attendant upon things" (*er dai wu zhe ye* 而待物者也). That is, it is open and expansive yet completely responsive. Mind-fasting, then, is emptying the mind of artificial constraints to open it up and make room for the appropriate natural response to occur. It therefore involves the elimination of rigid, dogmatic, formulaic attitudes and habits and our self-identification with them. As Kuang-ming Wu points out, "To empty oneself is to become oneself; to become oneself is thus to go along with the world; to go along thus with the world of inevitables is to be free in it. Therefore to empty oneself is to be free in the world."[30] This process enables frictionless (effortless: *wuwei*) and immediate response to circumstance. A. C. Graham suggests that "the Daoist is somewhere where this dichotomy [between rational detachment and decision making on the one hand, and romantic indulgence on the other] does not apply." I would add that this "somewhere" is in the socket of the hinge, at the fulcrum of all dichotomies. When we occupy that space, all things revolve around us, and we remain balanced and well-adjusted despite the unpredictability and inevitability presented by the world. We become at ease and comfortable (*shi*) with our surroundings and so seem invisible, or at least inconspicuous, to others.

We find expressions of this idea of open-mindedness in the "Qiwu-lun" chapter. Watson's translation is as follows: "Great Understanding is broad and unhurried; little understanding is cramped and busy. Great words are clear and limpid; little words are shrill and quarrelsome."[31]

What he translates as "great understanding" (*dazhi* 大知) could just as easily mean "vast comprehension" or open-mindedness. The phrase reads "*dazhi xianxian*." If *xian* 閑 means, as many (though not all) commentators suggest, "broad" or "leisurely," then the doubling of the word suggests "expansive" or "broadly accommodating." Kuang-ming Wu, following Akatzuka Tadashi 赤塚忠,[32] suggests that both *dazhi* and its opposite (*xiaozhi* 小知, small- or narrow-mindedness) are meant pejoratively, in the sense that all kinds of knowledge and discourse have problems associated with them.

Whether or not this is true, Watson's translation of the last sentence of this phrase is open to question. The characterization given for *dayan* 大言 ("great words") is that they are *yanyan* 炎炎 (fiery, brilliant, explosive). Watson substitutes without explanation a different character (*dan* 淡: clear, transparent, pale) for the doubled *yan*. It is not clear what is gained by this. *Yanyan* can effectively and coherently be understood as language that is deconstructively performative. Its performative aspect in this case refers to its *trans*-formative function, its seductive and subtle effect on the sensibilities of the reader. In other words, reading the text transforms the reader. Its deconstructive aspect refers to its self-erasing function, its ability to burn itself up after it performs its function, leaving behind no traces in the world, like the fish net that is discarded once the fish has been caught. Despite its incendiary quality, since it leaves no mark behind, this can still truly be called an unobtrusive use of language, and according to one passage in the text, it is the way the sage speaks. Zhuangzi laments, at the end of the "Waiwu" chapter: "The fish trap exists because of the fish; once you've gotten the fish, you can forget the trap. The rabbit snare exists because of the rabbit; once you've gotten the rabbit, you can forget the snare. Words exist because of meaning; once you've gotten the meaning, you can forget the words. Where can I find a man who has forgotten words so I can have a word with him?"[33] Such a person is a desirable partner for conversation because he or she has no preferences at stake and so will not insist on projecting any inappropriate meanings onto our statements. Such a person will be truly willing and able to come to *terms* with us, meet us on our own turf, and understand us as we understand ourselves, by using language without being hampered by or fixated on any favorite or popular usage. This limits misunderstanding and, since clarity is a privileged cognitive mode, is therefore of value. So the transparent person, the person whose cognitive filters are transparent or lacking, is the ideal conversational partner.

Watson, however, describes the freedom of the genuine person (*zhenren* 真人) as a "mindless, purposeless mode of life,"[34] but I have some trouble accepting that it is entirely "mindless" and "purposeless." Daoist sages do not walk around bumping into things in a foggy haze. Clarity is privileged. As we have already pointed out, though a river may meander, following the path of least resistance, it still always manages to get to the sea. On the basis of the story of Cook Ding, at least, I would say that Zhuangzi values the overcoming of conflict and friction. This is to say, we need to find our place (*shi*)—to reconcile ourselves to that which is outside of our control and operate *within* our parameters, instead of thinking of the limits as limitations and consequently struggling obstinately and vainly against them. As Roger Ames says, "the profile which emerges [of Zhuangzi's ideal person] is not inconsistent with that of the sage-ruler of the *Laozi*—a consummate person whose catholicism, tolerance, and ability enable him to respond appropriately and efficaciously to any set of circumstances."[35]

This image of the well-adjusted person serves nicely to describe the genuine person, who has become balanced and centered. He or she is then able to experience the pitch and roll of oppositions (*taiji* 太極),[36] the ebb and flow of a constantly changing world, without being thrown off-balance. In a cognitive sense, the goal seems to be a kind of open-minded equanimity that is not flustered or disturbed by the unexpected. This is the example set by Cook Ding.

This kind of centering, as has often been noted, is also emphasized in many forms of Asian martial arts, such as Chinese *taijiquan* 太極拳 or Japanese *aikido*. In both of these, the goal is to become completely centered, so as to become rooted and immovable. Furthermore, those who master these techniques are also able to uproot others by entering into and appropriating their opponents' center. In fact, many aspects of Zhuangzi's concept of the ideal or "genuine person" (*zhenren*) correspond to the ideal of mastery in the martial arts. This is the case because the martial arts master is generally considered to have learned how to harmonize with his or her surroundings[37] and is therefore able to *avoid* friction or conflict. Traditionally, the highest form of mastery in the martial arts is modeled on the image of water, which overcomes by yielding, and in this way avoids injury without causing harm to others.[38]

This sense of balance is acquired by becoming comfortable with shifting foundations. For example, one common training method in *taijiquan* is to train on the beach so that the sand shifts underfoot and requires attention to balance. In this sense, it seems the *Zhuangzi* is endorsing the vertigo that results from shifting foundations or at least attempting to make it familiar enough not to cause fear or forced response. We can, in fact, learn from our vertigo—we can use it to cultivate and develop a sense of balance, which then allows us to adapt and conform to circumstances and conditions as they arise and change. To cling to our distinctions and their consequent evaluations is a form of rigidity, which inevitably leads to dissonance, friction, and conflict. Vertigo teaches us fluidity and balance. So Zhuangzi constantly keeps us off-balance. As one recent commentator puts it, "He disorients us so he can reorient us,"[39] though it seems more likely, in terms of this current discussion, that he disorients us so that we can learn to orient ourselves in any novel situation, without relying on him.

Conclusion

Many interpreters will agree that the *Zhuangzi* is concerned with freedom. Since the idea of a "fit" implies a reciprocal interrelation between the various components of a situation, freedom in this sense is constituted by lack of constraints which might inhibit or impede natural response. Usually, these constraints take the form of the burden of convention, expectation, and social artifice. Therefore freedom does not necessarily imply the freedom to do whatever we want. One must acknowledge and accommodate the real inevitabilities and limitations one encounters. This is because one cannot *force* the "fit," one must rather *find* it, which involves meeting the world at least halfway.

The text as a whole encapsulates this idea, because it is written in such a way that the text responds to the reader just as the reader responds to the text. In this sense I would suggest that, just as text and reader constitute a reciprocally responsive whole, the same can be said of all human experience. As a result, suggests Zhuangzi, the most effective mode of human experience is to blend or "fit" (*shi*) into any given situation in such a way as to allow ourselves to respond (*ying* 應) effortlessly and spontaneously, just like the hinge. This mode of nonobtrusive experience is what we might call "*wuwei.*"

Many commentators on the text understand the *Zhuangzi* as advocating some form of abstract mysticism, which devalues the world of concrete realities. There are several difficulties with this approach, however, which may lead one to overlook much of the subtlety of the text. For example, Burton Watson, one of the foremost translators of the *Zhuangzi*, describes its attitude as one of "skepticism and mystical detachment."[40] He also claims that "Zhuangzi's answer to the question [of how to live in a world dominated by chaos, suffering, and absurdity] is: free yourself from the world."[41] More recent translators such as Victor Mair also make this assumption: "Above all, Master Zhuang emphasized spontaneity. He was a mystic who recommended freedom from the world and its conventions."[42] Watson does acknowledge that the sage does not "in any literal sense withdraw and hide from the world—to do so would show that he still passed judgment upon the world."[43] However, he still insists that in the state of *wuwei*, "Man becomes one with Nature, or Heaven, as Zhuangzi calls it, and merges himself with Dao, or the Way, the underlying unity that embraces man, Nature, and all that is in the universe."[44]

I would say therefore that these readings are somewhat problematic, in two ways. First of all, representing *dao* 道 as some kind of abstract, transcendental entity with which the sage merges overlooks the emphasis on concrete immanence found throughout the text. For example, Zhuangzi says about *dao* that "*dao*(s) is (are) established as it is (they are) performed" (*dao xing zhi er cheng* 道行之而成). Watson's reading of this phrase is "A road is made by someone walking on it,"[45] rendering *dao* as "road" even though, in the very next paragraph, he translates it in its more technical sense (in Zhuangzi's discussion of the *daoshu* 道樞 or "hinge of *dao*"). But it is unnecessary to posit an eternal or abstract *dao* that exists apart from things, the behavior or quality of which is different than all the various possible concrete *dao*s operating in the world. If Zhuangzi's *dao* is not abstract but rather totally concrete, then this distinction between the technical (abstract) and ordinary (concrete) uses of the word *dao* becomes unnecessary. A concrete *dao* cannot be said to exist somewhere else before it operates in the world—its operation establishes its presence (*dao xing zhi er cheng*). Any *dao*, then, can be said to exist to the extent that it functions or operates in some way, since it *is* the way things work. That is, it *is* what it *does*. The way, in this sense, is then not something ontologically distinguishable from the things which are working in that way.

Some scholars argue that the *dao* is some special category of thing, whose transcendent nature renders it ineffable. For instance, Philip Ivanhoe says "Zhuangzi shared with Laozi the belief that words can never adequately describe the Dao,"[46] as though there were a single absolute Dao underlying all reality though not present in it. And even though Ivanhoe suggests that Zhuangzi was "fundamentally skeptical about language in general,"[47] he still finds it necessary to single out *dao* as somehow being more ineffable than the rest of reality.

Second, Zhuangzi does not merely tolerate the world; he actually affirms it as wonderful and enjoyable, once one learns to fit in. The important thing is to find the "fit."

Watson's approach allows him to dismiss some of what Zhuangzi says:

> Zhuangzi invents a variety of mysterious and high-sounding pseudo-technical terms to refer to the Way or the man who has made himself one with it. I have given a literal translation of such terms, and capitalized them in order to indicate their special character—e.g., Great Clod, Supreme Swindle, True Man. The reader need not puzzle over their precise meaning, since in the end they all refer to essentially the same thing—the inexpressible Absolute.[48]

As we have already suggested, Zhuangzi's so-called Absolute, if he posits one at all, is almost certainly not transcendent; its operation constitutes its establishment. Furthermore, it is not clear how "True Man" (*zhenren*) comes to be included in Watson's list of expressions for the "inexpressible ultimate," except to the extent that Watson insists that this genuine person is one who has reached a certain level of identification with the abstract entity he seems to describe as the "Absolute Dao."

But the *Zhuangzi* actually inspires us, not to remove or distance ourselves from the day to day world by identifying with some transcendental Dao, but rather to immerse ourselves *in* the world. Rather than understanding ourselves as *apart from* the world, we should understand ourselves as *a part of* it, fully and completely integrate ourselves *within* it. As Kuang-ming Wu says, "one becomes free *in* the hustle and bustle of worldly activities."[49]

Therefore it can be said that the *Zhuangzi* describes the behavior and attitude of what we might call the "perfectly well-adjusted person," someone who is perfectly at ease in all situations. It is not clear, however, if Zhuangzi thinks that everyone *should* be like this, or that everyone *could* be like this, or that *anyone* could be like this. To generalize in this fashion would itself be inconsistent with the nonformulaic personality of the text. Instead, the text simply presents us with strange and unsettling, though ultimately fascinating and compelling, stories that disturb our balance and force us to adjust. In this way, reading the text becomes a transformative project in itself.

Notes

This piece has been previously published, under the same title, in *Asian Philosophy* 6:1 (1996), pp. 59–72. We are grateful to Taylor & Francis Ltd. (http://www.tandf.co.uk) for agreeing to let us republish the piece in the present volume.

1. This chapter will refer, for the most part, only to the Inner Chapters, so as to avoid having to complicate matters with debates over authorship and authenticity. The Inner Chapters are the first seven, mostly believed to be the work of the actual Zhuangzi himself, while the rest of the chapters, according to some scholars, seem to represent a number of different authorial hands, agendas and styles. For a thorough discussion of this, see, for example, A. C. Graham, *Studies in Chinese Philosophy and Philosophical Literature* (Albany: State University of New York Press, 1990), pp. 283–321.

2. ZZJS 40; HY 3/1/47. Translations are taken from the following works: Victor Mair, *Wandering on the Way: Early Taoist Tales and Parables of Chuang Tzu* (New York: Bantam Books, 1994); Burton Watson, *The Complete*

Works of Chuang Tzu (New York: Columbia, 1968); Kuang-ming Wu, *The Butterfly as Companion* (Albany: State University of New York Press, 1990); Fung Yu-lan, *Chuang-Tzu—A New Selected Translation with an Exposition of the Philosophy of Kuo Hsiang* (Beijing: Foreign Languages Press, 1989); and A. C. Graham, *Chuang Tzu—The Inner Chapters* (London: George Allen & Unwin).

3. Roger Ames, *The Art of Rulership—A Study in Ancient Chinese Political Thought* (Honolulu: University of Hawaii Press, 1983), p. 43.

4. ZZJS 268; HY 18/6/70. Wing-tsit Chan, *Sourcebook in Chinese Philosophy* (Princeton: Princeton University Press, 1963).

5. As Roger Ames says, "'*Xiaoyaoyou*' ('wandering in unconditioned freedom') is a happy exchange for *wuwei*" (Ames, *The Art of Rulership*, p. 218, note 20.

6. Kuang-ming Wu, *Chuang Tzu: World Philosopher at Play* (New York: Scholars Press, 1982), p. 19.

7. Watson 34–35; ZZJS 36–37; HY 2–3/1/35–42.

8. Although one reasonable translation for the word *laozi* is "old master(s)," another is "mature child." The *Daode Jing* explains that the sage is childlike in precisely this sense of seeing the resonant and pregnant possibilities in things. The child is "mature," on the other hand, in the emotional sense, that is, not childish, able to postpone gratification, etc.

9. Watson 50–51; "Yangshengzhu," ZZJS 117–19; HY 7/3/2–10.

10. Ibid.

11. A. C. Graham, *Disputers of the Tao* (Illinois: Open Court, 1989), p. 186.

12. ZZJS 146; HY 10/4/55 (my translation).

13. "Dasheng," ZZJS 662; HY 50/19/62–64 (my translation).

14. Or, to paraphrase Heidegger, you never really know the hammer until it breaks.

15. Mair, *Wandering on the Way*, pp. 12–13; ZZJS 51; HY 3–4/2/10–13.

16. "Obstinate progression" is a phenomenon demonstrated, for instance, in the case of laboratory rats with a certain kind of brain lesion, who run into the walls of mazes and keep pushing against the wall, rather than turning in the direction of nonobstruction.

17. Kuang-ming Wu, *The Butterfly as Companion*, p. 81.

18. In electronics, a superconductor is a medium that conducts energy with little or no resistance. This enables a signal to be maximally effective over long distances without decay and with a minimum of energy expended.

19. Watson, 40; "Qiwulun," ZZJS 66; HY 4/2/30–31.

20. Kuang-ming Wu, *The Butterfly as Companion* (Albany: State University of New York Press, 1990), p. 161.

21. Mircea Eliade, *The Sacred and the Profane* (New York: Harcourt Brace Jovanovich, 1959).

22. Absolute value is the value of a number independent of its positive or negative quality. That is, the absolute value of both "one" and "negative one" is "one."

23. Watson 39; "Qiwulun," ZZJS 63; HY 4/2/26–27.

24. A. C. Graham, "Taoist Spontaneity and the Dichotomy of 'Is' and 'Ought,'" in Victor Mair, *Experimental Essays in Chuang Tzu* (Honolulu: University of Hawaii Press, 1983), p. 9; ZZJS 539; HY 40/15/11. The phrase *budeyi* is elsewhere (ZZJS 234; HY 15/6/15) translated by Watson (p. 79) as "reluctant, he could not help doing certain things," and Fung Yu-lan as "he responded spontaneously, as if there were no choice" (Fung Yu-lan, *Chuang-Tzu*, p. 93).

25. Graham, "Taoist Spontaneity," p. 9.

26. This is also similar, by the way, to the way phonograph arms are designed in order to minimize friction of the stylus against the side of the groove in the record to minimize wear and tear on both the record and the stylus.

27. Mair, *Wandering on the Way*, pp. 44–45.

28. Another relevant phrase that is even more ubiquitous is *wang* 忘 (forgetting), which shows up, among other places, in the story of Yan Hui and Confucius, found in the "Dazongshi" chapter. The conversation ends in the following exchange: "Yan Hui said, 'I smash up my limbs and body, drive out perception and intellect, cast off form, do away with understanding, and make myself identical with the Great Thoroughfare. This is what I mean by sitting down and forgetting everything.' Confucius said, 'If you're identical with it, you must have no more likes! If you've been transformed, you must have no more constancy! So you really are a worthy man after all! With your permission, I'd like to become your follower'" Watson, 90–91; ZZJS 284–85; HY 19/6/92–93. [For a discussion of this and related passages, see the first section of Yang Rur-bin's chapter in this volume.—ed.]

29. Watson 57–58; "Renjianshi," ZZJS 147; HY 9/4/26–28.

30. Kuang-ming Wu, *Chuang Tzu: World Philosopher at Play* (New York: Scholars Press, 1982), p. 126.

31. Watson 37; ZZJS 51; HY 3/2/9–10.

32. Kuang-ming Wu, *The Butterfly as Companion*, p. 157.

33. Watson 302; ZZJS 944; HY 75/26/48–49. Since this is from a chapter other than the "Inner" ones, its attribution is disputable, but I include it anyway because it expresses so well an idea found in the Inner Chapters. A more reliable example would be from "Yingdiwang": "The Perfect Man uses his mind like a mirror—going after nothing, welcoming nothing, responding but not storing." Watson, 97; ZZJS 307; HY 21/7/32–33.

34. Watson 6.

35. Ames, *The Art of Rulership*, p. 44.

36. Perhaps this is an idiosyncratic rendering, but *taiji*, at least in some sense,

refers to the relationship between, or unity of, yin and yang. As a principle, especially in the martial arts, it refers to the fact that everything that reaches its extreme turns into its opposite. The world of *taiji*, then, is the world of fluctuation and change, and the "perfectly adjusted person" is the one who most easily adapts and keeps his or her balance in the face of this "pitch and roll of oppositions." Roger Ames says: "This natural *dao* reflects what the *Laozi* perceives to be the order and regularity of natural change: the reversion principle, natural equilibrium, implicit opposites, impartiality, and so on." (ibid, p. 37).

37. The word *aikido* (*heqidao* 合氣道), for example, translates as the "way of harmonizing energy" and suggests that success in the martial arts is a matter of overcoming by means of conforming to the movements of the opponent. Similarly, one sign of mastery in *taijiquan* is the ability to perform the exercises outdoors among the birds and animals without creating a disturbance among them. This requires that one's movements be perfectly natural and inconspicuous so as to blend in completely with one's environment.

38. As the *Laozi* (ch. 50) suggests, "He who knows how to live can walk abroad without fear of rhinoceros or tiger. He will not be wounded in battle. For in him rhinoceroses can find no place to thrust their horn, tigers no place to use their claws, and weapons no place to pierce. Why is this so? Because he has no place for death to enter." Gia-fu Feng and Jane English, *Tao Tè Ching* (New York: Vintage Books, 1972), p. 52.

39. Bryan W. Van Norden, "Competing Interpretations of the Inner Chapters of the 'Zhuangzi,'" *Philosophy East and West* 46:2 (1996), pp. 247–69.

40. Watson 2.

41. Ibid. 3.

42. Mair, *Wandering on the Way*, p. xliii.

43. Watson 5–6.

44. Ibid. 6.

45. ZZJS 69; HY 4/2/33; Watson 40.

46. Philip J. Ivanhoe, "Zhuangzi on Skepticism, Skill, and the Ineffable *Dao*," *Journal of the American Academy of Religion* 61:4 (1993), p. 639.

47. Ibid.

48. Watson 25

49. Kuang-ming Wu, *Chuang Tzu*, p. 63.

8

A Mind–Body Problem in the *Zhuangzi*?

PAUL RAKITA GOLDIN

Chapter 18 of the *Zhuangzi*, "Zhi le" 至樂 (Supreme joy), contains some of the most memorable passages articulating a characteristic theme in the compendium.[1] All matter is in constant flux, changing from form to form constantly and inexorably. The chapter ends with a vivid description of the recycling of matter throughout the universe:

> There are originative germs for all species. When they obtain water, they become silky filaments 續斷.[2] When they are between water and land, they become "frog's-clothing" 蛙蠙之衣 [i.e., moss]. When they grow on elevated ground [by the riverbank], they become plantains 陵舄. When plantains obtain fertile soil, they become "crow's-feet" 烏足 [i.e., another kind of aquatic plant]. The roots of the "crow's-feet" become maggots 蠐螬 and the leaves become butterflies 胡蝶. The butterflies quickly transform into insects that are born beneath stoves; they appear as though having shed their skin, and are called *quduo* 鴝掇. In a thousand days, the *quduo* becomes a bird called *ganyugu* 乾餘骨. The spittle of the *ganyugu* becomes a *simi* 斯彌; the *simi* become "pickle-flies" 食醯. The *yilu* 頤輅 is born of the "pickle-fly"; the *huangkuang* 黃軦 is born of the *jiuyou* 九猷; "grain-grubs"[3] 瞀芮 are born of "rot-worms" 腐蠸. When the "goatherd" 羊奚 is paired with the "no-shoots" 不筍, the "enduring-bamboo" 久竹 produces the *qingning* 青寧. The *qingning* produces leopards 程; leopards produce horses; horses produce people; and people finally return to the originative germs [of nature]. The Myriad Things all emerge from the originative germs and return to the originative germs.[4]

The details in this playful passage are obviously not intended to be precise. One could hardly imagine any ancient writer earnestly believing that horses give birth to humans.[5] But the larger point is clear and squares well with the rest of the *Zhuangzi*: we are all born of an endless sequence of mysterious transformations, of which our existence as human beings represents only one temporary stage. When we die, our material will be transformed again into some other entity somewhere in the universe.

The chapter expands on this idea to argue against excessive displays of mourning for a loved one. Thus we read that when Zhuangzi's wife died, his boon friend Huizi 惠子 (i.e., Hui Shi 惠施) came to offer his condolences and was shocked to find Zhuangzi banging on a basin and singing.

> Huizi said: "She lived with you, raised your children, and grew old. Now that she is dead, it is enough that you do not weep for her; but banging on a basin and singing—is this not extreme?"
>
> Zhuangzi said: "It is not so. When she first died, how indeed could I not have been melancholy? But I considered that in the beginning, she was without life; not only was she without life, but she was originally without form; not only was she without form, but she was originally without *qi* 氣. In the midst of mixing with cloud and blur, there was a change and there was *qi*; the *qi* changed and there was form; the form changed and there was life; and now there is another change, and there is death. This is the same as the progression of the four seasons, spring, summer, autumn, winter.[6] Moreover, she sleeps now, reclining in a giant chamber; if I were to have accompanied her, weeping and wailing, I would have considered myself ignorant of destiny. So I stopped."[7]

Zhuangzi's point is that mourning is irrational, because his wife's death not only is inevitable but is caused by the same cosmic transformations that originally brought about her very life. To love his wife entails accepting her death as another one of the world's mysterious processes, and our unreflective differentiation between "life" and "death" is shown to be one of those artificial distinctions that the text loves to discredit. Life and death are nothing more than two complementary aspects of the same ineffable cosmic truth.[8]

The *locus classicus* of this view is found in the "Dazongshi" chapter. Four illustrious (and thoroughly fictitious) gentlemen—Zisi 子祀, Ziyu 子輿, Zili 子犁, and Zilai 子來—make a pact:

> "Whoever can take non-action as his head, life as his backbone, death as his buttocks—whoever knows that death, life, existence, and non-existence are one body—we will be friends with him." The four men looked at each other and smiled; none had anything contrary in his mind,[9] so they became friends with each other.

228PAULRAKITAGOLDIN

ZiyubecameZisiwenttovisithim.[Ziyu]said:"Greatisthe Creator of Things—putting me out of shape like this! My back is hunched; my five sense-organs are on top; my chin is hidden in my navel; my shoulders are higher than the crown of my head; my neck-bones point to Heaven." There was a disorder in his *yin* and *yang qi*, but his mind was at ease, as though there was nothing the matter. He limped over to a well and saw his reflection; he said: "Alas! The Creator of Things has put me out of shape like this!"

Zisi said: "Do you hate it?"

"No, how could I hate it? Suppose my left arm is transformed into a rooster; I would comply and keep track of the time of night.[10] Suppose my right arm is transformed into a crossbow; I would comply and look for an owl to roast. Suppose my buttocks are transformed into wheels and my spirit into a horse; I would comply and ride—why would I ever need a car? Moreover, what we obtain, we obtain because it is the right time; what we lose, we lose because we must follow [the flow of Nature]. If we are at peace with our time and dwell in the flow, sorrow and joy cannot enter into us. This is what the ancients called "unencumbered." Those who are unable to release themselves are tied down by objects. Moreover, things do not last longer than Heaven. So why should I hate it?"[11]

The intended point of this passage is the same as that of Zhuangzi's lecture to Huizi: death is merely another cosmic transformation that we must accept with equanimity. Ziyu's brilliant speech, however, raises certain problems that one suspects the author has not entirely thought through. The first indication comes in the statement that "there was disorder in his *yin* and *yang qi*, but his mind was at ease, as though there was nothing the matter" 陰陽之氣有沴，其心有閒而無事. In other words, although something very unusual has happened to his material substance—his *yin* and *yang qi*—this irregularity has not affected his mental processes. But then what material is his mind made of? It seems as though the author presupposes a disembodied mental power within Ziyu that can continue to function despite massive corporeal decay. This is a significant point, because it appears that we have encountered a mind-body problem—the arch-vexation of Western philosophy. (In what follows, I will use the term *mind-body problem* to refer specifically to the suggestion that the mind and the body may be metaphysically distinct entities. There are, of course, other possible interpretations of the phrase.)

The mystery only deepens when Ziyu avers cheerfully that if his buttocks were to be made into wheels, and his spirit into a horse 以神為馬, he would simply comply with his destiny and ride around, with no further need of a carriage. Whatever this "spirit" refers to, it cannot be a designation for the mental faculty that remains unperturbed in the face of terrifying transformations of matter—because even after his spirit is transformed into a horse, he still retains the power to assess his situation calmly and make the best of it.[12] It is hard to escape the conclusion that he conceives of his "mind" as an entity with no physical material at all.

Ziyu's speech raises several further questions. First, how does the *Zhuangzi* account for intelligence within its theory of cosmically recycling matter? For modern readers, part of the allure of that view, with its "crow's-feet" and "pickle-flies," must be that it is so strikingly similar to our own. To be sure, we do not believe that maggots and butterflies are born of the roots and leaves of a plant, but how different is the idea, in its essentials, from what we read in *Hamlet*?

> *Hamlet:* Your worm is your only emperor for diet: we fat all crea-
> tures else to fat us, and we fat ourselves for maggots; your
> fat king and your lean beggar is but variable service, two
> dishes, but to one table—that's the end.
>
> *King:* Alas, alas!
>
> *Hamlet:* A man may fish with the worm that hath eat of a king,
> and eat of a fish that hath fed of that worm.[13]

And of course, the *Zhuangzi* contains another famous scene with an identical point:

> Zhuangzi was about to die, and his disciples wished to bury him richly. Zhuangzi said: "I take Heaven and Earth as my coffin and sarcophagus, the sun and moon as my linked jade disks, the stars and constellations as my pearls, and the Myriad Things as my mortuary gifts. Will the accoutrements of my burial not be sufficient? Why add all this?"
>
> The disciples said: "We are afraid that the crows and kites may eat you, Master."
>
> Zhuangzi said: "Above, it will be the crows and kites that eat me; below, it will be the crickets and ants that eat me. Why be partial?"[14]

Zhuangzi, Hamlet, and we ourselves—with our concepts of the "food-chain" and the "law of the conservation of matter"—observe rightly enough that we are made of the same material as the animals and vegetables that we eat and the worms and maggots that eat us after death. But *none* of these schemes explains very clearly why—if the same basic stuff can appear equally in fish, worms, and human beings—neither fish nor worms, nor "crow's-feet" nor "pickle-flies," possess intelligence or consciousness! Where in the great process of material transformation do inanimate objects like "silky filaments" obtain the capacity to reflect on their condition, to utter oaths and speeches, to philosophize with an unmoved mind? This is as serious a problem for Zhuangzi's view of the world as it is for our own.

One possible solution, for Zhuangzi's case, may be that *all* material, in all its forms, possesses these complex mental faculties—that is to say, mental processes are simply an attribute of material. After all, the text is filled with such images as philosophical butterflies,[15] laughing cicadas, and talking metal. The *Zhuangzi* may imagine the world to be inhabited by untold billions of minds, residing in moss, residing in rot-worms. In this case, the consciousness of human beings would not present a particular problem.

However, there are reasons why it is doubtful that this is how the *Zhuangzi* conceives of the world. First, the fact that self-conscious butterflies may appear in dreams does not mean that self-conscious butterflies must exist in nature. It is reasonable to interpret the references to dreaming butterflies and talking cicadas as illustrative examples that the author or authors use, *when it suits them,* to convey the larger philosophical points. Otherwise, when the figure of Zhuangzi bangs on his basin, we should expect the basin to squawk back. Such events do not occur often enough in the text for us to believe that the authors really conceive of animate basins.

Second, and more important, the text regularly describes the "mind" in contexts where it can only be construed as entirely disembodied. Consider the following anecdote from "Zhi le:"

> Zhuangzi went to Chu and saw a hollow skull; it was brittle, but retained its shape. He tapped it with his riding-crop, and then he asked it: "Sir, was it because of your greed for life and loss of principles that you ended up like this? Or was it because you were involved in the affairs of a doomed state, and were executed with an axe, that you ended up like this? Or was it because you were involved in evil conduct, bringing shame on the reputation of your father, mother, wife, and children, that you ended up like this? Or was it because you had the misfortune to freeze or starve that you ended up like this? Or maybe your years just came to an end?" When he was done talking, he picked up the skull, and used it as a pillow to sleep.
>
> At midnight, the skull appeared in a dream, saying: "You speak like a sophist! I perceive that your words are all born of the encumbrances of humanity. In death there is none of this. Would you like to hear an explanation of death?"

Zhuangzi said: "Yes."

The skull said: "In death, there is no ruler above, no subject below. There is also no such thing as the four seasons; one simply follows Heaven and Earth as one's spring and autumn. Even the joys of a south-facing king cannot exceed this."

Zhuangzi did not believe him, and said: "If I commanded the Director of Destiny 司命 to restore your body to life;[16] to make bones, flesh, meat, and skin for you; to return your father, mother, wife, children, and village acquaintances; would you wish it?"

The skull frowned in deep vexation, and said: "How could I abandon the joys of a south-facing king and return to the toils of life among men?"[17]

The "person" pertaining to this skull will evidently enjoy the rest of eternity in a kind of timeless Never-never-land. Zhuangzi's interlocutor looks suspiciously like an immaterial soul. Similarly, we remember that when his wife dies, Zhuangzi remarks that she now "sleeps, reclining in a giant chamber." But according to the earlier theory of the transformation of matter, all of one's material should be reconstituted into some other physical object at the moment of death. This is, after all, Zili's point when he consoles his friend Zilai, who is lying deathly ill: "Great is the Creator and Transformer! What will you be made into next? Where will you be sent? Will you be made into a rat's liver? Will you be made into an insect's leg?"[18] Rat's livers and insect's legs manifestly do not live in the carefree death-world of Zhuangzi's wife and the hollow skull from Chu. What, then, do we have to look forward to after death: coming back as a rat's liver or spending eternity in supreme and somnolent bliss?

I think the only way to reconcile this problem is to assume that our *material* will be recycled into something phenomenal like a rat's liver, but that our *disembodied minds* live on in some mysteriously timeless and immaterial place. This is not only an identity problem—are "we" the substance that will be transformed into a rat's liver or the ghost that will survive forever?—it is also a mind-body problem.

Moreover, this conundrum is not unique to the *Zhuangzi*. One of the most remarkable examples of an unacknowledged mind-body problem appears in the writings of Xunzi 荀子 (third cent. B.C.). The relevant passage appears in a philosophical discussion of abdication: "They say: 'When [the king] is old and decrepit, he should abdicate.' This is also not so. In his blood, *qi*, sinews, and energy, there may be decay; but in his wisdom, deliberations, choices, and rejections, there is no decay."[19] In Xunzi's system, the *qi* and the mind appear to flourish and decay independently of each other. He does not address the evident difficulty: what material, then, is the mind made of? I believe Xunzi means to say that the mind and the body are metaphysically distinct substances. In particular, his calculated use of the term *qi* emphasizes his view that the mind cannot be composed of the same material as the rest of the body.[20]

The suggestion that there is an unacknowledged mind-body problem (or call it a "folk-psychological" dualism)[21] in certain ancient Chinese philosophical texts is likely to prove controversial. In a sense, this is curious, because if one were to make the same claim about ancient Greek philosophy—or about Augustine, or any number of pre-Cartesian thinkers—one might not expect much objection. In the study of traditional Chinese philosophy however, the very suggestion of a mind-body dichotomy has attained the status of a taboo. This is because the most authoritative textbooks, insofar as they discuss the issue at all, agree that no such problem ever haunted Chinese philosophy and that reading it into the Chinese context represents an unwarranted imposition of Western concerns. To quote A. C. Graham, who is perhaps the single most influential critic:

> [The mind-body dichotomy] never emerged in pre-Han philosophy; the word *xin* 心 "heart" is sometimes translated as "mind," reasonably enough in later philosophy influenced by Indian Buddhism, but in the classical period it refers only to the heart as the organ with which one thinks, approves and disapproves. (Thinking is not in traditional China located in the brain.) . . . Confucius is not a victim of the post-Cartesian superstition of mind as "ghost in the machine"; he does not conceive the difference between ritual as dignified and reverent performance and as empty formality in terms of the presence or absence of dignity and formality in the performer's mind.[22]

These strictures can be traced back directly to Herbert Fingarette, an insightful Western philosopher who, late in life, attempted to explain the philosophy of the Confucian *Analects* 論語 (and who, it should be remarked, was not trained as a scholar of Chinese). According to Fingarette, when Confucius refers to the virtue of *ren* 仁 (humanity), he does not imply anything like an inner mental condition; he means nothing more than submitting to *li* 禮 (ritual). Fingarette emphasized this point to show that Confucius did not partake of a conception of human nature that was "psychologized" along the lines so familiar from Western philosophy and that most previous interpreters made the mistake of simply assuming that he did.

> Thus *li* and *ren* are two aspects of the same thing . . . *Li* refers to the act as overt and distinguishable pattern of sequential behavior; *ren* refers to the

act as the single, indivisible gesture of an actor, as his, and as particular and individual by reference to the unique individual who performs the act and to the unique context of the particular action.

Our more familiar Western terminology would be misleading. We are tempted to go further than I have above and say *ren* refers to the attitudes, feelings, wishes and will. This terminology is misleading. The thing we must *not* do is to psychologize Confucius's terminology in the *Analects*. The first step in seeing that this is so is to recognize that *ren* and its associated "virtues," and *li* too, are not connected in the original text with the language of "will," "emotion," and "inner states." The move from *ren* as referring us to a person on to *ren* as "therefore" referring us to his inner mental or psychic condition or processes finds no parallel in the *Analects*. Certainly there is no systematic or even unsystematic elaboration of any such connections.[23]

Insofar as I understand his argument, Fingarette seems to be saying that Confucius neither accepts nor rejects an image of the mind as the locus of inner mental states: the whole idea of such an alternative never even occurs to him. As a virtue, *ren* does not presuppose any mental states whatsoever; it is merely another term for the skillful practice of *li*. Moreover, when Confucius appears to discuss various "emotions," these are really nothing more than observable conditions. For example, when it says in *Analects* 2.6 that parents are "worried" (*you* 憂) about their child's illness, this is to be understood as a "response to trouble" and should not be "conceived as rooted in troubled 'inner' states."[24]

Fingarette constructed this argument in 1972, at a time when many Western philosophers were, for their own reasons, particularly irritated by traditional Western mentalism. One can only imagine how refreshing it must have been to discover that Confucius was innocent of "Cartesian superstitions." But Fingarette's account of *ren* is controversial[25] and was originally intended, in any case, to apply only to the *Analects*—which are sufficiently vague as to allow for a number of mutually incompatible interpretations, some of them "psychologized," some of them not. In any case, whether or not Fingarette's contention is tenable in the context of the *Analects*, I think Graham and others have erred in extending Fingarette's contention to cover *all* of traditional Chinese thought.

To be sure, it is certain that no Chinese philosopher ever problematized the notion of inner mental states in any manner remotely like that of Descartes. It is also plain that many Chinese philosophers conceived of the heart-mind as just another organ of the body and not an immaterial ghost or spirit. And then there were those schemes that did not conceive

of a mind (in any philosophical sense) whatsoever. The *Huainanzi* 淮南
子, for example, expounds a thoroughgoing materialism (inherited, no
doubt, from the *Zhuangzi*) in which human beings, like all other physical
objects, are thought to be made up of *qi*. Since *qi* obeys certain constant
and knowable physical laws, a skillful ruler can make his subjects do anything he wants them to, merely by stimulating their *qi* in the appropriate
manner. The idea is especially well illustrated in the phenomenon of
sympathetic musical vibrations.

> The lord—oh how he is like an archer! A minute [error] here counts for
> feet and yards there [by the target]. Therefore [the lord] is cautious about
> how he stimulates [the people]. When Rong Qiqi 榮啓期 plucked [his
> instrument] once, Confucius was joyous for three days; he was stimulated
> by harmony. When Zou Ji 鄒忌 (385–319 B.C.)[26] strummed once wildly,
> King Wei (of Qi 齊威王, r. 357–320 B.C.) was sorrowful all night; he was
> stimulated by melancholy.[27] If one moves them with the lute and zither,
> and forms them with tones and sounds, one can make the people grieve
> or be joyous.[28]

In this chillingly regulated world, the sovereign simply strikes the
appropriate chord, and his subjects assume perforce the intended attitude.
These claims are all presented without any consideration of the people's
ability or even *will* to resist this form of control. The text grants only that
the people may be disaffected and cause trouble if they are mistreated.
What the *Huainanzi* refuses to accept is the notion that people may have
any kind of spiritual life, that they may have likes and dislikes that are not
motivated solely by their five senses, and that they have the capability and
obligation of moral development.[29]

It was even possible for Mencius, a Chinese philosopher with a very
sophisticated concept of 'mind,' to avoid entirely the problem of dualism
by conceiving of the heart (the locus of the mind) as a part of the body
with a specific function, like all others.

> Gongduzi 公都子 asked: "Though we are equally human, why is it that
> some become greater people, and others become lesser people?"
> Mencius said: "Those who follow their greater parts become greater
> people; those who follow their lesser parts become lesser people."
> "Though we are equally human, why is it that some follow their greater
> parts, and others follow their lesser parts?"
> "The ears and eyes, as organs, do not think, and they become clouded by
> objects. When an object engages [the sense organ], it simply leads it away.
> The heart, as an organ, thinks. If it thinks, then it obtains [what it seeks];

if it does not think, then it does not obtain it. This is what Heaven has imparted to me. If one takes one's stand first on [the part] that is greater, then the parts that are lesser cannot snatch it away. This is simply the way to become a greater person."[30]

With this elegant formulation, Mencius is able to fulfill two competing philosophical obligations. On the one hand, he remains true to his conviction that the difference between humans and animals—and between moral and immoral people—lies in the mind. On the other hand, he avoids the problem of an immaterial spirit or a "ghost in the machine" by asserting that the mind is simply a part of the body: it is the organ of the body that "thinks" 思 (in Mencius's special moral sense), just as the eyes and ears are the organs that perceive objects. In other words, while Mencius may or may not believe in the possibility of inner mental states, it is clear that he does not see any need to separate the mind and the body on a metaphysical level.

However, while these passages from *Huainanzi* and Mencius appear to bear out Graham's claims, the examples of Xunzi and Zhuangzi demonstrate that we need not retain the familiar assessment, "pre-Han philosophy knows nothing of a mind-body dichotomy."[31] Indeed, Xunzi's sophisticated conception of the mind as spectator and director is so "mentalist" that it is hardly surprising he should find it impossible in the passage discussed above to locate even the most basic mental faculties in the normal substance of the body.[32] His notion of "knowing the Way" is distinctive and comes close to the Western idea of cognizing truths of nature within an inner mental theater.

> One might sit in a room and still see the Four Seas; one might reside in the present and still expound on bygone and distant times. If one is conversant with the Myriad Things and knows their essence, if one tests order and disorder and is conversant with their systems, then one can treat Heaven and Earth as one's warp and woof and assign the proper roles to the Myriad Things.[33]

When a philosopher declares that one might sit inside one's chamber and still "see" everything within the Four Seas, there cannot be much doubt that he conceives of a mind with an actively theatrical imagination, with entire worlds and fantasies parading before a disembodied mental "viewer." This is not a mind that is unfamiliar with what Fingarette calls "inner mental states."[34]

But it is never clear in Xunzi precisely how these mental processes function. How is it possible that the outside world can be viewed from

within the confines of one's room? Where does the "viewing" take place?
He simply did not ask the necessary questions that show he was aware
of a mind-body problem. On the basis of his statement about the aged
king with his unimpeded mind, one must presume that Xunzi simply
takes it as a matter of course that the mental world is a world of its own,
fundamentally separate from the physical world. This is to say that Xunzi
subscribed intuitively to "folk psychology" (as the term is currently used).
I believe the *Zhuangzi* did so as well, and I suspect that the same general
view can be found in still other ancient Chinese texts.[35]

These issues are brought into clear focus in the following anecdote
from the *Mozi* 墨子:

> In the past, in the time of Bao 鮑, Lord Wen of Song 宋文君 (r. 610–
> 589 B.C.), there was a functionary named Priest Guangu 觀辜 who was
> following the service for a ghost.[36] The medium[37] emerged with a staff; he
> said to him: "Guangu, why are the jade tablets and disks not up to their
> full measure? Why is the wine and millet unclean? Why are the sacrificial
> victims not unblemished and fat? Why are the offerings of spring, summer,
> autumn, and winter[38] not timely? Did you do this, or did Bao do this?"
>
> Guangu said: "Bao is young and immature; he is still in his diapers. What
> could Bao know about this? This was done specifically by the functionary
> in charge, Guangu."
>
> The medium lifted his staff and beat him, killing him on top of the altar.
> At the time, those people in Song who were participating in the ceremony
> all saw it; those who were far away all heard it. It is written in the annals
> of Song. The feudal lords transmitted [the story] and commented: "For
> whoever is not reverent and cautious about sacrifices, the punishment of
> the spirits is even as swift as this." Seeing that the story is in several books,
> one can hardly doubt that ghosts exist.[39]

Here we have, in the starkest possible terms, a ghost in a machine.
The function of the "medium" 祝子 in this ceremony is to serve as a
physical receptacle for the spirit being cultivated. This particular spirit was
evidently dissatisfied with the lassitude of the "functionary in charge" 官
臣 and punished him by using the body of the medium to kill him. As
far as the viewers were concerned, the medium himself played no part in
the gruesome affair; his own mental processes were somehow temporarily shut off. It was obvious to everyone present that the offended spirit
exercised its will and bludgeoned Guangu to death. Just how this could
all happen is never explained, because the operative worldview, again, is
unproblematized. After all, it is only a philosophical materialist who could
ask how spirits or souls might animate bodies and effect their intentions

through them. The author of this particular text apparently had no difficulty in conceiving of a dualistic universe populated by material bodies and immaterial spirits.[40] And this particular story is by no means unusual; the ancient literature abounds with similar tales of ghosts and spirits, some beneficent, some malevolent, some thoroughly inscrutable.[41]

The tale of Guangu and the ghost transcending matter reveals a dualistic conception of the world that is a necessary condition for the notion of a metaphysical mind-body dichotomy. The world of the ghost who killed Guangu is the same as the world where Zhuangzi believes his wife sleeps peacefully and where the skull from Chu enjoys its timeless bliss, free from the cares of human existence. It is the world of the spirit. So the orientation of the *Zhuangzi* is at once materialistic and dualistic. We are told, on the one hand, that all matter constantly cycles and recycles through various shapes and combinations and, on the other hand, that our immaterial spirit escapes this process and lives on *in essentially the same form* after death. All in all, this conception is not so surprising: we know of a similar idea from Western religious philosophy, namely the doctrine of the "immaterial soul."[42] We ourselves commonly express a compatible worldview, when, after the death of a loved one, we console ourselves by saying that he or she is still present with us, still "looking down at us" from Heaven. Even people who do not take such statements seriously have heard them before and should have no trouble understanding them.

Appendix:
The Dream Problem in the *Zhuangzi*

There is one other important respect in which the *Zhuangzi* broaches philosophical problems associated with the mind-body dichotomy. The text is notable for its recurring dream sequences, in which the apparent reality of reality is questioned by comparing it to the apparent reality of a dream. Yet as famous as these passages are, their philosophical significance is still frequently overlooked.[43] The butterfly dream is probably the most oft-cited example of this theme in the *Zhuangzi*:

> Once Zhuang Zhou dreamt that he was a butterfly, a butterfly fluttering happily, and he was aware that this is what he wanted to be. He did not know that he was Zhou. Soon he awoke, and, startled, he was Zhou. He did not know whether he was Zhou dreaming that he was a butterfly, or whether he was a butterfly dreaming that he was Zhou.[44]

And similarly:

> Who dreams of wine weeps in the morning; who dreams of weeping hunts
> in the morning. While one is dreaming, one does not know that it is a
> dream, and in the middle of the dream one may even divine one's dream.
> Only after waking does one know that it was a dream. Soon there will be
> a Great Awakening, after which we will know that this is a Great Dream.
> And fools think themselves "awake," confident that they know things: this
> is a lord, this a shepherd. How obtuse! Confucius and you are all dreaming.
> When I say that you are dreaming, I am also dreaming.[45]

The point of these passages is that it is not so self-evidently true that
we are what we think we are. Perhaps our existence and experiences are
nothing more than the dreams of a butterfly—for how can we tell the
difference between our perceptions of reality and the unreal experiences
of dreams?[46] The issue here is the same as what Gareth B. Matthews[47] has
called the "epistemological dream problem" in Descartes:

> How often, asleep at night, am I convinced of just such familiar events—
> that I am here in my dressing-gown, sitting by the fire—when in fact I
> am lying undressed in bed! Yet at the moment my eyes are certainly wide
> awake when I look at this piece of paper; I shake my head and it is not
> asleep; as I stretch out and feel my hand I do so deliberately, and I know
> what I am doing. All this would not happen with such distinctness to
> someone asleep. Indeed! As if I did not remember other occasions when
> I have been tricked by exactly similar thoughts while asleep! As I think
> about this more carefully, I see plainly that there are never any sure signs by
> means of which being awake can be distinguished from being asleep. The
> result is that I begin to feel dazed, and this very feeling only reinforces the
> notion that I may be asleep.[48]

Strictly speaking, the "dream problem" ("How do I know whether I
am now dreaming?") is not the same as the mind-body problem, but the
two are related in that they both hinge on the reflexive use of the first-
person pronoun, *I*.[49] That is to say, when I ask, "How do I know whether
I am dreaming?" I do not mean, "How do I know whether Paul Rakita
Goldin is dreaming?"—for I can still ask the dream question without
any external knowledge of who I am. I mean: "How do I know, from
my own point of view, whether I am dreaming?" This special, "reflexive"
use of '*I*' has been distinguished from regular uses of *I* ("I am hungry,"
etc.) by means of the conventional marker '*I★*'.[50] Remarkably, it has
been suggested that the *Zhuangzi* makes effectively the same distinction
through its complementary usage of the first-person pronouns *wo* 我 (I)
and *wu* 吾 (I★).[51] In any case, what is clear is that the *Zhuangzi* uses the

"epistemological dream problem" to ask the type of skeptical question that Richard Rorty identifies as the watershed in the history of Western philosophy:"How do we know that anything which is mental represents anything which is not mental?"[52]

Unlike Descartes, however, the Zhuangzi makes no explicit attempt to solve the dream problem.[53] This difference should come as no great surprise, since it is well established that the Zhuangzi prefers to ask epistemological questions rather than to answer them. (This is the sense in which the skepticism of the Zhuangzi has been called "therapeutic.")[54] But the fact that Zhuangzi does not solve the dream problem ought not prevent us from recognizing that he raises it, and in this respect, comes closer to the Cartesian mode of skepticism than any other Chinese philosopher.

Notes

I would like to thank Bryan W. Van Norden for helpful comments on an earlier version of this chapter.

1. Most commentators agree that "Zhi le" is a later chapter with close philosophical links to the so-called *neipian* 內篇 (Inner Chapters), especially chapter 6, "Dazongshi" 大宗師 (The great ancestral teacher). It is justifiable, therefore, to use the famous images in "Zhi le" as illustrative examples of a Zhuangzian theme, even though it is extremely unlikely that the chapter was written by Zhuang Zhou 莊周 himself. See, e.g., Liu Xiaogan, *Classifying the Zhuangzi Chapters*, Michigan Monographs in Chinese Studies 65 (Ann Arbor: Center for Chinese Studies, University of Michigan, 1994), p. 100; Zhang Hengshou 張恒壽, *Zhuangzi xintan* 莊子新探 (Wuhan: Hubei renmin, 1983), p. 198; A. C. Graham, "How Much of *Chuang-tzu* Did Chuang-tzu Write?" *Journal of the American Academy of Religion* 47.3 (1979), reprinted in Graham, *Studies in Chinese Philosophy and Philosophical Literature* (Albany: State University of New York Press, 1990), p. 283; Hu Yüan-chün 胡遠濬, *Zhuangzi quangu* 莊子詮詁 (Taipei: Shangwu, 1967), p. 141; Guan Feng 關鋒, "*Zhuangzi* waizapian chutan" 莊子外雜篇初探, in Zhexue yanjiu bianji bu 哲學研究編輯部, *Zhuangzi zhexue taolun ji* 莊子哲學討論集 (Beijing: Zhonghua, 1962), pp. 61–98; Lin Yunming 林雲銘 (fl. 1663), *Zhuangzi yin* 莊子因, in *Wuqiubei zhai Zhuangzi jicheng chubian* 無求備齋莊子集成初編, ed. Yen Ling-feng 嚴靈峰 (Taipei: Yiwen, 1972), 18, 4, p. 26b; and Chen Zhi'an 陳治安 (fl. 1632), *Nanhua zhenjing benyi* 南華真經本義, in *Wuqiubei zhai Zhuangzi jicheng xubian* 續編, ed. Yen Ling-feng 嚴靈峰, (Taipei: Yiwen, 1974), 26, 11, p. 1a. On the other hand, Jiang Fucong 蔣復璁, "*Zhuangzi* kaobian" 莊子考辨, *Tushuguan xue jikan* 圖書館學季刊 2.1, reprinted in

Xu Weishu tongkao 續偽書通考, ed. Cheng Liang-shu 鄭良樹 (Taipei: Xue-sheng, 1984), 2, p. 1382, considers the chapter "overdone" 矯枉過直 and "the fabrication of a shallow scholar" 淺學者之所為.

2. Following the commentary in Guo Qingfan 郭慶藩 (1844–1896), *Zhuangzi jishi* 莊子集釋, ed. Wang Xiaoyu 王孝魚, Xinbian Zhuzi jicheng (Beijing: Zhonghua, 1961), p. 625, note 2. Most commentators read *jue* 絕 here, but Guo Qingfan's "father" 家世父 (Guo Songtao 郭嵩燾) explains the merits of the reading *xuduan* 續斷, which are silky filaments found in water. See also the commentary in Wang Shu-min 王叔岷, *Zhuangzi jiaoquan* 莊子校詮, 2nd edition, Zhongyang Yanjiuyuan Lishi Yuyan Yanjiusuo zhuankan 88 (Taipei, 1994), 2, p. 659, note 6.

3. I assume that the *maorui* 瞀芮 is the same creature known in Modern Mandarin as the *maozei* 蟊賊.

4. ZZJS 624–25; HY 47–48/18/46. All translations in this chapter are my own unless otherwise indicated. Cf. the translations in Victor H. Mair, *Wandering on the Way: Early Taoist Tales and Parables of Chuang Tzu* (New York: Bantam, 1994; rpt., Honolulu: University of Hawaii Press, 1998), pp. 172 f.; and Wing-tsit Chan, *A Source Book in Chinese Philosophy* (Princeton: Princeton University Press, 1963), p. 204.

5. Nevertheless, we must not overestimate the ancients' knowledge of nature and ecology. As late as the eleventh century, for example, Cheng Yi 程頤 (1033–1107) suggested in all seriousness that fireflies are born of decaying grass and that lice are born spontaneously in new clothes. See Zhu Xi 朱熹 (1130–1200), *Henan Chengshi yishu* 河南程氏遺書 (*Guoxue jiben congshu* 國學基本叢書), 18, p. 220. Cf. also A. C. Graham, *Two Chinese Philosophers: The Metaphysics of the Brothers Ch'eng*, 2nd edition (La Salle, Ill.: Open Court, 1992), p. 36.

6. There is an anacoluthia in the original: "spring, autumn, winter, summer" 春秋冬夏.

7. "Zhile," ZZJS 614–15; HY 46/18/15–19. Compare the translations in Mair, *Wandering on the Way*, pp. 168 f., and Chan, *A Source Book in Chinese Philosophy*, p. 209.

8. This interpretation is by no means novel; see e.g., Chen Guying 陳鼓應, *Zhuangzi qianshuo* 莊子淺說 (Hong Kong: Shang-wu, 1991), pp. 27 ff.; A. C. Graham, *Disputers of the Tao: Philosophical Argument in Ancient China* (La Salle, Ill.: Open Court, 1989), pp. 202–04; and Fung Yu-lan, *A History of Chinese Philosophy*, tr. Derk Bodde, 2nd edition (Princeton: Princeton University Press, 1952), 1, pp. 236–39. Cf. also, e.g., "Zhi beiyou" 知北遊, ZZJS 733; HY 58/22/11–12: "The birth of a human being is the accumulation of *qi*. When it accumulates, there is life; when it dissipates, there is death. Since death and life are in league with each other, what should I be vexed about?"

9. That is, they did not harbor any notions that were "contrary" 逆 to the "mysterious principles" 玄理 of the Way, as Cheng Xuanying 成玄英 (fl.

630–60) explains in his commentary. The idea here is that the four gentlemen have overcome the blinkered human tendency to formulate one's own private opinions—one's own "completed mind" (*chengxin* 成心), in the language of the *Zhuangzi*. For more on this idea in the *Zhuangzi*, see e.g., Graham, *Disputers of the Tao*, pp. 191 ff., and Harold H. Oshima, "A Metaphorical Analysis of the Concept of Mind in the *Chuang-tzu*," in *Experimental Essays on Chuang-tzu*, ed. Victor H. Mair, Asian Studies at Hawaii 29 ([Honolulu]: University of Hawaii Press, 1983), pp. 63–84. Cf. also Wang Fuzhi 王夫之 (1619–1692), *Zhuangzi jie* 莊子解 (Beijing: Zhonghua, 1961), p. 16.

10. I believe the character *qiu* 求 in *yu yin yi qiu shi ye* 予因以求時夜 is excrescent, by confusion with *qiu* in the next clause. The commentary of Lu Deming 陸德明 (556–627) notes that one edition omits *qiu*. See also the commentary of Yu Yue 俞樾 (1821–1907), *Zhuangzi jiaoquan*, 1, p. 245, note 10.

11. "Dazongshi," ZZJS 258–60; HY 17/6/45–53. Cf. the translations in Mair, *Wandering on the Way*, pp. 57 f., and Chan, *A Source Book in Chinese Philosophy*, pp. 196 f.

12. According to the conventional worldview of the Six Dynasties, this "spirit" 神 was conceived unproblematically as another kind of *qi* that is subject to the same transformations as all other kinds of matter. In other words, it was not understood as an immaterial spirit. See especially the view attributed to the interlocutor of Huiyuan 慧遠 (A.D. 334–416) in "Shamen bujing wang zhe lun" 沙門不敬王者論, which is preserved in Seng You 僧祐 (445–518), *Hongming ji* 弘明集 (Taipei: Zhonghua, 1983), 5, p. 9a. Cf. also Charles Holcombe, *In the Shadow of the Han: Literati Thought and Society at the Beginning of the Southern Dynasties* (Honolulu: University of Hawaii Press, 1994), pp. 100 f. For an overview of the concept of '*shen*' in early traditions of meditation, see Harold D. Roth, "The Early Taoist Concept of *Shen*: A Ghost in the Machine?" in *Sagehood and Systematizing Thought in Warring States and Han China*, ed. Kidder Smith Jr. (Brunswick, Maine: Asian Studies Program, Bowdoin College, 1990), pp. 11–32. However, this later conception of the "spirit" is firmly in line with the general materialist tendency of the Six Dynasties and therefore may not reflect the original viewpoint of the *Zhuangzi*.

13. *Hamlet* IV.iii,21–28; text in G. Blakemore Evans, ed., *The Riverside Shakespeare* (Boston: Houghton Mifflin, 1974), p. 1171.

14. "Lie Yukou" 列禦寇, ZZJS 1063; HY 90/32/47–50. Compare the translation in Mair, *Wandering on the Way*, p. 332.

15. See the appendix to this chapter.

16. On the idea of resurrection in the Warring States and the power of the divinity known as the "Director of Destiny" 司命, see e.g., Mu-chou Poo, *In Search of Personal Welfare: A View of Ancient Chinese Religion* (Albany: State University of New York Press, 1998), p. 66. A recently excavated text from

Fangmatan 放馬灘, Gansu Province, tells a gripping story of resurrection; see Donald Harper, "Resurrection in Warring States Popular Religion," *Taoist Resources* 5:2 (1994), pp. 13–28; Li Xueqin 李學勤, "Fangmatan jian zhong de zhiguai gushi" 放馬灘簡中的志怪故事, *Wenwu* 文物 1990.4, pp. 43–47; and He Shuangquan 何雙全, "Tianshui Fangmatan Qinjian jiazhong rishu kaoshu" 天水放馬灘秦簡甲種日書考述, in *Qin-Han jiandu lunwen ji* 秦漢簡牘論文集, ed. Gansu Sheng Wenwu Kaogu Yanjiusuo ([Lanzhou]: Gansu renmin, 1989), pp. 7–28.

17. "Zhi le," ZZJS 617–19; HY 46–47/18/22–29. Compare the translation in Mair, *Wandering on the Way*, p. 170.

18. "Dazongshi," ZZJS 261; HY 17/6/55–56.

19. "Zhenglun" 正論; text in Wang Xianqian 王先謙 (1842–1918), *Xunzi jijie* 荀子集解, ed. Shen Xiaohuan 沈嘯寰 and Wang Xingxian 王星賢, Xinbian Zhuzi jicheng (Beijing: Zhonghua, 1988), 12.18, p. 333. Cf. the translation in John Knoblock, *Xunzi: A Translation and Study of the Complete Works* (Stanford: Stanford University Press, 1988–94), 3, p. 41.

20. I have drawn attention to this passage in Paul Rakita Goldin, "Insidious Syncretism in the Political Philosophy of *Huai-nan-tzu*," *Asian Philosophy* 9:2 (1999). Mark Edward Lewis, *Sanctioned Violence in Early China* (Albany: State University of New York Press, 1990), p. 224, and Sawada Takio 澤田多喜男, "*Junshi* 荀子 to Ryoshi Shunjū 呂氏春秋 ni okeru ki," in *Ki* 氣 *no shisō* 思想—*Chūgoku* 中國 *ni okeru shizenkan* 自然觀 *to ningenkan* 人間觀 *no tenkai* 展開, ed. Onozawa Seiichi 小野澤精一, et al. (Tokyo: Tōkyō Daigaku, 1978), pp. 85 f., both discuss this passage, but without considering its relevance to the mind-body problem.

For another early example, consider the following lines from the *Chuci* 楚辭: "When people are born, they all have something in which they take their pleasure; I have taken it as my rule only to be fond of elegance. Though my body be dismembered, I would still not change; for how could my mind reform through punishment?" In Jin Kaicheng 金開誠, et al., *Qu Yuan ji jiaozhu* 屈原集校注, Zhongguo gudian wenxue jiben congshu (Beijing: Zhonghua, 1996), 1, p. 48. The author is evidently denying that his mind can be affected by stimuli applied to his body. Nevertheless, the metaphysical underpinnings of this passage are far less clear, and it may not be necessary to presuppose an immaterial mind in this case.

21. For a seminal but controversial view of "folk psychology," see Paul M. Churchland, "Eliminative Materialism and the Propositional Attitudes," *Journal of Philosophy* 78 (1981), pp. 67–90; and Churchland, *Scientific Realism and the Plasticity of the Mind* (Cambridge: Cambridge University Press, 1979). It is not often observed that the term *folk psychology* (which is evidently intended to be disparaging) is infelicitous and extremely misleading. First, the presence of the word *folk* (on analogy with *folk music, folk wisdom*, etc.) implies that different "folks" may have different "folk psychologies." But it has been sug-

gested by certain "innatists" that something akin to the "folk-psychological" paradigm is actually wired into the human brain. See, e.g., Jerry A. Fodor, *The Language of Thought* (Cambridge: Harvard University Press, 1975). Moreover, one fundamental premise of "eliminative materialism" is that "folk psychology" represents a coherent and homogeneous theory. This supposition is not uncontested—in part because of observed differences in the content of "folk psychology" among various cultures. See, e.g., Roy G. D'Andrade, "A Folk Model of the Mind," in *Cultural Models in Language and Thought*, ed. Dorothy Holland and Naomi Quinn (Cambridge and New York: Cambridge University Press, 1987).

22. *Disputers of the Tao*, pp. 25 f., with the Romanization converted. Cf. also Chad Hansen, *A Daoist Theory of Chinese Thought: A Philosophical Perspective* (New York and Oxford: Oxford University Press, 1992), esp. pp. 75 ff.; and Hansen, "Language in the Heart-mind," in *Understanding the Chinese Mind: The Philosophical Roots*, ed. Robert E. Allinson (Oxford: Oxford University Press, 1989), esp. pp. 84 ff. Similarly, Chris Jochim, "Just Say No to 'No Self' in *Zhuangzi*," in *Wandering at Ease in the* Zhuangzi, ed. Roger T. Ames (Albany: State University of New York Press, 1998), pp. 50 ff., denies that there is any place for a "mind-body dualism" in the *Zhuangzi*'s concept of '*xin*.'

23. Herbert Fingarette, *Confucius—The Secular as Sacred*, Harper Torchbooks (New York: Harper & Row, 1972), pp. 42f., with Romanization emended; emphasis in original. Fingarette is surely influenced here by Gilbert Ryle, *The Concept of Mind* (London: Hutchinson, 1949), esp. pp. 11 ff.

24. Fingarette, *Confucius*, pp. 44 f. Incidentally, the implicit interpretation of *Analects* 2.6 here is debatable; many commentators take this passage to refer to the *parents'* illness, and not that of the child. See Cheng Shude 程樹 德 (1877–1944), *Lunyu jishi* 論語集釋, ed. Cheng Junying 程俊英 and Jiang Jianyuan 蔣見元, Xinbian Zhuzi jicheng (Beijing: Zhonghua, 1990), 3, pp. 83 ff.

25. For some responses to Fingarette's thesis, see, in addition to the works mentioned in note 22, above, Benjamin I. Schwartz, *The World of Thought in Ancient China* (Cambridge and London: Harvard University Press, Belknap Press, 1985), pp. 71 ff.; Herrlee G. Creel, "Discussion of Professor Fingarette on Confucius," in *Studies in Classical Chinese Thought*, ed. Henry Rosemont Jr., and Benjamin I. Schwartz, *Journal of the American Academy of Religion*, Thematic Issue 47:3 (1979), pp. 407–16; the review article by Henry Rosemont Jr. in *Philosophy East and West* 26:4 (1976), pp. 463–77; as well as Fingarette's response and Rosemont's counter-response, *Philosophy East and West* 28:4 (1978), pp. 511–19.

My own view is that Fingarette underestimates the importance of such passages as the "triple self-examination" in *Analects* 1.4, *Lunyu jishi* 1, p. 18: "Zengzi 曾子 said: 'Everyday I examine myself on three counts. In planning for others, have I failed to be sincere? In my intercourse with friends, have I failed to be trustworthy? Do I fail to practice what I teach?'" Zengzi's notion of "self-examination" implies certain cognitive faculties, and the idea makes very little sense unless we imagine something akin to a Cartesian theater, wherein Zengzi's mind observes dispassionately the conduct of the self.

26. See Ch'ien Mu 錢穆, Xian-Qin zhuzi xinian 先秦諸子繫年, 2nd edition, Canghai congkan (Hong Kong: Hong Kong University Press, 1956; rpt., Taipei: Dongda, 1990), p. 617, for Zou Ji's dates.

27. See Roger T. Ames, The Art of Rulership: A Study of Ancient Chinese Political Thought (Honolulu: University of Hawaii Press, 1983; rpt., Albany: State University of New York Press, 1994), p. 242, note 40 f., for classical sources of these two anecdotes.

28. "Zhushu" 主術; text in Liu Wendian 劉文典, Huainan Honglie jijie 淮南鴻烈集解, ed. Feng Yi 馮逸 and Qiao Hua 喬華, Xinbian Zhuzi jicheng (Beijing: Zhonghua, 1989), 9, p. 275. Compare the translation in Ames, The Art of Rulership, pp. 172 f.

29. Cf. Goldin, "Insidious Syncretism."

30. Mencius 6A.15; text in Jiao Xun 焦循 (1763–1820), Mengzi zhengyi 孟子正義, ed. Shen Wenzhuo 沈文倬, Xinbian Zhuzi jicheng (Beijing: Zhonghua, 1987), 23, p. 792. Cf. the translation in D.C. Lau, Mencius (New York: Penguin, 1970), p. 168.

31. Thus Graham, Disputers of the Tao, p. 103.

32. On Xunzi's concept of 'mind,' see, e.g., Paul Rakita Goldin, Rituals of the Way: The Philosophy of Xunzi (Chicago and La Salle: Open Court, 1999), pp. 21 ff.; Uchiyama Toshihiko 內山俊彥, Chūgoku kotai shisōshi 中國古代思想史 ni okeru shizen ninshiki 自然認識, Tōyōgaku sōsho (Tokyo: Sōbunsha, 1987), pp. 83 ff.; Lee H. Yearley, "Hsün Tzu on the Mind: His Attempted Synthesis of Confucianism and Taoism," Journal of Asian Studies 39:3 (1980), pp. 465–80; and Tang Chün-yi 唐君毅, Zhongguo zhexue yuanlun: Yuanxing pian 中國哲學原論: 原性篇 (Hong Kong: Xinya, 1968), pp. 57 f.

33. "Jiebi" 解蔽, Xunzi jijie 15.21, p. 397. Cf. the translation in Knoblock, 3, p. 105.

34. Xunzi's idea that moral action represents a rational choice sheds further light on his implicit acceptance of cognitive faculties and propositional attitudes. According to Xunzi, we are free to follow the rituals or not, but one of Xunzi's most basic arguments is that following the rituals is prudent. This argument presupposes an element of rationality that seems incompatible with Fingarette's reconstruction of the Confucian concept of 'mind.' For more on this issue in Xunzi, see e.g., Goldin, Rituals of the Way, pp. 17 ff. and 68 ff.

35. One prime candidate is the "Nei ye" 內業, which postulates famously that the "mind" must have another "mind" within it. See the text in Dai Wang 戴望 (1783–1863), Guanzi jiaozheng 管子校正, Zhongguo sixiang mingzhu (Taipei: Shijie, 1990), 16.49, p. 270. These two minds can be interpreted as the

material mind (i.e., the heart), which is of the same order as the other body organs, and the immaterial mind, which is unlike any part of the body.

36. Following the commentary of Lu Wenchao 盧文弨 (1717–1796). *Li* 厲 is often explained as a "temple," but Lu argues that the meaning "ghost" is probably intended.

37. Following the commentary of Sun Yirang 孫詒讓 (1848–1908).

38. Once again, the order of the seasons is skewed in the Chinese: 春秋 冬夏.

39. This appears in the "Minggui xia" 明鬼下 chapter of the *Mozi*; text in Wu Yujiang 吳毓江, *Mozi jiaozhu* 墨子校注, ed. Sun Qizhi 孫啓治, Xinbian Zhuzi jicheng (Beijing: Zhonghua, 1993), 8.31, p. 338. Cf. the translation in Yi-pao Mei, *The Ethical and Political Works of Motse*, Probsthain's Oriental Series 19 (London, 1929), pp. 163 f., where the term *zhuzi* 袾子 is miswritten as 袾子. The story is also retold, with further reflections, in the "Siyi" 祀義 chapter of the *Lunheng* 論衡; text in Huang Hui 黃暉, *Lunheng jiaoshi (fu Liu Pansui jijie)* 論衡校釋 (附劉盼遂集解), Xinbian Zhuzi jicheng (Beijing: Zhonghua, 1990), 25.76, pp. 1051 ff., where the unfortunate priest's name is given as "Yegu" 夜姑. The name "Guangu" 觀辜, incidentally, may be allegorical: "Faulty Observance"; see Paul Rakita Goldin, "Personal Names in Early China—A Research Note," *Journal of the American Oriental Society* 120:1 (2000). Cf. also Henri Maspero, *China in Antiquity*, tr. Frank A. Kierman Jr. ([Amherst]: University of Massachusetts Press, 1978), pp. 116 f.

40. For more on the idea of souls and the afterlife in ancient China, see e.g., Yü Ying-shih, "O Soul Come Back! A Study of the Changing Conceptions of the Soul and Afterlife in Pre-Buddhist China," *Harvard Journal of Asiatic Studies* 47:2 (1987), pp. 363–95; Yü Ying-shih, "New Evidence on the Early Chinese Conception of Afterlife," *Journal of Asian Studies* 41:1 (1981), pp. 81–85; and Michael Loewe, *Chinese Ideas of Life and Death: Faith, Myth and Reason in the Han Period (202 BC–AD 220)* (London: George Allen & Unwin, 1982), pp. 25–37.

41. See, e.g., Poo, *In Search of Personal Welfare*, pp. 53 ff.; Poo, "The Completion of an Ideal World: The Human Ghost in Early-Medieval China," *Asia Major* 10:1–2 (1997), pp. 71–73; and Alvin P. Cohen, "Avenging Ghosts and Moral Judgement in Ancient China: Three Examples from the *Shih-chi*," in *Legend, Lore, and Religions in China: Essays in Honor of Wolfram Eberhard on His Seventieth Birthday*, ed. Sarah Allan and Alvin P. Cohen (San Francisco: Chinese Materials Center, 1979), pp. 97–108.

42. See, e.g., Richard Swinburne, *The Evolution of the Soul*, revised edition (Oxford and New York: Oxford University Press, 1997).

43. Consider, e.g., Hansen, *Daoist Theory*, p. 52: "Dream arguments and sense skepticism play major roles in Western thought; they are at best minor refrains in Chinese thought." But the dream problem, with its associated

problem of sense skepticism, far from representing a "minor refrain," is a central theme in the philosophy of the *Zhuangzi*.

44. "Qiwulun" 齊物論, ZZJS 112; HY 7/2/94–96. Cf. the translations in Mair, *Wandering on the Way*, p. 24; and Chan, *A Source Book in Chinese Philosophy*, p. 190.

45. "Qiwulun," ZZJS 104; HY 6/2/81–83. Cf. the translations in Mair, *Wandering on the Way*, pp. 22 f.; and Chan, *A Source Book in Chinese Philosophy*, p. 189.

46. Cf. also the statement attributed farcically to Confucius in "Dazong-shi," ZZJS 275; HY 18/6/81: "You dream that you are a bird and soar up to the sky; you dream that you are a fish and dive into a pool. But I do not know whether the present speaker is awake or dreaming." On dreams in the *Zhuangzi* in general, see, e.g., Robert E. Allinson, *Chuang-Tzu for Spiritual Transformation: An Analysis of the Inner Chapters* (Albany: State University of New York Press, 1989), pp. 78–110.

47. Gareth B. Matthews, *Thought's Ego in Augustine and Descartes* (Ithaca, N.Y., and London: Cornell University Press, 1992), p. 54 et passim.

48. René Descartes, *Oeuvres de Descartes*, ed. Charles Adam and Paul Tannery (Paris:Vrin, 1964–76), 7, p. 19; tr. John Cottingham, et al., *The Philosophical Writings of Descartes* (Cambridge: Cambridge University Press, 1985), 2, p. 13. (The passage appears in the *First Meditation*.)

49. Cf. e.g., G. E. M. Anscombe, "The First Person," in *Mind and Language*, ed. Samuel Guttenplan (Oxford: Clarendon, 1975), pp. 45–65.

50. Matthews, *Thought's Ego*, p. 4, following Hector-Neri Castañeda's distinction between *he* and *he**.

51. See esp. Kuang-ming Wu, *The Butterfly as Companion: Meditations on the First Three Chapters of the* Chuang Tzu (Albany: State University of New York Press, 1990), p. 416, note 28: "*Wo* is an identifiable self, which others can identify as a subject as well as an object. *Wu* is an identifying agent, but itself not identifiable as such." Kuang-ming Wu's own interpretation of the dream sequences in the *Zhuangzi* differs from the above, and he does not compare them to the similar passages in Descartes. Wu's more recent book, *On Chinese Body Thinking: A Cultural Hermeneutic*, Philosophy of History and Culture 12 (Leiden: Brill, 1997), was not available to me at the time of this writing.

Note that Kuang-ming Wu's understanding of *wu* and *wo* is controversial; see e.g., Paul Kjellberg's review in *Philosophy East and West* 43:1 (1993), p. 113, as well as Jochim, "Just say No," pp. 55 f., for recent criticism. For *wu* and *wo* generally, see Ann Heirman and Bart Dessein, "*ngo 吾 and *nga 我," *Asiatische Studien/Etudes Asiatiques* 52:3 (1998), pp. 695–761; R. H. Gassman, "Eine kontextorientierte Interpretation der Pronomina *wu* und *wo* im *Meng-tzu*," *Asiatische Studien/Etudes Asiatiques* 37:2 (1984), pp. 129–53; A. C. Graham, "The Archaic Chinese Pronouns," *Asia Major* 15:1 (1969), pp. 17–61; Jin Shouzhuo 金守拙 (i.e., George A. Kennedy), "Zai lun wu wo" 再論吾我,

Bulletin of the Institute of History and Philology 28 (1956), pp. 273–81, reprinted in *Selected Works of George A. Kennedy*, ed. Tien-yi Li (New Haven: Far Eastern Publications, 1964), pp. 434–42; and Bernhard Karlgren, "Le proto-chinois, langue flexionelle," *Journal Asiatique* 11 (1920), pp. 205–32.

52. Richard Rorty, *Philosophy and the Mirror of Nature* (Princeton: Princeton University Press, 1979), p. 46.

53. Descartes proposes various solutions to the dream problem (indeed, he proposes at least two distinct kinds of dream problems). See e.g., Matthews, *Thought's Ego*, pp. 55 ff.; and Bernard Williams, *Descartes: The Project of Pure Enquiry* (New York: Penguin, 1978), pp. 51 ff. and 309–13.

54. Cf. e.g., Philip J. Ivanhoe, "Was Zhuangzi a Relativist?" in *Essays on Skepticism, Relativism, and Ethics in the* Zhuangzi, ed. Paul Kjellberg and Philip J. Ivanhoe (Albany: State University of New York Press, 1996), p. 200; and Mark Berkson, "Language: The Guest of Reality—Zhuangzi and Derrida on Language, Reality, and Skillfulness," in Kjellberg and Ivanhoe, p. 109. This notion of the "therapy" of skepticism derives from the Hellenistic Skeptics. See e.g., Paul Kjellberg, "Skepticism, Truth, and the Good Life: A Comparison of Zhuangzi and Sextus Empiricus," *Philosophy East and West* 44:1 (1994), pp. 111–33, revised as "Sextus Empiricus, Zhuangzi, and Xunzi on 'Why Be Skeptical?'" in Kjellberg and Ivanhoe, pp. 1–25; and Martha C. Nussbaum, "Skeptic Purgatives: Therapeutic Arguments in Ancient Skepticism," *Journal of the History of Philosophy* 29 (1991), pp. 1–33, revised in Nussbaum, *The Therapy of Desire: Theory and Practice in Hellenistic Ethics*, Martin Classical Lectures: New Series, 2 (Princeton: Princeton University Press, 1994), pp. 280–315.

9

"Nothing Can Overcome Heaven": The Notion of Spirit in the *Zhuangzi*

MICHAEL J. PUETT

One of Zhuangzi's anecdotes opens with a description of a certain ritual specialist named Ji Xian 季咸: "In Zheng there was a specialist on spirits named Ji Xian. He could tell whether a man would live or die, survive or be destroyed, have good fortunate or bad, live long or die young, and he could predict the year, month, week, and day as though he were a spirit (*shen* 神)."[1]

Ji Xian's powers, indeed, were such that the apprentice Liezi felt him to be superior to Liezi's own master. The remainder of the anecdote goes on to show that the powers of the spirit specialist are, counterintuitively, quite limited and that Liezi's master is indeed far more impressive.

I will trace the details of the argument below. Here, it is sufficient to mention that this critique of the ritual specialists of the day is a recurrent theme within the "Inner Chapters." In another anecdote, Zhuangzi, in the midst of a discussion of how trees useful for man are inevitably cut down, concludes with another such critique:

> Therefore, before they have lived out their years given by Heaven, they are cut down by axes in mid-journey. This is the danger of being something that can be used. Thus, in the Jie sacrifice, oxen with white foreheads, pigs with upturned snouts, or a man with piles cannot be offered to the river. This is something that all ritual specialists and invocators know, as they are considered inauspicious. But this is why the spirit-man considers them greatly auspicious.[2]

Here the contrast is drawn between the "ritual specialist" and "invocator" (*wuzhu* 巫祝), on the one hand, and on the other, a "spirit-man" (*shen ren* 神人), a term that appears frequently in the "Inner Chapters" of the *Zhuangzi*. Unlike the ritual specialists, Zhuangzi informs us, the spirit-man does not distinguish objects in terms of what is useable or unusable for man's sacrifices. Why this is significant is, again, something I will put off for the moment. Here, I simply wish to point out Zhuangzi's object of criticism.

This critique of ritual specialists is a common theme in several texts from the fourth century B.C. Like the *Zhuangzi*, many texts from the period opposed the relationships between humans and spirits assumed by the ritual specialists of the day, and many claimed that humans had more direct access to spiritual powers than was accepted in contemporary ritual practices.[3] As we shall see, however, Zhuangzi, while borrowing a great deal of vocabulary from these other texts, also opposed many of the claims at the time concerning such access to spiritual power. In fact, much of the power of Zhuangzi's arguments comes precisely from the degree to which he builds upon, while questioning, contemporary views concerning the implications of gaining this power.

In this chapter, I will look in detail at Zhuangzi's vision of spiritual power—how he defines it, why he so defines it, and how it compares with other definitions at the time.[4] This will entail an analysis of many of the anecdotes in which Zhuangzi discusses the notion of "spirit" (*shen*), as well as an analysis of the cosmology posited by Zhuangzi. I will conclude with a brief discussion of the implications this has for Zhuangzi's supposed relativism.

To trace the theme of spiritual cultivation in full, let us turn to other passages in which Zhuangzi discusses the "spirit-man," a term he reserves for some of the figures he most admires. I will begin with another anecdote concerning Liezi 列子, a figure, as we saw above, characterized in the *Zhuangzi* as an apprentice in self-cultivation:

> Liezi rode the wind with great skill. He only returned after fifteen days. He brought good fortune, but not in great amounts. And, although he avoided walking, he still had that upon which he depended (*you suo dai* 有所待). As for he who ascends the correctness of Heaven and Earth and rides the give and take of the six *qi* 氣 in order to wander without limit—what does he depend upon? Thus I say: the perfect man has no self, the spirit-man has no merit, the sagely man has no fame.[5]

Liezi's failure lies in the fact that he still depended upon something. In opposition to this, Zhuangzi holds up the "perfect man," the "sage," the "spirit-man": those who do not rely on things, do not depend on things, and wander without limit.

The author then elaborates the argument in a dialogue between Lian Shu 連叔 and Jian Wu 肩吾. A disbelieving Jian Wu begins by quoting the words of a certain Jie Yu 接輿:

> He said, "On the distant Gushe 姑射 Mountain there lives a spirit-man. His flesh is like ice and snow, and he is modest as a virgin. He does not eat the five grains but sucks in the wind and drinks the dew, ascends the vaporous *qi*, rides the flying dragons, and wanders beyond the four seas. When his spirit is concentrated, he makes things free from flaws and makes the harvests ripen."[6]

The description is one of a full lack of dependence and lack of boundaries: the spirit-man is not bound by the four seas, does not depend on the ground to walk, does not require agriculture produce.

Moreover, the text tells us, it is by concentrating his spirit that he exercises potency over the natural world as well. Such potency, however, does not consist of an ability to prognosticate—the power possessed by the spirit specialist from Zheng. Instead, the potency of the spirit-man resides in his ability to cause things (*wu* 物) to be free from flaws and to make the harvests plentiful. Put in other words, the spirit-man, by concentrating his spirit, is able to make things flourish as they naturally ought, free from harm.

Zhuangzi then narrates Lian Shu as supporting Jie Yu's words and building upon these claims:

> As for this man, nothing can harm him. Great floods can reach Heaven, but he will not drown; great droughts can melt metal and stone and scorch the earth and mountains, but he will not burn ... Why would he worry about things? (孰肯以物為事)[7]

Spirit-men are not dependent in the specific sense that they are not controlled by, nor do they bother themselves with, things (*wu*). As he elsewhere states: one should be "able to overcome things and not be injured by them" (能勝物而不傷).[8]

Yet another anecdote makes the point even more forcefully:

> Wang Ni 王倪 said: "The perfect man is spiritual! (*zhiren shen yi* 至人神矣) If the great swamps catch fire, he cannot be burned. If the Yellow and Han Rivers freeze, he cannot be made cold. If swift lightening strikes mountains and the gale winds shake the sea, he cannot be frightened. A man such as this rides the vaporous *qi*, mounts the sun and moon, and wanders beyond the four seas. Death and life do not alter him—how much less the principles of benefit and harm!"[9]

The perfect man is spiritual (*shen*). As such, natural phenomena—things—have no effect on him. Moreover, he is not contained by any boundaries: neither the four seas nor even death itself constrain him. The latter point is of particular interest: whereas the spirit specialist Ji Xian possessed knowledge over life and death, Zhuangzi claims that he who is spiritual is unaffected by life and death. Those who are spiritual for Zhuangzi do not possess special knowledge of, nor power over, things; instead, they are simply unaffected by things. The distinction will prove to be crucial.

The point comes out clearly in a quotation attributed to Confucius:

> Do not listen with your ears but listen with your heart; do not listen with your heart but listen with *qi* . . .
>
> To stop from leaving tracks is easy; to not walk on the ground is difficult. When acting for the sake of man it is easy to deceive; when acting for the sake of Heaven it is difficult to deceive. You have heard of using wings to fly; you have never heard of flying without using wings. You have heard of using knowing to know; you have not heard of using not knowing to know. . . Allow your ears and the eyes to penetrate on the inside, and place the understanding of the mind on the outside (徇耳目內通而外於心知). Ghosts and spirits will come to dwell (鬼神將來舍), not to mention the human. This is the transformation of the myriad things (*wanwu zhi hua* 萬物之化).[10]

The particular phrasing here continues the general perspective we have seen before: the sage can walk without depending upon the ground, like a bird should be able to fly without depending upon wings. Through cultivation with *qi*, the text argues, one reaches a point where ghosts and spirits will dwell within oneself.

This terminology of spirits coming to "dwell" (*she* 舍) within the adept calls to mind the "Nei ye 內業" chapter of the *Guanzi* 管子, a text that is probably slightly earlier than the Inner Chapters of the *Zhuangzi*.[11] The "Nei ye" is one of those texts, mentioned earlier in this chapter, that attempts to claim a more direct access to spiritual powers than that supported by the ritual specialists of the day. A brief comparison of the claims given in the "Nei ye" with those found in the *Zhuangzi* will help us to understand the significance of Zhuangzi's arguments concerning spirits. I will begin with a passage in the "Nei ye" similar to the *Zhuangzi* passage just quoted: "There is a spirit that of itself resides within the body, at times leaving, at times entering. No one is able to contemplate it. If you lose it, there will be disorder; if you obtain it there will be order. Carefully clean its resting place, and the essence (*jing* 精) will of its own enter."[12] There is a concern here with using self-cultivation techniques to bring "spirits" (*shen*) and "essence" (*jing*) to "dwell" (*she*) within oneself.[13] Elsewhere in the "Nei ye," the reasons for this concern are laid out: *shen* and *jing* are nothing but highly refined *qi*, and the more of this highly refined *qi* that one gains, the more power of and knowledge about the world that one attains.[14]

Thus, although the terminology of bringing spirits to come and dwell is similar in the *Zhuangzi* and "Nei ye," the ultimate goals of the two texts are radically different. As the "Nei ye" further argues:

> To unify things and be able to transform is called spirit (一物能化謂之神). To unify affairs and be able to alter is called craft (一事能變謂之智). Transforming but not altering the *qi*, altering but not changing one's craft: only the superior man holding fast to the one is able to do this! By holding fast to the one and not losing it, he is able to rule over the myriad things. The superior man controls things; he is not controlled by them (*junzi shi wu, bu wei wu shi* 君子使物，不為物使).[15]

In the "Nei ye," the goal of the superior man is to unify and control things (*shi wu* 使物), and, indeed, to gain the power to rule over the myriad things. Whereas the potency of the spirit-man in the *Zhuangzi* is described as serving to allow things to be as they naturally ought, the "Nei ye" claims that the adept can possesses direct control over things.

The difference becomes only the more glaring as we move farther into the "Nei ye:"

> When awareness (*yi* 意) of *qi* is obtained, all under Heaven will submit; when the awareness of the mind is stabilized, all under Heaven will listen. Concentrate the *qi* as if a spirit, and the myriad things will all reside within. Can you concentrate? Can you unify? Can you not engage in crackmaking and milfoil divination and yet understand auspiciousness and inauspiciousness? Can you stop? Can you reach an end? Can you not seek from others and obtain it in yourself? Think about it (*si zhi* 思之), think about it, and think about it again. If you think about it but do not penetrate, the ghosts and spirits will penetrate it. This is not due to the power of the ghosts and spirits; it is due to the ultimate point of essential *qi* (*jingqi* 精氣).[16]

The "Nei ye" is teaching one to use self-cultivation through *qi* to gain power and knowledge over things. Through this technique, the text claims, one can make all under Heaven submit, make the myriad things reside within, and gain an understanding of auspiciousness and inauspiciousness without resorting to divination.

The argument of the "Nei ye," then, is that by relying upon *qi*, one can attain the powers that spirit specialists can only achieve through magical arts of working with spirits. In other words, one can have direct access to those powers of controlling phenomena and foretelling the future that are possessed by spirits and that spirit specialists can only achieve through magical arts. If a spirit specialist would have to resort to divination to understand auspiciousness and inauspiciousness, the adept in the "Nei ye" could do so through *qi*. But, it is important to note, the end result would be the same: both the spirit specialist and the practitioner described in the "Nei ye" are seeking power over and knowledge about things (*wu*). This point is underlined in the fact that the terms used to describe the adept are in fact quite similar to those used by Zhuangzi in describing the spirit specialist from Zheng (in the anecdote with which I opened this essay): as with the spirit specialist from Zheng, the adept in the "Nei ye" can become "like a spirit" (*ru shen* 如神) and can understand auspiciousness and inauspiciousness.

Thus, although the *Zhuangzi* is using a terminology very similar to the self-cultivation literature, it is in fact offering a gnosis different both from that obtainable by the spirit specialists and that described in the self-cultivation literature itself. Indeed, the passage quoted above concerning spirits coming to dwell closed not with a discussion of controlling the myriad things but rather with a reference to the transformation of the myriad things. But what precisely does this mean? And, if the gnosis offered by the *Zhuangzi* is supposed to be superior to that in which one gains the powers of prognostication held by spirits, then what precisely does it involve?

To answer these questions, let us turn to an anecdote that explicitly discusses the proper relationship humans should have to the differentiated world of things (*wu*). The anecdote concerns two figures, Zisi 子祀 and Ziyu 子輿. The latter is being refashioned by the Fashioner of Things (*zaowuzhe* 造物者) and is queried by Zisi as to his feelings concerning such a refashioning:

> "The Fashioner of Things is making me all rolled up like this." Zisi said: "Do you detest this?" Ziyu replied: "No—how could I detest it? . . . One obtains life at the proper time; one loses it when it is fitting. If you are content with the time, and if you dwell in what is fitting (*an shi er chu shun* 安時而處順), then anger and joy will be unable to enter you. This is what of old was called 'untying the bonds' (*xuan jie* 縣解). If you are unable to untie them yourself, then you will be bound by things. But things cannot ultimately overcome Heaven. What is there for me to detest?"[17]

The concern here is for those who are "bound by things"—a concern in some ways similar to that seen in the "Nei ye" for those who are controlled

by things. But the thrust of the argument is in many ways the opposite.
The goal of the cultivation is not to learn to control things; instead, the
goal is to liberate oneself (literally: untie oneself *zi jie* 自解) by no longer focusing on things. Such things, Ziyu assures us, can never overcome
Heaven (*sheng tian* 勝天): all things will inevitably be transformed into
other things. To bind oneself to any one thing (including one's human
form) is to commit oneself to cycles of joy and sorrow; only by complying
with this ceaseless transformative process can one avoid resentment.

Unlike the "Nei ye," which is concerned with making all under
Heaven submit, the *Zhuangzi* calls on one to side with the ceaseless transformation itself. Whereas the "Nei ye" teaches one to control things,
the *Zhuangzi* teaches one to accept the ceaseless flux of the world. And
whereas the "Nei ye" teaches one to understand good and bad fortune, the
Zhuangzi teaches one to accept these as fate: "Life and death are fated (*ming*
命). That they have the regularity of day and night is a matter of Heaven
(*tian* 天). As for that with which man cannot interfere, it all belongs to
the essential qualities of things. They only take Heaven as their father, and
yet we still love them. How much more that which surpasses them!"[18] It
is Heaven that governs the ceaseless transformation of things, including
human life, and it is accordingly Heaven that we should support.

The argument continues. If one hides one's possessions (for example,
a boat), they may still be stolen. But if one hides all under Heaven in all
under Heaven, then nothing will ever be lost.[19] In other words, if one
defines one's gaze to include everything, then the disappearance of single
things is not a problem. The same point holds for the human form: one
would not mourn the loss of one's form with death if one embraced
the transformations of everything.[20] Accordingly, the author concludes,
"Therefore the sage will roam where things cannot be hidden and where
all exist. He takes pleasure in dying young, he takes pleasure in old age. He
takes pleasure in beginnings, he takes pleasure in ends. If men take him
as a model, how much more that to which the myriad things are tied and
that to which each single transformation depends" (*yi hua zhi suo dai* 一
化之所待).[21]

The cosmology of the *Zhuangzi* is thus coming into focus. All things
(*wu*) are tied to Heaven, and all things ceaselessly transform. The goal of
the adept is not to control things—an act that would be portrayed within
this cosmology as an attempt to overcome Heaven. One must rather take
pleasure in the ceaseless transformations of the universe—including those
of one's own life and death. Instead of attempting to overcome Heaven,
one should seek to glory in the transformations of Heaven. The goal, as

Zhuangzi puts it elsewhere, is to "use to the utmost what one receives from Heaven" (盡其所受乎天).[22]

And with this cosmology clarified, we can begin to see what Zhuangzi is getting at in his discussion of spirit. For spirit too is associated not with control but rather with properly following that which one is given from Heaven:

> When Gongwen Xuan 公文軒 saw the Commander of the Right 右師, he was alarmed and said: "What sort of man is this? Why is he one-legged?[23] Is this due to Heaven or man?" The Commander replied, "It is due to Heaven, not man. When Heaven generates something, it makes it unique (*du* 獨). Man's appearance is something given to him. This is how I know it is from Heaven, not man. A swamp pheasant walks ten paces for one peck and a hundred paces for one drink. But it does not seek to be nourished in a cage. Its spirit, even if treated as a king, would not be happy."[24]

The moral of the anecdote is that we must accept what Heaven has given. As we are told in the closing analogy, the spirit of the pheasant cannot be content unless it does what it is supposed to do—even if what it is supposed to do seems absurd, and even if placing it within human constraints would result in it being treated as a king. The contentment of the spirit, then, depends upon an acceptance of the order of Heaven.

At first glance, such a stance might appear to be at odds with many of the statements quoted earlier in this chapter. Before, we were confronted with a vocabulary of lack of dependency, even of liberation: those of us who become spirit-men will roam freely, will no longer depend on things, will no longer be bound by things—will become, in fact, untied. In these most recently quoted passages, however, the vocabulary has shifted to one of acceptance: just as the spirit of the pheasant can only be content if it follows what it is supposed to do, so must we learn to accept our fate, accept what Heaven has ordained for us.

For Zhuangzi, however, these two seemingly contradictory stances are in fact flip sides of the same coin: the liberation that comes from no longer being dependent upon things precisely involves an acceptance of the order of Heaven. Hence the significance of the statement quoted above that nothing can overcome Heaven (*sheng tian*). To be dependent on the world of things is, for Zhuangzi, to attempt to overcome the order of Heaven. This would be equally true of someone who strongly hoarded possessions as it would be of those who would try to control things through gaining supernatural powers—regardless of whether such powers were gained through magical acts or through the cultivation of *qi*.

Zhuangzi is indeed calling on the spirit to become untied, but for Zhuangzi this means that the spirit can properly follow the order of the world. He wants the pheasant to be uncaged, but, Zhuangzi would emphasize, only so that it may walk "ten paces for one peck and a hundred paces for one drink." The spirit untied will naturally do what it naturally ought.

This connection of the liberated spirit with the order of Heaven is seen perhaps most forcefully in the famous Cook Ding anecdote. A certain Lord Wenhui has just commented on the tremendous skill of Cook Ding, and the Cook offers his response: "I am fond of the Way, which advances beyond skill. When I first started carving oxen, I could only see the ox. After three years, I never saw the whole ox. Nowadays, I follow along using my spirit, and I don't use my eyes to look at all. My senses and knowledge have stopped, but my spiritual desires move along. I accord with the Heavenly patterns."[25] Cook Ding's greatness lies in the fact that he uses his spirit, not his eyes. By allowing the "spiritual desires" (*shen yu* 神欲) to go where they wish, Cook Ding accords with the "Heavenly patterns" (*tian li* 天理).[26]

Following the Way, in "accord with the Heavenly patterns," means, in the case of a butcher, an ability to move flawlessly through the natural shifts in the carcass. It does not, in other words, involve any form of transcendence, nor does it involve any form of control over things. Following the desires of the spirit means following the patterns of Heaven.

At this point, we are finally in a position to understand both why and how Zhuangzi is so critical of the ritual specialists. In both of the anecdotes quoted at the beginning of this chapter, the ritual specialists were being singled out for their incorrect support for the proper order of Heaven. In the second anecdote, ritual specialists and invocators are presented as preventing things from living out their years given by Heaven (*wei zhong qi tiannian* 未終其天年), whereas the spirit-man wishes them to live out the years fated for them. The criteria for valuation, in other words, is the degree to which the figures in question support the order of Heaven.

A similar argument underlies the anecdote concerning Liezi and the spirit specialist from Zheng. In the next part of the anecdote, Liezi tells his master, Huzi, about the great spirit specialist Ji Xian. Huzi tells Liezi to invite the spirit specialist over so that the spirit specialist may use physiognomy on Huzi. On four separate occasions, Huzi presents a different face to him; each is clearly meant to signify an ever deeper stage of self-cultivation. On the first occasion, Huzi shows him the patterns of earth (*diwen* 地文),[27] which Ji Xian misinterprets as meaning that Huzi will soon die. On the second, Huzi shows him "Heavenly, fertilized ground" (*tianrang* 天壤),[28] which Ji Xian misinterprets as signifying that Huzi is revivifying. On the third, Huzi presents him with the "great void that none can overcome" (*taichong mosheng* 太沖莫勝),[29] which the spirit specialist cannot read at all. This latter state, it should be noted, was achieved by Huzi "balancing the impulses of the *qi*" (*heng qiji* 衡氣機).[30] Finally, Huzi presents Ji Xian "not yet having emerged from one's ancestor" (*weishi chu wu zong* 未始出吾宗),[31] after which Ji Xian runs away.

The spirit specialist, whose art is concerned only with attaining a knowledge over life and death, fails before Huzi. Not only is Ji Xian unable to foretell the life and death of Huzi, but Huzi, through cultivation of his *qi*, is able to reach a state in which he is not bound by things, in which the very concerns of life and death become irrelevant. The state that Huzi has attained is one in which he can reach back to that point before things were differentiated—symbolized here as the void that cannot be overcome and the state prior to the generation of things. And note here that the term for "overcome" is again *sheng* 勝—the same word used in the dictum that things cannot overcome Heaven. Once again, the cultivated figure for Zhuangzi is one who gains access to that point that nothing can overcome.

This same point may explain the differences between Zhuangzi and a text like the "Nei ye." Just as Zhuangzi opposes any attempt to focus too fully on things, so would he oppose any attempt to transcend the human form, become like a spirit, and gain control over things: he neither wants man to lose sight of Heaven nor for man to transcend himself and become like Heaven. If one is a human, then one should remain a human until the proper time given by Heaven occurs for one to be transformed into something else.[32] In other words, the sage for Zhuangzi does not attempt to transcend humanity. As he argues explicitly: "When neither Heaven nor man overcome (*sheng* 勝) the other—this is called the True Man" (*zhenren* 真人).[33] Here again we see the recurrent call on man not to attempt to overcome Heaven (*sheng tian*), only now it is linked with the concurrent concern that man should also not be overcome by Heaven—which is to say that man should not strive to reject his humanity and simply become Heaven.

This framework also explains the famous anecdote at the end of the "Dechongfu" chapter.[34] Zhuangzi calls on man to go without his dispositions (*qing* 情) and thus to prevent the "right and wrong" (*shi fei* 是非) from entering; as a consequence, man will be able to perfect his

Heaven (*cheng qi tian* 成其天).[35] Zhuangzi then narrates Huizi 惠子 as questioning the meaning of such a stance. Huizi asks how a man who goes without his dispositions can still be called a man (人而無情，何以 謂之人).[36] Zhuangzi responds in full:"Distinguishing'right' and'wrong' is what I mean by the dispositions. What I mean by being without disposi- tions is that man should not allow likes and dislikes to enter and thus harm himself. He should always accord with the spontaneous and not add to life" (常因自然而不益生).[37] Huizi then questions him on what it would mean to add to life, and Zhuangzi responds as follows:"The Way gave us appearance, and Heaven gave us form. Do not use likes and dislikes to enter and harm the self. Now, you are putting your spirit on the outside, and wearing out your essence."[38]

The call here is for man to accept that which is given to him and not to add to life by categorizing things according to humanly constructed distinctions of right and wrong. To do so is to harm the self, thus prevent- ing one from fully living out one's Heavenly given lifespan. Instead, one must accord with the spontaneous, keep one's spirit internalized, and not wear out one's essence.

Here again, then, the notion of spirit is connected directly with using properly that which was given from Heaven and according with the spontaneous way. The gnosis called upon is not a transcendence of the human but rather a continuation and perfection of the Heaven within man—a continuation that requires us to stop imposing distinctions upon things and rather to cultivate that with which we were endowed.

Considering this, it should be clear that we should read the term *spirit-man* literally. Zhuangzi is not calling on humans to become spirits; he is calling on humans to no longer be dependent upon artificial attempts to either reify things or categorize things according to artificial standards. A spirit-man is not a man who becomes a spirit. A spirit-man is rather a man who fully cultivates his spirit and thus wanders free from things while enabling things (including his own human form) to fulfill their natural endowment.

For Zhuangzi, then, the ultimate goal is to no longer be dependent on things, but also not to attempt to control things or transcend the human form. He would thus oppose either trying to impose artificial distinctions on things or trying to become a spirit and gain control over things. In- deed, by the way Zhuangzi has defined his terms, *both* of these would be a failure to maintain the proper relationship with Heaven. It is wrong to be bound to things, and it is wrong to attempt to transcend the human; for Zhuangzi, becoming bounded and being overreaching are directly related. Just as Zhuangzi will portray unloosening and accepting the order of things as flip sides of the same coin, so will he see boundedness and hubris as linked as well.

꙳ ꙳

We often associate Zhuangzi with liberation, with a denial of boundaries, with a call for humanity to become uncaged. And, indeed, all of these images do certainly appear regularly in the text. Zhuangzi is clearly concerned that most humans live their lives fully dependent on things, foolishly clinging to their life and possessions. But as we have seen, this concern with not being dependent on or bound by things, with becoming untied, with wandering beyond any boundary, is intimately and directly tied to a cosmological claim: the liberated spirit will accord with Heavenly patterns, help things be as they naturally ought, and allow things to fulfill fully their Heavenly given allotment. As Zhuangzi repeatedly argues, we cannot overcome Heaven, we must accept fate, and we must accord with the order of Heaven.

By presenting his argument in this way, Zhuangzi is able to call on man to cultivate himself and to strive to perfect his spirit and the Heaven within him, and yet Zhuangzi is able to make this call in such a way as to undercut many of the claims being made at the time concerning the ability of man to gain the powers of spirits—whether through magic or cultivation of the *qi*. Zhuangzi is arguing against any attempt to gain knowledge or control over the universe and is instead calling on the spiritual man to take pleasure in the patterns of Heaven.

Somewhat counterintuitively, then, Zhuangzi turns out to be strongly committed to the notion that there are proper patterns in the natural world that a cultivated person will inherently follow. This is a point, I think, that has been missed by those scholars who would portray Zhuangzi as a relativist. For example, Robert Eno has argued that Zhuangzi is calling for man to engage in skill-based activities that would lead to a state of spiritual spontaneity. And, according to this reading, any skill-based activity would work: "Dao-practices can be adapted to any end: the dao of butchering people might provide much the same spiritual spontaneity as the dao of butchering oxen—as many a samurai might testify."[39] I would argue, on the contrary, that Zhuangzi is indeed asserting that the cultivated human spirit will act in certain ways rather than others. He does so not by asserting that particular activities are ethically better than others, but rather by making a cosmological claim: the authoritative person will inherently behave in certain ways rather than in other ways. Just as the pheasant, if it is allowed to do as Heaven means it to do, will walk ten paces for one peck and a hundred paces for one drink, so will a human, if he uses his endowment properly, act in conformity with the Heavenly patterns as well. In this sense, Zhuangzi is not a relativist; he is, on the contrary, a cosmologist with a strong commitment to a certain definition of the proper place of humanity in the universe.[40]

Zhuangzi's calls for liberation can thus be read as involving a careful redefinition of notions current at the time—spirit, Heaven, and man—to argue for a particular type of gnosis—a gnosis involving a breaking of boundaries and yet, at the same time, an acceptance of the patterns of Heaven. For Zhuangzi, liberation involves a proper and spontaneous acceptance of the order of the world. Anything else is an attempt to overcome Heaven—a project doomed to failure.

Notes

1. "Yingdiwang," ZZJS 297; HY 20/7/15–16. Cf. Burton Watson, *The Complete Works of Chuang Tzu* (New York: Columbia University Press, 1968), pp. 94–95, and A. C. Graham, *Chuang -tzu: The Seven Inner Chapters and Other Writings from the Book of Chuang-tzu* (London: George Allen & Unwin, 1981), p. 96.

2. "Renjianshi," ZZJS 177; HY 12/4/80–83. Cf. Watson 65–66, Graham 74.

3. For a discussion of this theme, see my "Humans and Gods: The Theme of Self-Divinization in Early China and Early Greece," in *Thinking through Comparisons Ancient Greece and China*, ed. Stephen Durrant and Steven Shankman (Albany: State University of New York Press, 2002).

4. My understanding of these issues has been greatly enhanced by Lee H. Yearley's "Zhuangzi's Understanding of Skillfulness and the Ultimate Spiritual State," in *Essays on Skepticism, Relativism, and Ethics in the Zhuangzi*, ed. Paul Kjellberg and Philip J. Ivanhoe (Albany: State University of New York Press, 1996), pp. 152–82.

5. "Xiaoyaoyou," ZZJS 17; HY 2/1/19–22. Cf. Watson 32, Graham 44.

6. "Xiaoyaoyou," ZZJS 28; HY 2/1/28–30. Cf. Watson 33, Graham 46.

7. "Xiaoyaoyou," ZZJS 30–31; HY 2/1/32–34. Cf. Watson 33–34, Graham 46.

8. "Yingdiwang," ZZJS 307; HY 21/7/33. Cf. Watson 97; Graham 98.

9. "Qiwulun," ZZJS 96; HY 6/2/71–73. Cf. Watson 46; Graham 58.

10. "Renjianshi," ZZJS HY 147, 150; HY 9/4/26–27, 30–33. Cf. Watson 57–58, Graham 68–69.

11. For a discussion of the dating of the "Nei ye," see Harold Roth, "Re-

daction Criticism and the Early History of Taoism," *Early China* 19 (1994), pp. 14–17, and Rickett's discussion in W. Allyn Rickett, trans., *Guanzi: Political, Economic, and Philosophical Essays from Early China*, volume II (Princeton, Princeton University Press, 1998), pp. 32–39. For a fuller discussion of the "Nei ye," see my "Humans and Gods: The Theme of Self-Divinization in Early China and Early Greece," in *Thinking through Comparisons*.

12. "Nei ye," *Guanzi*, Sibu beiyao edition, 16.3a–3b.

13. See also "Xin shu, shang," *Guanzi*, 13.1b: "If one empties one's desires, the spirit will enter and dwell (虛其欲，神將入舍). If in clearing one does not cleanse fully, the spirit will leave."

14. See "Nei ye," *Guanzi*, 16.2b.

15. "Nei ye," *Guanzi*, 16.3a.

16. "Nei ye," *Guanzi*, 16.4b–5a.

17. "Dazongshi," ZZJS 259–60; HY 17/6/49–53. Cf. Watson 84–85, Graham 88.

18. "Dazongshi," ZZJS 241; HY 16/6/20–22. Cf. Watson 80, Graham 86.

19. ZZJS 243; HY 16/6/25–26.

20. ZZJS 243–44; HY 16/6/26–27.

21. ZZJS 244; HY 16/6/27–29. Cf. Watson 81, Graham 86.

22. "Yingdiwang," ZZJS 307; HY 21/7/32. Cf. Watson 97, Graham 98.

23. Following the traditional emendation of *wu* 兀 for *jie* 介.

24. "Yangshengzhu," ZZJS 124–26; HY 8/3/12–14. Cf. Watson, 52, Graham, 64.

25. "Yangshengzhu," ZZJS 119; HY 7/3/5–6. Cf. Watson, 50–51, Graham, 63–64.

26. For an excellent discussion of this passage, see Scott Cook, "Zhuang Zi and His Carving of the Confucian Ox," *Philosophy East and West* 47:4 (October 1997), pp. 536–39.

27. "Yingdiwang," ZZJS 299; HY 20/7/21.

28. ZZJS 300–01; HY 20/7/23.

29. ZZJS 302; HY 20/7/25–26.

30. ZZJS 301; HY 20/7/26.

31. ZZJS 304; HY 20/7/28–29.

32. For a careful discussion of the relations between Heaven and man in the *Zhuangzi*, see the introduction in Graham 15–19.

33. "Dazongshi," ZZJS 241; HY 16/6/20. Cf. Watson 80, Graham 85.

34. For an excellent discussion of this passage, see A. C. Graham, "The Background of the Mencian Theory of Human Nature," in *Studies of Chinese Philosophy* (Singapore: The Institute of East Asian Philosophies, 1986), pp. 61–63.

35. ZZJS 217; HY 14/5/54–55. For the reasons behind my translation of *qing* as "dispositions," see my "Ethics of Responding Properly: The Notion

of *Qing* in Early Chinese Thought," in *Emotions in Chinese Culture*, ed. Halvor Eifring (Leiden: Brill, 2003).

36. ZZJS 220–21; HY 14–15/5/56–57.

37. ZZJS 221; HY 15/5/57–58. Cf. Watson 75–76, Graham 82.

38. ZZJS 222; HY 15/5/58–59. Cf. Watson 76, Graham 82.

39. Robert Eno, "Cook Ding's Dao and the Limits of Philosophy," in *Essays on Skepticism, Relativism, and Ethics in the Zhuangzi*, ed. Kjellberg and Ivanhoe, p. 142. For another argument that Zhuangzi is a relativist, see Chad Hansen, "A Tao of Tao in Chuang-tzu," in *Experimental Essays on Chuang-tzu*, ed. Victor Mair (Honolulu: University of Hawaii Press, 1983), pp. 24–55.

40. My conclusions are thus largely in line with those of Philip J. Ivanhoe, even though our respective conclusions were achieved through different routes. See his "Was Zhuangzi a Relativist?" in *Essays on Skepticism, Relativism, and Ethics in the Zhuangzi*, pp. 196–214.

10

Transforming the Dao:
A Critique of A. C. Graham's Translation
of the Inner Chapters of the *Zhuangzi*

SHUEN-FU LIN 林順夫

Frederick Henry Balfour published his book *The Divine Classic of Nan-hua, Being the Works of Chuang Tsze, Taoist Philosopher* in 1881.[1] This was the very first complete translation of the *Zhuangzi* 莊子 (traditionally attributed to Zhuang Zhou 莊周, ca. 369–286 B.C.) into any Western language.[2] Although the *Zhuangzi* has not enjoyed as great a popularity as the *Daode jing* 道德經 has among Western translators, it has, for more than a century, attracted many admirers of its own in the West as a text that appeals equally to the reader's rational faculty and imagination. To date, there exist in the English language alone six complete translations and numerous partial translations by such distinguished scholars and skilled translators as Herbert A. Giles, James Legge, Fung Yu-lan, Arthur Waley, Wing-tsit Chan, Burton Watson, A. C. Graham, Victor H. Mair, and David Hinton.[3] It can be said that twentieth-century translators of this immensely complex Daoist classic have in one way or another attempted to reproduce the original Chinese text into the English language with some fidelity. Published exactly one hundred years after Balfour's translation, the book *Chuang-tzu: The Seven Inner Chapters and Other Writings from the Book of Chuang-tzu* (which is four-fifths of the original) by the late A. C. Graham—an expert in ancient Chinese thought and a remarkable translator of classical Chinese poetry and philosophical texts—represents not only one of the latest but also the most important attempt to move the translation ever closer to the original source-language text. This chapter intends to review Graham's criticism of several significant previous English translations of the *Zhuangzi*, his own strategy in translating the *neipian* 內篇 or Inner Chapters, and the strengths and possible flaws of his efforts.

I shall begin with a brief discussion of some aspects of recent trans-lational thinking in the West that bear special relevance to my examination of Graham's translation of the Inner Chapters. It has been pointed out that the history of translation theories from the age of the Romans to the second half of the eighteenth century is one of a gradual shift from a view of translation as the appropriation of the content of the original without any real concern for its stylistic and linguistic idiosyncrasies, to one of exploitation of the original in order to enrich the linguistic and aesthetic dimensions of one's own language, and finally to one of respect for the foreign in the original source-language text.[4] The new respect for the foreign that had emerged during the second half of the eighteenth century was then "followed by the courage to move toward the foreign."[5] During the subsequent nineteenth and twentieth centuries, this sense of responsibility toward the foreign in the original source-language text continues as a strong undercurrent in the theory and practice of transla-tion in the West.[6]

The sense of responsibility toward the foreign can be expressed in two different ways.[7] The majority of writers in the West believe that it is impossible to find precise equivalencies from one language to another and consequently emphasize fidelity to the totality of the source-language text rather than to its parts and details. The major exception to this practice is the Russian American novelist Vladimir Nabokov, who insists that only a "literal translation" is valid because "anything but that is not truly a translation but an imitation, an adaptation or a parody."[8] Nabokov is very critical of those translators who simply substitute "easy platitudes for the breathtaking intricacies" of the texts they translate.[9] For him, "The person who desires to turn a literary masterpiece into another language, has only one duty to perform, and this is to reproduce with absolute exactitude the whole text, and nothing but the text."[10]

One should note here that what Nabokov considers as a literal translation is different from the kind of "literal rendering of the syntax" and of "individual words" of the source-language text attacked by Walter Benjamin.[11] For Benjamin, a literal translation aims at "rendering the sense" of the original only, while a real translation "must lovingly and in detail incorporate the original's mode of signification."[12] As we shall see later, Graham's concept of 'translation' comes closer to Nabokov's "literal translation" or Benjamin's emphasis on incorporating "the original's mode of signification" than to that of the majority of translators and writers from the nineteenth century into the twentieth.

One important new development in twentieth-century translational thinking in the West is the consideration of the translation process in the broader perspective of the nature of language and human communication.[13] Octavio Paz, the Mexican poet who won the Nobel Prize in literature in 1990, has offered brilliant insights into the nature of language and translation. He says, "When we learn to speak, we are learning to translate; the child who asks his mother the meaning of a word is really asking her to translate the unfamiliar term into the simple words he already knows. In this sense, translation within the same language is not essentially different from translation between two tongues, and the histories of all peoples parallel the child's experience."[14] According to Paz, then, translation is fundamental to all acts of human communication. He extends this idea further to note that the very tool we use in communication is itself already a translation: "No text can be completely original because language itself, in its very essence, is already a translation—first from the nonverbal world, and then, because each sign and each phrase is a translation of another sign, another phrase."[15] These observations of Paz's can be used to illuminate a common ancient Chinese view of language.

Various thinkers in ancient China regard language as essentially a tool—and more often than not, a rather inadequate tool—for the communication of ideas and experiences.[16] This functional view of language is tersely expressed in a remark attributed to Confucius 孔子 (551–479 B.C.): "Writing does not fully express speech and speech does not fully express ideas" (shu bu jin yan, yan bu jin yi 書不盡言，言不盡意).[17] "Writing" in this passage corresponds to Paz's "text" and "speech" to the spoken component of his "language." The word yi 意 (rendered "ideas" here for the sake of simplicity) is used by ancient Chinese thinkers to refer to ideas of things, thoughts, and intentions in a person's mind.[18] Of course, the ideas of things are images of them to begin with.[19] To follow Paz's insight, these ideas of things already constitute a translation of our experience and understanding of the world. In the quoted remark, Confucius is said to be talking about the difficulty of transferring the ideas, thoughts, and intentions in the mind into speech and writing. Therefore, we can say that speech and writing are essentially "further translations" of the ideas, thoughts, and intentions a person wishes to convey, even though the concept of translation is not used in this ancient Chinese passage.[20]

If Confucius is said merely to complain about the inadequacy of language as a translation of a person's ideas and experiences, the Daoist thinkers are adamant in denying language any ultimate validity. The *Daode jing* opens with this startling statement:

> The way that can be spoken of
> Is not the constant way;
> The name that can be named
> Is not the constant name.[21]

Laozi 老子 cannot find a sufficient way to designate the ultimate reality of nature and the cosmos that he perceives in the nonverbal world, so he gives it merely the makeshift names of "Dao" ("the Way") and "the great."[22] Similarly, in the "Qiwulun" 齊物論 chapter, we find the following comment by Zhuangzi: "Speech is not just blowing breath, speech has something to say; the only trouble is that what it says is not fixed. Do we really say something? Or have we never said anything? If you think it different from the twitter of fledglings, is there proof of the distinction? Or isn't there any proof?"[23] Zhuangzi argues that, unless what our speech says can be fixed, we might as well regard human language as essentially the same as the twittering of fledglings. What our speech says can never be fixed because it is never an exact representation of our experience in the first place, and it can be understood and interpreted differently by different listeners. Thus, according to Laozi and Zhuangzi, language is at best a "makeshift translation" of a person's original ideas, thoughts, or experiences.

Ancient Chinese thinkers generally exhibit a kind of what Graham calls "naive realism" in their epistemology, despite their common belief in the inadequacy of language. Graham uses Zhuangzi to represent this naive realism and says, "[Zhuangzi] has a perfect confidence that not only things but our ideas (*yi* 意) of them—which in the first place would be their images—would still be there if we could get rid of the nuisance of having to talk about them."[24] The following passage from the *Analects* of Confucius seems to illustrate the same confidence: "The Master said, 'I'm about to give up speech.' Zigong said, 'If you do not speak, what would there be for your disciples to transmit?' The Master said, 'What does heaven ever say? Yet the four seasons go round and the hundred things come into being. What does heaven ever say?'"[25]

With some exceptions, modern writers and thinkers in the West generally do not seem to hold such a negative view of language itself, but they are as keenly aware as ancient Chinese philosophers of the inevitability of the process of transformation involved in all acts of human communication. The German philosopher Hans Georg Gadamer, for instance, says, "Reading is already translation, and translation is translation for the second time ... The process of translating comprises in its essence the whole secret of human understanding of the world and of social communication."[26] And in reviewing recent translational thinking, Rainer Schulte and John Biguenet conclude, "At all times, translation involves an act of transformation."[27]

In light of this line of argument, we can say that the various English translations of the *Zhuangzi* are different transformations of the Chinese classic, none of which is, and can ever be, an exact equivalent of the original. It is awesome to realize that these translations can actually be transformations upon transformations, when we take into account the whole spectrum of relevant factors ranging from the nature of all languages (and the impossibility of finding word-to-word equivalents in English) to the transmission through the centuries of the *Zhuangzi* with the numerous commentaries on which the translators have based their reading and interpretation. A. C. Graham is clearly aware of this problem when he says, "Zhuangzi illustrates to perfection the kind of battering which a text may suffer between being written in one language and being transferred to another at the other end of the world some two thousand years later."[28] This is not to say that none of the translations has conveyed any of the philosophy of the Chinese text, because a perceptive reader will always be able to grasp some of the ideas (意) of the original author(s). Nor is this to say that no translation can be considered a closer approximation to the original Daoist classic than the others. The fidelity to the original can be determined by the translator's competence in both the source language and the target language, by his knowledge of Zhuangzi's ideas and of the text associated with his name, by his approach to the translation, and by his notion of what the text is. As stated earlier, Graham's translation of the Inner Chapters of the *Zhuangzi* has moved considerably closer than previous English translations to that portion of the original Chinese text. Nonetheless, because of his conception of what the text is composed of, his translation is not as close an equivalent of the original as we would like this exceptional scholar and translator to have produced. His criticisms of several important English translations and his own method in translating the Inner Chapters are both closely related to his conception of this Daoist classic. Indeed, Graham's view of the nature of the *Zhuangzi* as a text is the key to a proper assessment of his translation.

Graham devotes section 8 in the introductory chapter of *Chuang-tzu: The Inner Chapters* to a discussion of the textual complexities of the Chinese book and the problem of translation.[29] In this brief section, he discusses the nature of ancient Chinese texts in general and of the *Zhuangzi* in particular, reviews together in a general but pointed manner the three English translations by James Legge, Herbert A. Giles, and Burton Watson, and then sets forth in detail his own strategy in translating this early Daoist text. Brief as it is, this section represents the result of many years of Graham's efforts in trying to come "to grips with the outstanding textual, linguistic and philosophical problems"[30] of the *Zhuangzi*. Comments presented here are largely Graham's original conclusions drawn from his own intensive study of ancient Chinese thought and texts, but he has also been influenced by the views of modern scholars such as Fu Ssu-nien 傅斯年, Guo Moruo 郭沫若, Ch'ien Mu 錢穆, Wang Shu-min 王叔岷, Zhang Hengshou 張恆壽, Ren Jiyu 任繼愈, Takeuchi Yoshio 武內義雄, and especially Guan Feng 關鋒, scholars who hold views radically different from the traditional ones regarding the composition of the book.

Graham offers the following general observation on the nature of early Chinese philosophical texts:

> [A]ncient Chinese thinkers did not write books, they jotted down sayings, verses, stories, thoughts and by the third century B.C. composed essays, on bamboo strips which were tied together in sheets and rolled up in scrolls. A chapter of Zhuangzi would have originated as an item or collection of items making up a single scroll. Collections of scrolls ascribed on good or bad authority to one author or school grew up gradually and did not assume a standard form until Liu Xiang 劉向 (77–6 B.C.) edited them for the Imperial library of the Han dynasty.[31]

Few scholars would probably find fault with the above general remarks. It is true that the essays by Xunzi 荀子 (ca. 298–238 B.C.) and HanFeizi 韓非子 (280?–233 B.C.) are the earliest examples of rigorously structured argumentative essays in the Chinese tradition. Graham is also right about the way writings were preserved and edited systematically for the first time by Liu Xiang 劉向 in ancient China. Questions only begin to arise when he presents his ideas about the actual composition of the *Zhuangzi* text.

Today, scholars generally agree that the *Zhuangzi* is not the collected works of a single author named Zhuang Zhou, but a collection of philosophical writings of the fourth, third, and perhaps even second centuries B.C., which largely belong to the Daoist school of thought. Regardless of whether Graham's dating and division of the materials into six strata and groups are ultimately valid, they are done by a careful and insightful intellectual historian of ancient China. I am concerned solely with those of his speculations regarding how the chapters might have come into being that have affected his translation.

   Just as most modern Chinese scholars do, Graham recognizes the Inner Chapters "as substantially the work of Zhuangzi himself."[32] But quite unlike them, Graham does not consider these first seven chapters of the book as essentially integral pieces of fantastic prose composed by Zhuang Zhou himself with some tampering by later scholars and some textual corruptions. He speculates that Zhuangzi probably "left behind only disjointed pieces, mixed up perhaps with his disciples' records of his oral teaching, and it was a Syncretist editor of the second century B.C. who devised the headings, grouped the relics under them, and relegated the unusable bits to the Mixed chapters."[33] Sometimes he thinks that more than just one editor is to be credited with assembling the bits and pieces Zhuangzi left behind. As he says later in the headnote to the text of his translation of the "Xiaoyaoyou" 逍遙遊 (Going rambling without a destination, chapter 1): "The pieces which the compilers of Zhuangzi assembled in 'Going rambling without a destination' are all on the theme of soaring above the restricted viewpoints of the worldly."[34] Here some troubling questions immediately suggest themselves. Were these apparently "disjointed pieces" jotted down by Zhuangzi on different occasions? Could someone other than the "author" actually group together these pieces presumably from different contexts into quite coherent discourses? How come the Inner Chapters do not read like the *biji* 筆記 or "random jottings" of later historical time? Since Huang Tingjian 黃庭堅 (1045– 1105) of the Song dynasty, Chinese literary scholars through the ages have admired the unity and structure of the Inner Chapters.[35] If Graham is indeed correct about the nature of the Inner Chapters, the Syncretist editor and/or compilers deserve more credit than Zhuangzi does for producing these examples of brilliant early Chinese philosophical prose. I shall return later to examine the evidence that the Inner Chapters are not just series of disjointed or discontinuous pieces and episodes grouped under seven headings because there is a subtle kind of "inner logic" in the unfolding of ideas running through each of them. For now, let me first comment on Graham's lack of a clear notion of the development of ancient Chinese philosophical prose.

   The first of Graham's statements quoted in the preceding paragraph may lead one to think that by the third century B.C Chinese thinkers all

of a sudden began to compose well-developed discursive essays of the
kind found in the *Xunzi* and the *HanFeizi*. This is, of course, contrary
to fact. Of the philosophical works up till the time of Zhuangzi, the
Lunyu 論語 or *Analects of Confucius* and the *Mencius* 孟子 (attributed to
a contemporary of Zhuangzi, the Confucian thinker Meng Ke 孟軻, ca.
372–289 B.C.) contain mainly recorded aphorisms, sayings, dialogues, and
debates, the last of which are only found in the latter work. Although in
form the *Mencius* is modeled upon the *Analects*, it is no longer aphoristic,
as the sections are much longer, and the arguments are usually extensively
developed. Each section in the *Mencius* is also generally focused on one
central issue.[36] But these two early Confucian texts are not two collections
of "philosophical essays."[37] With the earliest portions of the *Mozi* 墨子,
which were probably written by the followers of Mo Di 墨翟 (fl. 479–438
B.C.) during the late fifth and the early fourth centuries B.C., there appeared
the longer discursive "essays," each of which carried a title and focused
on a particular topic. Dialogues and anecdotes still figure importantly in
these early examples of the ancient Chinese philosophical essay because
philosophical discourse was still primarily oral. And the writers of these
essays also began to pay attention to the logical method of developing an
argument.[38] In terms of the development of early Chinese philosophical
prose, the Inner Chapters of the *Zhuangzi* represent a significant stage between the early works such as the *Analects* and the *Mozi* and the later well-
evolved argumentative essays of Xunzi and HanFeizi. The Inner Chapters
can be considered as "philosophical essays" of a very special kind. They
are series of stories—largely fables, brief anecdotes, and parables—intermixed with passages of discursive prose, designed for the articulation of
philosophical ideas. In the absence of real hard evidence, there does not
seem to be any justification for Graham to replace the traditional view
of Zhuangzi's authorship of the Inner Chapters with his radical notion
of the compilation by later editors of Zhuangzi's jottings and notes.

   Graham further believes that the *Zhuangzi* also suffers from the muti-
lation of editors and commentators and from the transposition of bamboo
strips (*cuojian* 錯簡) in the hands of those who handled the scrolls of this
text, resulting in a very badly mutilated and corrupt text. This belief is
based on modern Chinese and Japanese textual scholarship as well as on
Graham's own investigation. Graham is so confident of his findings that
he proceeds to "restore" the corrupt text by moving "occasional passages"
to "more suitable contexts"[39] within the Inner Chapters and transposing
fragments from the Mixed Chapters (Miscellaneous chapters; *zapian* 雜篇)
to the Inner Chapters. The issue for us here is not one of whether or not

the *Zhuangzi* is a mutilated and corrupt text. Nobody in his or her right mind today can argue that a text transmitted down to us from so long ago is pristine. Rather, the issue is: to what extent is the *Zhuangzi* mutilated and tampered with by later editors and commentators? More important, is it valid for Graham to restore what he regards as the "corrupt" Inner Chapters purely on what he considers as "internal grounds"[40] without any hard external evidence? This related question constitutes my main reservation regarding Graham's translation and will be dealt with later. Here let us discuss first the issue of the condition of the *Zhuangzi* text.

In a recent publication, Liu Xiaogan 劉笑敢 has presented an enormous amount of convincing evidence that the mutilated and corrupt condition of the *Zhuangzi* has perhaps been greatly exaggerated by modern Chinese scholars. Most important in his textual study of the *Zhuangzi* is his careful examination of six key single-character philosophical terms—namely, *dao* 道, *de* 德, *xing* 性, *ming* 命, *jing* 精, and *shen* 神—and three compound terms made from them—namely, *daode* 道德, *xingming* 性命, and *jingshen* 精神—in early Chinese texts.[41] Liu Xiaogan discovers that single-character terms (except *xing*) appear in the Inner Chapters but not their compounds (which appear thirty-six times in the Outer and Mixed Chapters). At the same time, single-character terms (and not their compounds) appear in *Zuo zhuan* 左傳, *Analects*, *Daode jing*, *Mencius*, and *Mozi*, texts that are traditionally believed to date before the middle of the Warring States period; however, the compound terms of *daode*, *xingming*, and *jingshen* are found in such texts as *Xunzi*, *HanFeizi*, and *Lüshi chunqiu* 呂氏春秋 from the late Warring States era. Liu Xiaogan's findings support the general rule of the evolution of terminology for philosophical discourse: single-character terms would appear in earlier texts while the more elaborate compound terms would appear in later texts. They also significantly weaken modern scholars' claims that the division of the *Zhuangzi* into Inner, Outer, and Mixed Chapters was done rather late in time and that the text has been severely mutilated and tampered with by editors and commentators. Liu Xiaogan also evaluated some of the most important pieces of evidence on whose basis Wang Shu-min has asserted that the *Zhuangzi* text we now have is the product of Guo Xiang 郭象 (died A.D. 312), who transposed materials among divisions at will.[42] For example, Wang Shu-min mentions that in the *Bailunshu* 百論疏, the Buddhist monk Jizang 吉藏 of the Sui dynasty says, "[It is said in] the Outer Chapters (*waipian* 外篇) of the *Zhuangzi* that for twelve years Cook Ding did not see the whole ox." He then speculates that because the Cook Ding story appears in the "Yangshengzhu" 養生主 chapter in the Inner Chapters, Guo Xiang must have moved that chapter from the Outer into the Inner Chapters.[43] Liu Xiaogan points out that this remark does not resemble in either content or actual wording any statement in the Cook Ding story in our present "Yangshengzhu" chapter and suggests that Jizang might have referred to an actual passage in the Outer Chapters that is now lost, since different versions of the same stories or metaphors do exist in various parts of the present *Zhuangzi* text.[44] I might add that it is also possible that Jizang could have simply misquoted from memory, and therefore his remark cannot be taken as hard evidence of textual transposition done by Guo Xiang.

Perhaps someday very ancient texts of the *Zhuangzi* might turn up to prove that Liu Xiaogan is totally wrong. But until then, the conservative attitude toward the text is to be recommended; after all, we do have the following remark from Lu Deming 陸德明 of the Tang dynasty, who had seen the various editions of the *Zhuangzi* from Jin 晉 times: "The Inner Chapters in the various editions are the same" (其內篇眾家並同).[45] In an article on the Mawangdui 馬王堆 texts of the *Daode jing*, the late Hsü Fu-kuan 徐復觀 cautions people not to regard the many textual emendations by scholars through the ages as too significant because "out of ten incidences one or two are effective while the other eight or nine all prove to be a waste of time," when checked against the two excavated early Han texts.[46] I wonder if we will ever have the opportunity to judge whether Graham's "radical reconstructions"[47] are valid or a waste of time.

Graham criticizes previous complete English translations of the *Zhuangzi* chiefly on the basis of what he takes to be the nature of the text. He finds fault with James Legge, Herbert A. Giles, and Burton Watson on the ground that they mainly follow the traditional commentators without paying heed to unique textual, linguistic, and philosophical problems. He says that all three translators have committed a single basic error of policy:

> They treat Zhuangzi as though it were what is nowadays understood by a "book," and present it as written in prose and divided into chapters composed of paragraphs; and they assume that, however disjointed, mutilated, even frankly unintelligible the original may be, however much its parts may differ in date, in thought and style, it is their duty to trudge forward from sentence to sentence, disguising the breaks, blurring the differences, assimilating the verse to the prose, in order to sustain the illusion of a smooth flow.[48]

These serious charges are largely valid. The three translators do indeed attempt to render the chapters as consisting of well-arranged paragraphs of prose. Even in the admirable translation by Burton Watson, who is clearly aware of the textual problems (as he has briefly discussed them in the introduction to his translation),[49] there is a very high degree of readability and uniformity in style. Graham actually praises Watson "for his consistent treatment of the main philosophical terms as well as for his deftness in picking the apt and vivid word."[50] It goes without saying that it is far easier to read these three English translations than the original *Zhuangzi* because Legge, Giles, and Watson have each worked hard to make sense out of a very difficult old text. In the remark below Graham further notes the effect of the translators' attempt to produce a smooth equivalent in English of the ancient Chinese text:

> A quite eerie effect is that the smoother the English the more Zhuangzi will assume the persona of someone who could have written that English—intermittently lively, more often verbiage, expressing even at its most coherent incompatible opinions from 200 years of Chinese intellectual history. It is in the best translations that Zhuangzi suffers a strange mutation into a whimsical, garrulous old wiseacre to whose ramblings you listen with half an ear in the confidence that every now and then he will startle you awake with a vivid phrase, a striking aphorism or a marvelous story. But this image of the great Daoist, at once affectionate and profoundly insulting, has no relation to Zhuangzi or any other writer in the book, no relation to anything except the situation of a translator cracking under the multiple strains of his craft.[51]

The irritation with smooth translations displayed in the above quotation reminds one of the following comment by Nabokov: "I constantly find in reviews of verse translations the following kind of thing that sends me into spasms of helpless fury: 'Mr. (or Miss) So-and-so's translation reads smoothly.'"[52] Graham has no patience for these smooth or "literary" translations because they usually transform the original authors beyond recognition. Thus in his opinion Zhuangzi is transformed in the best English translations from an astonishingly original Daoist thinker and poet into a "whimsical, garrulous old wiseacre"! After briefly reviewing the three translations, Graham sets forth toward the end of the introductory chapter the details of his own strategy in translating this great ancient Chinese book.[53] I shall summarize here only those details most relevant to my concerns in this chapter.

First, Graham states that he will offer integral and complete translations of only homogeneous blocks such as the Inner Chapters and chapters 8 through 10, 12 through 16, and 33, instead of the entire book. Second, he will translate only those chapters that are true essays as consecutive

paragraphed prose. By "true essays" he means those chapters that resemble
the argumentative essays by Xunzi and HanFeizi. The Inner Chapters will
be treated differently because:

> The Inner Chapters are collections of isolated episodes probably grouped
> together by a later editor, and including, for example, sequences of rhymed
> quatrains, stories in which speakers may burst into song, didactic verses with
> scattered prose comments, strings of aphorisms, provisional formulations
> of ideas followed by criticisms, propositions which Zhuangzi (or a disciple
> perhaps) proceeds to annotate phrase by phrase. Each requires a correspond-
> ing form in English, with a typographic layout suited to its structure.[54]

Third, he will try his best to do equal justice to Zhuangzi as a philosopher and as a poet. He makes an interesting and incisive observation that
"a Daoist is a thinker who despises thoughts, yet values, and finds the
imagery and rhythm to convey, any spontaneously emerging process of
thinking which he senses is orienting him in the direction of the Way."[55]
He confesses that this is almost impossible to do and that at times he has
to resort to something awkward in English in order to render precisely the
philosophical language that is in fact quite poetic in the original Chinese.
Fourth, since not even the text of the homogeneous Inner Chapters is
pristine, he will attempt to restore the "corrupt" text by moving materials to suitable contexts. Finally, the "ideal version" he aims at producing
"would, like the original, have items which are delightful and illuminating
at first reading, and others which are elliptical, difficult, enigmatic, to be
skipped or to be wrestled with in the light of introduction and notes."[56]
He indicates modestly that he is not confident of having attained that
aim and offers "apologies to the ghost of Zhuangzi."[57]

It is clear that the ideal version Graham strives to come up with is
one that is as close an approximation in a foreign language of the original
as possible. To borrow a term from Walter Benjamin, Graham strives in his
translation to reproduce with as much fidelity as possible the "mode of
signification" of the Inner Chapters. Although Graham does not use the
term *literal translation* to describe his own efforts, he does refer to Herbert
Giles and Burton Watson as "primarily literary" translators.[58] Thus it seems
best to apply Nabokov's conception of a "literal translation" (that remains absolutely faithful to the original source-language text) to describe
Graham's work. *Chuang-tzu: The Inner Chapters* is a remarkable achievement in the field of Western sinology. With the exception of the small
amount of his tampering with the Chinese text (which I shall elaborate
below), I would say that Graham has almost fully attained the goal he set

out to reach. Both Zhuangzi the philosopher and Zhuangzi the poet are as vividly represented here as in the original text. I am simply amazed by the precision with which Graham has translated the key concepts in Daoist vocabulary. His renderings of *shi bi* 是彼 as "'it' and 'other,'" *shi fei* 是非 as "'That's it' and 'That's not,'" *yin shi* 因是 as "'That's it' which goes by circumstance" and *wei shi* 為是 as "'That's it' which deems," all from his translation of the "Qiwulun" chapter ("The sorting which evens things out"), are a few of the most unforgettable examples. These renderings may seem awkward in English, especially at first reading, but they are exactly what the Chinese counterparts say. Graham's application of the term *daemonic* as used by Johann Wolfgang von Goethe (1749–1832) in the sense of "that which cannot be accounted for by understanding or reason"[59] to translate the Chinese term *shen* 神 also shows the tremendous care he pays to selecting *le mot juste*. For the students of Chinese literature, Graham's most important contribution resides in his unrelenting policy (which is stated in a passage quoted previously) to preserve the forms of language such as rhymed quatrain, song, aphorism, and anecdote as they are used in the original text. How can the English reader fully appreciate the *Zhuangzi* as a monument of ancient Chinese prose literature without seeing these different forms transferred into his or her language? Furthermore, Graham's reproduction of these literary forms enhances the reader's grasp of one important part of Zhuangzi's philosophy, his mistrust for the adequacy of language, which we have briefly touched upon earlier. The goal of Daoism is to gain an understanding of the Dao, the great Way of nature and the cosmos, in order to attain spiritual freedom and to acquire a knack for living and a pristine perspective on the world. The Dao is spontaneous, indivisible, unlimited, and unconditioned, but unfortunately, human language chops things up by imposing artificial categories on them that destroy the clarity and oneness of the Daoist vision. Zhuangzi's mistrust for language makes him even more aware of the need to use all the resources of language and the literary art he can get as tools for pointing in the direction of the Dao.[60] The spirit of playfulness and the talent for variety in the use of language as displayed in the Inner Chapters are largely the result of Zhuangzi's awareness of both the limitations and the powers of words. In Graham's translation, the English reader can see for the first time this important aspect of Zhuangzi's thought and language fully reproduced.

Graham is not exacting only when dealing with key terms and larger matters of literary forms. He has applied a very high standard of precision and accuracy to his entire project. Throughout the Inner Chapters, I have found only a small numbers of places where I disagree with his reading of particular words. Let us look at one such example to show not Graham's imperfection but the high standard he has set for himself. The following is a passage from the "Xiaoyaoyou" chapter (Going rambling without a destination): "A cicada and a turtle-dove laughed at it, saying, 'We keep flying till we're bursting, stop when we get to an elm or sandalwood, and sometimes are dragged back to the ground before we're there. What's all this about being ninety thousand miles up when he travels south?'"[61] This passage comes after the paragraph in which Zhuangzi talks about the relativity of things to conclude the opening story about the Kun fish and the Peng bird. The author seems to be drawing a comparison between Peng's immense power to travel and the two little creatures' limited ability to fly. But the contrast here is only relative because Peng can only make its distant journey when there is enough wind to bear its wings. Graham's "We keep flying till we're bursting" is slightly off, resulting in an omission of the parallel between Peng's action and that of the two creatures. The Chinese original is as follows: "我決起而飛." Graham apparently takes *jue* 決 to mean "burst" as in the sense of *juelie* 決裂 and leaves out the word *qi* 起 or "to rise up" entirely. However, Lu Deming cites a gloss from Li Yi 李頤 to note that *jue* 決 means *ji* 疾 or "swiftly" in the passage. Wang Shu-min has further provided a useful gloss that Wang Niansun 王念孫 has already explained why *jue* 決 is interpreted as *ji* 疾 by alluding to the *Guangya shigu* 廣雅釋詁 to note that 決 is a loan word for 趹 (which means 疾) in the present context.[62] Therefore, the original line should read: "We swiftly rise up and fly off." It is used to parallel Peng's rising up from the ocean after having changed from a fish into a bird, especially in the lines of "怒而飛" ("When it puffs out its chest and flies off") and "搏扶搖而上者九萬里" ("it mounts spiraling on the whirlwind ninety thousand miles high."). In the subsequent repeated passage, there is also this line "我騰躍而上" ("I do a hop and skip and up I go."), which exactly parallels these sets of descriptions. I believe these parallels are important and should be preserved in a translation. But one has to split hairs to recognize Graham's oversight in the translation here.

Let us now turn to examine the more seriously questionable parts of Graham's translation of the *Zhuangzi*, namely, his tampering with the source text. As noted earlier, Graham's emendations are motivated by his desire to restore what he considers a badly corrupt and mutilated early Daoist text to a closer approximation of its original shape. His tampering can be divided into two kinds: (1) moving passages and fragments to more suitable contexts, either within the Inner Chapters or from the Mixed into the Inner Chapters; and (2) relegating occasional passages in the text to Zhuangzi's afterthoughts or annotations by Zhuangzi himself, his disciples, or later editors and putting them in brackets. He has identified in his book transpositions and questionable passages in about a dozen places. I find all of Graham's tinkerings are open to question.

As mentioned earlier, Liu Xiaogan has taken Graham to task for moving a passage from chapter 24, "Xu Wugui" 徐無鬼, and inserting it before the Cook Ding story in chapter 3, "Yangshengzhu." He observes,

> There are indeed some occurrences of the same words in both, such as *youya* (有涯) and *wuya* (無涯), but the writing style is different. In the passage from "Xuwugui" we read "*zhi dayi, zhi dayin, zhi damu, zhi dajun, zhi dafang, zhi daxin, zhi dading, zhiyi* (知大一, 知大陰, 知大目, 知大均, 知大方, 知大信, 知大定, 至矣)." (Knowing the ultimate One, knowing the ultimate Yin, knowing the ultimate eye, knowing the ultimate adjuster, knowing the ultimate in scope, knowing the ultimate truthful, knowing the ultimate fixed, you have reached the perfect point.) It mechanically repeats seven parallel sentences without any development of ideas, followed by seven equally stiff sentences. These rigid language patterns are evidently different from the general style of the Inner Chapters which are imaginative, fantastic, free and unrestrained. Thus, Graham's judgment in this case is to be questioned.[63]

In addition to Liu's observation on writing style, I might add that chapter 3 is focused on knowing "what matters in the nurture of life," that is, to "Trace the vein which is central and make it your standard"[64] (*yuan du yi wei jing* 緣督以為經) or to find the space in life (the Daoist middle way) so that one can move about freely without running into conflict with anything. The present text, containing some opening statements, followed by several anecdotes and a few lines of concluding remarks, is integral and sufficient in itself. The passage Graham inserts from chapter 24, which describes a variety of knowledge, looks in reality very out of place in this short but nonetheless complete and integrated chapter. Just as in this case, most of Graham's transpositions are based on some occurrences of the same words in two contexts. Because of the limitation of space, I shall examine only one other incidence. The examination of all of the textual reconstructions should be the subject of another study.

Graham moves a "poem" that begins chapter 14, "Tianyun" 天運 (Circuits of Heaven), to serve as the conclusion of the dialogue between Ziqi of Nanguo 南郭子綦 and Yancheng Ziyou 顏成子游 that opens chapter 2, "Qiwulun" (The sorting that evens things out"). The following is the transposed "poem":

Heaven turns circles, yes!
Earth sits firm, yes!
Sun and moon vie for a place, yes!
Whose is the bow that shoots them?
Whose is the net that holds them?
Who is it sits with nothing to do and gives them the push that
    sends them?

Shall we suppose, yes, that something triggers them off, then seals
    them away, and they have no choice?
Or suppose, yes, that wheeling in their circuits they cannot stop
    themselves?
Do the clouds make the rain?
Or the rain the clouds?
Whose bounty bestows them?
Who is it sits with nothing to do as in ecstasy he urges them?

The winds rise in the north,
Blow west, blow east,
And now again whirl high above.
Who breathes them out, who breathes them in?
Who is it sits with nothing to do and sweeps between and over
    them?[65]

Whether the above is indeed constructed as a poem is open to question, but the lines do show more regulation. Graham's skillful rendering captures the spirit of the original very well. He feels that his transposition is particularly justified in this case because the Tang monk Zhanran's 湛然 *Zhiguan fuxing chuanhong jue* 止觀輔行傳宏訣 cites the three lines of "雨為雲乎? 雲為雨乎? 孰降施是?" from it, saying that they are from the Inner Chapters.[66] Zhanran's remark is not hard enough evidence for Graham to insert the passage in the "Qiwulun," however. Zhanran might have quoted those three lines from an edition of the *Zhuangzi* that existed in his time but has been lost since that carried them in one Inner Chapter. Since Zhanran's book appears to be for personal use, he might have misquoted from memory without checking against the particular edition of the *Zhuangzi*. His brief remark certainly cannot be considered as hard evidence in textual criticism in the same way Liu Xiaogan's statistical study of key philosophical terms can. In any case, Zhanran has not indicated from which Inner Chapter he is quoting those three lines.

It seems clear that Graham believes this section in chapter 14 belongs here in chapter 2 because of the shared images of "wind" (*feng* 風), "breathing in and out" (*xuxi* 噓吸) and "sealing up" (*jian* 緘) and the question concerning the force that controls the process of nature. He speculates that this "poem" must have been excised by later editors to avoid duplication.[67] Upon closer scrutiny, we find problems in this suggested transposition.

In the first place, the passage previously quoted from the "Tianyun" chapter ends with the question "May I ask why?" (敢問何故), which Graham has not included in his transposition. Why? Second, Graham translates Ziqi's reply (which immediately precedes the inserted passage in Graham's translation) to Yancheng Ziyou as follows: "Who is it that puffs out the myriads which are never the same, who in their self-ending is sealing them up, in their self-choosing is impelling the force into them?"[68] For a long time, I could not figure out from where Graham derived the phrase "sealing them up." It is now clear to me that Graham uses "sealing them up" to render the character *xian* 咸 in the line "咸其自取" so that there is one more link between the two passages. But to my knowledge, *xian* cannot be taken to mean, or to serve as a loan word, for *jian* 緘, which appears in the passage from the "Tianyun" chapter. Last, the most important objection to inserting the passage from the "Tianyun" chapter is that it does not suit the local context between the first two sections of the "Qiwulun." Graham himself correctly explains the meaning of the opening sections of chapter 2: "Zhuangzi's parable of the wind compares the conflicting utterances of philosophers to the different notes blown by the same breath in the long and short tubes of the pan pipes, and the noises made by the wind in hollows of different shapes."[69] In the present text of the "Qiwulun," the Ziqi story is followed by the passage describing the variegated phenomena of the human mind, which produce the conflicting utterances of the philosophers. The variegated phenomena of the mind also resemble the notes made by the pan pipes and the noises by the wind in hollows. This is why Zhuangzi uses the phrase "music coming out of emptiness (i.e., hollows)" (*yue chu xu* 樂出虛) in the second section to serve as an integrative element. The first two sections of chapter 2 are well integrated by the paralleling images of the wind, the notes, the noises, and the variegated states of the mind. There is no gap to be filled between them. In actual fact, Graham's insertion of the "Tianyun" passage with its focus on cosmic order and its inclusion of images of "clouds," "rain," and "net" creates a digression and destroys the existing integrity in the text. Therefore, this attempted reconstruction is not built upon solid internal ground.

Let us now turn to examine passages that are bracketed by Graham in his translation as representing the Daoist thinker's afterthoughts or

annotations made by him or others on his remarks in the text. I shall use
examples from the "Xiaoyaoyou" chapter since our received text appears
to be in pretty good shape. In the opening paragraph of his translation, Graham has rearranged a couple of places and put three fragments
in parentheses:

> In the North Ocean there is a fish, its name is the Kun; the Kun's girth
> measures who knows how many thousand miles. It changes into a bird,
> its name is the Peng; the Peng's back measures who knows how many
> thousand miles. When it puffs out its chest and flies off, its wings are like
> clouds hanging from the sky. This bird when the seas are heaving has a
> mind to travel to the South Ocean. (The South Ocean is the Lake of
> Heaven.) In the words of the Tall Stories, "When the Peng travels to the
> South Ocean, the wake it thrashes on the water is three thousand miles
> long, it mounts spiraling on the whirlwind ninety thousand miles high, and
> is gone six months before it is out of breath." (The Tall Stories of Qi is a
> record of marvels.) Is the azure of the sky its true colour? Or is it that the
> distance into which we are looking is infinite? It never stops flying higher
> till everything below looks the same as above (heat-hazes, dust-storms, the
> breath which living things blow at each other).[70]

There is nothing intrinsically wrong in regarding the two sentences about
Tianchi (the South Ocean) and *Qixie* (the Tall Stories of Qi) as the
author's afterthoughts, if the latter was indeed originally where Graham
has placed it but somehow got dislocated in our received text (the line
"The Tall Stories of Qi is a record of marvels" actually appears right after
the line "The South Ocean is the Lake of Heaven" in the text we now
have). The line "*nanming zhe tian chi ye*" (南冥者天池也) does look like a
thought added after having finished the story about the Peng to explain
the place to where the bird has just traveled. Graham's rearrangement does
make the entire paragraph seem more logical. But if Graham is right that
Zhuangzi is a "thinker who despises thought," would he care about this
sort of logical sequencing of the sentences? The point I want to make
is that, it is possible—preferable, in fact—to read the opening passage in
the present text as an expression of the author's ideas as they emerge in
his mind. The line "*Qixie zhe zhiguai zhe ye*" (齊諧者志怪者也) belongs
in that context because it parallels the previous line in syntactic structure.
These two lines serve as an effective link between the two halves of the
paragraph, presenting two clusters of the author's thoughts. Moving the
poetic images "heat-hazes, dust-storms, the breath which living things
blow at each other" to the end of the paragraph also ruins the depiction
of the author's thought process. It seems that after quoting from the *Qixie*,

Zhuangzi goes on to describe a view from above as if he is the Peng, returns to his own perspective again to ask the questions about the color of the sky, and ends the paragraph with the remark "When it (the Peng) looks down, all it sees is the same." Thus the paragraph concludes with the implication that the Peng is actually just as limited in perception as we are down below on the ground. Graham's rendering has limited the perspective to that of the Peng bird. The abrupt shifts in the paragraph can be interpreted as acute depictions of Zhuangzi's lyrical visions. The rearrangement in Graham's first paragraph completely destroys this lyrical quality. Graham is actually sensitive to Zhuangzi's deftness in expressing his lyrical visions as he has observed in the headnote to the "Qiwulun" chapter: "It contains the most philosophically acute passages in the Inner Chapters, obscure, fragmented, but pervaded by the sensation, rare in ancient literatures, of a man jotting the living thought at the moment of its inception."[71] It is a pity that Graham has not applied the same kind of insight to his interpretation of other Inner Chapters in the book.

The next chunk of text that Graham has bracketed is the section concerning "Tang's questions to Ji" (湯之問棘也).[72] This section is largely a summary of the story about the Kun, the Peng, and the little creatures that precedes the discursive paragraph about the relative conditions in space (i.e., distances in travel) and time (i.e., the amounts of time required to travel to different distances and the life spans of living things). If we believe as Graham does that the "Xiaoyaoyou" is assembled by compilers, we certainly could regard this whole paragraph as an afterthought of the author or a later annotation on the story that begins the chapter. But to do so is to ignore completely the nature and function of the passage. The summary differs from the previous account of the Peng story in several significant details. The North Ocean, not the South Ocean, is now called the "Lake of Heaven"; the Kun and the Peng are not clearly related; the power, rather than the condition required, for Peng's journey is emphasized: "It mounts the whirlwind in a ram's horn spiral ninety thousand miles high, cutting through clouds and mist, shouldering the sky, and then he sets its course southward to journey to the South Ocean";[73] and most important of all is the tone of arrogance in the little quail's comment on Peng's journey: "Where does he think he's going? I do a hop and a skip and up I go, and before I've gone more than a few dozen yards come fluttering down among the bushes. That's the best kind of flying, where does he think he's going?"[74] The purpose of this paragraph is to introduce those who are involved in official service as Zhuangzi says at the beginning of the next paragraph: "Those, then, who are clever enough to do well in one office or efficient enough to protect one district, whose powers suit one prince and are put to the test in one state, are seeing themselves as this little bird did, and Song Rong smiled at them in disdain."[75] If this whole paragraph is an afterthought, or—worse—only a later annotation, the sense of unity and continuity in the writing up till this point would be completely lost. Actually, these two passages about the story of the Peng constitute an explicit example of an organizational device which may be called "musical structure" used in the Inner Chapters. The organizational device can be called "musical" because it relies on "variation on themes" for coherence within a piece of prose.[76] I borrow the term *variation on a theme* from music to refer to a similar process of modifying a theme or passage in the Inner Chapters in such a way that the product can be recognized as having derived from a prior passage. The variation must be made for the new treatment of the same theme to function in a different context. But the recurrence of whole or partial phrases, sentences, and/or motifs is what defines the current passage as a variation on the same theme that has been depicted before. There is no question that the "Tang's questions to Ji" passage can be seen as a variation on the account of Peng's journey that begins the chapter.[77]

Graham's last tinkering with the text of the "Xiaoyaoyou" occurs right after the mention of Song Rong. Here is the rest of Graham's paragraph in full:

> Not only that, he [Song Rong] refused to be encouraged though the whole world praised him, or deterred though the whole world blamed him, he was unwavering about the division between inward and outward, discriminating about the boundary between honour and disgrace—but then he soared no higher. (He was too concerned about the world to break clean away.) Or that Liezi now, he journeyed with the winds for his chariot, a fine sight it must have been, and did not come back for fifteen days. (Even so, there was something he failed to plant in his own soil.) The former of them, in the hope of bringing blessing to the world, failed to break clean away; the latter, even if he did save himself the trouble of going on foot, still depended on something to carry his weight. As for the man who rides a true course between heaven and earth, with the changes of the Six Energies for his chariot, to travel into the infinite, is there anything that he depends on? As the saying goes,
>
> > The utmost man is selfless,
> > The daemonic man takes no credit for his deeds.
> > The sage is nameless.[78]

There are several changes Graham has made to the original Chinese text. First, he moves the comment on Song Rong—"Even so, there was something he failed to plant in his own soil" (雖然，猶有未樹也)—to a later context about Liezi and replaces it with "but then he soared no higher," a phrase that is not in the original at all. Since Song Rong is obsessed with "fixing (*ding* 定) the division between inward and outward, and discriminating about the boundary between honour and disgrace," the choice of the planting imagery with its sarcastic tone here seems especially appropriate. The comment is totally out of place where Graham has inserted it. Second, the line "He was too concerned about the world to break clean away" seems to say just the opposite of the Chinese, which can be rendered as "He was not too eager about pursuing worldly things." Finally, the two comments—"He was not too eager about pursuing perfections" (Graham's "in the hope of bringing . . . failed to break clean away") and "even if . . . weight"—which seem to be both aimed at Liezi in the original, are now divided evenly between Song Rong and Liezi. The result of these changes is that Graham's passage now appears to be focused on a comparison between Song Rong and Liezi. The original, however, is an enumeration of different personalities in the ascending order of their spiritual attainment, from the arrogant officials to the man who is able to roam in the boundless realm.

Before I close this chapter, I would like to return to Graham's view regarding the composition of each of the Inner Chapters. Since we have been looking at Graham's reconstruction of the "Xiaoyaoyou," let us continue to use it as an example. Earlier I quoted a statement from Graham's headnote to this chapter, saying that the pieces assembled by compilers "are all on the theme of soaring above the restricted viewpoints of the worldly." To be sure, soaring is the central idea and image that integrates the sections into a whole. But the "pieces" are not just disjointed thoughts and notes on the theme of soaring above the restricted viewpoints of the worldly that Zhuangzi jotted down at various times in his life. If this were the case, there would not be any sense of order in which these pieces are arranged and related to each other. Although the chapter does not follow the logical organization of ideas in an argumentative essay, it does have an intricate logic of its own in the unfolding of ideas. I shall follow Ch'ien Mu's division of the chapter into six sections and examine the inner logic that brings the seemingly disjointed pieces together.

Ch'ien Mu takes the long part ending with the line "The sage is nameless" as constituting the first section.[79] Zhuangzi begins the chapter

with the story about the Peng's astonishing power to travel.The reader may
be misled to think that the Peng is used to serve as a metaphor for freedom.
But Zhuangzi is quick to remind us that space and time impose boundaries and conditions of relativity on things. Peng's distant journey depends
on enormous conditions, while the limited flying of the cicada and the
turtle-dove requires very little effort. From these creatures Zhuangzi then
turns to talk about human beings and concludes that just like the Peng,
the little birds, Song Rong and Liezi (who can actually fly) do not have
the ability to "go rambling without any restriction" (*xiaoyao you* 逍遙遊)
as the utmost man, the daemonic man, and the sage can. Only at the end
of this long section do we realize that the kind of "soaring" or spiritual
freedom Zhuangzi advocates is of an absolute kind that does not depend
on anything and transcends all restrictions, boundaries, and limitations.

The second section is about the Confucian sage King Yao who
attempts to yield the throne to Xu You, but the latter refuses to take it,
regarding it as totally useless, and asserts his preference to lead a selfish
and simple life.[80] This second section is only loosely connected with the
last paragraph of the previous section by its concern with involvement
in government, but the idea of soaring is not commented on at all.

The third section records a conversation between Jian Wu and Lian
Shu concerning Jie Yu's wild story about the daemonic man of Guyi
whose great power resembles the utmost man, the daemonic man, and
the sage described at the end of section 1.[81] And this daemonic man does
not concern himself with affairs of the world. His indifference toward
human affairs parallels Xu You's lack of interest in accepting the throne
described in the preceding section.

It is not until the fourth section that we realize that uselessness, indifference to human affairs, and spiritual freedom are intimately related.[82]
In this brief section, Zhuangzi first uses the Man of Song to bring up the
idea of usefulness and ends with Yao's forgetting his empire after meeting
with "the Four (daemonic men?) in the mountains of Guyi."

The themes of usefulness and uselessness dominate the last two
sections of the chapter, in each of which Zhuangzi engages the logician
Hui Shi 惠施 in a lively debate.[83] Hui Shi is scolded by his friend for
being clumsy "in finding uses for something big" and apparently "useless" from a practical and utilitarian point of view. Here in the end, we
finally realize that being socially useless is fundamental to the absolute
freedom—the rambling through life without limitation—that Zhuangzi
wishes to enjoy.The last section is a brilliant conclusion to the chapter.
The ideas of "big and useless" and of "rambling in the boundless realm"

are brought together. The images of the big tree, small animals, and the big yak also hark back to the beginning of the chapter. Zhuangzi even uses the phrase "as a cloud hanging from the sky" to describe the size of the yak to tighten the connection between the beginning and the ending of the chapter. Above all, the central idea of the chapter, *xiaoyao*, or "unlimited rambling," is even embedded in the last few lines of the text here. In the last analysis, it is interesting to note that the more carefully we read the six seemingly random pieces of prose, the more we feel that there is an intricate kind of unity within them. There is clearly an "inner logic" to the chapter's organization. The seemingly haphazard elements within it do relate to each other in a kind of "mysterious resonance," and this "mysterious resonance" is closer to the structure of music than to argumentative prose. I wonder if we follow Graham's advice to take the "pieces" or sections separately, will we still be able to say that each is "on the theme of soaring above the restricted viewpoints of the worldly?"

Notes

This piece was presented at The Second International Conference on the Translation of Chinese Literature, held in Taipei, Taiwan, December 19–21, 1992. I wish to thank Carol Rosenthal Kaufmann for carefully going over an earlier version and making suggestions for stylistic improvement. This chapter has been published in *Translation Quarterly* 13, 14 (1999), pp. 63–96. For inclusion in the present volume, I have made slight changes in several places, changed the romanization system from Wade-Giles to pinyin, and slightly revised several footnotes as well as added a couple of new ones. I am grateful to the editors of *Translation Quarterly* for agreeing to let me publish the piece in this volume on the *Zhuangzi*.

1. Frederick Henry Balfour, tr., *The Divine Classic of Nan-hua, Being the Works of Chuang Tsze, Taoist Philosopher* (Shanghai and Hong Kong: Kelly and Walsh, 1881).

2. Helmut Wilhelm mentions that the German scholar Ernst Faber (1839–1899) completed a translation into German of the entire *Zhuangzi* before 1881, but unfortunately the manuscript of his translation "fell victim to a fire before it went to print." See "Chuang-tzu Translations: A Bibliographical Appendix" in Victor H. Mair, ed., *Experimental Essays on Chuang-tzu* (University of Hawaii Press, 1983), p. 158.

3. To my knowledge, there exist to date these six complete translations of the *Zhuangzi* in the English language: (1) Frederic Henry Balfour, tr., *The Divine Classic of Nan-hua, Being the Works of Chuang Tsze, Taoist Philosopher;*

(2) Herbert C. Giles, tr., *Chuang Tzu: Mystic, Moralist, and Social Reformer*, re-printed as *Chuang Tzu: Taoist Philosopher and Chinese Mystic*; (3) James Legge, tr., "The Writings of Kwang-Tze," in *The Sacred Books of China, The Texts of Taoism*, reissued with revised romanization by Clae Waltham as *Chuang Tzu: Genius of the Absurd, Arranged from the Work of James Legge*; (4) Burton Watson, tr., *The Complete Works of Chuang Tzu*; (5) Victor H. Mair, tr., *Wandering on the Way: Early Taoist Tales and Parables of Chuang Tzu*; (6) Martin Palmer with Elizabeth Breuilly, Chang Wai Ming, and Jay Ramsay, trs., *The Book of Chuang Tzu*. For full references see the bibliography to this volume.

4. This history has been reviewed in a speech given by Hugo Friedrich on July 24, 1965, in Heidelberg. The speech has been translated into English as "On the Art of Translation" by Rainer Schulte and John Biguenet and included in their book, *Theories of Translation: An Anthology of Essays from Dryden to Derrida* (Chicago and London: University of Chicago Press, 1992), pp. 11–16. This collection of twenty-one essays with a very useful introductory essay by the editors provides an excellent overview of the evolution of translational thinking in the West.

5. Ibid., p. 15.

6. Rainer Schulte and John Biguenet, eds., *Theories of Translation*, "Introduction," p. 3.

7. These different ways are discussed in ibid., pp. 3–6.

8. Vladimir Nabokov, "Problems of Translation: Onegin in English," in *Theories of Translation*, p. 134.

9. Ibid., p. 127.

10. Ibid.

11. Walter Benjamin, "The Task of the Translator," in *Illuminations*, tr. Harry Zohn and ed. Hannah Arendt (New York: Schocken Books, 1969), p. 78.

12. Ibid.

13. See the editors' review of essays by Arthur Schopenhauer, Roman Jakobson, Jacques Derrida, Michael Riffaterre, and Octavio Paz represented in their book, *Theories of Translation*, pp. 6–10.

14. Octavio Paz, "Translation: Literature and Letters," tr. Irene del Corral, *Theories of Translation*, p. 152.

15. Ibid., p. 154.

16. See Chang Heng 張亨, "XianQin sixiang zhong liangzhong dui yuyan de xingcha" 先秦思想中兩種對語言的省察, *Si yu Yan* 思與言 8:6 (March 1971), pp. 283–92.

17. This remark appears in the "Xici" 繫辭 (Appended words) to the *Yi Jing* 易經 (Book of Changes). For the Chinese passage, see Sun Xingyan 孫星衍, *Zhouyi jijie* 周易集解 (Congshu jicheng edition), p. 604. This remark is rendered as follows in the Richard Wilhelm/Cary F. Baynes translation of the *Yi Jing*: "Writing cannot express words completely. Words cannot express thoughts completely." See the *I Ching or Book of Changes*, translated into

English from the German translation of Richard Wilhelm by Cary F. Baynes (Princeton: Princeton University Press, 1950), p. 322.

18. See A. C. Graham, *Disputers of Tao* (La Salle: Open Court Publishing Company, 1989), pp. 133, 154, 200.

19. Ibid., p. 200.

20. The word *yi* 譯 has been used in some early Chinese texts to mean "translation" or "interpretation." For instance, in the "Wang zhi" 王制 chapter of the *Li ji* 禮記, we find the following passage: "五方之民，言語不通，嗜欲不同，達其志，通其欲···北方曰譯." See *Shisan jing zhushu* 十三經注疏 (Taipei: Yiwen yinshuguan, 1965), 5, p. 248. Again, in the "Kao ji" 考績 chapter of Wang Fu's 王符 *Qianfu lun* 潛夫論, we find the following statement: "夫聖人為天口，賢者為聖譯。是故聖人之言，天之心也，賢者之所説，聖人之意也。" See Wang Fu, *Qianfu lun*, with a commentary by Wang Jipei 王繼培 (Shanghai: Guji chubanshe, 1978), p. 83.

21. D. C. Lau, tr., *Lao Tzu: Tao Te Ching* (Penguin Books, 1963), p. 57.

22. Ibid., p. 82. For convenience sake, I will refer to Laozi as the author of the *Daode jing*, despite the problems surrounding the authorship of this early Daoist text.

23. ZZJS 63; HY 4/2/23–24. This is a slightly modified version of A. C. Graham's translation of the passage. See Graham, *Chuang-tzu: The Seven Inner Chapters and Other Writings from the Book Chuang-tzu* (London: George Allen & Unwin, 1981), p. 52.

24. A. C. Graham, *Disputers of Tao*, p. 200.

25. This is adapted from D. C. Lau, *Confucius: The Analects* (Penguin, 1979), p. 146.

26. This remark is quoted in Rainer Schulte and John Biguenet's introduction to their book, *Theories of Translation*, p. 9.

27. Ibid.

28. Graham 27.

29. Ibid., pp. 27–33. Graham's opinions on the date and composition of the book are presented in his long article "How Much of *Chuang-tzu* Did Chuang-tzu Write?"

30. Graham 30.

31. Ibid., p. 27.

32. Ibid.

33. Ibid., p. 29.

34. Ibid., p. 43.

35. Huang Tingjian 黃庭堅 has remarked on how well knit the Inner Chapters are. To my knowledge, he is the first scholar in history to have made an observation on the structure of the Inner Chapters. His remark can be found quoted in Ch'ien Mu 錢穆, *Zhuangzi zuanjian* 莊子纂箋 (Taipei: Dongda tushu gongsi, 1989), p. 1.

36. For a useful discussion of these general features, see Xu Hanwei 許漢

威, *XianQin wenxue ji yuyan lilun* 先秦文學及語言例論 (Henan: Zhongzhou guji chubanshe, 1984), p. 115.

37. Brief "discursive essays" can be found in the *Mencius*. The two sections that begin with "Mencius said, 'Fish is what I want'" and "Mencius said, 'Shun rose from the fields'" respectively are good examples. See D. C. Lau, tr., *Mencius* (Penguin, 1970), book 6, part A, section 10, pp. 166–67; and book 6, part B, section 15, p. 181.

38. Xu Hanwei, *XianQin wenxue ji yuyan lilun*, p. 151.

39. Graham 32.

40. Ibid.

41. Liu Xiaogan 劉笑敢, *Zhuangzi zhexue ji qi yanbian* 莊子哲學及其演變 (Beijing: Zhongguo shehui kexue, 1988), pp. 3–13. The textual study portion of this book has been translated by William Savage and published under the title of *Classifying the Zhuangzi Chapters* by the Center for Chinese Studies at the University of Michigan. For Liu Xiaogan's study of the six terms, see *Classifying the Zhuangzi Chapters* (Ann Arbor: The University of Michigan Center for Chinese Studies, 1994), pp. 4–16.

42. Ibid., pp. 28–31.

43. Wang Shu-min expresses this opinion in his influential *Zhuangzi jiaoshi* 莊子校釋 of 1947. He includes this argument in *Zhuangzi jiaoquan* 莊子校詮 (1988), his definitive work on this Daoist classic.

44. Liu Xiaogan's critique can be found in his book *Zhuangzi zhexue ji qi yanbian*, pp. 29–30.

45. See "Jingdian shiwen xulu" 經典釋文敘錄 included in Guo Qingfan 郭慶藩, *Zhuangzi jishi* 莊子集釋, p. 6.

46. Hsü Fu-Kuan, "Boshu Laozi suo fanyingchu de ruogan wenti" 帛書老子所反應出的若干問題, *Mingbao yuekan* 明報月刊 114 (June 1975), p. 99.

47. Graham uses this term to refer to the extensive reconstruction of a passage in the "Dechongfu" 德充符 chapter. See Graham 81.

48. Ibid., p. 30.

49. Burton Watson's introduction first appeared in his *Chuang Tzu: Basic Writings* (1964) and then again in his *Complete Works of Chuang Tzu* (1968).

50. Graham 30.

51. Ibid., p. 31.

52. Vladimir Nabokov, "Problem of Translation: Onegin in English" in Rainer Schulte and John Biguenet, eds., *Theories of Translation*, p. 127.

53. Graham 31–33.

54. Ibid., p. 31.

55. Ibid., p. 33.

56. Ibid., p. 32.

57. Ibid., p. 33.

58. A. C. Graham refers to Giles and Watson as "primarily literary" translators. See ibid.

59. Quoted by Graham in a footnote in Graham 35.
60. Ibid., p. 25.
61. Graham 44–45; ZZJS 9; HY 1/1/8–9.
62. All of the details can be found in Wang Shu-min, *Zhuangzi jiaoquan,* 1, p. 11.
63. Liu Xiaogan discusses this particular transposition in his afterword written in English and published with the translation of his book *Classifying the Zhuangzi Chapters,* p. 171. For the line from "Xu Wugui," see ZZJS 871; HY 69/24/106–07; for the Cook Ding story, see ZZJS 117–24; HY 7–8/3/2–12.
64. Graham 62.
65. Graham 49; "Tianyun," ZZJS 493; HY 36/14/1–4. For the "Qiwulun" dialogue, see ZZJS 43–50; HY 3/2/1–9.
66. Wang Shu-min is probably the first scholar to identify this citation and published it in his *Zhuangzi jiaoshi* in 1947.
67. Graham 49–50.
68. ZZJS 50; HY 3/2/9.
69. Graham 49.
70. Graham 43; ZZJS 2; HY 1/1/1–4.
71. Graham 48.
72. ZZJS 14; HY 1/1/13–17.
73. Graham 44; ZZJS 14; HY 1/1/14–15. I have altered Graham's rendering of 絕雲氣 to reflect more closely the sense of the passage.
74. Graham 44; ZZJS 14; HY 1/1/15–16. Again I have made a slight alteration to capture the tone of the passage better.
75. Graham 44; ZZJS 16; HY 1–2/1/17–18. I changed Graham's "the little birds" to "this little bird."
76. Professor Kuang-ming Wu has applied the idea of music to describe the structure of the *Zhuangzi* text. He compares the book of *Zhuangzi* to "musical scores and sounds" because our reading of this text can be likened to the experience of creating, performing, or listening to music: "There is no musical structure apart from its being experienced by the composer, by the performers, and by the participating audience. The three parties are not mere instruments of music: they are music." Kuang-ming Wu, *Chuang Tzu: World Philosopher at Play* (New York: The Crescent Publishing Company, 1982), p. 108. While Professor Wu focuses on the mode of experiencing in his analogy of the *Zhuangzi* text with music, I focus on the organizational strategy Zhuangzi seems to have employed in writing the Inner Chapters.
77. I first used the idea of "variation on themes" to describe the "musical structure" of the Inner Chapters in my article "The Language of the 'Inner Chapters' of the *Chuang Tzu*" included in Willard J. Peterson, Andrew H. Plaks, and Ying-shih Yu, eds., *The Power of Culture: Studies in Chinese Cultural History* (Hong Kong: The University of Hong Kong Press, 1991), p. 69. I am delighted to report that to my knowledge at least one other scholar of the

Zhuangzi has applied the concept of "variations on a theme" to examine the elemental organizational pattern found in the *Zhuangzi* text. In his recent book *Zhuangzi de wenhua jiexi—qiangudian yu houxiandai de shijie ronghe* 莊子的文化解析——前古典與後現代的視界融合, Ye Shuxian 葉舒憲 uses the term *biandiao* 變調 (variations on a theme) to discuss what he regards as the main theme of this Daoist classic, that of "the pattern of eternal return," of "the eternal cycle of life, death, and rebirth." The concept of *biandiao* is used in many places throughout Professor Ye's brilliant book. The reader could read in particular these two chapters for an understanding of Professor Ye's discussions of the patterns of "variations on a theme" in the *Zhuangzi*: "Chapter 1: The Recurrence of Dao" ("Dao zhi huigui 道之回歸") and "Chapter 2: The Structure of Recurrence in the *Zhuangzi*" ("Zhiyan yu tianjun: *Zhuangzi* de huixuan jiegou 卮言與天鈞:《莊子》的回旋結構") in *Zhuangzi de wenhua jiexi—qiangudian yu houxiandai de shijie ronghe* (Wuhan: Hubei renmin chubanshe, 1997), pp. 35–97. It should be noted here that Professor Ye and I have separately arrived at this similar view about one important organizational pattern found in the *Zhuangzi* text. We were not aware of each other's work until the fall of 1999.

78. Graham 44–45; ZZJS 16–17; HY 2/1/18–22.
79. ZZJS 2–22; HY 1–2/1/1–22.
80. ZZJS 22–26; HY 2/1/22–26.
81. ZZJS 26–31; HY 2/1/26–34.
82. ZZJS 31; HY 2/1/34–35.
83. ZZJS 36–39, 39–42; HY 2–3/1/35–42, 3/1/42–47.

References to Works on
the *Zhuangzi*

Allinson, Robert E. "On the Origin of the Relativistic Thesis for Interpretations of the Chuang-tzu." *Hanxue yanjiu* (1988), pp. 275–298.

———. *Chuang-tzu for Spiritual Transformation.* Albany: State University of New York Press, 1989.

———. "On the Question of Relativism in the Chuang-tzu." *Philosophy East and West* 39:1 (1989), pp. 13–26.

Alt, Wayne. "Logic and Language in the Chuang-tzu." *Asian Philosophy* 1:1 (1991), pp. 61–76.

Ames, Roger T. "Knowing in the *Zhuangzi*: 'From Here, on the Bridge, over the River Hao.'" In Ames, *Wandering at Ease in the Zhuangzi*, pp. 219–230.

———, ed. *Wandering at Ease in the Zhuangzi.* Albany: State University of New York Press, 1998.

Balfour, Frederick Henry, tr. *The Divine Classic of Nan-hua, Being the Works of Chuang Tsze, Taoist Philosopher.* Shanghai and Hong Kong: Kelly and Walsh, 1881.

Berkson, Mark. "Language: The Guest of Reality—Zhuangzi and Derrida on Language, Reality, and Skillfulness." In Kjellberg and Ivanhoe, *Essays on Skepticism, Relativism and Ethics*, pp. 97–126.

Cao Dalin 曹大林. "Luelun fandui jueduizhuyi de Zhuangxue renshilun 略論反對絕對主義的莊學認識論." *Jilin daxue xuebao* 吉林大學學報, 1982.2.

Chang Heng 張亨, "XianQin sixiang zhong liangzhong dui yuyan de xingcha 先秦思想中兩種對語言的省察." *Si yu Yan* 思與言 8:6 (March 1971), pp. 283–292.

Chen Guying 陳鼓應. *Zhuangzi jinzhu jinyi* 莊子今註今譯. Taipei: Shangwu yinshuguan 1975; 9th edition, 1989.

———. *Zhuangzi qianshuo* 莊子淺説. Hong Kong: Shangwu, 1991.

Chen Zhi'an 陳治安 (fl. 1632). *Nanhua zhenjing benyi* 南華真經本義. In *Wu-qiubei zhai Zhuangzi jicheng xubian* 無求備齋莊子集成續編, ed. Yen Ling-feng. Taipei: Yiwen yinshuguan, 1974, 26, p. 11.

Chiao Hung 焦竑. *Zhuangzi yi* 莊子翼. Taipei: Guangwen shuju, 1970.

Ch'ien Mu 錢穆. *Zhuangzi zhuanjian* 莊子纂箋. Taipei: Dongda tushu gongsi, 1985; 3rd edition, 1989.

Chinn, Ewing Y. "Zhuangzi and Relativistic Scepticism." *Asian Philosophy* 7:3 (1997), pp. 207–221.

———. "The Natural Equality of All Things." *Journal of Chinese Philosophy* 25:4 (1998), pp. 471–482.

Cook, Scott. "Zhuang Zi and His Carving of the Confucian Ox." *Philosophy East and West* 47:4 (October 1997), pp. 521–553.

Eno, Robert. "Cook Ding's Dao and the Limits of Philosophy." In Kjellberg and Ivanhoe, *Essays on Skepticism, Relativism and Ethics*, pp. 127–151.

Fung, Yu-lan 馮友蘭. *Chuang-Tzu—A New Selected Translation with an Exposition of the Philosophy of Kuo Hsiang*. Shanghai: Commerical Press, 1933; Rprt. Beijing: Foreign Languages Press, 1989.

Giles, Herbert C., tr. *Chuang Tzu: Mystic, Moralist, and Social Reformer*. London: Bernard Quaritch, 1889.

———. *Chuang Tzu: Taoist Philosopher and Chinese Mystic*. London: George Allen & Unwin, 1961 (reprint of his 1889 work [above]).

Graham, A. C. (Angus Charles). "Chuang-tzu's Essay on Seeing Things as Equal." *History of Religions* 9:2 and 3 (November and February 1969–70), pp. 137–159.

———. *Chuang-tzu: The Seven Inner Chapters and Other Writings from the Book of Chuang-tzu*. London: George Allen & Unwin, 1981.

———. "How Much of *Chuang-tzu* Did Chuang-tzu Write?" In Benjamin I. Schwartz, *Journal of the American Academy of Religion Thematic Issue* 47:3 (September 1979), pp. 459–502. Reprinted in A. C. Graham, *Studies in Chinese Philosophy and Philosophical Literature*. Singapore: Institute of East Asian Philosophies, 1986, pp. 283–321.

Guan Feng 關鋒, "Zhuangzi zhexue pipan 莊子哲學批判." *Zhexue yanjiu* 哲學研究, no. 7.8 (1960).

———. "*Zhuangzi* waizapian chutan" 莊子外雜篇初探. In *Zhuangzi zhexue taolun ji* 莊子哲學討論集, ed. Zhexue yanjiu bianji bu 哲學研究編輯部. Beijing: Zhonghua shuju, 1962, pp. 61–98.

Guo Qingfan 郭慶藩 (19th c.). *Zhuangzi jishi* 莊子集釋 (1895) (ZZJS). Wang Xiaoyu 王孝魚, ed.; Beijing: Zhonghua shuju, 1961.

Hansen, Chad. "A Tao of 'Tao' in *Chuang Tzu*." In Mair, *Experimental Essays*, pp. 24–55.

Hanshan [Deqing]'s 憨山 [德清]. *Guan Lao-Zhuang yingxiang lun* 觀老莊影響論. Taiwan: Liulijingfang photocopy ed., 1972.

———. *Zhuangzi neipian Hanshan zhu* 莊子內篇憨山註.Taipei:Xinwenfeng chuban gongsi, 1994.

Harvard-Yenching Institute. *Zhuangzi yinde* 莊子引得 (*A concordance to Chuang Tzu*) (HY). Beijing:Yanjing daxue tushuguan yinde bianzuanju, 1947.Taipei reprint: Chengwen, 1966.

Hu Annan 狐安南 (Fox, Alan). "*Zhuangzi* zhong de jingyan xingtai: Ganying yu fanying《莊子》中的經驗形態: 感應與反映." In *Zhongguo gudai siwei fangshi tansuo* 中國古代思維方式探索, ed. Yang Rur-bin 楊儒賓 and Huang Chün-chieh 黃俊傑.Taipei: Zhengzhong shuju, 1996, pp. 183–200.

Hu Yüan-chün 胡遠濬. *Zhuangzi quangu* 莊子詮詁. Taipei: Shangwu yinshuguan, 1967.

Ivanhoe, Philip J. "Zhuangzi's Conversion Experience." *Journal of Chinese Religions* 19 (1991), pp. 13–25.

———. "Skepticism, Skill, and the Ineffable Dao." *Journal of the American Academy of Religion* 64:4 (1993), pp. 639–654.

———. "Was Zhuangzi a Relativist?" In Kjellberg and Ivanhoe, *Essays on Skepticism, Relativism and Ethics*, pp. 197–214.

Jiang Fucong 蔣復璁. "*Zhuangzi kaobian*" 莊子考辨. In *Tushuguan xue jikan* 圖書館學季刊 2.1, reprinted in Cheng Liang-shu 鄭良樹, ed., *Xu Weishu tongkao* 續偽書通考.Taipei: Xuesheng, 1984.

Jochim, Chris. "Just Say No to 'No Self' in *Zhuangzi*." In Ames, *Wandering at Ease in the Zhuangzi*, pp. 35–74.

Kjellberg, Paul. "Skepticism, Truth and the Good Life: A Comparison of Zhuangzi and Sextus Empiricus." *Philosophy East & West* 44:1 (1994), pp. 111–133.

———. "Sextus Empiricus, Zhuangzi and Xunzi on 'Why Be Skeptical.'" In Kjellberg and Ivanhoe, *Essays on Skepticism, Relativism and Ethics*, pp. 1–25.

Kjellberg, Paul, and Ivanhoe, Philip J., eds. *Essays on Skepticism, Relativism, and Ethics in the Zhuangzi*. Albany: State University of New York Press, 1996.

Legge, James, tr. "The Writings of Kwang-tze." In *The Sacred Books of China, the Texts of Taoism.* 1891. See Waltham.

Lin, Shuen-fu 林順夫. "The Language of the 'Inner Chapters' of the Chuang Tzu." In *The Power of Culture: Studies in Chinese Cultural History*, ed. Peterson, Plaks, and Yu. Hong Kong: Chinese University Press, 1994, pp. 14–21.

Lin Yunming 林雲銘 (fl. 1663). *Zhuangzi yin* 莊子因. In *Wuqiubei zhai Zhuangzi jicheng chubian* 無求備齋莊子集成初編 ed. Yen Ling-feng, Taipei:Yiwen yinshuguan, 1972, 18, p. 4.

Liu Wu 劉武. *Zhuangzi jijie neipian buzheng* 莊子集解內篇補正. Taipei: Wenjin, 1988.

Liu Xiaogan 劉笑敢. *Zhuangzi zhexue ji qi yanbian* 莊子哲學及其演變. Beijing: Zhongguo shehui kexue, 1988.

———. *Classifying the Zhuangzi Chapters*. Tr. William Savage. Michigan Monographs in Chinese Studies 65. Ann Arbor: Center for Chinese Studies, University of Michigan, 1994.

Lu Xixing 陸西星. *Nanhua zhenjing fumo* 南華真經副墨. In *Wuqiubeizhai Zhuangzi jicheng xubian* 無求備齋莊子集成續編, ed. Yen Ling-feng. Taipei: Yiwen yinshuguan, 1974, v. 7.

Lusthaus, Dan. "The Overflowing of Oppositions (*Fan-yen*): The Structures of Zhuangzi's Arguments in 'Autumn Floods.'" Paper delivered at the Eastern Division Meeting of the American Philosophical Association, Washington, D.C., Dec. 1992.

Mair, Victor H., ed. *Experimental Essays on Chuang-tzu*. Honolulu: University of Hawaii Press, 1983.

———, tr. *Wandering on the Way: Early Taoist Tales and Parables of Chuang Tzu*. New York: Bantam Books, 1994. Reprint. Honolulu: University of Hawaii Press, 1998.

Nivison, David. "Hsun Tzu and Chuang Tzu." In *Chinese Texts and Philosophical Contexts: Essays Dedicated to A. C. Graham*, ed., Henry Rosemont Jr. La Salle: Open Court, 1991, pp. 129–142.

Oshima, Harold. "A Metaphorical Analysis of the Concept of Mind in the *Chuang-tzu*." In Mair, *Experimental Essays*, pp. 63–84.

Palmer, Martin, with Elizabeth Breuilly, Chang Wai Ming, and Jay Ramsay, trs. *The Book of Chuang Tzu*. Arkana: Penguin Books, 1996.

Raphals, Lisa. "Skeptical Strategies in *Zhuangzi* and Theaetetus." In Kjellberg and Ivanhoe, *Essays on Skepticism, Relativism and Ethics*, pp. 26–49.

Roth, Harold. "Who Compiled the Chuang Tzu?" In *Chinese Texts and Philosophical Contexts*, ed. Henry Rosemont Jr. LaSalle: Open Court Press, 1991, pp. 79–128.

———. "The Yellow Emperor's Guru: A Narrative Analysis from Chuang Tzu 11." *Taoist Resources* 7.1 (April, 1997), pp. 43–60.

Schwitzgebel, Eric. "Zhuangzi's Attitude toward Language and His Skepticism." In Kjellberg and Ivanhoe, *Essays on Skepticism, Relativism and Ethics*, pp. 68–96.

Shen Yiguan 沈一貫. *Zhuangzi tong* 莊子通. In *Wuqiubei zhai Zhuangzi jicheng* 無求備齋莊子集成, ed. Yen Ling-feng. Taipei: Yiwen yinshuguan, 1972, v. 9.

Van Norden, Bryan W. "Competing Interpretations of the Inner Chapters of the 'Zhuangzi.'" *Philosophy East and West* 46:2 (1996), pp. 247–269.

Waltham, Clae, ed. *Chuang Tzu: Genius of the Absurd, Arranged from the Work of James Legge*. New York: Ace Books, 1971. (Legge's 1891 work with revised romanization.)

Wang Fuzhi 王夫之. *Zhuangzi jie* 莊子解 (A.D. 1709). Wang Xiaoyu 王孝魚, ed. Beijing: Zhonghua shuju, 1964.

Wang Shu-min 王叔岷. *Zhuangzi jiaoshi* 莊子校釋. Shanghai: Shangwu yin-shuguan, 1947.

———. *Zhuangzi jiaoquan* 莊子校詮. Taipei: Zhongyang yanjiuyuan Lishi yuyan yanjiusuo, monograph no. 88, 1988.

Watson, Burton, tr. *The Complete Works of Chuang Tzu*. New York: Columbia University Press, 1968.

Wong, David. "Zhuangzi on the Dilemma of Value Pluralism." (forthcoming)

Wu, Kuang-ming 吳光明. *Chuang Tzu: World Philosopher at Play*. New York: Crossroad, 1982.

———. *The Butterfly as Companion: Meditations on the First Three Chapters of the Chuang Tzu*. Albany: State University of New York Press, 1990.

Wuqiubei zhai Zhuangzi jicheng 無求備齋莊子集成. See Yen Lingfeng.

Yang, Rur-bin. *Zhuang Zhou xin mao* 莊周新貌. Taipei: Liming wenhua gongsi, 1991.

Ye Shuxian 葉舒憲. *Zhuangzi de wenhua jiexi—qiangudian yu houxiandai de shijie ronghe* 莊子的文化解析—前古典與後現代的視界融合. Wuhan: Hubei renmin chubanshe, 1997.

Yearley, Lee. "The Perfected Person in the Radical Chuang-tzu." In Mair, *Experimental Essays*, pp. 125–139.

———. "Zhuangzi's Understanding of Skillfulness and the Ultimate Spiritual State." In Kjellberg and Ivanhoe, *Essays on Skepticism, Relativism and Ethics*, pp. 152–182.

Yen Ling-feng 嚴靈峰. "Zhuangzi Qiwulun pian zhi gaiding yu jiaoshi 莊子齊物論篇之改定與校釋, pt. 1." *Dalu zazhi* 24:3.

Yen Ling-feng 嚴靈峰, ed. *Wuqiubei zhai Zhuangzi jicheng chubian* 無求備齋莊子集成初編. Taipei: Yiwen yinshuguan, 1972.

———. *Wuqiubei zhai Zhuangzi jicheng xubian* 無求備齋莊子集成續編. Taipei: Yiwen yinshuguan, 1974.

Zhang Dainian 張岱年. "Lun Zhuangzi 論莊子." *Yanyuan lunxueji* 燕園論學集 (1984).

Zhang Hengshou 張恒壽. *Zhuangzi xintan* 莊子新探. Wuhan: Hubei renmin, 1983.

Zhexue yanjiu bianji bu 哲學研究編輯部, ed. *Zhuangzi zhexue taolunji* 莊子哲學討論集. Peijing: Zhonghua shuju, 1962.

Zhuangzi jiaoquan 莊子校詮. See Wang Shu-min.

Zhuangzi jishi 莊子集釋 (ZZJS). See Guo Qingfan.

Zhuangzi yinde 莊子引得 (HY). See Harvard-Yenching Institute.

Ziporyn, Brook. "The Self-So and Its Traces in the Thought of Guo Xiang." *Philosophy East & West*, n. 43 (July, 1993), pp. 511–539.

———. *The Penumbra Unbound: The Neo-Daoist Philosophy of Guo Xiang*. Albany: State University of New York Press, 2003.

Contributors

SCOTT COOK 顧史考 received his Ph.D. in Chinese from the University of Michigan in 1995 and is currently associate professor of Chinese at Grinnell College. He specializes in pre-Qin textual studies and early Chinese intellectual history. His articles have appeared in such journals as *Asian Music*; *Chinese Literature: Essays, Articles, Reviews*; *Harvard Journal of Asiatic Studies*; *Monumenta Serica*; *Philosophy East and West*; *[Taida] Wenshizhe xuebao* [台大] 文史哲學報 (*Humanitas Taiwanica*); and *Zhongguo dianji yu wenhua luncong* 中國典籍與文化論叢; as well as in various conference volumes in both Taiwan and mainland China. He is currently finishing up work on his manuscript *Harmony and Discord: Musical Thought in Warring States China*.

ALAN FOX 狐安南 earned his Ph.D. in religious studies from Temple University in 1988 and is currently associate professor of philosophy at the University of Delaware. He has published articles in such journals as *Asian Philosophy* and *Journal of Chinese Philosophy* and has a chapter, "*Zhuangzi* zhong de jingyan xingtai: ganying yu fanying" 《莊子》中的 經驗形態:感應與反映 (Modes of experience in the *Zhuangzi*: Reaction and reflection), in Yang Rur-bin and Huang Chün-chieh, eds., *Zhongguo gudai siwei fangshi tansuo* (Zhengzhong, 1996).

PAUL RAKITA GOLDIN is associate professor of Chinese thought in the Department of Asian and Middle Eastern Studies at the University of Pennsylvania. He is the author of *Rituals of the Way: The Philosophy of Xunzi* (Open Court, 1999) and *The Culture of Sex in Ancient China* (Hawaii, 2002) and is also a coeditor of the forthcoming *Reader of Traditional Chinese Culture* (Hawaii). His articles have appeared in such journals as *Asian Philosophy; Chinese Literature: Essays, Articles, Reviews; Early China; Journal of Asian History; Journal of the American Oriental Society; Monumenta Serica;* and *T'ang Studies.*

CHAD HANSEN recevied his Ph.D. in philosophy from the University of Michigan and is currently professor of philosophy at the University of Hong Kong. He is author of *Language and Logic in Ancient China* (Michigan, 1983) and *A Daoist Theory of Chinese Thought* (Oxford, 1992). He has written numerous articles on Chinese philosophy, which have appeared in such journals as *Philosophy East and West, Journal of Chinese Philosophy,* and *Journal of Asian Studies.* His article "A Tao of 'Tao' in *Chuang Tzu*" appears in Victor Mair, ed., *Experimental Essays on Chuang Tzu* (Hawaii, 1983).

SHUEN-FU LIN 林順夫 received his Ph.D. degree from Princeton University and is now Professor of Chinese literature at the University of Michigan. He is the author of *The Transformation of the Chinese Lyrical Tradition: Chiang K'uei and Southern Sung Tz'u Poetry* (Princeton, 1978) and *Lixiangguo de zhuixun* 理想國的追尋 (The pursuit of utopias) (Tunghai University, 2002). He is also cotranslator of *The Tower of Myriad Mirrors: A Supplement to Journey to the West (Hsi-yu pu),* Second Edition (Michigan Publications on China, 2000); coeditor and author of *The Vitality of the Lyric Voice: Shih Poetry from the Late Han to the T'ang* (Princeton, 1986); coeditor of *Constructing China: The Interaction of Culture and Economics* (Michigan Publications on China, 1998); and author of numerous articles on Chinese poetry, fiction, aesthetics, literary theory, philosophical prose, and dream literature.

DAN LUSTHAUS earned his Ph.D. in religion at Temple University in 1989 and is currently visiting assistant professor of religion at the University of Missouri. He has previously taught at such institutions as the University of California, Los Angeles, and the University of Illinois. He is author of *Buddhist Phenomenology: A Philosophical Investigation of Yogācāra Buddhism and the Ch'eng Wei-Shih Lun* (Routledge-Curzon, 2002) and *A Comprehensive Commentary on the Heart Sutra (Kuiji's Commentary, T.33.1710)* (Numata Center, 2001). His articles on Daoist and Buddhist thought have appeared in a variety of journals, including *Journal of Chinese Philosophy.*

MICHAEL J. PUETT is professor of Chinese history in the Department of East Asian Languages and Civilizations at Harvard University. He received his Ph.D. in 1994 from the Department of Anthropology at the University of Chicago. His research interests are focused primarily on the intellectual, cultural, and political history of early China. He is the author of *The Ambivalence of Creation: Debates concerning Innovation and Artifice in Early China* (Stanford, 2001) and *To Become a God: Cosmology, Sacrifice, and Self-Divinization in Early China* (Harvard, 2002), as well as articles appearing in such journals as *Harvard Journal of Asiatic Studies*.

HAROLD D. ROTH is Professor of East Asian studies and religious studies at Brown University. He received his A.B. in Religion from Princeton University in 1970 and Ph.D. from the University of Toronto in 1981. He is author of *The Textual History of the Huai-nan Tzu* (AAS, 1992) and *Original Tao: Inward Training (Nei-yeh) and the Foundations of Taoist Mysticism* (Columbia, 1999). He is also coeditor of *Daoist Identity: History, Lineage, and Ritual* (Hawaii, 2002) and editor of *A Companion to Angus C. Graham's Chuang Tzu: The Inner Chapters* (Hawaii, 2003). His previous articles on the *Zhuangzi* include "The Yellow Emperor's Guru" (*Taoist Resources* 7.1 [April 1997]) and "Who Compiled the Chuang Tzu" (in Henry Rosemont Jr. ed., *Chinese Texts and Philosophical Contexts* [Open Court, 1991]); he has also written entries on the *Zhuangzi* for the *Stanford Encyclopedia of Philosophy* (2001 [online]) and Michael Loewe, ed., *Early Chinese Texts* (IEAS/SSEA, 1993).

RUR-BIN YANG 楊儒賓 received his Ph.D. in Chinese literature in 1987 from National Taiwan University and is currently professor in the Department of Chinese Language and Literature at National Tsinghua University in Hsinchu, Taiwan. He is author of *Zhuang Zhou xin mao* 《莊周新貌》 (*Zhuangzi* in a new guise) (Liming wenhua, 1991) and *Rujia shenti guan* 《儒家身體觀》 (The Confucian conception of the body) (Zhongyanyuan Wenzhesuo, 1996); editor of *Zhongguo gudai sixiang zhong de qi lun yu shenti guan* 《中國古代思想中的氣論與身體觀》 (Discourse on *Qi* and the concept of body in ancient Chinese thought) (Juliu tushu, 1993); and coeditor of *Zhongguo gudai siwei fangshi tansuo* 《中國古代思維方式探索》 (Investigations of modes of thinking in ancient China) (Zhengzhong, 1996). He has also translated into Chinese such works as C. G. Jung, *The Psychology of Eastern Meditation*; W. T. Stace, *Mysticism and Philosophy*; and Wing-Tsit Chan, *A Sourcebook in Chinese Philosophy* (part 1).

BROOK ZIPORYN 任博克 is assistant professor in the Department of Philosophy and Department of Religion at Northwestern University. He has previously served as visiting assistant professor in Chinese philosophy at the University of Michigan and Harvard University. He attained his Ph.D. in Chinese in 1996 from the Department of Asian Languages and Cultures at the University of Michigan. His major works include: *Evil and/or/as the Good: Omnicentrism, Intersubjectivity and Value Paradox in Tiantai Buddhist Thought and Its Antecedents* (Harvard CEAS, 2000); *The Penumbra Unbound: Guo Xiang and the Neo-Taoist Philosophy of Freedom* (State University of New York, 2003); and *The Ubiquity of the Otherwise: Neo-Tiantai Meditations on the Self-overcoming of Context, Identity and Desire* (Open Court, forthcoming).

Index of *Zhuangzi* Citations

Index

adaptation. *See* responsiveness; *shi* 適; *ying*
aesthetics, of life, 5, 67–68, 75–78
ai 哀, 67
aikido 合氣道, 219, 225 n. 37
Akatsuka Tadashi 赤塚忠, 217
Allinson, Robert E., 155 n. 3, 246 n. 46
Ames, Roger T., 2–3, 157–58 (nn. 21, 32), 209, 219, 225 n. 36, 244 n. 27
Analects of Confucius. *See Lun Yu*
anarchism, 7, 129, 154
Anscombe, G. E. M., 246 n. 49
aporia, 7–8, 163–64, 169, 172, 186–88
apportionment. See *fen*
archaeology, 14 n. 6
archery, 108, 125 n. 57
argumentation. *See* disputation; essay form, development of
Aristotle, 6, 97
artistry, 125 n. 57. *See also* skillfulness
Augustine, 232
"axis at the center of the circle." See *daoshu*

ba de 八德, 196–200
Balfour, Frederick Henry, 263
Barry, Brian, 162 (nn. 71, 75)
Baxter, William H., 80 n. 12
bei 悲, 67

Benjamin, Walter, 10, 264–65, 274
Berkson, Mark, 202 n. 4, 247 n. 54
bian 辯, 136, 138, 152–53, 195, 196, 198–200
Biguenet, John, 267, 286 n. 4
bishi 彼是. *See shi/bi*
Blackburn, Simon, 156 n. 9
body (身, 體): concept of, 5–6, 89–90, 102–3, 117–18; dissolution of 90, 110, 117; orientation of, 197–98; perceptualization of, 6, 108; permeation and transformation of, 6, 94–95, 97–118; universal structure of, 92, 118. *See also* Dao, embodiment of
Bogaozi 伯高子, 96
Bohu Wuren 伯昏無人, 108
boundaries. *See* limits
Brandom, Robert, 139, 156 n. 13
breathing practices. *See* practices, meditative
Breuilly, Elizabeth, 286 n. 3
Bucke, Richard M., 120 n. 8, 125 n. 61
Buddhism, 98, 122 n. 34, 140, 203 n. 14, 204 n. 28; Chan 禪, 125 n. 57, 161 n. 62; Indian, 165, 185, 232
budeyi 不得已, 216, 224 n. 24. *See also* inevitability
Buliang Yi 卜梁倚, 18–19

305

Harper, Don, 30 n. 3, 242 n. 16

he 和. *See* harmony

He Bo 河伯 and Beihai Ruo 北海若, 172–75, 180, 183, 187, 188

He Shuangquan 何雙全, 242 n. 16

heart/mind. *See xin*

Heaven. *See tian*

"Heavenly mechanism." *See tianji*

"Heaven's panpipes." *See tianlai*

"Heaven's Pool." *See tianchi*

"Heaven's potter's-wheel." *See tianjun*

Heidegger, Martin, 104, 223 n. 14

Heirman, Ann, 246 n. 51

Henderson, John, 202 n. 6

Herder, Johann Gottfried, 121 n. 26

hermeneutics. *See* interpretation

Herrigel, Eugen, 125 n. 57

Heshang Gong 河上公, 88

hierarchy, 65–66, 76

"hinge of *dao*." *See daoshu*

Hinton, David, 263

Holcombe, Charles, 241 n. 12

holism: omnicentric, 4, 34–36, 40–41, 49; unicentric, 35, 38–42, 44–45, 53

Hsü Fu-kuan 徐復觀, 272

Hu Yüan-chün 胡遠濬, 239 n. 1

hua 化, 114–15, 254. *See also huasheng*; transformation

Huainanzi 淮南子, 16, 100–101, 104, 234–35

Huang Tingjian 黃庭堅, 269

Huang-Lao 黃老, 16, 88, 157 n. 16

huasheng 化聲, 74, 84–85 (n. 41, 45)

Hui Shi 惠施, 19–20, 22, 26–27, 48, 56, 57, 70, 86 n. 49, 117, 133, 140–41, 151, 205 n. 35, 210, 227, 258, 284

Huiyuan 慧遠, 241 n. 12

humanity, as principle in interpretation, 130–31

Hume, David, 94, 149

humility, 173

humor, 184

hundun 混沌, 39, 87 n. 49

Huxley, Aldous, 91–92

Huzi 壺子, 256–57

idealism, 127 n. 81, 139

identity: dissolution of, 91; nontransference of, 170

illumination. *See ming; yi ming*

Im, Manyul, 79 n. 9

impermanence, 5, 64, 77–78, 175, 185

imperturbability, 250–51

improvisation, of life, 68

inconstancy. *See* standards, conditions for; uncertainty

independence. *See* dependency; freedom

indeterminacy. *See* aporia; uncertainty

Indian philosophy, 165, 203 n. 14. *See also* Buddhism, Indian; mysticism, Indian

individuality, 91, 109–11, 115–16, 187

inevitability, 9, 183, 208, 210, 216–17, 220. *See also* fate

infinity (無窮), 49–51, 69, 109–10, 112, 175, 215. See also *qiong*

Inner Chapters (內篇), 3, 4, 10–12, 13–14 (nn. 1, 5, 6), 16, 17–19, 28, 33–36, 37, 39, 52–54, 164, 205 n. 33, 209, 222 n. 1, 224 n. 33, 239 n. 1, 248–49, 251, 264, 267, 270–78; unity and structure of, 269, 282, 283–85

"inner cultivation," 16, 18–19. *See also* self-cultivation; practices, meditative

interpretation: coherence principle and, 7, 130–34; norms of, 135; as process of translation, 1–2, 266–67

intersubjectivity, 41, 46

intuition. *See* intuitionism; knowledge, intuitive versus intellectual; mysticism

intuitionism, 48, 149

Ishida Hidemi 石田秀實, 123 n. 43

"It" and "Other." See *shi/bi*

Ivanhoe, Philip J., 2, 4, 15, 20–21, 29, 33, 154–55 (nn. 2, 3, 4), 159 (nn. 40, 48), 161 n. 57, 162 n. 69, 201 n. 1, 221, 247 n. 54, 262 n. 40

Jakobson, Roman, 286 n. 13

James, William, 120 n. 8

ji 己, 71, 75, 80 n. 19, 187. *See also* self

ji 技. *See* skillfulness

ji 機, 109

ji 濟, 75, 80 n. 17

Ji Xian 季咸, 248, 251, 253, 256–57

Printed in the United States
46375LVS00004B/70-129

9 780791 458662